AF608599

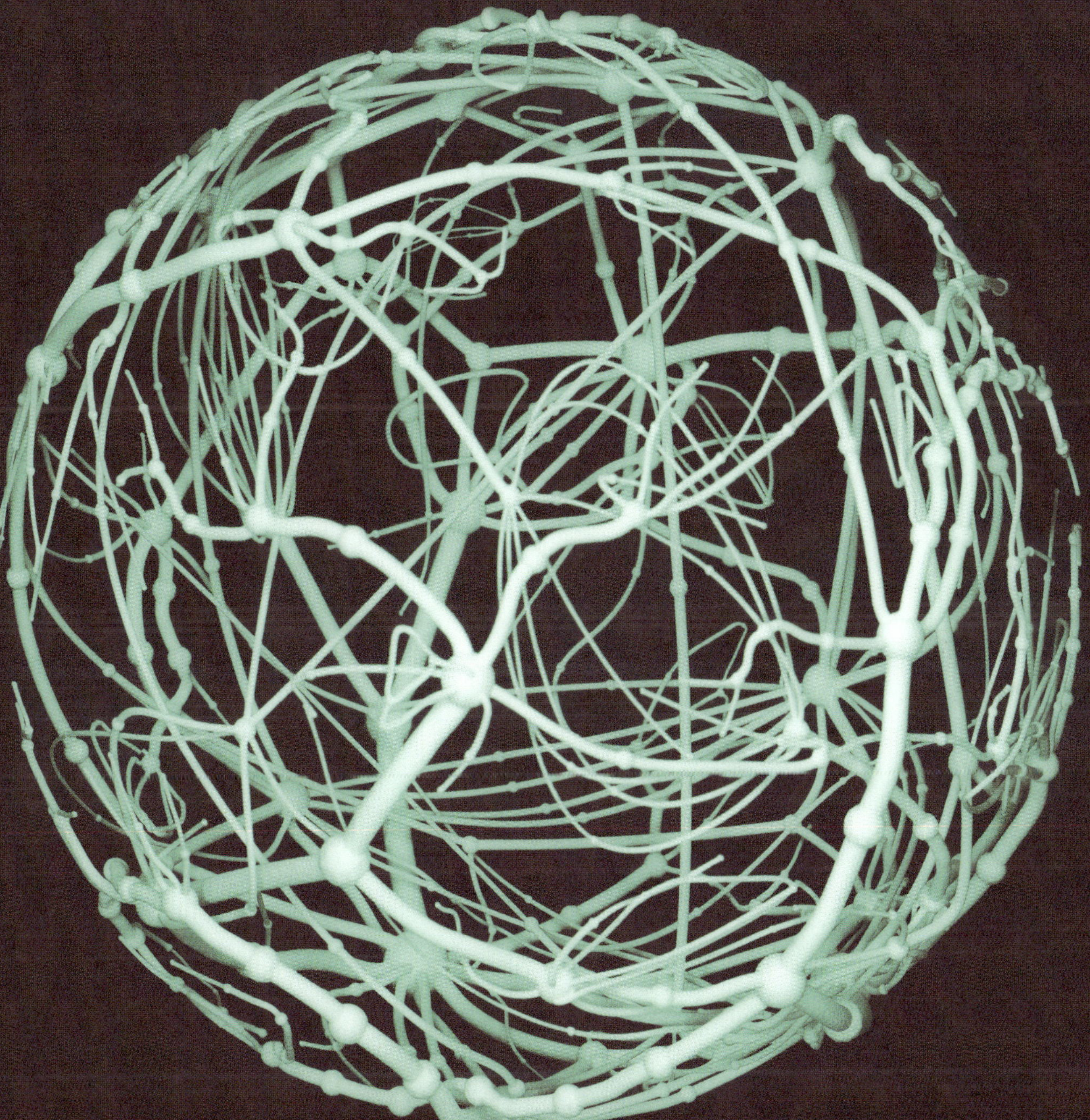

HIDDEN PATTERNS
VISUALIZING NETWORKS AT BARABÁSILAB

HIDDEN PATTERNS
VISUALIZING NETWORKS AT BARABÁSILAB

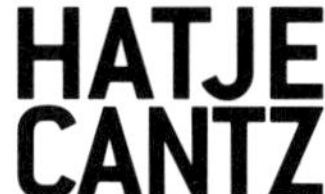

CONTENTS

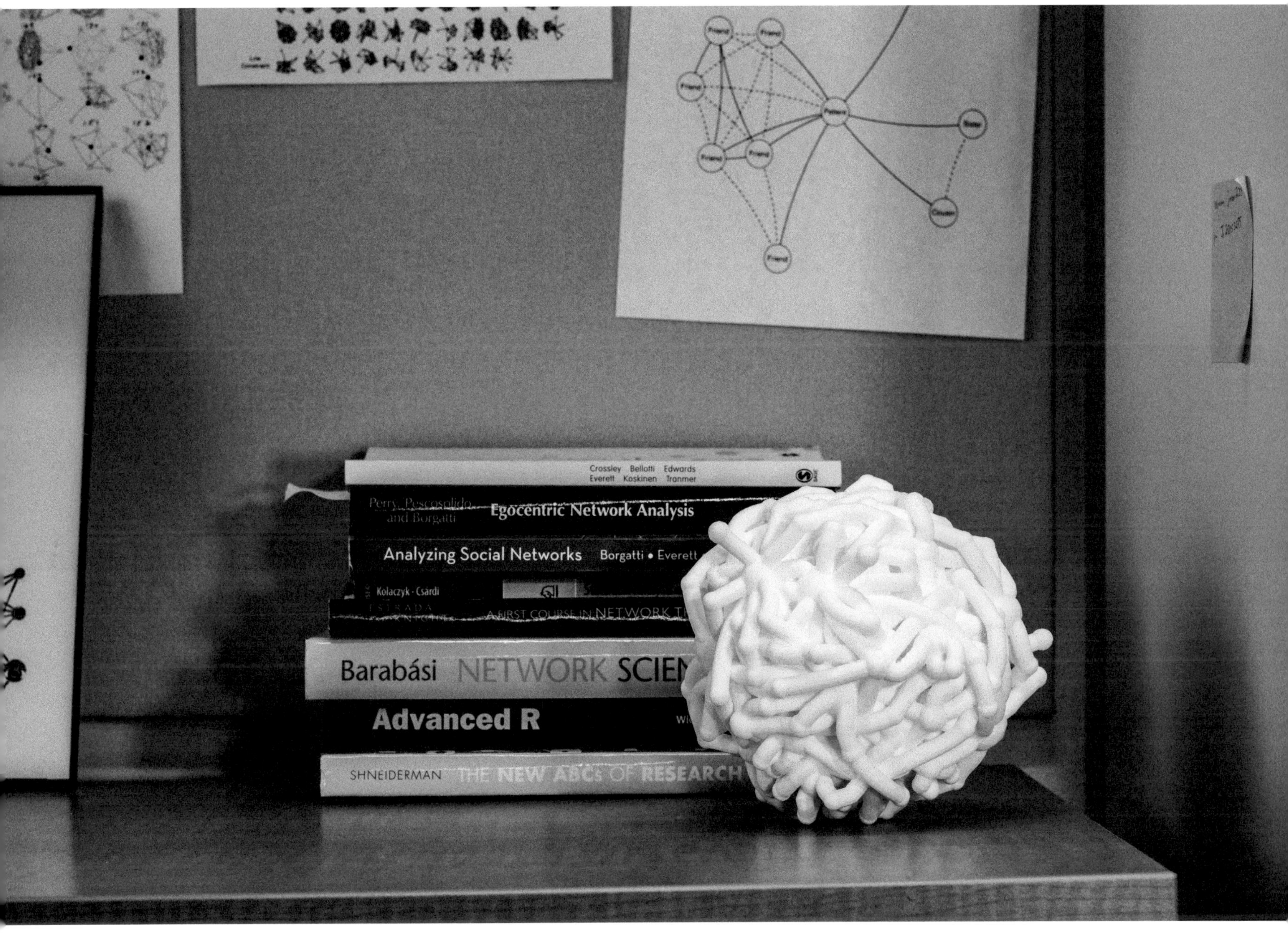
Crossley Bellotti Edwards
Everett Koskinen Tranmer
Perry, Pescosolido, and Borgatti
Egocentric Network Analysis
Analyzing Social Networks
Borgatti • Everett
Kolaczyk · Csárdi
A FIRST COURSE IN NETWORK
Barabási NETWORK
Advanced R
SHNEIDERMAN THE NEW ABCs OF RESEARCH

FOREWORD

The Polyphonic Museum Presents the BarabásiLab

It is the undisguised aim of contemporary-art museums to engage the present. This is true not only in regard to their fundamental task of collecting works, but also in terms of their functionality. Collecting and exhibiting institutions must provide opportunities that are in line with today's expectations for the presentation of art, and for other kinds of experiences and services that art museums have begun to offer. New strategies are constantly being developed to engage visitors with the latest mediation techniques and by using the language and terminology of the current moment.

The Ludwig Museum in Budapest is no exception. Our intent is to be an authentically pluralistic institution, by providing a framework for both the artwork and its perception. And, like other contemporary-art spaces, we take current artistic practice as a starting point as we ask and answer: *What makes an artwork relevant? What do new artistic approaches mean in a museum? How should a museum relate to, or embrace, a presentation practice that makes room for the artwork and its context, as well as for the sensibility of our time?*

Shortly after the founding of the Ludwig Museum in Budapest, in 1996, Peter Weibel organized his first large-scale exhibition here. *Beyond Art,* which featured the intellectual, scientific, and artistic values of the Austro-Hungarian monarchy, was of epoch-making significance because it positioned spirit, culture, science, and art as phenomena legitimately living side by side. With this exhibition, the Ludwig Museum declared its strategy to shift away from museumification and devote itself to experimentation. The parallel presentation of works of science, philosophy, and art theory became a recurring practice and a model in several subsequent exhibitions. The study of the science-art matrix is still a guideline of our institution. Our conferences and related exhibitions on media art and contemporary art over the past seven years all served as platforms for the meeting of art and science as interdisciplinary phenomena, and helped establish the methodology for the integrated presentation of these subjects.

As the first among a large network of Ludwig Museums around the world, the Ludwig Budapest—like our sister institutions in Havana, St. Petersburg, Beijing, and elsewhere, all of which were established after the fall of the Berlin Wall in 1989—focuses foremost on analyzing and reflecting neo-avant-garde tendencies in the former socialist countries. Displaying the connections between science and art also plays an important role in our approach to acquiring and staging art. In all of our shows, we draw on interdisciplinarity to create new narrative tools, with the intention of legitimating new-media art trends within the broader art scene. Which is why it is a thrill and an honor for the Ludwig Museum to exhibit twenty-five years of the BarabásiLab's visualizations.

Hidden Patterns promises to be a pivotal event for the art world's appreciation of the confluence of art and science, as it brings the aesthetic dimension of science to the fore. It is well known that network research—whether built on real, empirical data or, as occasionally happens, on fictional data—is not an uncommon subject in contemporary art. The BarabásiLab uses scientific tools to analyze networks. Its achievements, which take form as spectacular two- and three-dimensional visualizations, provide a new interpretive interface for the viewer—a kind of medium for understanding. By presenting this work, we hope to change the dialogue within the art world about how we define art, to reveal the dynamism of the art museum, and to bring the active experimenting spirit out of the passive spectator. Today, showing scientific subjects in an artistic field means—or can mean—that art has the capacity to simultaneously convey its own vision while embracing the forms of knowledge and discovery that scientific inquiry engenders. In other words, what *Hidden Patterns* demonstrates is that the language of art has corresponding potentialities in scientific practice.

We are pleased to co-present this exhibition with ZKM | Center for Art and Media in Karlsruhe, Germany, which, under the astute direction of Peter Weibel, has been a trailblazer in forging new connections between art, science, and technology. Most of all, we are immensely grateful to the BarabásiLab for allowing us to host this exhibition, as we can think of no clearer confirmation of the Ludwig Museum's commitment to operate as a laboratory than to present *Hidden Patterns*.

JULIA FABÉNYI, Director, the Ludwig Museum, Budapest

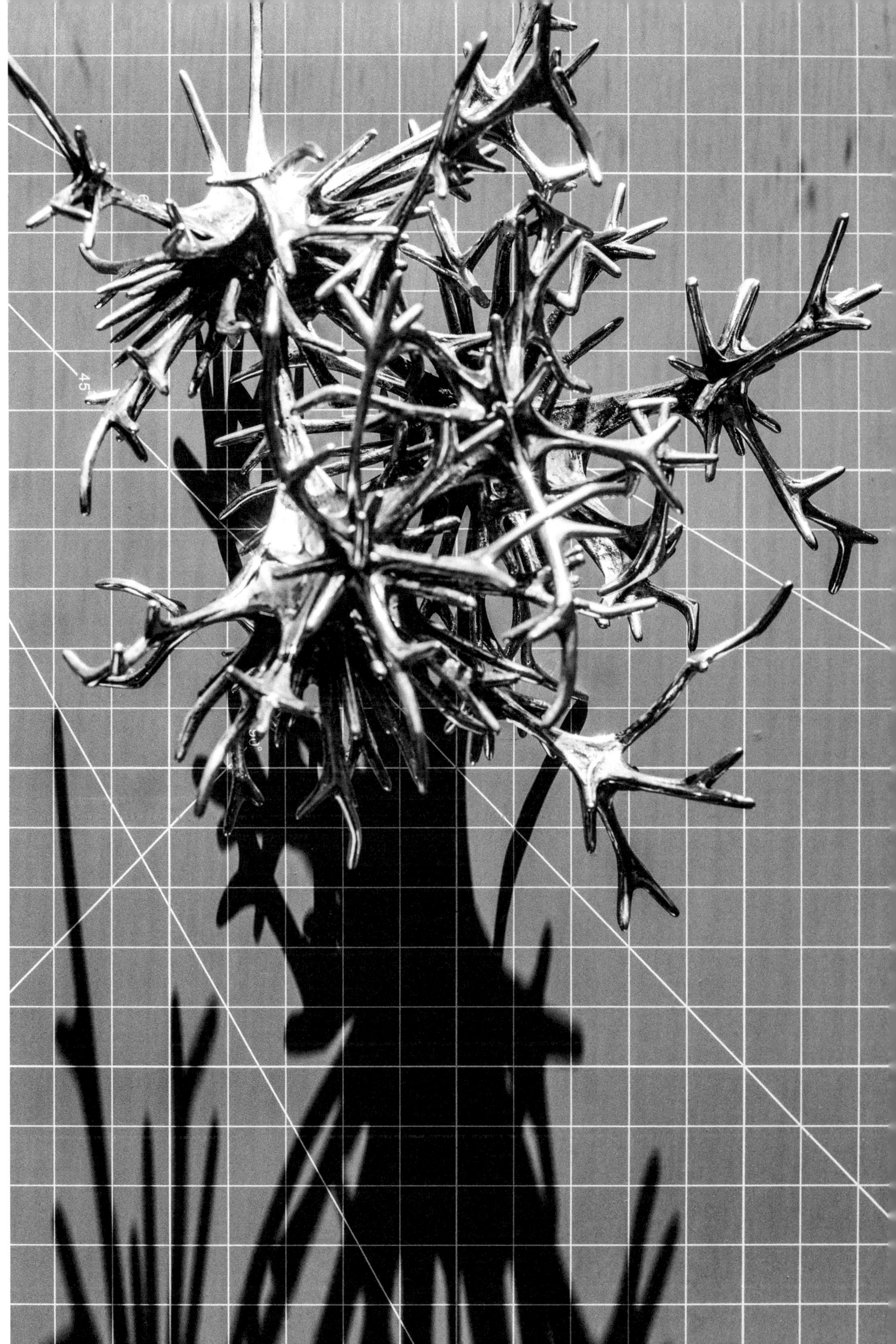

PREFACE

Martian Landing

Albert-László Barabási is part of a great tradition of Hungarian art and science. In *Hidden Patterns,* we see the convergence of science and art, which is so typical of the best part of European culture. If we have a closer look at the field of art, we realize that the scientifically based art movements such as Constructivism, Bauhaus, and De Stijl are all enriched by the pivotal contributions of Hungarian artists.

Several prominent members of the Bauhaus were Hungarians: László Moholy-Nagy, Ernő Kállai, Farkas Molnár, Sándor Bortnyik, Laszlo Péri, and others. The Bauhaus was domiciled in Weimar from 1919 to 1925, subsequently in Dessau from 1926 to 1932, and then in Berlin from 1932 to 1933, when the Nazis closed it down.

Bortnyik returned to Hungary, where in 1928 he founded and then directed the Műhely School of Commercial Art. Known as Little Bauhaus or Budapest Bauhaus, it produced many significant contributions to the field of art. Among the Műhely students was Victor Vasarely, born in Pécs, a founding figure of Op Art. Vasarely paved the way for the computer works of Vera and François Molnár, the French media artists of Hungarian birth who cofounded several artistic research groups, including GRAV (Groupe de Recherche d'Art Visuel).

László Moholy-Nagy immigrated to the United States after his western European period, and there he founded and directed the New Bauhaus in Chicago, which was later renamed School of Design, then Institute of Design, and finally the Illinois Institute of Design (IIT). He was succeeded as director by his student György Kepes, a painter, designer, and art theorist also born in Hungary. In 1967, Kepes was commissioned by the Massachusetts Institute of Technology (MIT) to establish a new center devoted to exploring the confluence of art and machines. Kepes taught at his initiative, the Center for Advanced Visual Studies (CAVS), a fellowship program that brought cutting-edge artists into contact with scientists and engineers (now part of MIT's visual arts program), until his retirement in 1974.

Another line of influence can be traced from Lajos Kassák, the Hungarian poet, to László Moholy-Nagy and Andor Weininger. Kassák founded a forum for Hungarian activism and published an avant-garde magazine—first in Budapest and later on in Vienna—called *MA: Internacionális Aktivista Művészeti Folyóirat* (International Activist Art Journal). Weininger, a Bauhaus student, demonstrated a conviction that the essence of artistic activity lay in the original idea for, and conceptual elaboration of, a work of art, and not in its technical realization, which reveals an intellectual proximity to the conceptual artists of a later generation.

An inclination to combine conceptual art with technical progress, to interlink rationality with innovation, is characteristic of all the aforementioned artists. No wonder image technology owes so much to Hungarian culture. The invention of holography by Nobel laureate Dennis Gabor (originally Gábor Dénes) is a case in point. And Gabor is just one of the many Hungarian Nobel laureates whose scientific discoveries have profoundly shaped our world. Albert Szent-Györgyi first isolated vitamin C; Georg von Békésy (originally Békésy György) enriched the knowledge of the functioning of the ear and the eye through his groundbreaking research on sensory inhibition mechanisms; Eugene P. Wigner introduced the theory of symmetry in physics, which led to a greater understanding of the atomic nucleus and the elementary particles. The construction of the atomic bomb, in Los Alamos, was more or less based on the theoretical work of four Hungarians: Leó Szilárd, who wrote the famous letter signed by Albert Einstein to US President Franklin D. Roosevelt arguing for a nuclear program; Eugene P. (originally Jenő Pál) Wigner; John von Neumann (originally Neumann János Lajos); and Elizabeth (originally Erzsébet) Róna. And the infamous Edward (originally Ede) Teller was the "father of the hydrogen bomb." Further, the reputations of Hungarian mathematicians, physicists, and chemists such as Alfréd Rényi, Lipót Fejér, László Lovász, Loránd Eötvös, Paul Erdős, Paul Halmos, Magdolna and István Hargittai, George de Hevesy, John G. Kemeny, and Theodore von Kármán have had such high standing in the scientific community that the myth of the Martians—namely, that Hungarians are Martians—was born.[1]

Enrico Fermi, the Italian physicist known as the architect of the atomic bomb, is credited with prompting that myth, probably in Los Alamos. After a long preamble about how the vast universe should have already produced intelligent living creatures that would have come to Earth, he posed the question of why this race of extraterrestrial intelligence had not yet appeared: "If all this has been happening," he said, "they should have arrived here by now, so where are they?" To which Leó Szilárd, a man known for his quick wit, replied: "They are among us, but they call themselves Hungarians."[2]

Albert-László Barabási is one of the Martians. Although he wasn't born in Hungary—his Transylvanian hometown was culturally Hungarian but technically Romanian at the time—and, like so many notable Hungarians, he achieved his breakthroughs far from its borders, Barabási clearly got the Hungarian DNA. His influential mathematical and visual models of the complex structures of social networks have changed our understanding of how things connect. He discovered that the sites that form the World Wide Web have three mathematical properties: 1. They expand, evolve, and adapt. 2. They aim to link themselves to hubs with the most connections (i.e., preferential attachment). 3. Their rate of attraction is governed by a fitness parameter. This connection between preferential attachment and fitness defines social media as closed spaces of feedback—or controlled, exponentially growing resonances. In plain terms, it's viral campaigning. Subsequently, he applied his theory to biological systems and epidemiology, to metabolic networks, and to protein interaction. Diseases link to each other through shared genes and other phenomena of a molecular network. In his book *The Formula: The Universal Laws of Success* (2018), he applied his insights about the science and practice of networks to social systems. His path from network science to network medicine to new foundations of social science in the form of data-crunching systems constitutes a remarkable cultural and scientific achievement.

ZKM | Center for Art and Media opened in Karlsruhe, Germany, in 1989. Its founder, Heinrich Klotz, often compared it to the Dessau Bauhaus, identifying the conceptual and ideal proximities between the two institutions. The drive to recognize and show the significance of future-oriented media and technologies by means of a broad spectrum of artistic and scientific approaches is reflected in the overall philosophy and practice of ZKM, which is why it has often been called "the digital Bauhaus." Whereas in the twentieth century, as reflected in the spirit of the Bauhaus, it was the material design of objects that stood at the center of artistic exploration, today it is digital design and the codification of data. Frank Lloyd Wright declared "machinery, materials and men"[3] to be the equation for the twentieth century. For the twenty-first century, I believe the formula to be "media, data, and men." Since the models for ZKM have been the Bauhaus and the Center for Advanced Visual Studies, which lived essentially from the contributions of so many Hungarian artists, it is only logical that ZKM devotes an exhibition to the outstanding artistic and scientific work of Albert-László Barabási.[4]

PETER WEIBEL, Chairman and CEO, ZKM | Center for Art and Media, Karlsruhe, Germany

---

1 See György Marx, *A marslakók érkezése – Magyar tudósok, akik Nyugaton alakitották a 20. század történelmét* (*Arrival of the Martians*) (Budapest, 2000).

2 György Marx, *The Voice of the Martians* (Budapest, 1997), p. 117.

3 "Machinery, Materials and Men" is the title of F. L. Wright's first of six lectures, known as *The Princeton Kahn Lectures* (1930) in Frank Lloyd Wright, *The Future of Architecture* (New York, 1953), pp. 68–90.

4 For example, György Kepes, ed., *The New Landscape in Art and Science* (Chicago, 1956); György Kepes, ed., *Structure in Art and in Science* (New York, 1965); or György Kepes, ed., *The Nature and Art of Motion* (London, 1965).

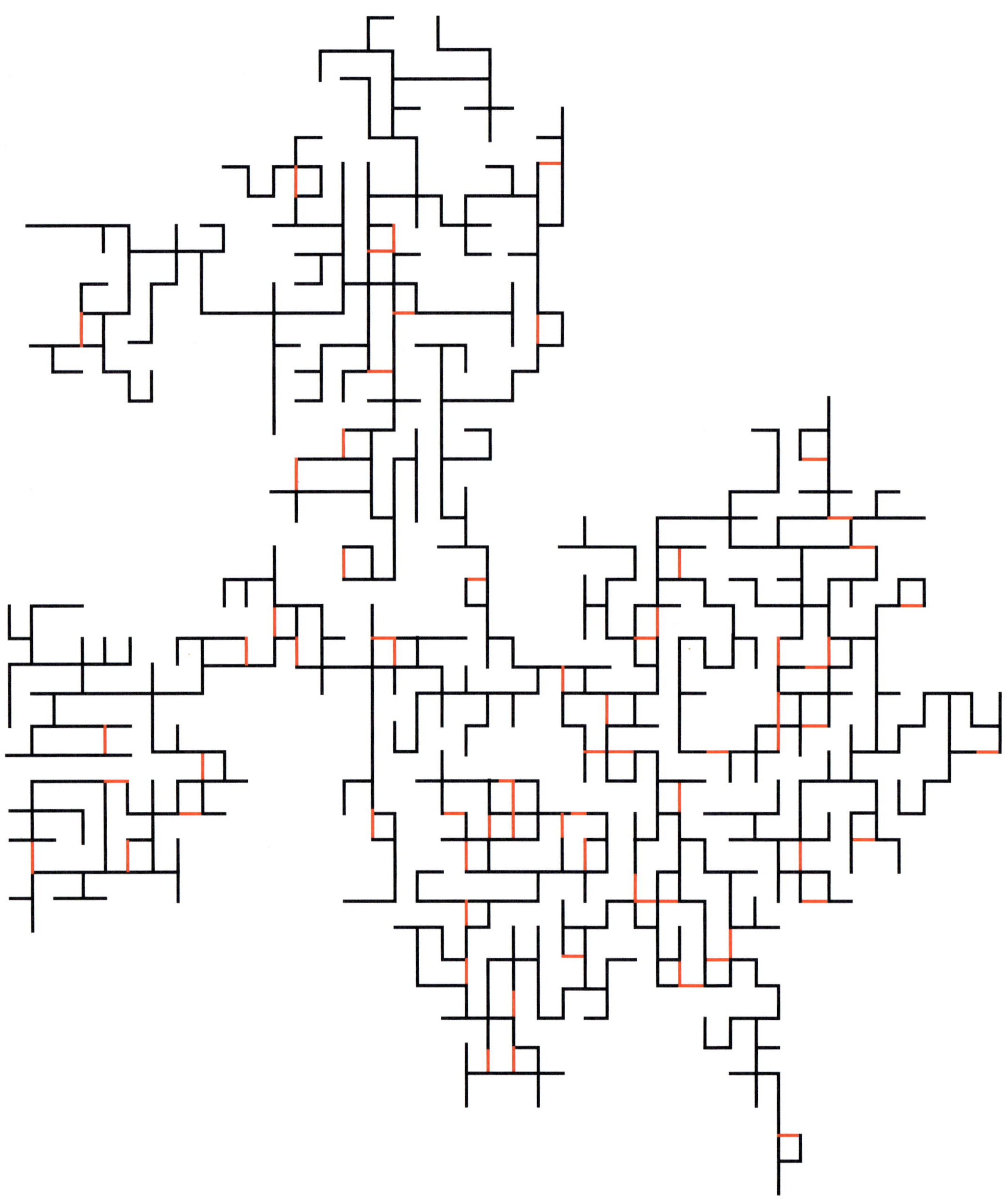

Fig. 1

INTRODUCTION

The Evolution of the BarabásiLab's Visual Language

BY ALANNA STANG

Albert-László Barabási's affinity for scientific thinking emerged early in life. He attended a math-and-physics high school in Csíkszereda, a small city in Transylvania, the culturally Hungarian region of eastern Romania, where in both ninth and twelfth grades he won the local Physics Olympiad. Yet Barabási planned to become an artist. The son of a museum chief and a theater director, he wanted to study sculpture and painting, not to become a scientist.

But it was easier for him to get into college for science than for art, and the rules-based take on the mystifying forces that govern our existence appealed to him deeply. He concentrated in physics and engineering at the University of Bucharest, publishing three papers on chaos theory as an undergraduate. After immigrating to Hungary, he earned his master's in theoretical physics from Eötvös Lóránd University in Budapest in 1989. By the time he was twenty-seven, he had a PhD in physics from Boston University. In 1995, after a stint as a postdoctoral associate at IBM's Watson Research Center, Barabási became an assistant professor of physics at the University of Notre Dame in Indiana. Four years later, he would upend decades of physics convention with his "scale-free" theory of real networks.

Over the course of the next twenty years, Barabási would not only invent a new field of network science, he would also evolve a graphic language for visualizing his research, first two-dimensionally, later as three-dimensional sculptures, and as of this writing—thanks to advances in virtual reality—in four dimensions.

First Attempts

Barabási produced his very first data visualization in 1995, just a month after he had begun exploring networks. The maze-like grid pattern (fig. 1), which showed a spreading pattern on a lattice, called invasion percolation in science, had to be printed in black and white—even though Barabási had rendered some of the connections in red—because *Physical Review Letters,* the preeminent physics journal at the time, wasn't yet being published in color.

By 2000, the BarabásiLab's experiments in network visualization had begun in earnest. A year earlier, but in a previous century, while Bill Clinton was being acquitted and Leo Castelli was being laid to rest and an upstart called Google was being introduced as AOL's search partner, Barabási—now at Notre Dame—and his team had already mapped the diameter of the World Wide Web. A massive undertaking, the study investigated the connectivity and large-scale topographical properties of the Web in order to understand its architecture. Barabási's analysis of linked

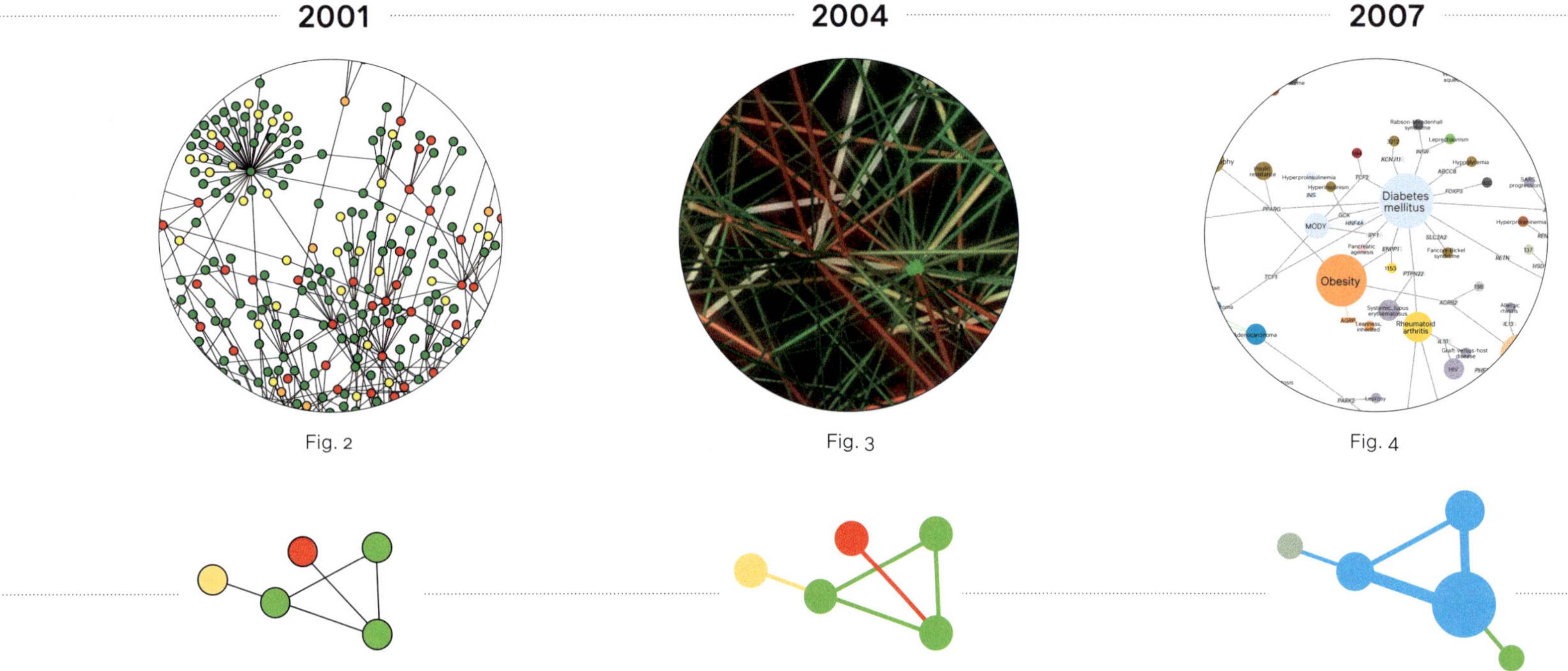

Fig. 2

Fig. 3

Fig. 4

pages—the documentation of which in the September 1999 issue of *Science* would become one of the most cited papers in science (more even than the Human Genome Project, published in 2001)—showed that the World Wide Web was what he termed a "scale-free" network. The prevailing theory at the time held that nodes of real networks are randomly linked to each other, resulting in a rather uniform network architecture. A scale-free network, by contrast, has distinct hubs, or nodes, with an exceptional number of links that hold the network together. When drawn side by side, the architecture of the two different models shows the importance of hubs in a scale-free network and their irrelevance in a random network.

The real discovery, of course, was that the Internet was not the only network that arranged itself according to this scale-free structure. Many, many systems, Barabási and others would go on to discover, from social networks to protein interactions in our cells, follow the same, non-random pattern.

After showing that certain nodes attract more connections and are therefore more critical to a network, Barabási started to examine network robustness. As he tried to understand how susceptible networks might be to failure or node breakdown, or how resilient they might be despite node or connection fragility, visualizing the structure—both for his own understanding and for explanatory purposes—was suddenly imperative.

The first visualization contrasting a random and a scale-free network, published in the July 27, 2000, issue of *Nature,* represented how complex networks tolerate error, attack, and interventions. Looking much as if a couple of Montessori-approved child's toys had exploded, the diagrams illustrate the important role the hubs play in a scale-free network and the absence of such hubs in a random network (see page 31, top). While neither of the two images reflected true scope or scale, they did convey the deep structural differences between the scale-free and the random models. The uneven, hub-dominant format of the scale-free network graphically explains why it would

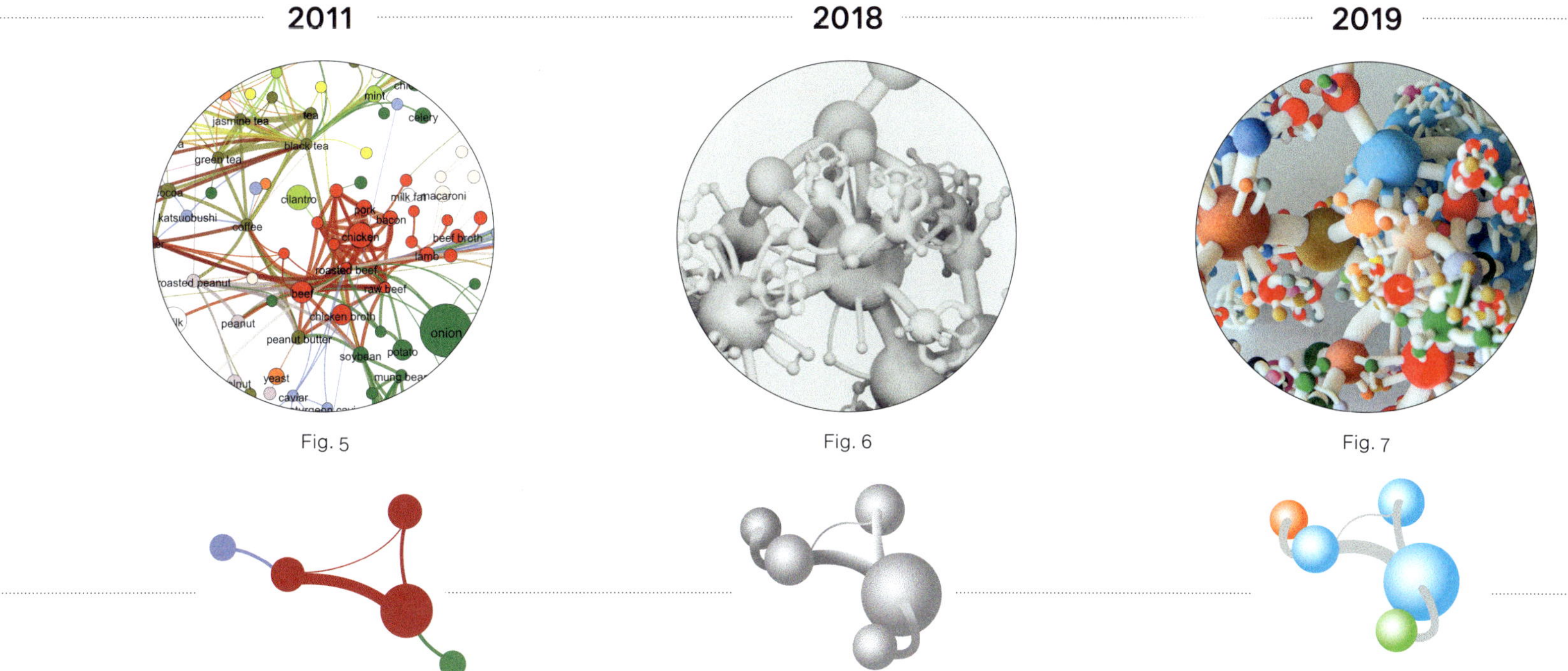

Fig. 5

Fig. 6

Fig. 7

be well-defended against random failures, but fragile in the face of an attack on a hub. More important, rudimentary though they were, these first diagrams showed Barabási and his team the profound value of bringing their work to life in visual form.

An Iterative Process

For the next study, the BarabásiLab focused on the role of the network in a cell's survival—in this case a yeast cell. To look at how its survival depends on its most highly connected proteins, the team took the visualization process a step forward by accurately representing the actual architectural arrangement of the cellular connections. But how to convey the fact that it was now possible to predict exactly which nodes would need to be eliminated to destroy a certain cell? How to configure the information? How to choose colors, shapes? How to use two-dimensional space to depict an inherently infinite dimensional network?

It was an iterative process. At first, the most connected (and most important) nodes in the protein-integration network—what biologists call the lethal or essential proteins, because of their ability to bring down the whole network—were clustered at the center of the diagram. The next attempt, using a network-visualization software tool designed to explore social networks, had a more realistic overall form but many hidden nodes. The final form (fig. 2, and see page 32), built with straight, unweighted links in 2001, communicates complexity through the multitude of the relationships they represent. It offered the first glimpse of the deeply interlinked architecture of living systems by explicitly showing how proteins in a cell interact with one another. This image advanced the lab's visualization progress because it worked on many levels: as a figure to illustrate the research findings, and as an illustration of the invisible forces—the connective tissues—that shape our biological existence. Furthermore, it had a presence, a visual draw, even when stripped of its legend, which was key to Barabási's desire to take the discourse about networks into a different dimension.

Link Think

The next major leap in the evolution of the BarabásiLab's visualizations was in 2004, with the encoding of information within the links. Previously, the diagrammatic links had simply represented connections. With Barabási's study of how energy flows through metabolic reactions inside a cell, the need arose to depict the various types of flows—or fluxes—and to distinguish them from one another within a single image.

By assigning different colors to the different fluxes of each reaction—represented as linear links—the team realized that new layers of visual information could be portrayed in a single image (fig. 3, and see pages 59–61). White was assigned to the most dominant fluxes, for example; green, orange, and pale pink to the subordinate ones. But it's the balance of multiple colors that captures the pulse of this particular network. Luminous, broad, and radiating with energy, these colored links have the appearance of a *Star Wars* lightsaber. Developed to depict the complexity and the diversity of observed flow patterns, the visual vocabulary of this image has reemerged in many subsequent network visualizations, because it allowed a whole different degree of information to be depicted.

Knowing the Nodes

In 2005, Barabási moved to the Dana-Farber Cancer Institute at Harvard Medical School to engage in a new research topic: human diseases. It was still the early stages of the genetics revolution. The Human Genome Project had been published only four years earlier, and genetics was searching for its role in medicine. Every week another gene was linked to another disease. For Barabási, the question became: *How do we conceptualize the many disease-gene associations that the medical community is reporting on a daily basis?*

The answer, which took form in 2007 as a map titled *The Human Disease Network* and captured the common genetic origins of different diseases (fig. 4, and see pages 63–65), was the first time that the BarabásiLab had encoded two sets of information in each node. Node size represented the number of genes linked to a particular disease. Node color, by contrast, signified the disease class. When Barabási first asked his postdoctoral associate Kwang-Il Goh to create node-size variations that would represent the number of genes associated with a disease, Goh implemented the changes. But the subtle variety had little impact on the visual content of the map. It was still too balanced, too uniform. So Barabási kept pushing. Eventually, he asked Goh to implement variations so extreme that a few diseases dominated the whole image. This radical version became the final representation. It not only required Goh to custom build code for its representation, it also necessitated a series of manual adjustments in which the node positions were altered, one by one, in order to eliminate node and link overlaps.

The Curveball

Up until 2011, all of the lab's network representations were composed of straight links—that is to say, only rigid lines connected the nodes. But as Barabási and his team worked on visualizing their latest area of investigation, the network of flavors, they found they could not achieve the visual clarity they were after with straight lines. Because so many food ingredients, which were represented as nodes, share the same flavor chemicals, the nodes were connected by numerous links. Accurate representation meant an unwieldly density of intersecting links. The visualization's effect was obfuscation, not illumination.

The team came up with a two-pronged approach to overcome this problem. The first innovation was the adoption of a statistical tool that enabled them to proportionately reduce the number of links without affecting the fidelity of the representation. The second breakthrough came via a newly released algorithm that they deployed to curve the links (fig. 5, and see page 33). By first diminishing the number of links represented, and then replacing straight links with arced connectors, the team could reduce the density of intersecting links around the hubs. Less visual clutter meant enhanced clarity for the visual representation of how foods are connected through common flavors, as it would for many other link-dense network visualizations down the road.

Depth Perception

The advent of three-dimensional printers represented a major turning point for the lab's visualizations. Barabási had been captivated by sculpture from a young age, and from the time he began visualizing his research, he was always disappointed that the ability to render networks was stuck in two dimensions. None of the existing network layout algorithms could account for the fact that in a network sculpture, link crossings violate our sense of physicality. Link crossings are forbidden in all physical networks, including the brain, where axons—the nerve fibers that act as neural transmitters—avoid other axons. So in 2007, as word of the first 3-D printers began to spread, he finally acted on his dream to turn his networks into sculptures and began developing the science of physical networks.

It took about a decade, however, for the mathematical tools necessary to lay out 3-D networks to catch up with the intricacies of the networks he wanted to produce. With the advent of widely available 3-D printers, he lost no time in rendering his visualizations in three dimensions. Initially, the team produced a study they called *Gurga*, Latin for "gorge," as its thick knot of interlacing links bend and weave the same way constrained water twists as it searches to find an opening to the land (see page 138).

The lab's first successfully rendered network sculpture was a 3-D version of *The Flavor Network* (fig. 6, and see page 137), which was originally produced in 2-D in 2011. Finalized in 2018, its play of intersecting shapes and negative space offered a whole new experience of how flavors connect. Without the color coding that so brilliantly brought it to life as a 2-D map, *The Flavor Network*'s distinct communities show the difference between the different food classes.

At that time, 3-D printing technology offered only single-color output. Less than a year later, however, color 3-D printers would enable the lab to produce data sculptures with a very different effect. In the 2019 version of *The Human Disease Network* (fig. 7, and see pages 66 and 67), color-coded nodes make it easy to spot the roots of the network's community structure: cancers in blue, and neurological disease in red. The many links between the members of the same community show that diseases of similar kind are caused by the same set of genes; thus they share symptoms and, eventually, treatment. The colored three-dimensional network makes the research finding not just easy to see, but easy to understand.

The next evolutionary stage of the BarabásiLab's visual language is taking shape in the form of 4-D experiments, the natural dimension of networks. As Barabási and his team experiment with augmented reality and virtual reality, the mediums that could bring such networks alive, they are forging new visual expressions for their research that will surely warrant new chapters in this ever-expanding story.

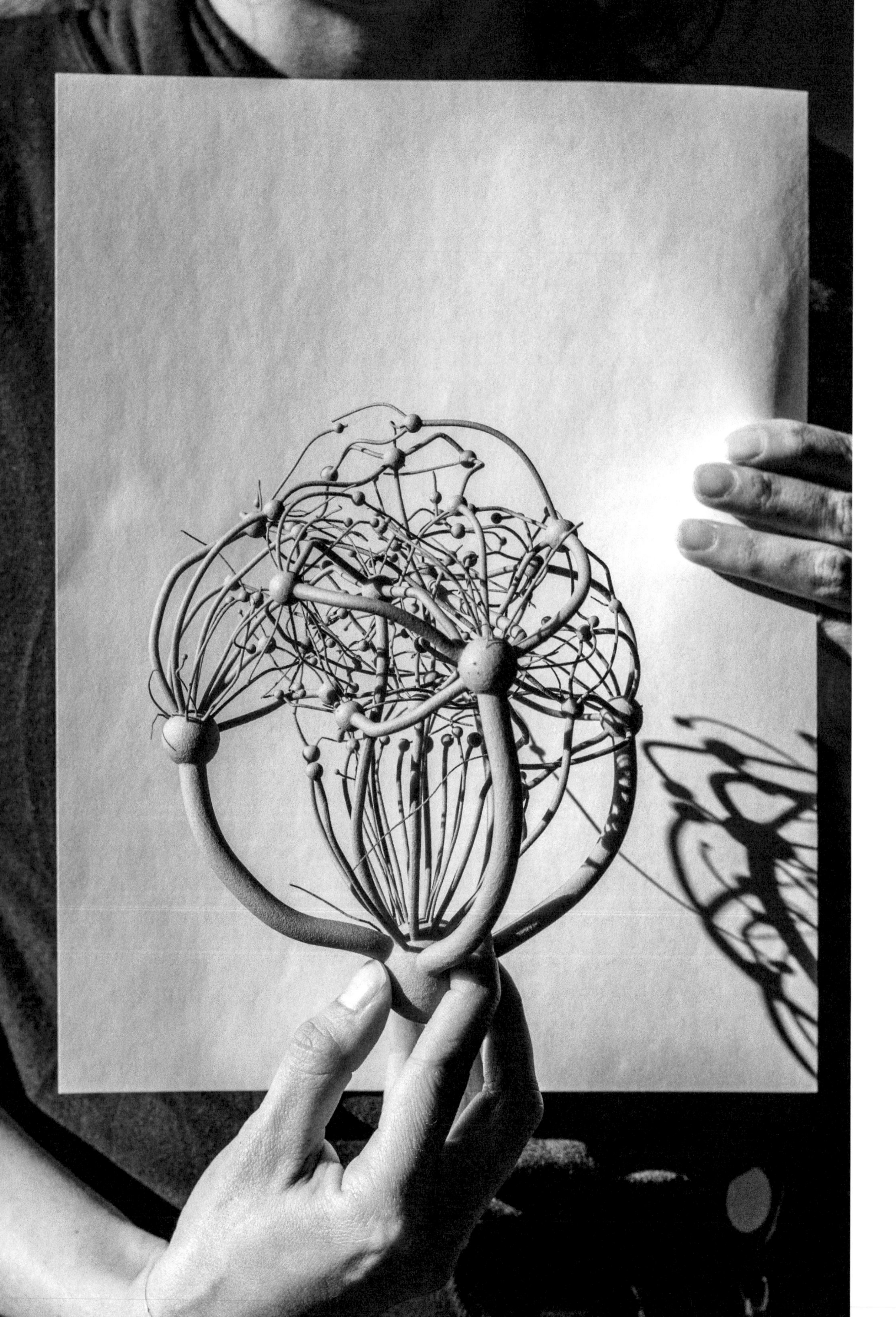

The Aesthetics of Connections:

A New Image of the World in Network Representation

BY JÓZSEF KÉSZMAN

Hidden Patterns, the inaugural exhibition of physicist Albert-László Barabási's artistic expression of network science, and the occasion for this publication, is an oddity in the life of the Ludwig Museum: a chimera that encompasses the methods and mentalities of several different types of knowledge. Comprising dozens of visually arresting images and objects rooted in empirical research, the show is a mosaic woven of science and art, in which elements of each domain intersect to form new offshoots and patterns. It is a proposition that may be divisive—presenting scientific findings in a museum—and that demands a clear answer to the question: *What has network science got to do with art?*

The exhibition is organized around the past twenty-five years of research from the Boston-based BarabásiLab, whose work focuses on the search for mostly unseen connections behind various phenomena. By revealing and analyzing repetitive patterns, Barabási's work demonstrates the true interconnectedness of all things, from nature and society to culture and art. This network approach holds out the promise of a universally applicable method that can be brought to bear on the precise scientific examination of almost any kind of relationship—the connection between a tennis player's performance and her popularity, or the outlooks for an individual artist's art-world success based on her educational and professional trajectory. Brought to life in the exhibition with state-of-the-art technology—including data sculptures, augmented reality (AR), virtual reality (VR), and a drawing robot—the network diagrams and structures vividly describe the hidden connections and relationships that underlie the real-world phenomena being observed. These representations offer new possibilities for visual expression for researchers and enthusiasts alike.

Yet even though these science-based visualizations have an aesthetic dimension, they don't necessarily read as artworks. And rightly so. Just as it is unnecessary to canonize scientific achievements in the language of art, the reverse doesn't make much sense either. Even so, both of these practices, visualization in scientific disciplines and the creation of artworks, fit into the same overarching field: the vast realm of visuality and visual expression. To put it another way, the moment of representation is key to both processes, making visualization the common denominator between the natural sciences and other segments of culture. And the subjective layer of that visualization is perfectly obvious in the works on view in this exhibition—let's not forget that Barabási, a world-renowned physicist, once aspired to be a sculptor. Visual art itself has for decades made use of complex visual diagrams and information graphics to give expression to various connections, processes, genealogies, degrees of kinship, and other types of relationships.[1] For the Fluxus group, whose experimental interdisciplinary work in the 1960s and 1970s emphasized process over product, graphic configurations, previously named *diagram(m)s*, were considered an artistic medium. This line can be traced back even further, to the Bauhaus, to occult representations, and beyond. In addition to their function, diagrammatic images were also formally classified by distinguishing points (places) and lines (connections). And by typifying them, we could speak of a tree-principle (temporal) or system-principle (spatial) division between the diagrams. The potential of diagrams soon became apparent: to see the whole in one, to have an overview, to map processes and phenomena and their interconnections, the relationship of the whole and each of its parts. Such insights can inform a completely different sort of knowledge than one obtained via a text-centric, discursive linguistic description and its linear narratives. It is a noteworthy coincidence that in parallel with the emergence of network research in the 1990s, relational aesthetics came to prominence in the art theory of the era. Describing new phenomena in contemporary art, relational aesthetics focused not on art objects but on the social connections, events, and contexts that are the networks of the art world.[2]

The visual renderings of the BarabásiLab's scientific projects that have previously appeared in an art-world context have done so mainly to represent a given topic as cultural practice. For example, the Serpentine Gallery's 2010 *Map Marathon: Maps for the 21st Century* included the lab's *The Human Disease Network*. At the Ludwig Museum in Budapest, and subsequently at the ZKM in Karlsruhe, Germany, where the *Hidden Patterns* exhibition will travel, the visualization models are being showcased independently, based on their own logic: tool, medium, language, template, model. These words sound familiar to us, as if they had freshly emerged from the conceptual apparatus of logical positivism. Just as Ludwig Wittgenstein saw language as a tool, so network research may be deployed as a new language, and we may discover a new face of the world in science and everyday life. "The limits of my language are the limits of my world," Wittgenstein famously wrote in his 1921 "Tractatus" (Treatise on Logic and Philosophy), suggesting that we can get to know the world only to the extent that our language is able to faithfully describe its phenomena and relationships. Compared to written and spoken language, the visual language of complex networks offers a different way of rendering and describing. We get a new image of the world through network representation.[3]

The BarabásiLab's visualizations are nothing short of a new model for learning. From a practical standpoint, they can be seen as a super-high-end tool or interface with seemingly limitless potential, a modus operandi that has an enormous range of action and impact, an almost universal applicability. Not only is network visualization among the most promising scientific methodological innovations of recent years, it is also an effective tool for studying cultural and social phenomena, including the dynamics of the art world.

The exhibition that inspired this book provides an overview of ongoing research processes and analyses at the BarabásiLab, among them the display of *The Art Network*, which depicts relationships between artists and institutions, and the timely topic of how the Covid-19 pandemic impacts human communication. Ultimately, *Hidden Patterns* is about bringing the spirit of network thinking closer to the world of art and to a broader, interested audience. Barabási's visualizations are in many respects already present in the potential tool kit of contemporary art. They are harbingers of an opportunity and a potential it would be foolish for us to ignore.

---

1 Annamária Szőke, "Diagramok: gondolat-térképek. Bevezető egy 'kép' esszéhez" ("Diagrams: Mind-Maps. Introduction to an 'Image' Essay"), in *Diagram,* Annamária Szőke, ed. (Budapest, 1998), pp. 3–34.

2 Nicolas Bourriaud, *Relational Aesthetics* (Dijon, 1998).

3 This phrase is a reference to György Kepes's *A Világ Új Képe a Művészetben és a Tudományban* (*A New Image of the World in Art and Science*) (Budapest, 1979).

Representing Complexity: An Ode to the Node-Link Diagram

BY ISABEL MEIRELLES

When phenomena are not inherently visible, finding a fitting image or a metaphor can be especially helpful. Literature in cognition suggests that key to problem-solving is finding an efficient representation with which to solve the problem. A representation that is "right" will foster new knowledge, insights, and creations.[1]

For the BarabásiLab, the node-link diagram, one of the most common visualizations in network science, has been very right. Used for millennia, node-links are simple yet powerful representations of relationships among a set of elements. With innate flexibility, the node-link works both as a metaphor of connectedness and as a picture of the connected system. Its associative power lies in the ease with which we understand and interpret its overall configuration. Like other types of diagrams, node-link diagrams abstract the data they represent by indexing them spatially, preserving explicitly the information needed for interpretation and inference given the simultaneous view of the whole.

Connecting the Dots

Composed of dots (the nodes) connected by lines (the links), the node-link is a schematic representation of relationships in a system, independent of the nature of the system, whether social, biological, or cultural. Though a simplification of the real system, it is an exact one-to-one representation describing the connections between elements, where the connections are defined a priori. Node-link diagrams depict both qualitative information: who/what is connected to whom/what; and quantitative metrics: how many connections, how central, and so on.

When we think of connections, we naturally think of lines. Paul Klee, the Swiss-born artist, famously described a line as a "dot that went for a walk."[2] Throughout history, lines have been drawn on paper to connect people (fig. 1), places (fig. 2), concepts (fig. 3), imagined worlds, and so on. Nature is filled with connected systems. We can see them in rivers, in veins and nerves (fig. 4), and in both plants and animals and their living environments, among others. We also encounter node-link diagrams in our constructed and cultural environments, from road systems (fig. 5) to communication networks, from artworks (fig. 6) to scientific projects (fig. 7).

It could be argued that the ubiquity of the node-link diagram is due to its qualitative value and its intuitive mapping. In any type of node-link diagram, we immediately understand that the lines stand for connections between the nodes, whatever they might represent. These are diagrams that truly enable us to "draw connections" or "connect the dots," in order to get the "big picture."

A Node-link Is Not the Network

In his pioneering 2016 textbook, *Network Science,* Barabási explains that notwithstanding real networks' "amazing differences in form, size, nature, age, and scope," most of them "are driven by common organizing principles."[3] Those principles are what enable us to study and understand diverse networks and complex systems. But not all maps of real-world systems can be complete or entirely known. Still, it is possible to study the fundamental laws and reproducible mechanisms underlying these complex systems by examining what is known of them, principally through partial data sets.

The node-links are even further removed from completeness, in that they depict only the set of elements that interact with one another within the already partial data set, leaving out the isolated nodes. This means that even the most complex-looking node-links are partial and incomplete representations of the systems they stand for. Or, as Polish-American scholar Alfred Korzybski wrote in a 1931 paper for the meeting of the American Association for the Advancement of Science, "a map is not the territory it represents, but, if correct, it has a *similar structure* to the territory, which accounts for its usefulness."[4] Take for example the animated visualization of the microscopic system of subcellular networks, which Barabási presented at his 2012 TEDMED Talk (fig. 8).[5] Despite its complexity, this visualization—a dense and intricate node-link—depicts only 5 percent of interactions within the cells (the known percentile at the time). Were it not for the strategy of highlighting one disease at a time, in this case asthma, the image would convey very little meaning.

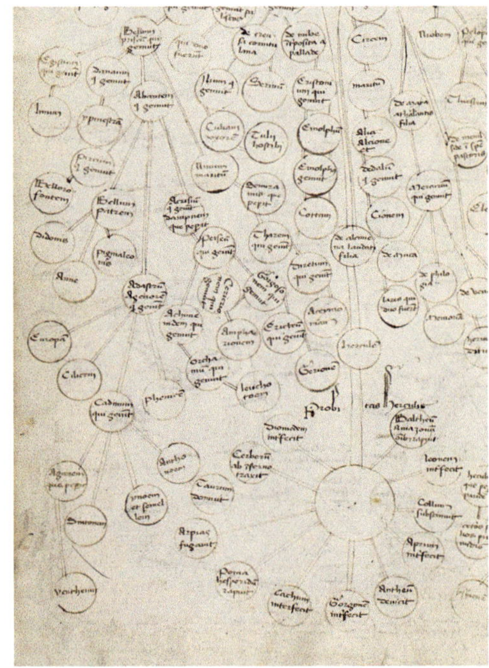

Fig. 1: *The Genealogy of Jupiter*, by Virgil and various authors, from a fifteenth-century codex.

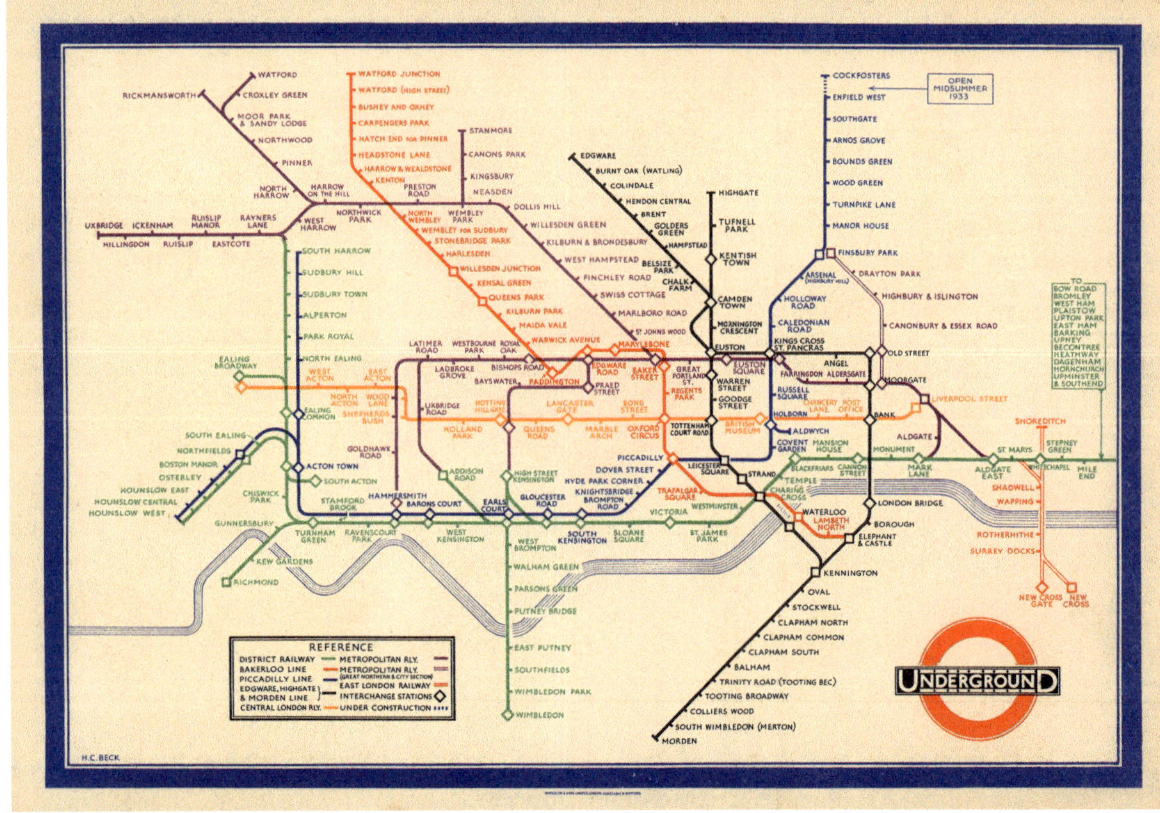

Fig. 2: *The Map of London's Underground Railways*, by Henry Charles Beck, 1933.

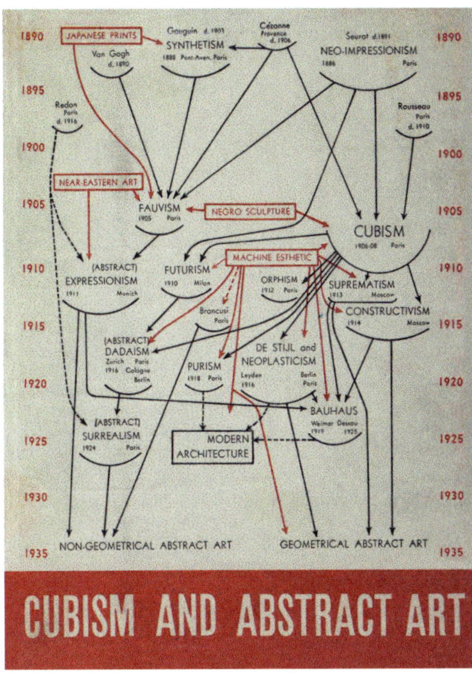

Fig. 3: Catalogue cover design from *Cubism and Abstract Art*, by Alfred H. Barr, Jr., 1936.

In short, while they depict the "real" world, node-link diagrams are not "the" world. They represent what we know of the systems they are mapping. Node-links are not alone in this. All types of visual representations, including maps, share this constraint. Argentine writer Jorge Luis Borges reminds us of the impossibility of one-to-one scale mapping in his 1946 story "On Exactitude in Science," which invites the reader to imagine an empire where "the Art of Cartography attained such Perfection that the map of a single Province occupied the entirety of a City, and the map of the Empire, the entirety of a Province. In time, those Unconscionable Maps no longer satisfied, and the Cartographers Guilds struck a Map of the Empire whose size was that of the Empire, and which coincided point for point with it."[6] The paragraph-long story is a parable of what happens when the representation coincides with its referent.

Getting Colorful

Creating visual representations of relational structures, especially those of large networks, presents many challenges, as most lack natural features that help organize them visually. This is evident when we compare such structures with hierarchical systems that offer intrinsic visual order, which makes them easier to perceive and interpret. The nerves in our body, for example, naturally organize in a tiered system, with visible ordered patterns. We can examine them in the work of Spanish neuroscientist Santiago Ramón y Cajal, who captured the nerve system of the human brain in thousands of drawings after intense and detailed observations (fig. 4).[7] Widely

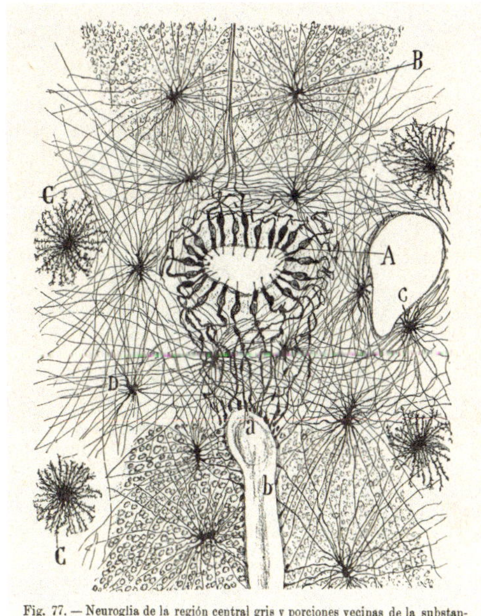

Fig. 4: *Neuroglia of the Grey Central Region and Neighboring Portions of the White Substance of the Spinal Marrow of a Boy of Eight Days*, by Santiago Ramón y Cajal, 1899.

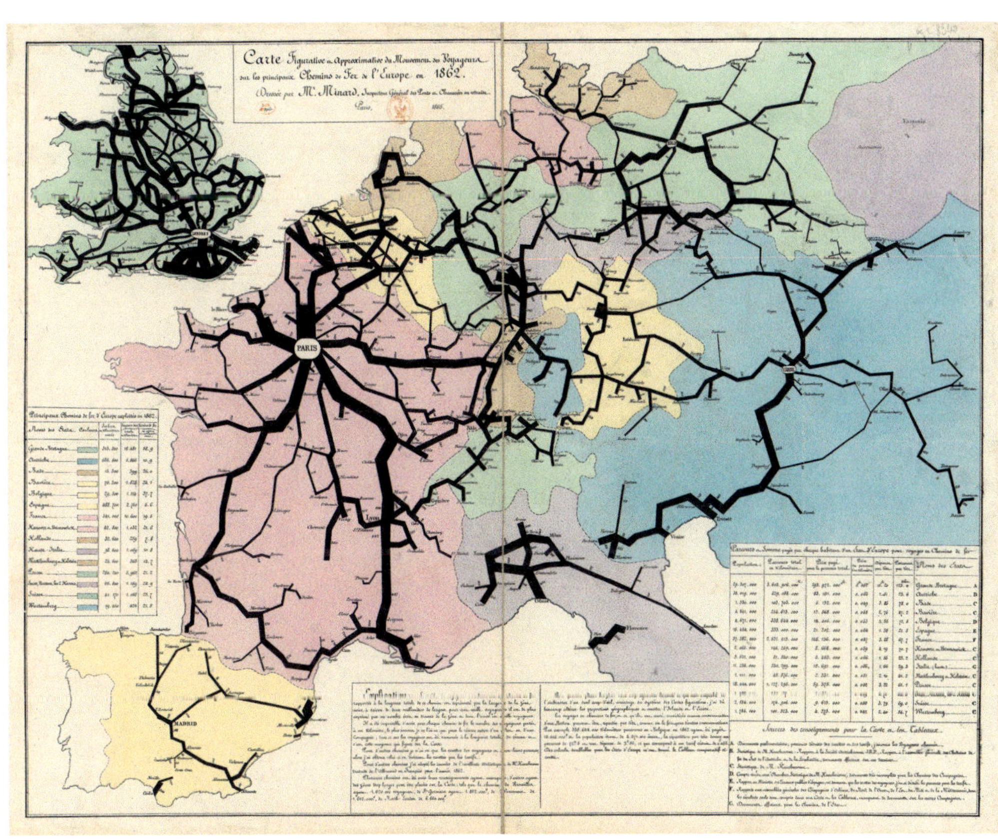

Fig. 5: *Figurative and Approximate Map of Travelers' Movements on the Main Railroads of Europe*, by Charles Joseph Minard, 1862.

considered the father of modern neuroscience, Cajal was one of two recipients of the 1906 Nobel Prize in Physiology or Medicine. Incidentally, before he began studying medicine, he trained to be an artist.

Interpreting the underlying structure of non-hierarchical representations, even those of small networks, can be tricky, especially when the overall interconnectedness between elements is impossible to unravel linearly or otherwise. Since his first forays into visualization, Barabási has used a series of visual strategies that aid in revealing the hidden structures of networks. Perhaps the simplest of all, yet one of the most effective, is the color encoding of nodes.

One of the lab's earliest node-link diagrams to be published in a paper, "Error and Attack Tolerance of Complex Networks," employed this strategy.[8] The visualization, which appeared in *Nature* in 2000, uses color to show levels of connectedness. The five nodes with the highest number of links are encoded in red, and their first neighbors in green (fig. 7). The image represents the lab's breakthrough discovery: that scale-free networks behave very differently from random networks. Barabási's subsequent visualization, published in *Nature* in the following year, was a map of the largest cluster of protein interactions (fig. 9). In that diagram, node colors stand for the phenotypic effect of removing the corresponding protein and, hence, are a fundamental feature of conveying the scientific findings. In general, colors can facilitate perception of many network features, such as patterns of connectedness behavior, distribution of nodes in different parts of the network, and the presence and location of clusters, among others.

In the BarabásiLab's 2007 *The Human Disease Network* (see page 62), which depicts the genetic origins of how diseases are related, disorders are grouped by

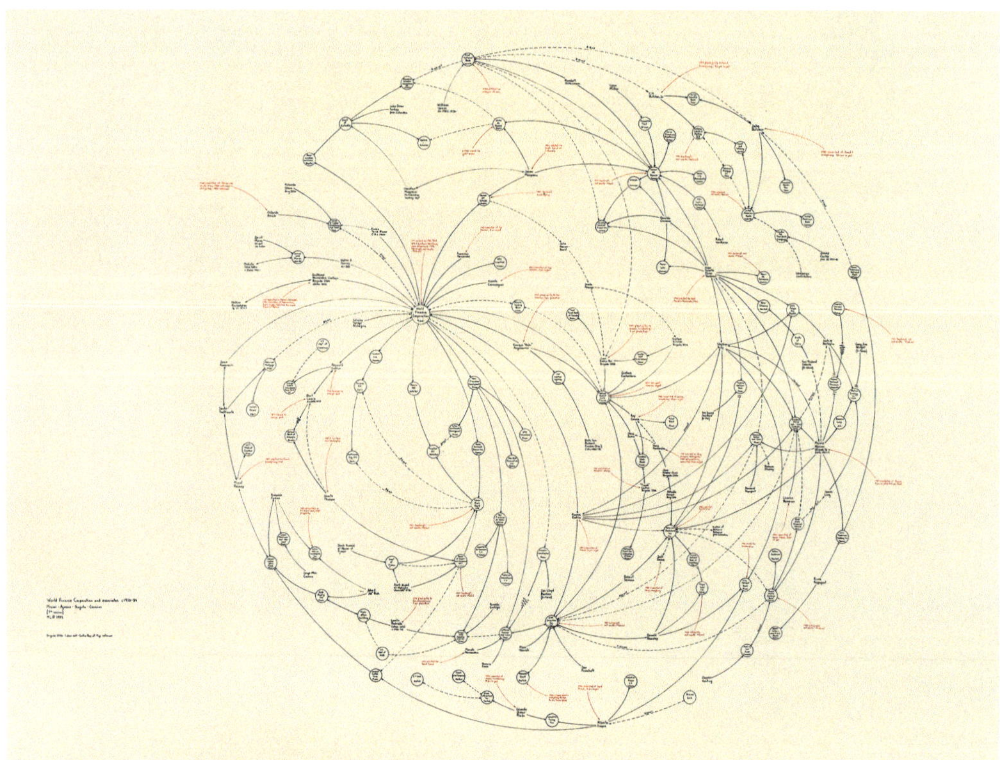

Fig. 6: *World Finance Corporation and Associates, c. 1970-84: Miami, Ajman, and Bogota-Caracas (Brigada 2506: Cuban Anti-Castro Bay of Pigs Veteran) (7th Version)*, by Mark Lombardi, 1999.

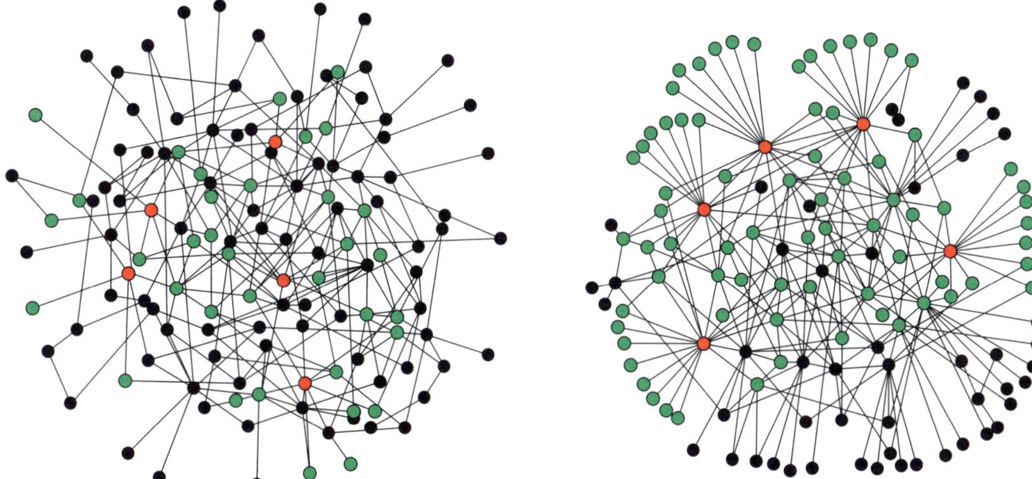

Fig. 7: The BarabásiLab's *Random vs. Scale-free Networks*, as published in "Error and Attack Tolerance of Complex Networks," in *Nature*, July 27, 2000.

color. We can examine the cyan cluster of cancers and even fathom the relationships between different types of cancers, as well as their connections to other morbidities, thanks in part to the color of nodes. In this diagram, the nodes also encode quantitative values, with their sizes standing for the number of genes associated with that disease. Adding to its communicative value is a clear layout with node overlaps avoided, and a minimum number of link crossings. In the early days, and whenever possible, researchers would painstakingly rearrange nodes to clarify the topology and highlight connectedness between elements. Such manipulation of nodes in the arts is still common practice.

The Human Disease Network is one of the lab's most iconic images. Its significance includes the different levels of knowledge and insight that it fosters—from the macro view of how diseases are interconnected to the micro understanding of particular genes. First published in 2007 in a paper for *Proceedings of the National*

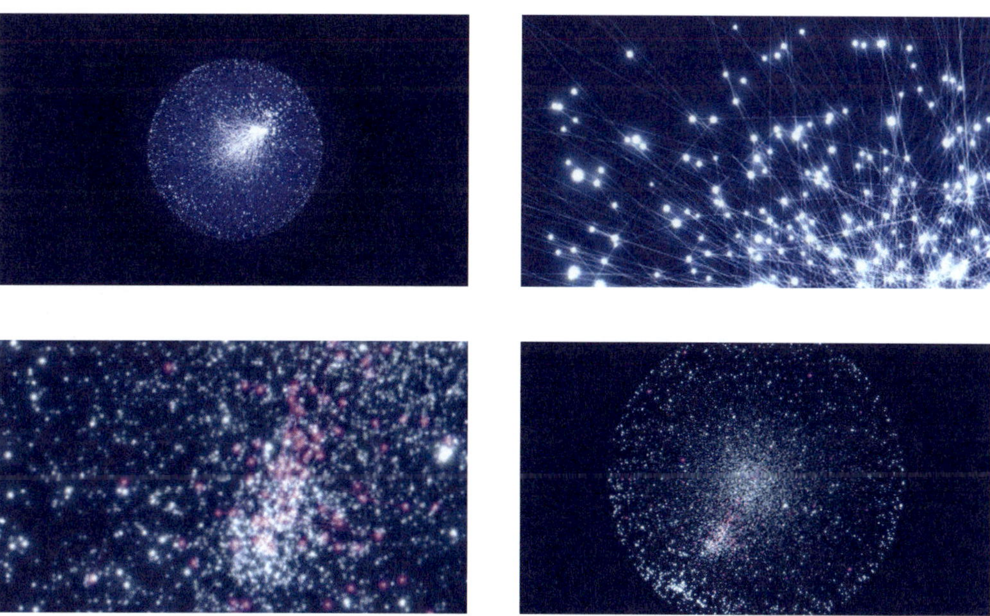

Fig. 8: Four stills from an animated digital visualization of the BarabásiLab's *The Human Disease Network*, which Barabási screened during his 2012 TEDMED Talk.

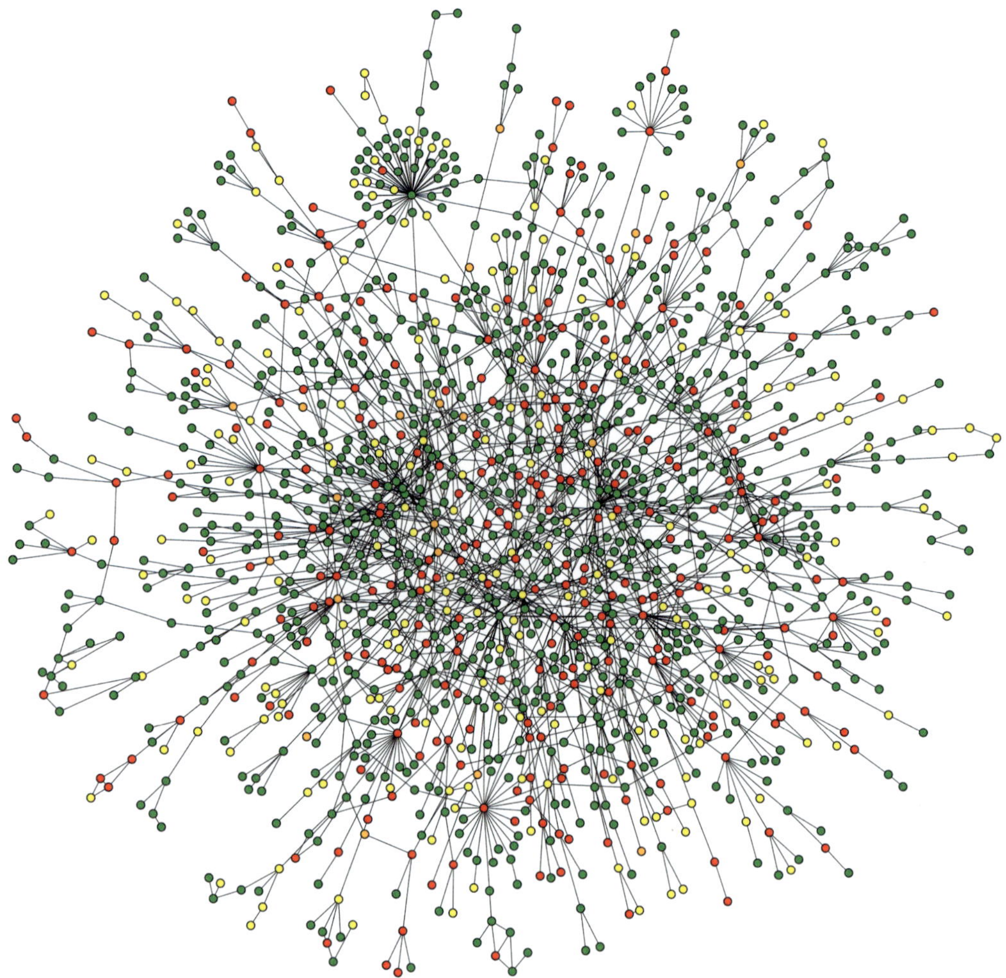

Fig. 9: The BarabásiLab's *Protein Interactions*, as published in "Lethality and Centrality in Protein Networks," in *Nature*, May 3, 2001.

Academy of Sciences, it was also reproduced as a large giveaway poster inside the publication.[9] The following year, the *New York Times* re-created it as an interactive online application, in which newspaper readers were able to zoom into areas of the network without losing the context of the whole graph.[10] And in 2010, it was displayed in *Map Marathon,* curated by Hans Ulrich Obrist, at the Serpentine Gallery, in London.[11]

Great Balls of Spaghetti

Overlapping nodes and links, and their resulting occlusions, are among the most challenging issues in network visualization. This is particularly true in the case of very large and complex systems, which tend to have dense areas crowded with large numbers of interconnected nodes. New techniques and algorithms are constantly being developed to make these frustrating "hairballs," or "spaghetti balls," easier to read and understand, since their visual clutter obliterates the structure they are supposed to reveal.

The Flavor Network, which the BarabásiLab's created in 2011, depicts how ingredients in food are connected through shared flavor chemicals. It was rendered with a technique called the hierarchical-edge bundle, which minimizes the number of crossing lines by grouping adjacent links (fig. 10).[12] This arrangement enhances the viewer's

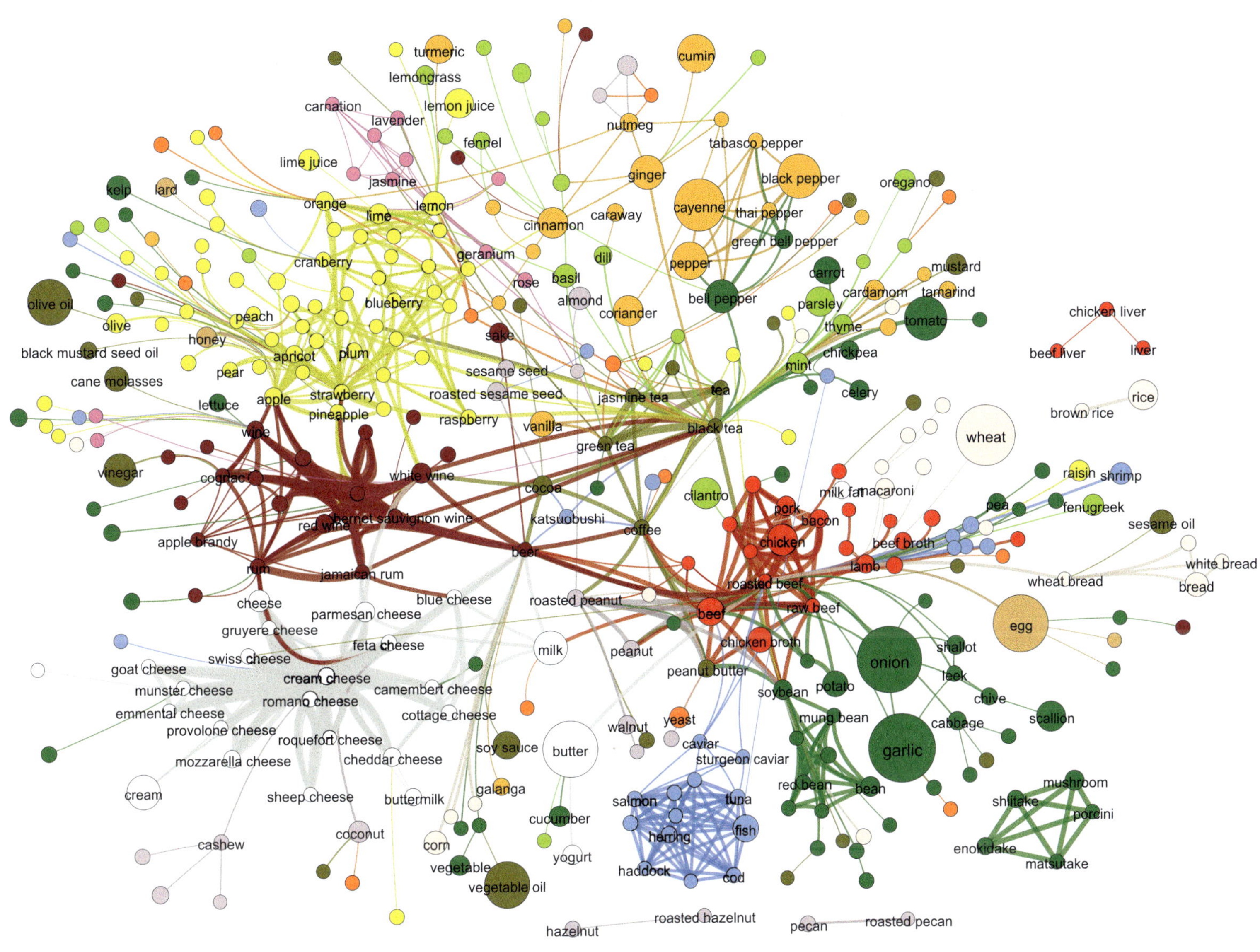

Fig. 10: *The Flavor Network*, by BarabásiLab, as published in "Flavor Network and the Principles of Food Pairing," in *Scientific Reports*, November 2011.

ability to follow connections, because the lines move in the same direction. Similarly, the lab's 2019 *150 Years of Nature*, which marked the journal's 150th anniversary, groups adjacent links in order to reveal meaningful patterns of connections (see page 164). The visualization's colored and curved lines are evocative of traces left behind by a living organism, suggesting the beautiful flow of knowledge and the passage of time.

The *Nature* network was not the first time the lab had depicted movement in a network, whether information, ideas, or money. In 2004, a set of visualizations titled *Flow* (see pages 58–61) revealed the movement of metabolic reactions by color encoding the connections responsible for the flow of energy. In the final version, multiple colored lines convey the pulse of the metabolic network, which is the source of life. A similar strategy was used in 2008, this time for the lab's research aimed at quantifying human dynamics. *Rhythm* is a set of visualizations depicting daily paths of individuals by color encoding their trajectories (see pages 84 and 85). Looking at the individuals' highlighted paths, we are confronted by their rhythms and repetitions, and how constrained and repetitive most lives actually are—the research showed that 93 percent of our movements are predictable.[13]

Escaping Flatland

While most node-link diagrams are attempts at flattening phenomena into the two dimensions of the plane, the BarabásiLab has ventured into three- and four-dimensional visualizations with sculptural renditions and experimentations in VR. Continuously pursuing new technologies, from the early days of network visualization software (such as Pajek) to pushing the boundaries of 3-D printing, the lab has enthusiastically explored and innovated a wide range of visual approaches. Its continuous experimentation with different dimensions has not only captured our imagination but expanded our understanding in a way similar to what Square, the main character in the nineteenth-century novella *Flatland,* by Edwin Abbott Abbott, experienced when he was visited by Sphere.[14] For Barabási, the attempt to dimensionalize scientific information and to expand scientific understandings for the non-scientific community is fundamental. His first book, *Linked: How Everything Is Connected to Everything Else and What It Means for Business, Science, and Everyday Life,*[15] conveys in clear prose and meaningful diagrams—including the *The Birth of a Scale-free Network* (fig. 11)—the ever-expanding nature of real networks and the power of connectedness. Barabási concludes the book, which was first published in 2002 and continues to inspire many in the arts and humanities today, by stating that the broad understanding of complexity depends on being able to envision it, and suggests that creating that vision will be his ongoing pursuit: "Looking back at the speed with which we disentangled the networks around us after the discovery of scale-free networks," he writes, "one thing is sure: Once we stumble across the right vision of complexity, it will take little to bring it to fruition. When that will happen is one of the mysteries that keeps many of us going."[15]

He has definitely kept going. Thanks to improvements in 3-D printing, combined with advanced mathematics, the BarabásiLab has not only proposed theoretical directions for the physicalization of networks, but also begun to produce them. *The Flavor Network,* which the lab successfully brought to life as a three-dimensional node-link in 2018 (see page 137), offers viewers a different understanding of the chemical origins of food combinations, because it allows them to move around the network and even manipulate it in their hands. What was originally a purely visual experience, imposed by the two-dimensional image, is now extended to other senses as a bodily experience. While this network is monochromatic, due to the restrictions of the three-dimensional powder printer at the time, the communities of flavors are still discernable by their physical location within the sculpture. This artful physicality enhances our ability to understand both the relationships between the flavor clusters and how they are positioned in the context of the whole structure.

Eyes Wide Open

Images have played a pivotal role in the development and communication of the sciences over time.[16] Barabási shares in that long-established scientific tradition of what science historian Peter Galison calls "wanting to know with eyes-open."[17] As they have been for other scientists before him, visual representations are central to Barabási's conceptualization process, as well as to his presentation of findings (figs. 12, 13). "My memory is visual, not auditory," he explained in a conversation we had recently. "If you tell me something, I don't retain it. If I look at a diagram, I never forget."

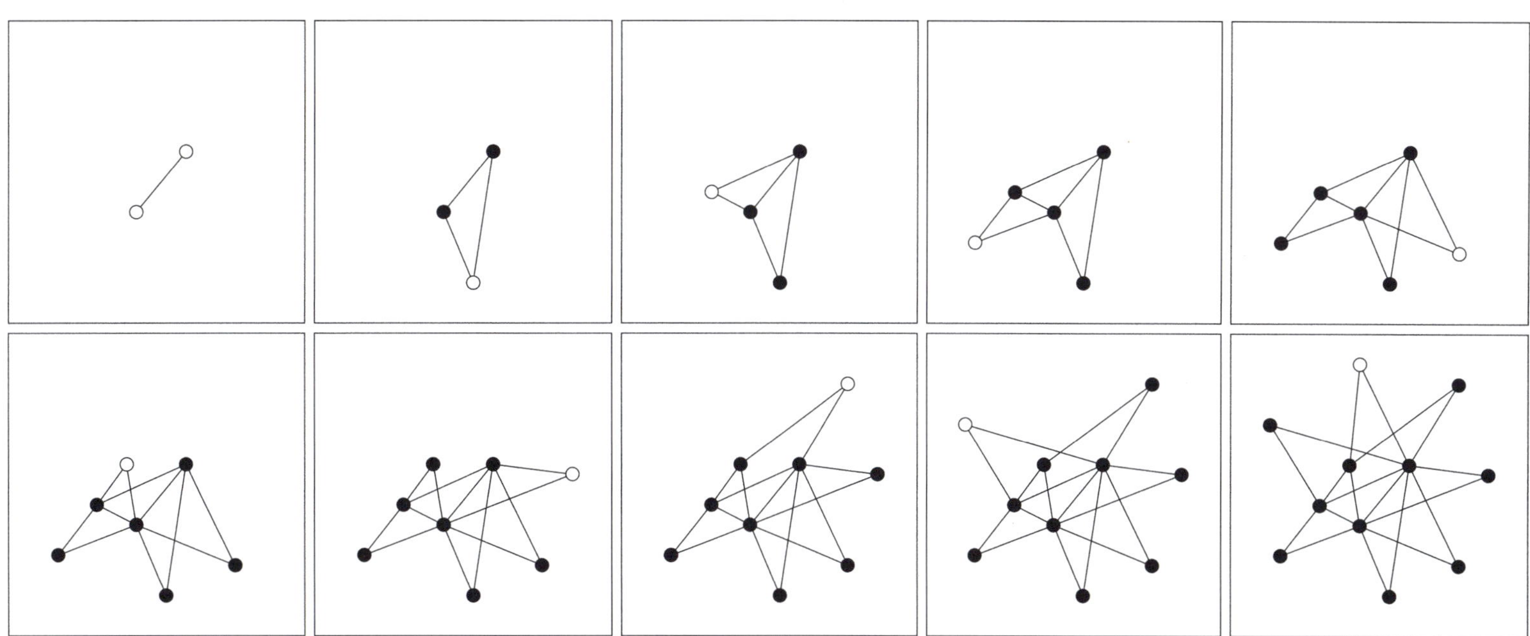

Fig. 11: *The Birth of a Scale-free Network*, from Barabási's 2002 book *Linked: How Everything Is Connected to Everything Else and What It Means for Business, Science, and Everyday Life*, which shows how highly connected hubs are the natural consequence of growth in the scale-free network topology.

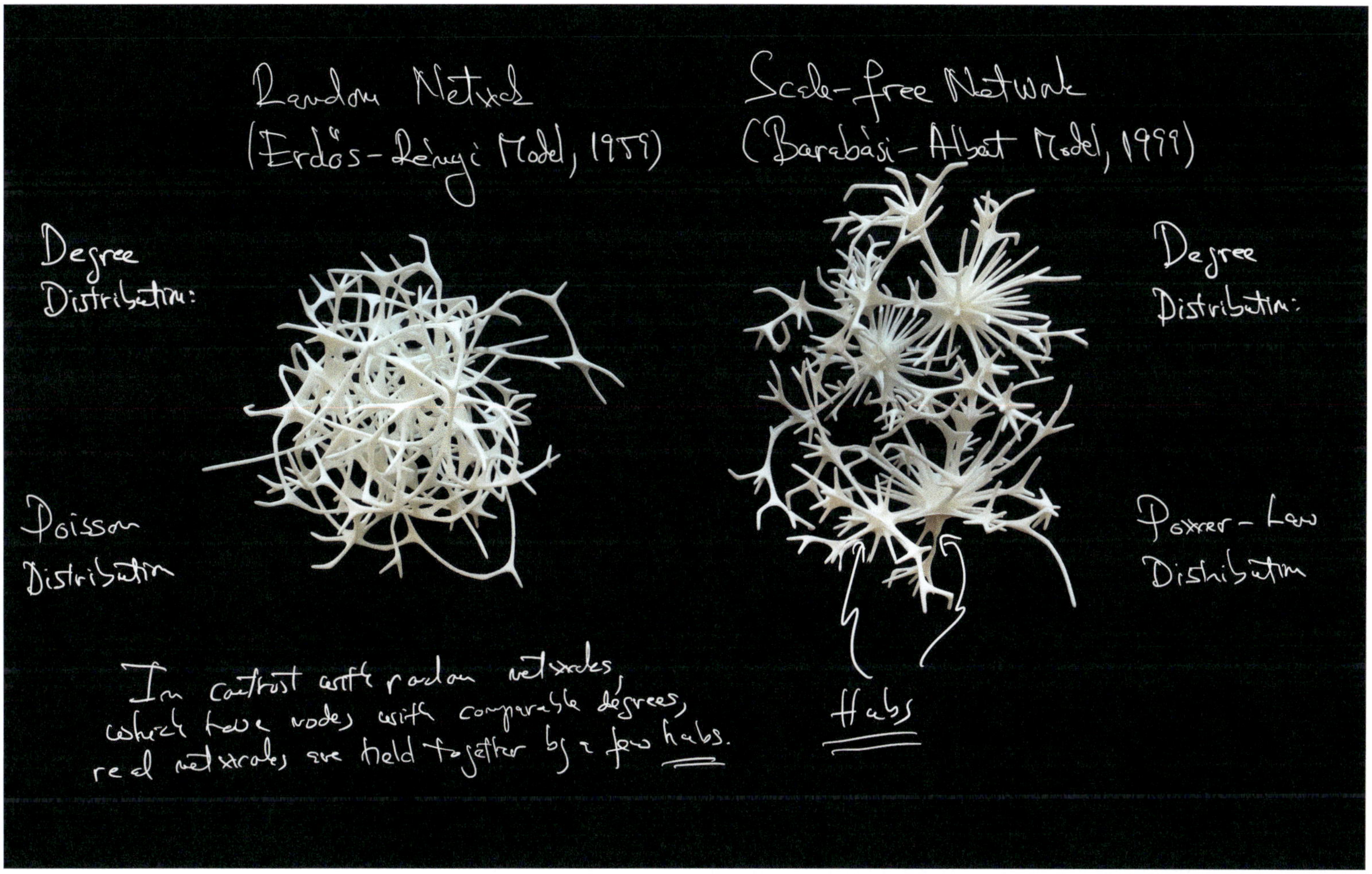

Fig. 12: A photograph of the 3-D-printed random and scale-free networks annotated by Barabási for Tomás Saraceno's Palais de Tokyo exhibition catalogue, *On Air*, 2018.

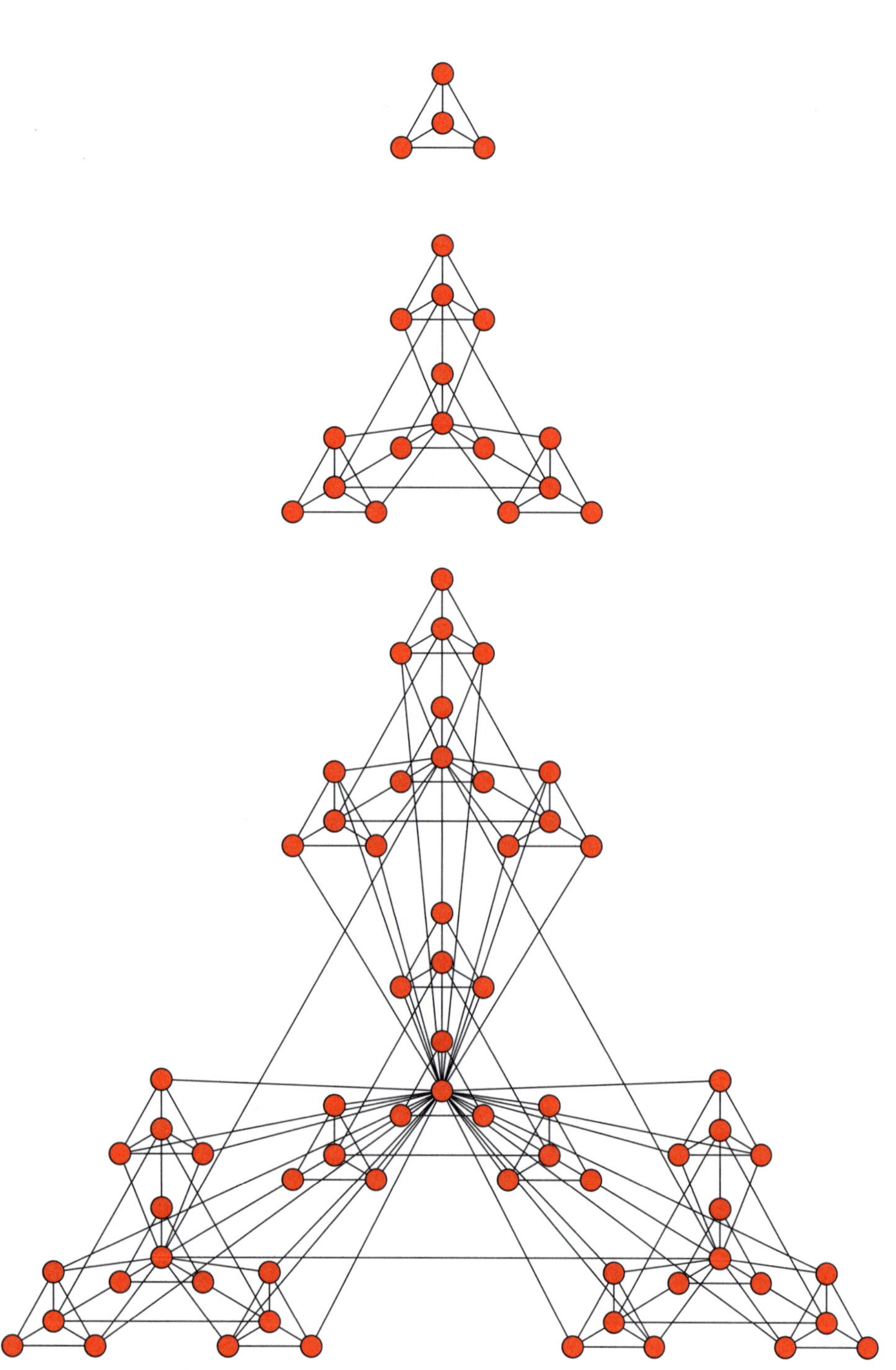

Fig. 13: The BarabásiLab's diagram *Hierarchical Networks*, as published in "Hierarchical Organization of Modularity in Metabolic Networks," *Science*, August 30, 2002.

Looking at the past twenty-five years of network-image production by the BarabásiLab, it is evident that node-link diagrams have occupied a central position in communicating relational structures of different nature and scales. From metabolic reactions (see page 59) to the cosmic web (see page 132), node-link diagrams have revealed invisible structures and patterns of connection. While the images help configure the science, the science untangles the images by directing our eyes toward what matters in them, even if what matters is dense, complex networks. Like some artists who are consumed by a particular shape or form, Barabási seems obsessed with the potentials offered by node-link diagrams. Indeed, and as we can see throughout this book, node-link diagrams are seductive both in their simplicity and their impenetrability. Having shaped the field of network science from its inception, and then persistently broadened our understanding and embrace of network thinking through meaningful and captivating images, Barabási's node-link-based visualizations have made an indelible mark on our memory and imagination. Their ever-evolving forms and subjects have inspired us to keep our eyes wide open, too.

---

1 See, for example, Herbert A. Simon, *The Sciences of the Artificial* (Cambridge, MA, 1981); and Barbara Tversky, *Mind in Motion: How Action Shapes Thought* (New York, 2019).

2 Paul Klee, *Cours du Bauhaus: Weimar 1921–1922, Contribuitions à la Thórie de la Forme Picturale* (Strasbourg, 2004).

3 Albert-László Barabási, *Network Science* (Cambridge, UK, 2016), pp. 24–25.

4 Alfred Korzybski, *Science and Sanity: An Introduction to Non-Aristotelian Systems and General Semantics* (Brooklyn, NY, 1933), p. 58.

5 Albert-László Barabási, "Do Your Proteins Have Their Own Social Network?" TEDMED Talks, May 31, 2012.

6 Jorge Luis Borges, *Collected Fictions,* trans. Andrew Hurley (New York, 1999).

7 Larry W. Swanson et al., *The Beautiful Brain: The Drawings of Santiago Ramón y Cajal* (New York, 2017).

8 Réka Albert, Hawoong Jeong and Albert-Laászló Barabási, "Random vs. Scale-free in Error and Attack Tolerance of Complex Networks," *Nature* 406 (July 27, 2000): 378–482.

9 Kwong-Il Goh et al., "The Human Disease Network," *Proceedings of the National Academy of Sciences* 104, no. 21 (May 22, 2007): 8685.

10 The interactive application "Mapping the Human 'Diseasome'" accompanied the article "Redefining Disease, Genes and All," by Andrew Pollack, *New York Times,* May 5, 2008.

11 Hans Ulrich Obrist, ed., *Mapping It Out: An Alternative Atlas of Contemporary Cartographies* (New York, 2014).

12 Danny Holten, "Hierarchical Edge Bundles: Visualization of Adjacency Relations in Hierarchical Data," *IEEE Transactions on Visualization and Computer Graphics* 12, no. 5, (September/October 2006): 741–748.

13 Chaoming Song et al., "Limits of Predictability in Human Mobility," *Science* 327, issue 5968 (February 19, 2010): 1018-1021.

14 Edwin Abbott Abbott, *Flatland: A Romance of Many Dimensions* (New York, 1998).

15 Albert-László Barabási, *Linked: How Everything Is Connected to Everything Else and What It Means for Business, Science, and Everyday Life* (New York, 2002).

16 See, for example, Lorraine Daston & Peter Galison, *Objectivity* (New York, 2007).

17 Peter Galison, "Image Scatter into Data, Data Gather into Images," in *Iconoclash: Beyond the Image Wars in Science, Religion, and Art,* Bruno Latour & Peter Weibel, eds. (Cambridge, MA, 2002) p. 301.

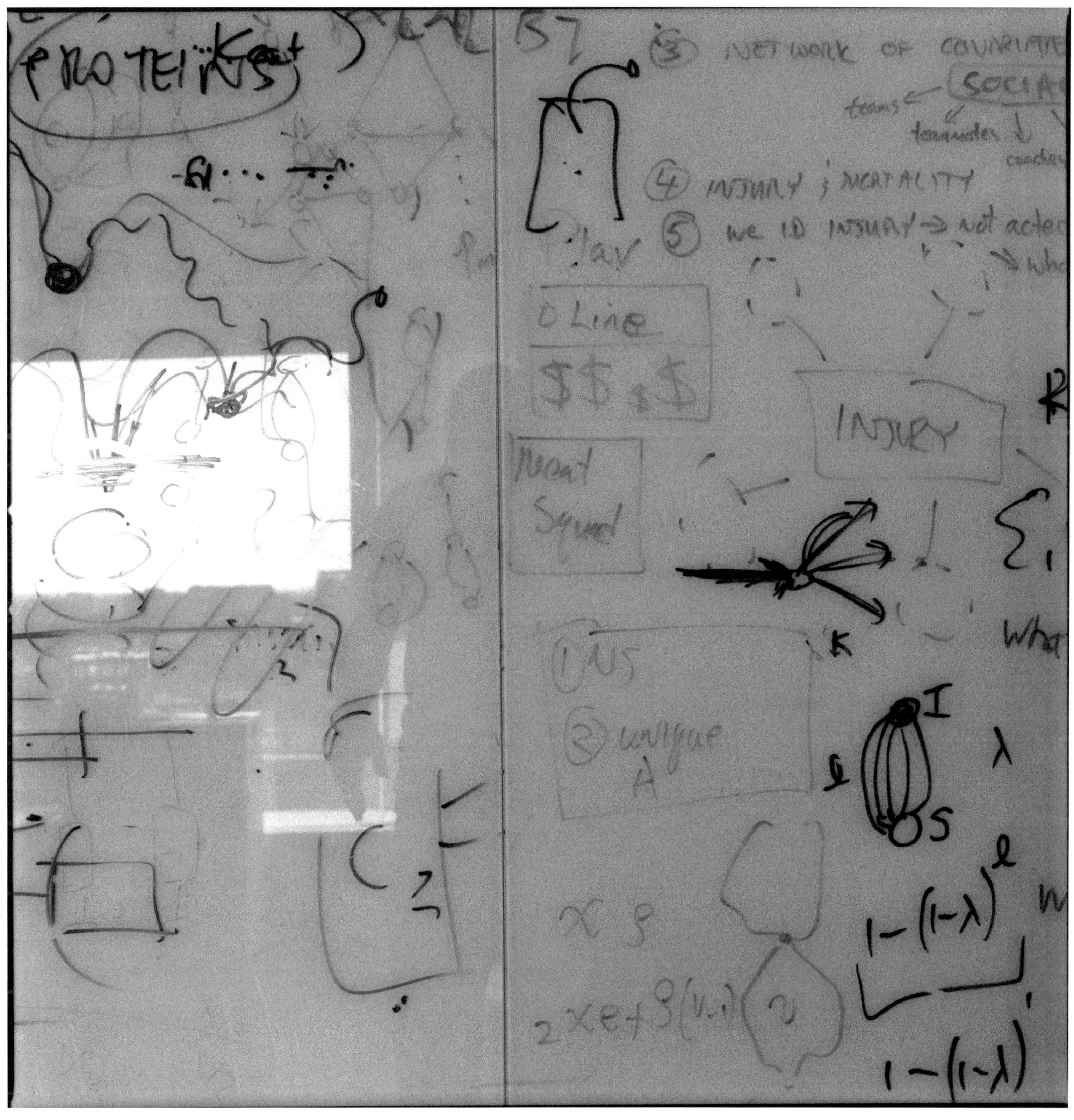
PROTEINS
NETWORK OF
teams
teammates
④ INJURY ; MORTALITY
⑤ we ID INJURY →
O Line
INJURY
① NS
② unique A
I
S
λ
1−(1−λ)

Where Randomness Ends and Order Begins

ALBERT-LÁSZLÓ BARABÁSI IN CONVERSATION WITH ANDRÁS SZÁNTÓ

Let's begin at the beginning. You have lived half a lifetime both inside and outside eastern Europe. You spend a lot of time in Budapest and hold an academic position there. What does that part of the world mean to you?

I am equally at home in Transylvania, Budapest, and Boston. And this plurality offers an opportunity for intellectual and cultural arbitrage, allowing me to immerse myself in different value systems and bring it all back to my life and my work. The collision of value systems is where the most interesting opportunities lie for people like me, who operate in the world of ideas.

From early on you excelled in science. And you were also drawn to art. How did the person that you are today come about?

I grew up in a family that eastern Europeans would call "intellectuals," in Csíkszereda, Romania, the heartland of Transylvania, in the Carpathian Mountains. My mother taught literature and was later a theater director. My father was a historian and a museum director. Every square centimeter in our house was covered with art. No surprise that by high school I wanted to become a sculptor. At the same time, I was winning physics competitions. When it came to a career choice, I had to contend with a competitive system for university admissions in Romania. There were five spots open for sculpting. There were seventy spots for nuclear physics. I chose science.

I got my master's in theoretical physics in Budapest, and my PhD in Boston. I was twenty-seven when I became an assistant professor, younger than some of my graduate students. And that's when art came back forcefully into my life. As a faculty member, I took a lot of classes at the university's art department—everything from photography to theater to film. At about the same time, my theoretical interest turned to networks. At first I didn't see a connection between these two pursuits. But already in 1999, when our work on networks started to make waves, I began pushing my lab to develop a visual language for representing networks.

Can you give me a capsule summary—a kind of elevator pitch—about the core ideas driving network science?

Our biological and physical existence depends on networks. Cells are networks of genes and molecules, and life as we know it is a result of interactions between them. Our consciousness is the result of the network of interactions of the billion or so

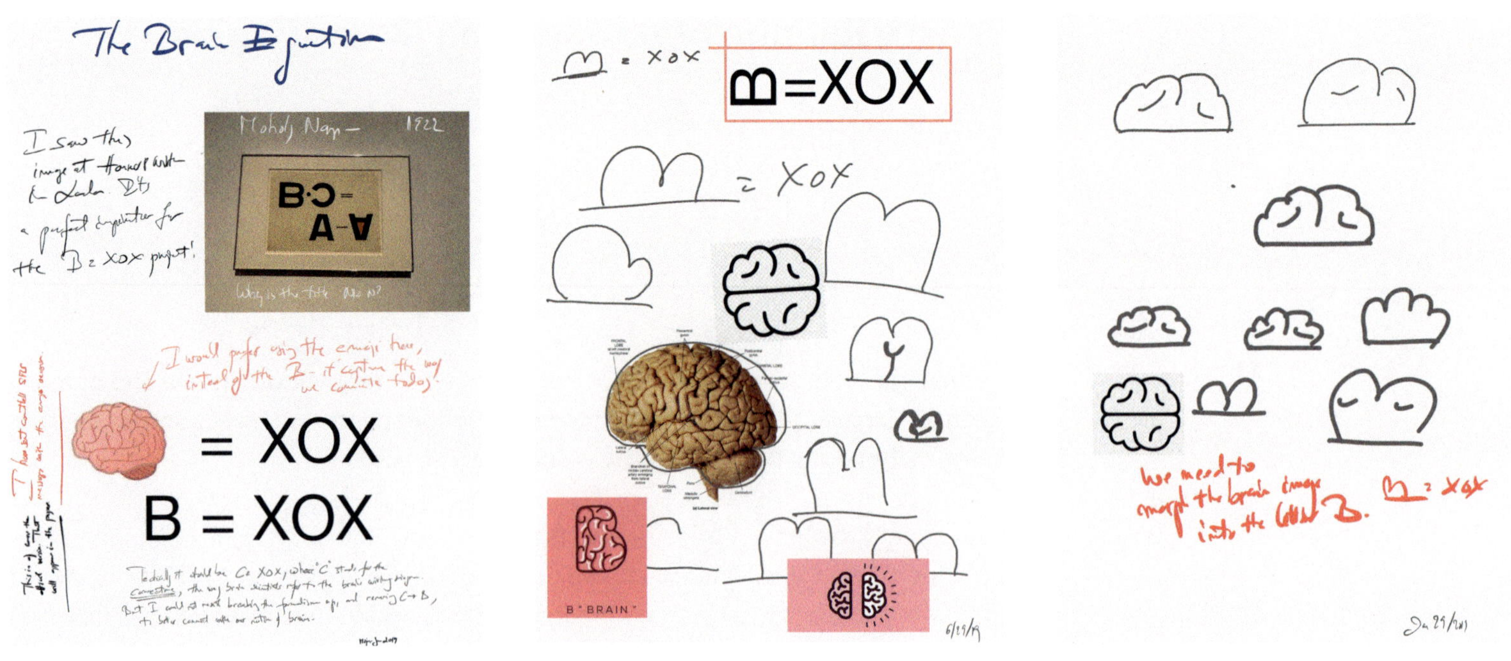

neurons in our brain. We communicate via networks: through telephone, email, and social networks. And our economy is a giant network of buyers and sellers, economic transactions connecting a vast layer of actors.

The twenty-first century is the century of networks. To be sure, some of these networks were in existence for over a billion years. Many, however, came about in the twentieth- and twenty-first centuries. And it was only in this century that we have truly come to understand the fundamental importance of connectedness—the way in which networks shape our lives. The science of networks has emerged as a response to this understanding.

And what are the basic building blocks of network science?

The building blocks are both empirical and mathematical. Empirical, because we rely on data to map out the networks that define us. Mathematical, because we use the tools of graph theory and physics to quantify and understand these large network maps. We are interested in their genesis, their evolution, and the role they play—as well as how they achieve the role they play—in everyday life.

Much of modern science is a reductionist enterprise. It tries to understand the components of a system—genes, atoms, even cells and humans—but none of these are meaningful in isolation. A molecule alone is not life. Not even the DNA is. Life emerges through interactions among molecules, just as society is the result of an exquisite layer of interactions among people. Network science conceptualizes these relationships. The core entities are the nodes (molecules, genes, humans, etc.), and our goal is to unveil how they interconnect in a meaningful way, to enable the emergence of something that is far more than the sum of the parts. We call these connections the links.

Obviously, the network of chemical reactions in our cells is very different from the World Wide Web, or a social network where people are connected by friendships or professional relationships. But the key discovery of network science—which came from my lab in the late 1990s—is that when you scrape away the details and just look at nodes connected by links, these networks are much more similar than they are different. There is a deep universality in networks.

Before we get into more detail on your work, who have been your intellectual or academic touchstones?

Having been trained as a theoretical physicist, my thinking is deeply inspired by physics. Perhaps the most defining influence on my work has been that of Ludwig Boltzmann, the Austrian physicist and philosopher who was the first to realize, when studying gases, that there was order behind randomness. His research defined the philosophy on which network science rests: you and I make our own choices about our friends and relationships, about whom to message, and what and where to purchase. Yet many of these independent and apparently random actions add up to something much bigger, thereby contributing to the emergence of networks, which can be described by universal laws.

Was there something you got from your immersion in art that helped to push or catalyze your thinking?

For me, the most inspiring thing about art is the fact that artistic expression lacks boundaries. It is willing to freely experiment with different media and technologies, and it possesses an unrestrained freedom to mix and utilize ideas. As soon as we started to study networks, I began appropriating concepts from the art world—not only to visualize networks, but also to think about them.

The story inside the art world in recent decades has been about breaking down universality, in search of a more diverse, decentered art discourse. There is much anxiety about universal laws in the humanities. You are arguing that behind the multitude of everyday occurrences, universal laws are alive and well.

Diversity can only be understood from the perspective of universality. You're diverse in comparison to what? Universality is the unavoidable reference frame if you want to talk about diversity.

I'll give you an example from physics: hundreds of years ago, people believed there were different gods responsible for tides and waves on the seas, for the movement of the stars, and for why we fall down if we don't pay attention. Then Newton came along and showed that all these phenomena have a single explanation: gravity. Once that was understood, it was possible to start exploring diversity, capturing the many different ways gravity manifests itself. Similarly, we cannot truly understand diversity and differences until we first understand what is universal about the human existence and experience. This is not to say there is no value to thinking about diversity—that is what I do every day. But these countless independent choices and actions

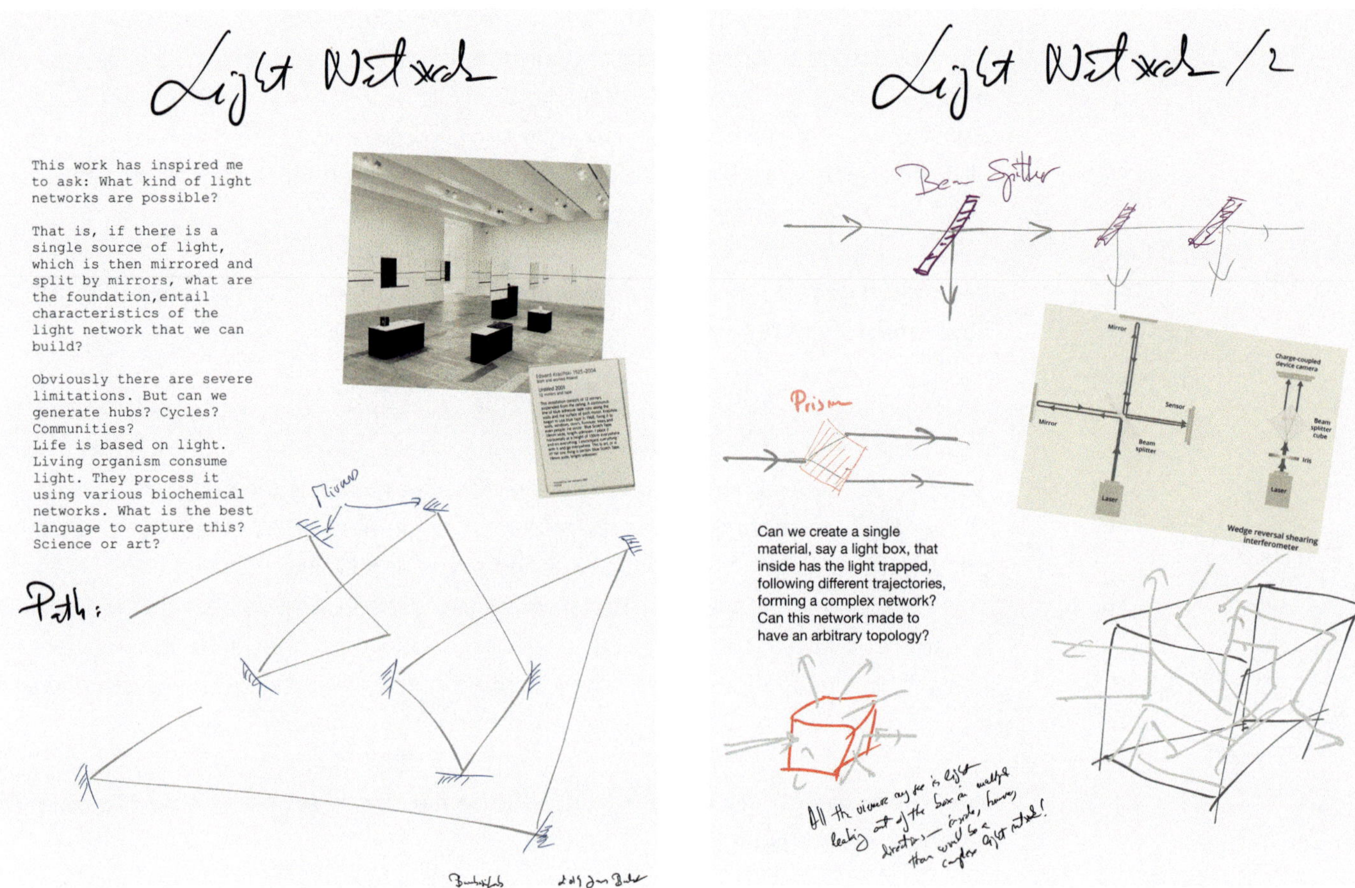

do add up to something larger than you and me. Which is why we must view diversity in the light of universality.

This book and the exhibition that occasions it are both titled *Hidden Patterns*. So what are the hidden patterns in the context you just described? Can we understand them? What are the limits of mapping the world this way?

My own intellectual pursuit is about pinning down the end of randomness and the beginning of order. Hence, for me, hidden patterns are about finding, quantifying, and then unveiling the order that is hidden inside complex systems. Art and science play a complementary role in this pursuit. Science allows me to pin down the quantitative signature of order. The language of art helps me unveil it, making it accessible—not just to scientists, but to everyone. Art also helps me ask questions that are not interpretable within the scientific framework.

Was there ever a "eureka" moment for you, an epiphany, when these ideas started really gelling together?

I first encountered networks as a postdoc at IBM, in 1995. I was living in New York City. Walking down the avenues, I was confronted with the many invisible networks that keep the city alive—from networks that bring water and electricity (the Internet was still emerging) to the social and professional networks that make things happen in the city. At the time, I was already reading the literature of graph theory and networks, connected to the great Hungarian mathematicians Paul Erdős and Alfréd Rényi. I realized that all the existing theories assumed that the networks we encounter in society and nature are fundamentally random. In other words, that the dice decide who my friends are, or where an Internet router connects to another router. That didn't make any sense to me.

That same year, I decided to study networks full-time. But for years, I could not get any of our findings published. A paper I wrote about networks was rejected by every science journal I sent it to. No one said there was anything wrong. What they said, effectively, was: "Why should we care?" It wasn't until 1999 that we managed to start publishing on networks. What had changed in the intervening four years? I had begun to move beyond theory and to look at real data. Notably, in 1998 we mapped out the World Wide Web, getting our hands on the map of a real network for the first time. Once we had that, we quickly realized that the properties we found had nothing to do with the properties predicted by the prevailing mathematical models.

This is when we discovered the so-called scale-free network property. To understand what that term means, you have to begin with the notion of randomness. For example, if the nodes in a social network were randomly connected then, at the end of the day, we all would be very similar in terms of the number of friends we have. What we discovered with the Web, by contrast, is that this is not the case in real life. The Web is dominated by a few massive hubs, or web pages, that have an exceptional number of links pointing to them. In subsequent years, we and others have shown repeatedly that these hubs are present in most naturally occurring networks—from cells in your body to social networks. Most real networks are dominated by hubs, and once hubs are present, they all follow the mathematical properties that we discovered in the Web.

Let's talk about the other aspect of your endeavor: visualization. How does visualization enable your understanding of the science?

What we do in the lab is rather abstract. As soon as we started working with network data, I started pushing the whole team to bring these networks to life. Our first successful attempt at visualization was in 2000, when we created two network maps to illustrate the difference between a random network and a hub-based, scale-free network [see page 31, top]. That same year, we got access to the first data about protein interactions, which maintain life in each cell. We worked for six months iterating different versions before we managed to obtain an elegant visual representation. It was published in *Nature* and has become an iconic image [see page 32], reproduced on many posters and book covers since. From that moment on, as we developed the mathematical tools, we simultaneously advanced the visual language for each project. We were often motivated by a desire to be on the cover of journals where our papers were being published. But over time, visualizing networks took on an intellectual and artistic pursuit of its own. Aesthetics became just as important as scientific accuracy.

But do you consider these visualizations art? If not, what would it take for them to be seen as art?

I made my career by defying scientific boundaries. My life goal has been to understand and depict the complexity of the world around us. This journey has been significantly inspired by art. And I have repeatedly appropriated the language of art and brought it back to science. For me, the question of whether this is art or science—or physics or network science—makes absolutely no sense. They are all part of the same journey of discovery.

That journey has recently led you to map the art world, creating the closest link yet between your two passions. How did you go about it? What have been your major insights from a network-science point of view?

Some years ago, I moved back to Budapest for an extended period, and during this time I began collecting works by leading Hungarian artists. I organized exhibitions in my home and in the courtyard of our building. These shows gave me an opportunity to interact with museums and galleries, as well as with artists themselves. And the more I learned about the inner workings of art as a profession, the more I saw how art works as a network. Then, four years ago, Sam Feinberger, who at that time was a postdoc in our institute at Northeastern University in Boston, mentioned that he had access, through the art entrepreneur Magnus Resch, to an exceptional data set that describes the exhibition history of all artists in the past forty years. I was intrigued. We immersed ourselves in the data, and it took us almost three years to figure out how we could use it to look at artistic processes and success.

At the beginning of any network-science project, we need to ask, "What are the nodes and links that most appropriately describe the system we are analyzing?" For art, the first instinct was that the nodes are the artists. As we dug into the data, however, we realized that although there is no art without artists, artistic success is determined not by artists but by the institutions. The artists and the art they create are the fuel, so to speak, of a complex institutional network. From the data, we were able to show that this hidden network determines what really happens in the long term in the art world, including the future of individual artistic careers.

What can we learn about art and the art world with the help of these analytical tools?

The question most artists want to know the answer to is: What does it take to be exhibited in MoMA or any other major institution? Obviously, you have to create great art. But who decides what is great art? Fundamentally, the institutions—or the curators and gallerists behind the institutions. They decide what fits the prevailing canon.

We asked where you have to be exhibited to get noticed by the curators of the most prestigious art institutions. We built a network in which organizations are connected when they are exhibiting the same artists. If the Ludwig Museum exhibits Dóra Maurer and then a few months later she is exhibited in MoMA, that is a signal MoMA considers Ludwig to be a reference institution. We crunched the data on the

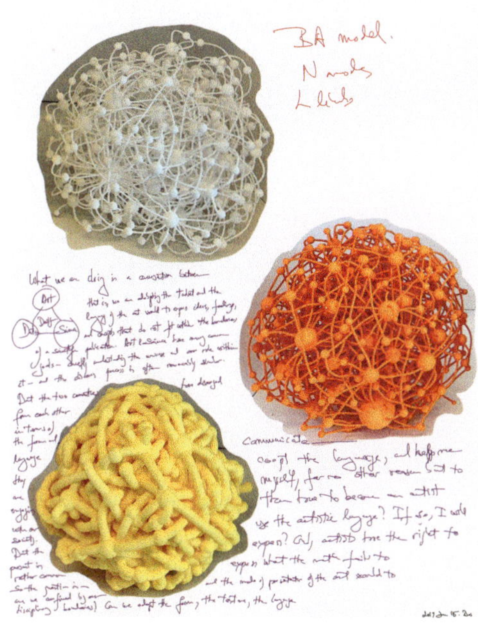

careers of half a million artists who exhibited in 20,000 institutions in 140 countries. This allowed us to map out those hidden paths of influence between museums and galleries [see pages 126–29].

Were there any surprises about the art-world data compared to other sets?

The big surprise was that the network is fragmented into different clusters of institutions. Some of these are geographic, such as Australian art organizations forming a compact cluster. Many of them are conceptual and market-driven. The A+ museums and galleries—MoMA, Centre Pompidou, Pace Gallery, Gagosian, etc.—together form a single, connected sub-cluster. Once an artist starts exhibiting in one of these places, the doors open to the other high-profile institutions. By contrast, if you start your career in a small gallery in Budapest, there are very few paths for you into these A+ institutions, because eastern European institutions form a separate cluster with few bridges to the A+ cluster. *The Art Network* enables us to predict artistic success. It is a meaningful and dynamic network, because if you place an artist on the map, we can predict her future trajectory. We know with a great deal of certainty whether she will rise or stagnate in terms of access to prominent and less prominent institutions.

Now is the moment to ask the big question: Is the art world any different from other networks?

In many ways, the structure of *The Art Network* is virtually indistinguishable from the networks we encounter in most social or biological systems. Just like the Web, the art world is dominated by hubs. On the Web, Google has hundreds of millions of links, making it a dominant hub. In the same way, the largest museums are the dominant hubs in the art space. *The Art Network* has islands of nodes that are densely connected, meaning they have many connections back and forth, to each other. These are parallel to thematic web pages on the Internet. This architecture is inescapable for "self-organized" systems in which the decision about where to connect stays at the level of the node. I decide who is my friend. The gallery or museum decides whom they will exhibit.

We can think of this universal structure like the architecture of a building: all buildings are alike when it comes to their architectural building blocks. But utility, purpose, and inhabitants differ from structure to structure. In this same way, the art world has many details that distinguish it, or explain why it diverges, from the other networks. Here, too, you first need to understand universality to be able to talk about uniqueness and diversity. Once we understand the universal properties of the network, we can ask how one particular artist's trajectory is different from another's, how a female artist's experience is different from a male's, or how the particular value system the art world represents is mirrored in the way the network is being used. These are the questions that fascinate me these days.

Since we started this project, the greatest epidemic of our lifetimes has emerged, spreading from Asia to Europe, North America, and around the world. It is a classic network phenomenon. I imagine it is also a great opportunity for network scientists.

Have you been involved in tracking and analyzing the novel coronavirus?

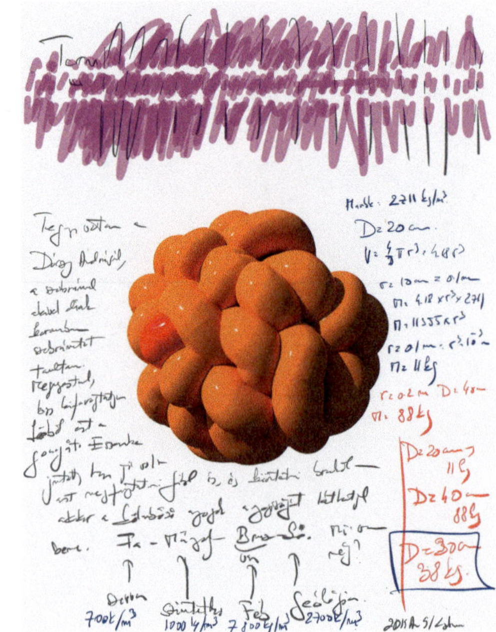

It is still too early to grasp the tragedy and the legacy of the Covid-19 pandemic. However, we can see that it has definitely put network science on the map. In the Network Science Institute at Northeastern University, where the tool set of epidemic forecasting has been developed for more than a decade, my colleagues are now predicting in real time how many people will be infected. Early on in the pandemic, they became the White House's prediction team, forecasting for the task force the expected impact of specific interventions, like the closing of schools or the resumption of air travel. I personally got deeply involved in another crucial problem, how to find drugs. The normal time frame to develop a new drug is ten years. Therefore, the only viable option is to identify existing drugs that may work for Covid-19 patients. So I have immersed myself in using network tools to identify which drugs may help save the lives of Covid-19 patients.

What does that mean exactly?

Drugs work by perturbing the network within cells. They do this by attaching to certain proteins. Similarly, the Covid-19 virus hijacks cells by attaching its proteins to certain human proteins. If we can find a drug that blocks the proteins and the resources the virus needs, we may be able to limit the virus's ability to invade our cells. We identified several hundred potential drugs and, working with colleagues at Harvard and Boston University, have been experimentally testing, finding that indeed many of the predicted drugs were able to kill the virus in infected cells.

What have we learned about the coronavirus as a network? Is it the same as other contagion networks? Or is it different?

Covid-19 follows the same spreading patterns as other biological and nonbiological viruses. We have been modeling these processes since 2009, when we started to track human mobility using mobile phones [see pages 88–93]. SARS-COV-2, the virus behind the Covid-19 epidemic, is fundamentally an influenza-like virus. What makes it so hard to stop is that, unlike most influenza viruses, it has a period of asymptomatic spread. That's why we are having such a hard time avoiding contagion and keeping people safe.

How does this network then cascade in influence on to other networks—social, economic, cultural? Or is it too early to tell?

Stopping the virus is a network-of-networks problem—meaning we need to simultaneously act on multiple networks. The first instinct was an intervention on the mobility network: by locking people up, we'd effectively kill human mobility. But this alone is not sufficient—we must acknowledge the deep interconnectivity of human existence and intervene at multiple networks, from limiting social interactions to economic transactions. Most European countries approached the pandemic as a holistic multinetwork problem, which is why they have done so much better than the US, which viewed it as only a mobility problem.

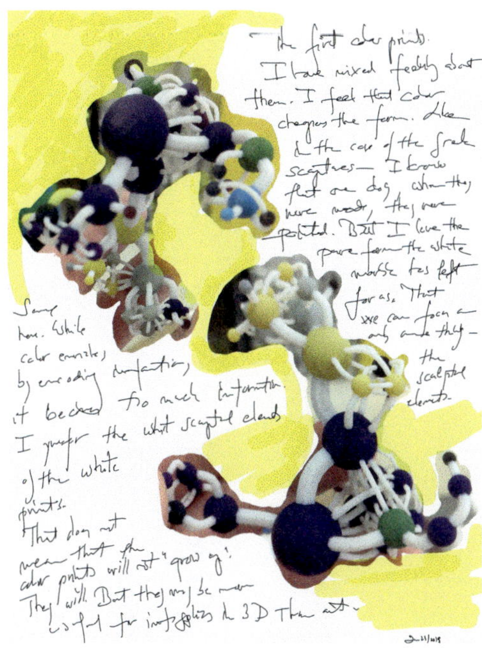

In the world of museums and cultural events, there is a lot of talk of a reversion to more local cultural networks and a corresponding decline in big global events, such as art fairs and biennials. Are these prognoses more a sign of present anxieties than of the realities of the future?

The more the world goes online, as it did during the pandemic, the more we miss and desire the experience of physicality, and the more we appreciate seeing something or someone in person. In the short run, there will certainly be a return to locality. That decoupling from the global canon could be very reinvigorating to the local communities. Yet, the more we stay online, the more we learn to appreciate aspects of human experience that cannot be replicated online. I expect that museums, galleries, nature, and other places that reveal the magic of physicality and materiality will be appreciated more than ever.

Has the epidemic forced some kind of reckoning for you and your lab? Has it brought to light something you missed before, or indicated that, as an organization, you now need to approach your remit differently?

The epidemic has put network science on the map in a big way. It would have taken another decade for us to achieve the kind of prominence, impact, and visibility the field is now experiencing. Everybody is a network epidemiologist now. Everybody understands mobility networks. The network-science community is at the forefront of the conversation in a way we never have been before. For the Budapest exhibit, we went back and pulled out some of the lab's decade-old work on epidemic spread, precisely because we had to reevaluate its relevance to the current conversation. The work we did on mobility around 2010 now plays a key role in how we understand and how researchers model the virus's spread. We even created a video about how mobility in New York changed during the lockdown. In sum, for network science in general, and for my own lab in particular, this moment has opened up many doors that would have stayed closed for many years.

Getting back to the art world, I want to drill down a bit on two propositions. One has to do with a widespread perception that over the past quarter-century there has been a great deal of consolidation around a small number of ever-larger entities in the art system (e.g., mega galleries, art fairs, auctions). Can you confirm or contextualize this in terms of network science?

The concentration of power is trivial from a network-science point of view. A unique feature of any scale-free network, like the art world, is that the size of the largest hubs is determined by the overall size of the network. However, another fundamental feature of this type of network is that when the network grows, for example if the number of art organizations doubles, the size and power of the largest institutions doesn't double. Their growth is sublinear. Art in the past thirty years has undergone a major process of globalization. Many more players have emerged. Institutions that had previously been geographically and conceptually isolated have joined the global art space. What art-world insiders experience as a power grab by a few major organizations is actually a completely predictable consequence of network growth. To be sure, the disparity between the big guys and the small guys creates tension and locks in opportunities. But the phenomenon of disparity is not unique to the art world. It is something we see in all large networks, as are the difficulties disparity ignites.

The second proposition I'd like to test relates to what you said a moment ago about artists being somewhat trapped in their regional sub-networks. We in the art world are proud that we have become more inclusive and polyphonic recently. We celebrate global artists entering the mainstream—just look at the new MoMA, which has committed itself to presenting parallel art histories to the established Western canon. But your data appear to tell a different story.

Both statements are true. There is globalization in the art world that naturally brings in players from the fringes of the system. But the numbers in which they come are not proportional to the presence in the system. I have watched with pride over the past five years as several Hungarian artists have entered the world's leading art institutions. But that number is a tiny fraction of the thousand-plus artists who have been showing their work in Hungary over the past decade. Space is limited at the top of the art world, especially because the top institutions grow at a slower rate than the whole system. The largest entities lock in a small number of artists who start their careers high up, exhibiting at the most highly regarded galleries and museums, and never exit that elite sphere. Once you factor in these artists, there is scant space for the artists who come from the periphery to claim top spots.

The inequality in access is an ongoing research subject in my lab. We recently published a major study on gender inequality in science and are finalizing a major study that uses network-based tools to explore gender-based access in the art world. A dream of mine is to expand this tool set to race as well so that we can understand the systemic issues that affect access to institutions of underrepresented groups.

We have not yet addressed commerce, prices, and values in the art world. We have seen enormous price inflation in the art market. How does that play out in light of the aforementioned network dynamics?

Every network's growth has to be fueled by resources. The growth of a cell or cell metabolism is fueled by ATP, adenosine triphosphate, the energy-carrying molecule in a cell. The growth of social networks is driven by jobs, economic opportunities, and access to learning. Money is one ingredient fueling the growth of the art world. But it is not the only one. From the data perspective, monetary value is virtually indistinguishable from prestige. The art world is the best example of a system where value emerges through the networks and not by some intrinsic, measurable characteristic. If you are an artist exhibited in the top hubs of *The Art Network*, then you will command high prices. This relationship is so symbiotic that it is impossible to find causality. Is it prestige that attracts money, or the money that attracts prestige? It's an inherently unsolvable chicken-or-egg problem. This pattern is widely observed when there is no objective measure of quality, but it is the network that creates value. When we rank

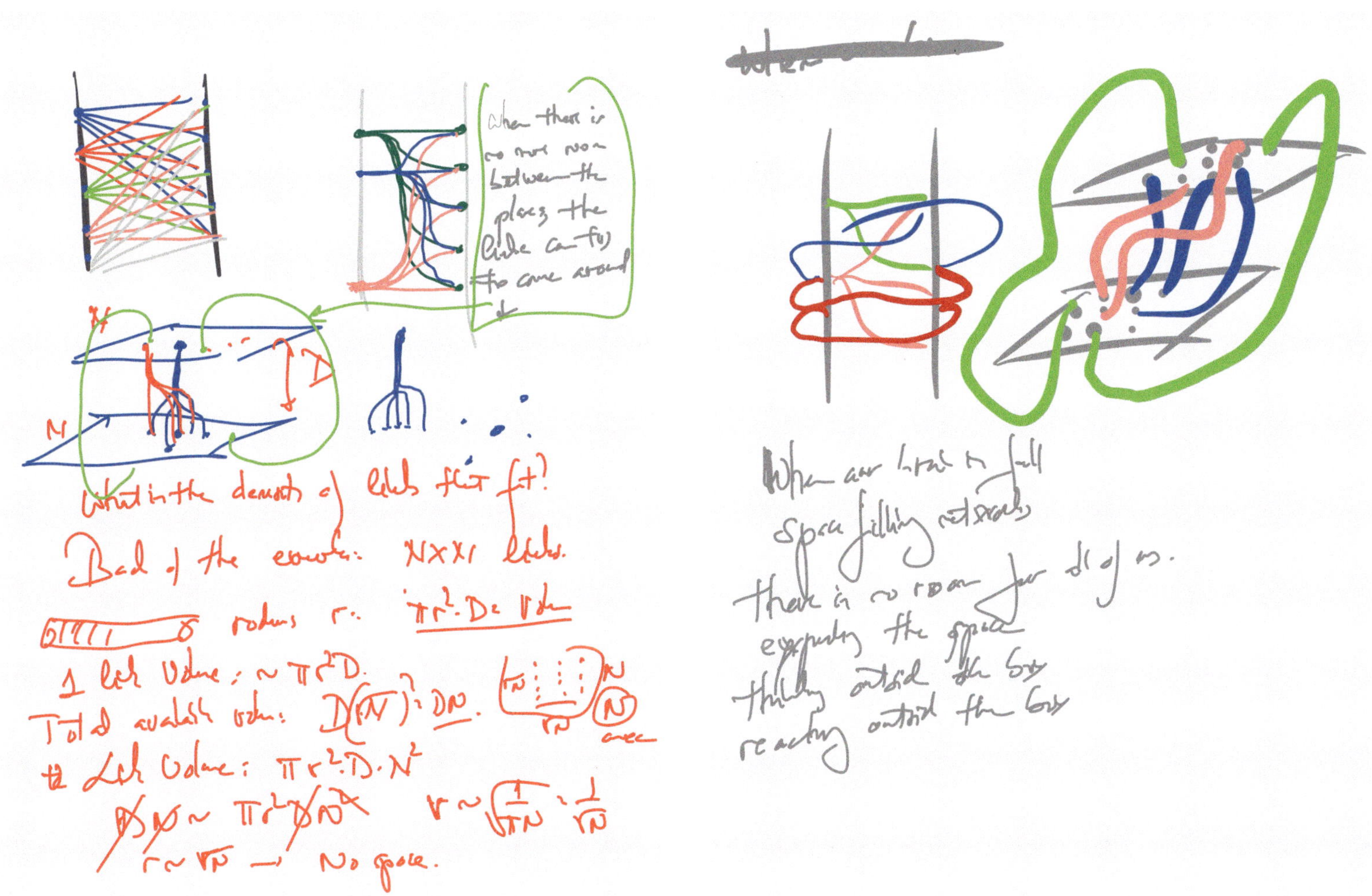

institutions based on what artists they exhibit, that ranking is perfectly aligned with the market prices of the artists they exhibit.

Let's turn now to your research process. Who works with you in your lab? How do you collaborate? How are visualizations produced as a practical matter?

The lab consists of postdoctoral researchers and students who are working toward their PhDs. They are physicists, computer scientists, neuroscientists, designers—even art historians. What differentiates us from other science labs is that when our researchers present results, it is not enough for them to push the science forward. We also expect them to break new ground in the visualization of the results. I personally get deeply involved in the visual narrative of the project, and, when needed, we bring in a designer as well. Right now, we have about thirty people in the lab, including two designers, and these numbers are growing steadily.

Over the past twenty years, our visual vocabulary has evolved together with our ability to bring network content to life. In 1995, I still put the network on a grid, without nodes [see page 16]. But by 1999, the nodes started to have an identity; they were circles of equal size connected by straight black lines. Then we started adding color to encode content. In 2007, we began to vary the node size and to codify other dimensions of the data. Four years later, the links started to curve in order to avoid each other and allow us to show increasingly dense and complex networks. In 2018, we stepped out of two dimensions and we now think in terms of 3-D, developing new tools to turn networks into "data sculptures" brought to life using 3-D printers. The science challenges us to keep pushing the boundaries in the way we depict our networks. We embrace this challenge by trying to develop not only the mathematical vocabulary of networks, but also their visual language.

How do you choose subjects? Does the potential for visualization play a role?

I look for opportunities that are ripe for exploration and can be studied with existing tools. And I always ask whether a certain problem will allow us to break new ground in terms of our conceptual and visual tool set. If a well-established community around a given problem already exists, I tend not to be interested. I get very excited about unexamined subjects that have a rich layer of meaning and societal impact and are challenging in their complexity. Once we satisfy these criteria, we try to establish a new visual and conceptual canon around the subject. That is what we did for networks in general, and then for human mobility, for network medicine, and now for art. We were among the first to study these problems, which helped turn many of them into well-established fields.

To what extent is what you do a function of the technology available today? Much of what the lab does simply couldn't be done even ten years ago. By extension, is what you are able to study now heavily limited by the tools available today?

Technological advances always open up new opportunities. Yet discoveries happen when the technology and the conceptual framework advance in tandem. That combination is what opens the door for researchers to take the next step. The same is largely true for art. In the history of art, new forms of expression were always pushed forward by advances in both tools and concepts. When a new form of expression emerges, it does so via multiple individuals who often live in the same environment but may be isolated from one another. In both science and art, innovation is limited by the technology and the conceptual frameworks that are available at a given moment. What we do in our lab is rely on technological advances to move the conceptual framework forward. We borrow from different scientific fields—we are just as likely to use mathematics as art—to achieve this.

Our data sculptures are a perfect example: there was a clear need to experience networks in their physical reality—to be able to walk around them and explore them from different perspectives—so as to understand the dynamics of their existence. I knew this in 2007, but it took ten years to develop the mathematical tools to achieve it. In parallel, the technology emerged with advances in 3-D printing. Around 2015, 3-D printers became much more accessible. But it was only in 2018 that we could develop the algorithms to design and print data sculptures. It was such a big development that our first data sculptures were featured on the cover of *Nature* magazine. Today, anyone can do it.

Yanchen

I was wondering if yould help me exeriment a little with three figures.

I am attaching them.

1. The first one, is a single line (with nodes, that I did not whow) and I would like to add a temperature gradient along the line, as shown.

I would like to try two versions:

A. The line also becomes thicker with the temperature.

B. The line thickness stays the same.

2. Is a variation on the first one, with a constant line thickness-- where the gradient is applied to multiple lines, arranged on a plane, like shown here, where there is a circular temperature gradient, as whown, so that the temerature is zero at the boundaries, and highest in the middle. Try about 32 lines, to have the sense of a lattice. If it is too much, try a fewer as well, say 16.

3. The this the 2d version of the previous one-- where the lines form a 2d lattice, and there is again a temperature gradient.

Here I am again looking for two versions:

A. when the lines are confined to the two dimensional plan.

B. When the lines can enter the z direction, perpendicular to the plane.

Can you play with these and send some images? I am really curious.

These can just be think black lines, do not need to be 3D tubes, maybe only the 3B needs to be in 3D.

On another note, how are you doing with the summary for Albert? As you say, we have a time to chat with him.

cheers I.

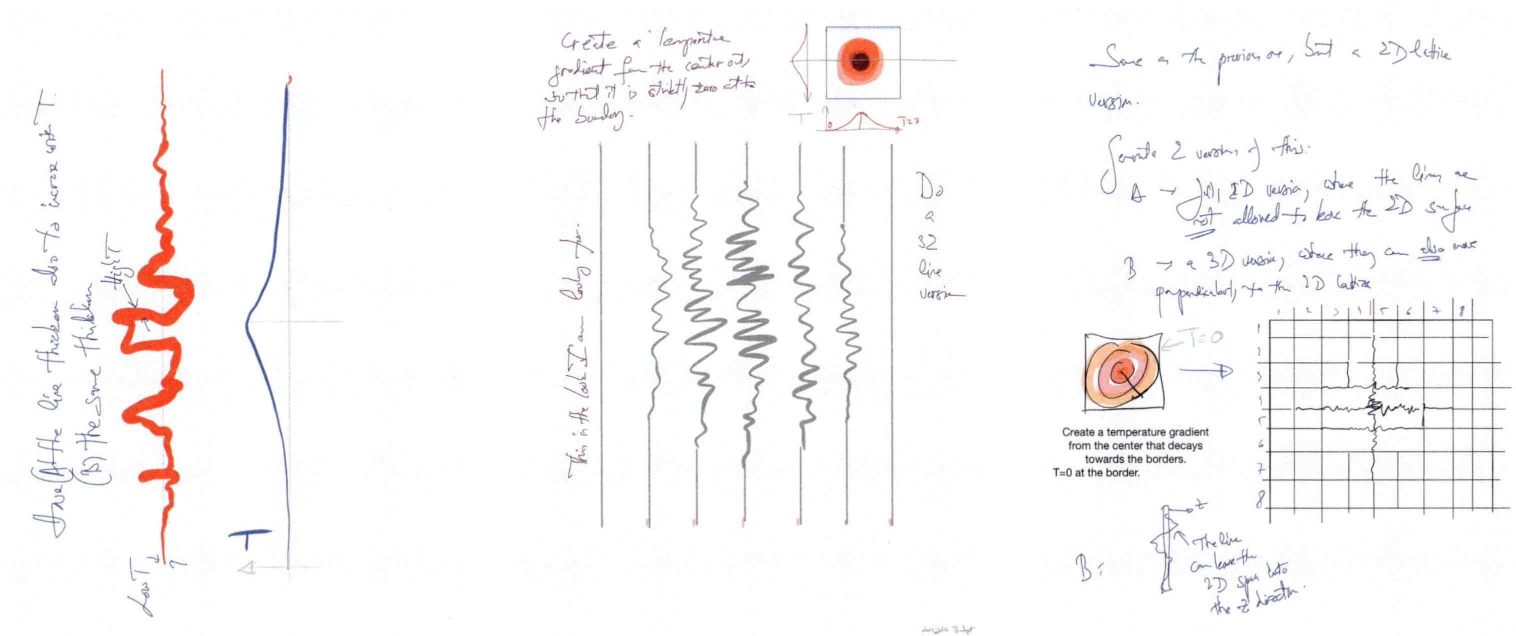

A leap in both visualization and understanding. What comes after 3-D?

We have an exciting project to represent networks in four dimensions. There is a compelling reason to do so. In four dimensions, the knots can unknot themselves—this is important because with entanglement the network can disappear. Let me explain: in two dimensions you can only draw “planar” networks, like the highways on a map. On a plane, the links cannot avoid each other. In three dimensions, you can always find a way around the links, so the links do not have to cross each other. However, in 3-D you are facing entanglement, when the links get caught up against one another. It's messy and requires time-consuming algorithms to sort them out and visualize them. In 4-D, these entanglements obtain an extra dimension to play with and can naturally disentangle themselves. It is rather magical.

If I look at the shadow of my two hands on the wall—that is, in two dimensions—it looks like one hand passes through the other. In reality, in three dimensions, they avoided each other. It's the same logic when you go from three to four dimensions. Ultimately, the best way to represent networks may be in four dimensions. Four-dimensional networks will make moves that appear non-physical to us, moves that make total sense in 4-D.

Could it be useful to have even more dimensions still? This is a question I am working on with László Lovász, a leading Hungarian mathematician. In the lab, we are now using AI to create the network's layout—it is fascinating to watch the speed with which it creates the data sculptures. Many networks of interest are still too large and complex to be 3-D-printed. *The Art Network* is one example. For these, we are now using virtual-reality tools to experience them.

Speaking of dimensions, art and science are often thought of as different dimensions, or different cultures, as British physicist and novelist C. P. Snow called them.

How do you see the connections between the two?

The creative process in art and science is identical. We are always looking for new forms of expression and new problems to attack with our tool set. But the outputs of artists and scientists are very different—and judged differently. For us, the work with the art space is symbiotic with the science we do. It is just another form of expression.

In my professional life, I use three languages—and I don't mean Hungarian, Romanian, and English. First, there is the scientific language, the language of mathematics and algorithms that furthers scientific inquiry. Second is a general-audience language, which I use in my books. Third is the visual language. All are rooted in the same desire to capture reality. All are part of a singular intellectual pursuit. They must all advance in parallel.

Based on your recent book, *The Formula,* am I right to conclude that while your success in the scientific world is likely to be long-lasting, your chances of succeeding in the conventional sense as an artist is still unknown? In other words, you did everything right for a career in science. But is it possible for a scientist to have a second career in art? Or is that a pipe dream?

I have been lucky in that our scientific work has had an exceptional impact. Yet success in science and in art is not about the individual who receives it, but about the community that offers it. So it is not up to me to decide if the work we do will be well-received in the art world. All I can do is put it out there and let the art community decide if they can build on it. In the past decade several of our works have been exhibited in major institutions, including the Serpentine Gallery in London and the Cooper-Hewitt, Smithsonian Design Museum in New York. Now my body of work is the subject of an exhibition that will debut at the Ludwig Museum in Budapest, and then go on to the ZKM | Center for Art and Media in Karlsruhe, Germany. None of this happened because I pushed for it. These institutions found us and asked for the work. We are at an early stage of this journey, and this is not a process I am interested in forcing. But I am enjoying it tremendously. The insights we get from networks only allow us to make informed choices. Those choices must naturally emerge. As with any kind of art, it's ultimately up to the institutional network to absorb and diffuse our work.

What's next? What still needs to be mapped? What are your dream projects? Dream collaborations? The holy grail?

There has been a major transformation in our lab's focus. For the past twenty years the visual part has been subjugated to the science. In the last few years, we have taken up projects that, while they continue to be rooted in science, are inspired by art. The art-network project and the 3-D-data-sculpture projects were examples of that. Both were motivated by art, and we then used science to bring a new perspective. You could say that artistic thinking was in the lead, and science came to help answer the questions posed by art. Many of the things we have done over the past two decades have no natural home in the scientific enterprise. Where do you put a data statue in the scientific world? What do you do with a video about a network's evolution?

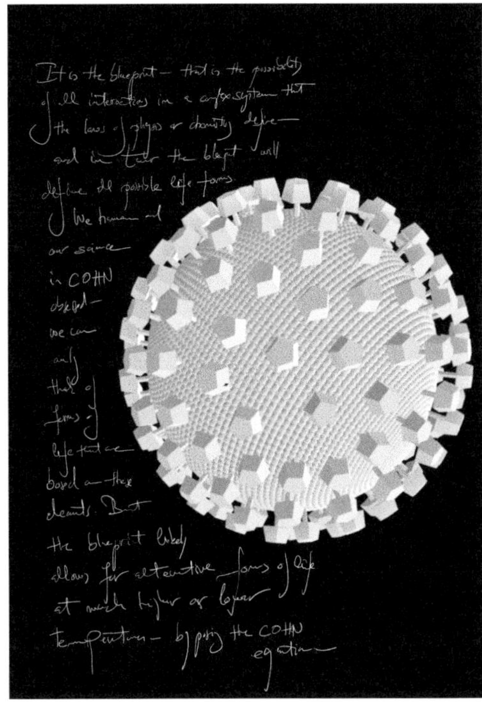

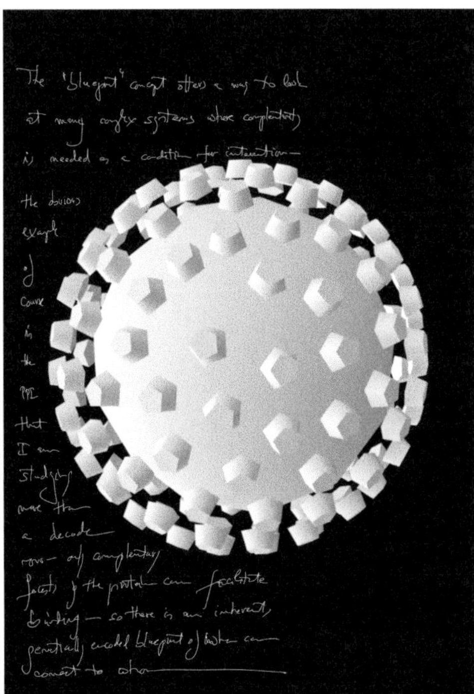

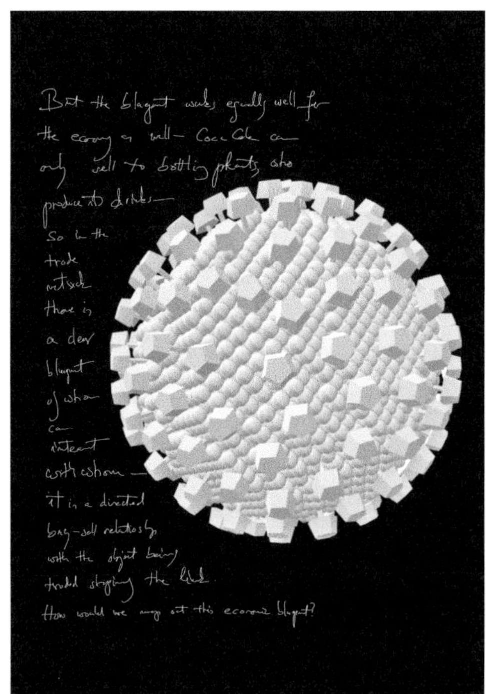

Many of these representations and mediums will find a better home in organizations that focus on art rather than on science. Embracing this new intellectual home and engaging with the very diverse and rich community behind the art world is a new and stimulating direction for the lab.

Finally, what are your hopes for the *Hidden Patterns* exhibition? Where do you see it taking you and your practice, both in terms of the science and in terms of the art?

I am humbled and excited about this opportunity. It allows me to look back at the past two and a half decades and re-curate the evolution of the language that we stumbled across in our scientific pursuit, and to explore its meaning as a comprehensive body of work. But more important, I hope that the exhibition will create a platform for an active and ongoing engagement with institutions in the art space and with artists. I hope it will open doors as I shift my lab toward a mutually rewarding engagement with the art world and turn what has been a largely solitary pursuit for the past twenty-five years into an active dialogue.

New York and Boston, spring 2020

PLATES

FLOW, 2004

Flow is the purpose of connectivity. The flow of ideas, electricity, blood, money, and information are all enabled by various social, infrastructural, or biological networks—which is why so many areas of science strive to understand how networks facilitate flow. In 2003, Barabási was exploring the flow of energy through a cell's metabolic network. Although by then the topological organization of individual reactions into metabolic networks was well understood, there were still many questions about the principles that govern their global functionality. To capture the complexity and diversity of observed flow patterns, Barabási wanted to develop a visual vocabulary that would describe the phenomena. But he didn't need the imagery to be explicit; its purpose was to be evocative, not explanatory. The images he and his team came up with were designed to be potential cover art, not diagrams of the research, for the issue of *Nature* in which his paper was being published. By color-encoding the predicted flux—or flow—of each reaction, the images illuminate the diversity of the flow patterns. The most dominant fluxes are represented by broad white lines that seem to radiate with energy. These lightbeams clearly stand out from the rest. The combination of colored links captures the pulse of the network. By illuminating the existence of a powerful flux backbone within the context of numerous low-flux links, the image illustrates how different types of flow inform a network's purpose and function—and how unequal flow can be inside any network.

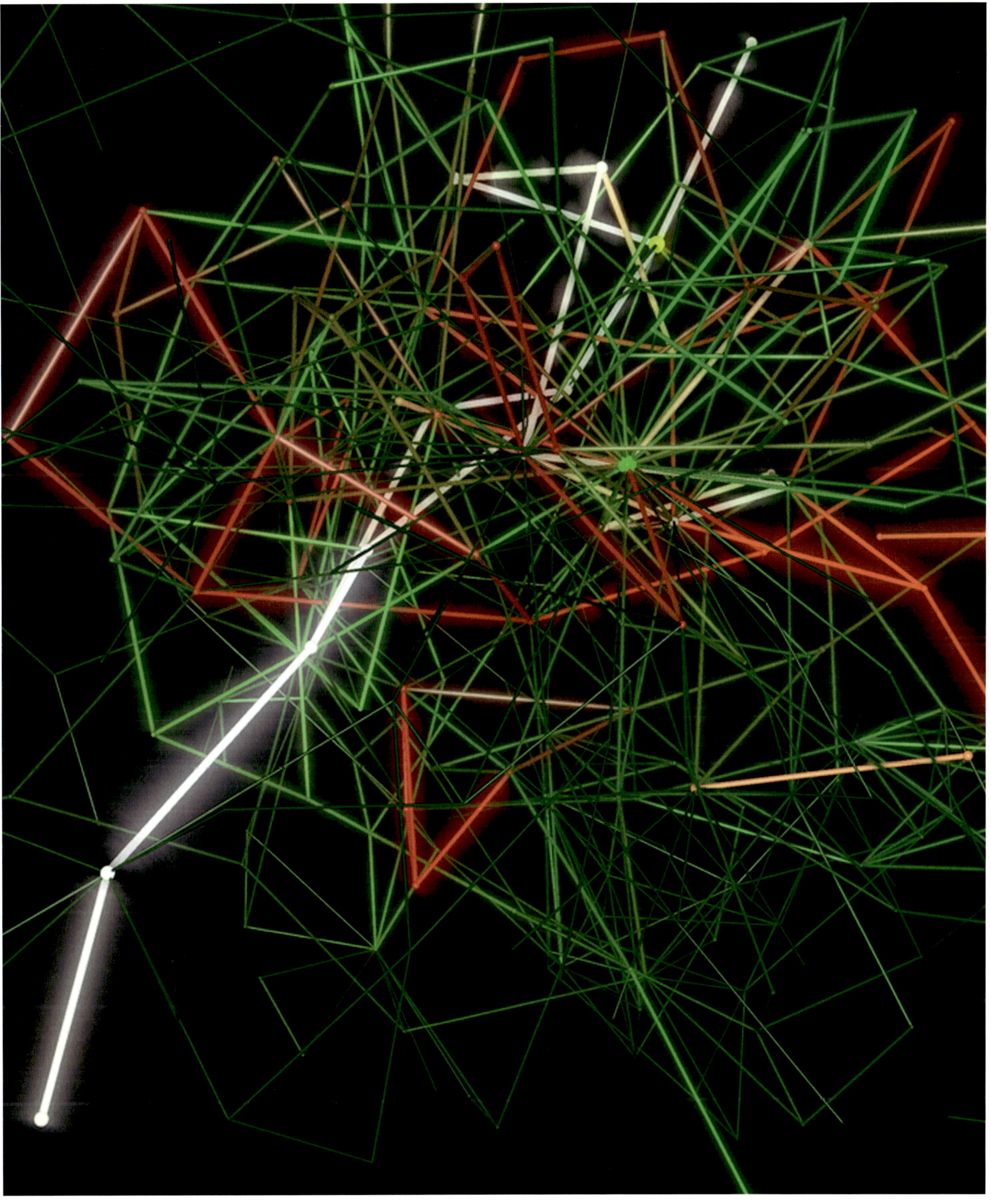

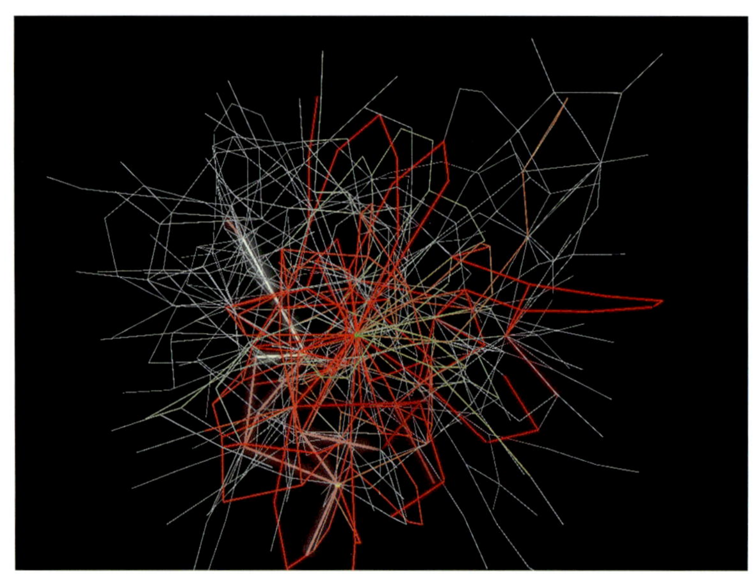

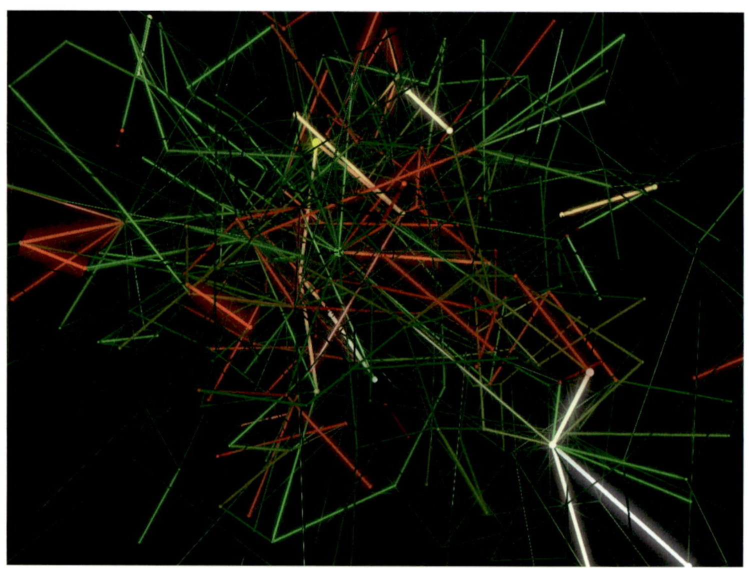

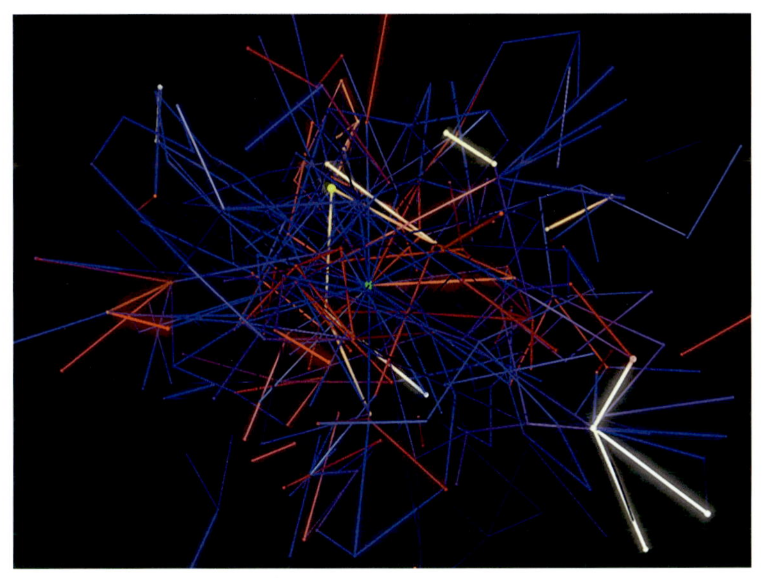
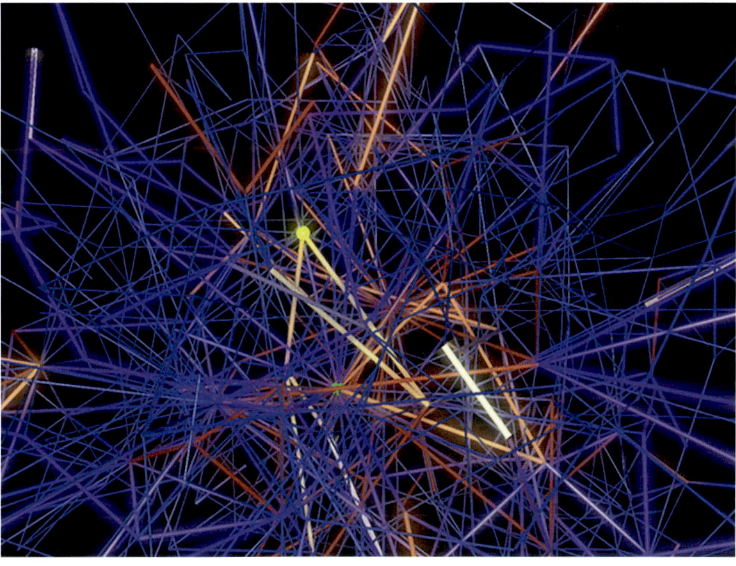

DISEASOME, 2007

The Human Disease Network is one of the BarabásiLab's most reproduced images. Originally printed by the National Academies of Sciences as a poster to accompany the publication of a research paper on how diseases connect, it was subsequently reproduced by the *New York Times* and included in the *Mapping It Out: Atlas of Contemporary Cartographies* exhibition at the Serpentine Gallery in London.

The project took form after the publication of the Human Genome Project in 2001, when it seemed like another gene was linked to another disease on a weekly basis. While on sabbatical at Harvard Medical School's Dana-Farber Cancer Institute during the 2005–06 academic year, Barabási found himself wondering what these many independent discoveries said about the relationships between diseases. The answer, he discovered, was a network in which two human diseases are connected through the genes implicated in both diseases. It took six months and many drafts to arrive at *The Human Disease Network*, which shows each node as a different disease. The size of the node reflects the number of genes responsible for the disease. Node color denotes the class to which each disease belongs. Cancers, for example, are blue nodes, as distinct from neurological diseases in red. The links correspond to the genes that connect the two diseases. The extreme node-size variation in this image represents a significant departure from previous visualizations. By enhancing the visibility of the largest hubs, the range of hub size allows the most explored diseases to dominate the visual space.

The visualization of this network further evolved in 2018, when 3-D color printing became accessible. It took many shattered prototypes to arrive at a viable data sculpture. But because of its spatial composition, the final 3-D color version, shown on pages 66 and 67, unveils certain relationships between disease classes that were largely hidden in the 2-D map.

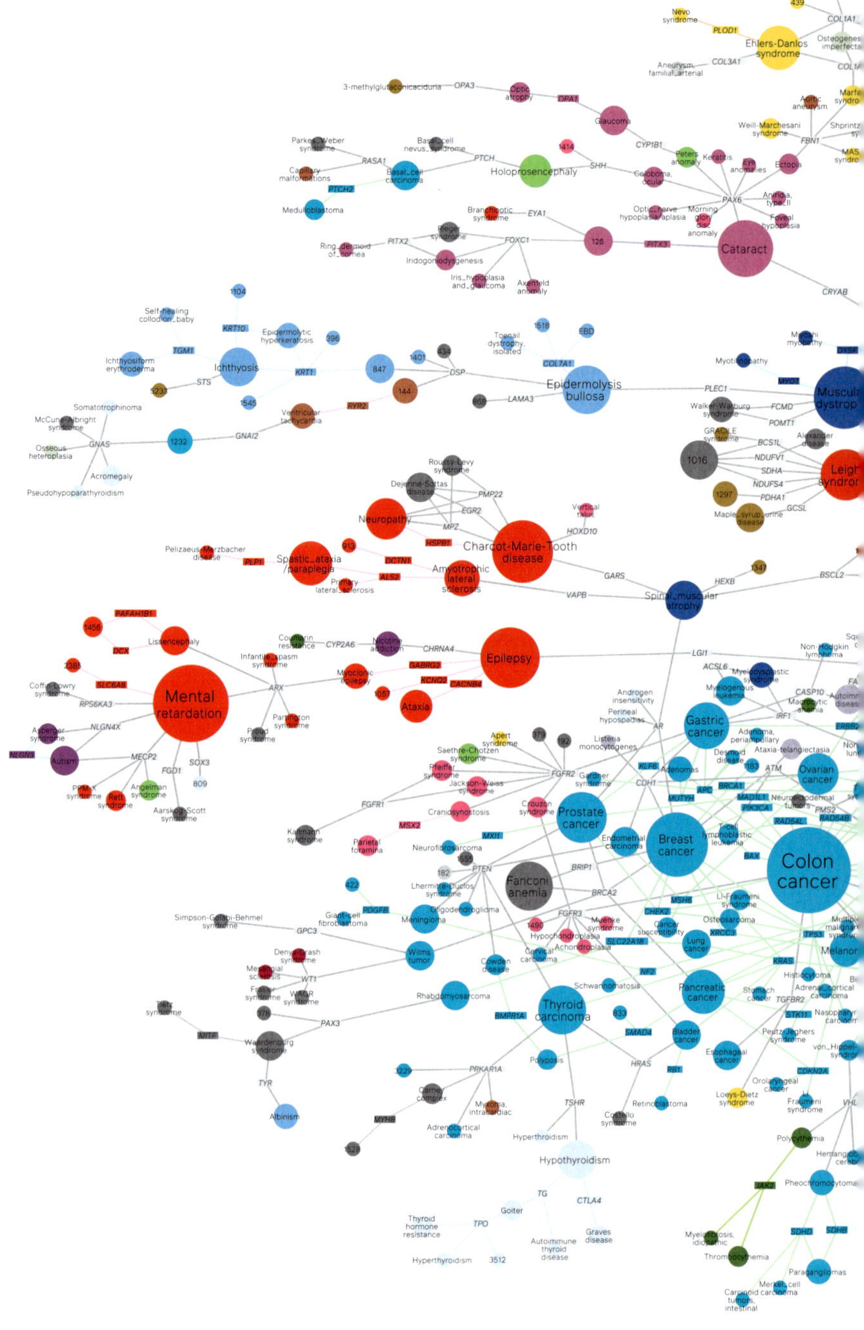

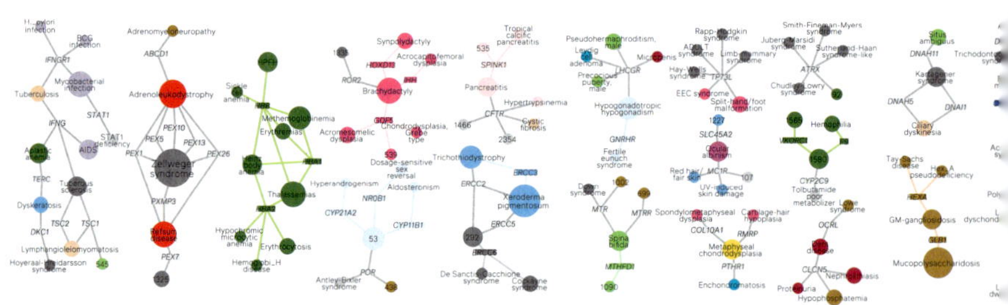

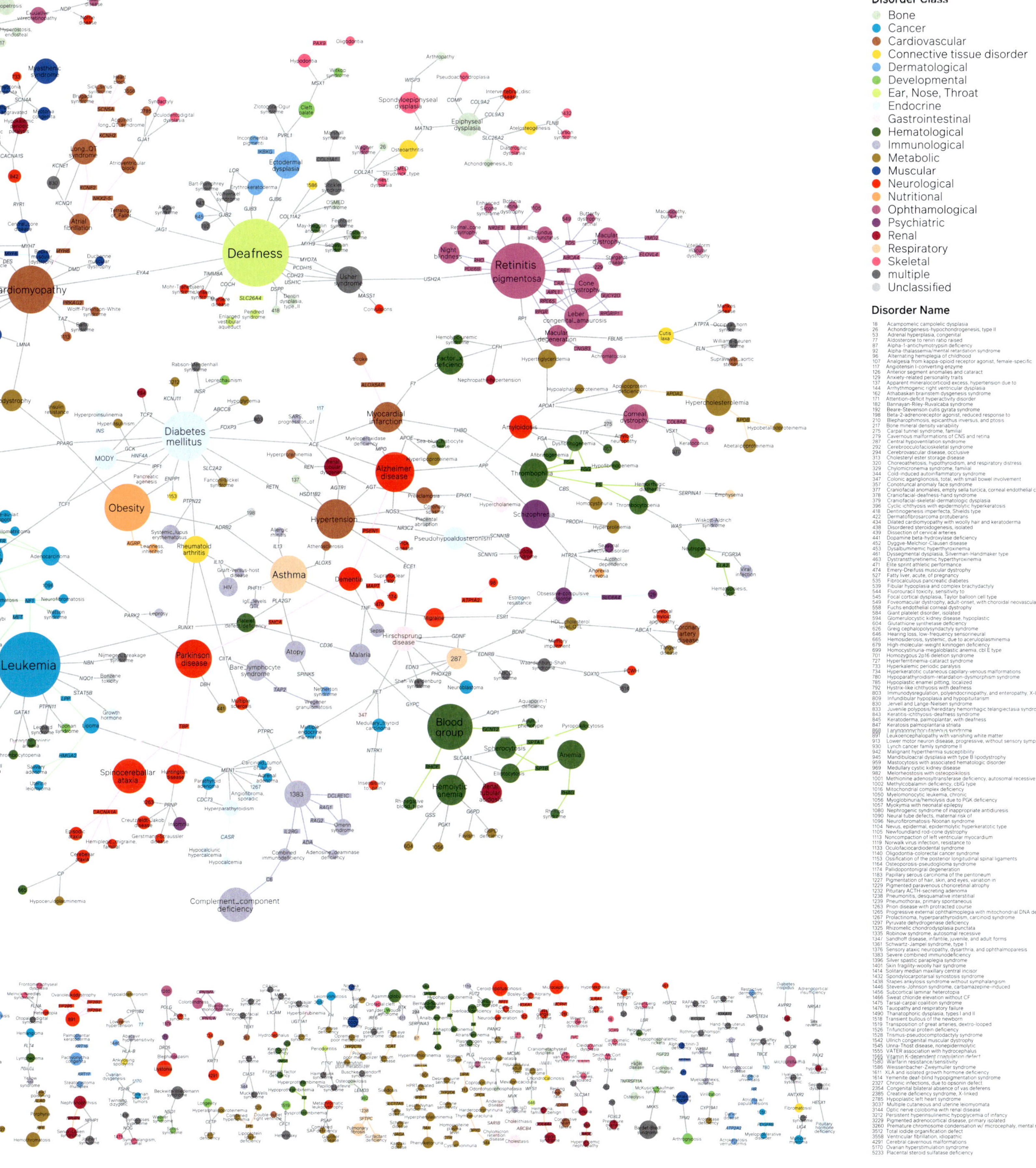
Deafness
Cardiomyopathy
Retinitis pigmentosa
Diabetes mellitus
Leukemia
Obesity
Asthma
Hypertension
Alzheimer disease
Myocardial infarction
Blood group
Parkinson disease
Spinocerebellar ataxia
Hemolytic anemia
Complement_component deficiency
Schizophrenia
Ectodermal dysplasia
Usher syndrome
Long_QT syndrome
Epiphyseal dysplasia
Spondyloepiphyseal dysplasia
Hypercholesterolemia
Amyloidosis
Thrombophilia
Anemia
Spherocytosis
Macular dystrophy
Cone dystrophy
Leber congenital_amaurosis
Macular degeneration
Night blindness
Pseudohypoaldosteronism
Rheumatoid arthritis
Dementia
Malaria
Atopy
Bare_lymphocyte syndrome
Migraine
Hirschsprung disease
Myasthenic syndrome
Atrial fibrillation
Factor_x deficiency
Corneal dystrophy
Coronary artery disease
Adenocarcinoma
MODY
1383
287
Disorder Class
Bone
Cancer
Cardiovascular
Connective tissue disorder
Dermatological
Developmental
Ear, Nose, Throat
Endocrine
Gastrointestinal
Hematological
Immunological
Metabolic
Muscular
Neurological
Nutritional
Ophthamological
Psychiatric
Renal
Respiratory
Skeletal
multiple
Unclassified
Disorder Name
18 Acampomelic campolelic dysplasia
26 Achondrogenesis-hypochondrogenesis, type II
53 Adrenal hyperplasia, congenital
77 Aldosterone to renin ratio raised
87 Alpha-1-antichymotrypsin deficiency
92 Alpha-thalassemia/mental retardation syndrome
96 Alternating hemiplegia of childhood
107 Analgesia from kappa-opioid receptor agonist, female-specific
117 Angiotensin I-converting enzyme
126 Anterior segment anomalies and cataract
129 Anxiety-related personality traits
137 Apparent mineralocorticoid excess, hypertension due to
144 Arrhythmogenic right ventricular dysplasia
162 Athabaskan brainstem dysgenesis syndrome
171 Attention-deficit hyperactivity disorder
182 Bannayan-Riley-Ruvalcaba syndrome
192 Beare-Stevenson cutis gyrata syndrome
198 Beta-2-adrenoreceptor agonist, reduced response to
210 Blepharophimosis, epicanthus inversus, and ptosis
217 Bone mineral density variability
275 Carpal tunnel syndrome, familial
279 Cavernous malformations of CNS and retina
287 Central hypoventilation syndrome
292 Cerebrooculofacioskeletal syndrome
294 Cerebrovascular disease, occlusive
313 Cholesteryl ester storage disease
320 Choreoathetosis, hypothyroidism, and respiratory distress
329 Chylomicronemia syndrome, familial
344 Cold-induced autoinflammatory syndrome
347 Colonic aganglionosis, total, with small bowel involvement
357 Conotruncal anomaly face syndrome
377 Craniofacial anomalies, empty sella turcica, corneal endothelial changes
378 Craniofacial-deafness-hand syndrome
379 Craniofacial-skeletal-dermatologic dysplasia
396 Cyclic ichthyosis with epidermolytic hyperkeratosis
418 Dentinogenesis imperfecta, Shields type
422 Dermatofibrosarcoma protuberans
434 Dilated cardiomyopathy with woolly hair and keratoderma
438 Disordered steroidogenesis, isolated
439 Dissection of cervical arteries
441 Dopamine beta-hydroxylase deficiency
452 Dyggve-Melchior-Clausen disease
453 Dysalbuminemic hyperthyroxinemia
461 Dyssegmental dysplasia, Silverman-Handmaker type
463 Dystransthyretinemic hyperthyroxinemia
471 Elite sprint athletic performance
474 Emery-Dreifuss muscular dystrophy
527 Fatty liver, acute, of pregnancy
535 Fibrocalculous pancreatic diabetes
539 Fibular hypoplasia and complex brachydactyly
544 Fluorouracil toxicity, sensitivity to
545 Focal cortical dysplasia, Taylor balloon cell type
549 Foveomacular dystrophy, adult-onset, with choroidal neovascularization
558 Fuchs endothelial corneal dystrophy
584 Giant platelet disorder, isolated
594 Glomerulocystic kidney disease, hypoplastic
604 Glutathione synthetase deficiency
626 Greig cephalopolysyndactyly syndrome
646 Hearing loss, low-frequency sensorineural
665 Hemosiderosis, systemic, due to aceruloplasminemia
679 High-molecular-weight kininogen deficiency
699 Homocystinuria-megaloblastic anemia, cbl E type
701 Homozygous 2p16 deletion syndrome
727 Hyperferritinemia-cataract syndrome
733 Hyperkalemic periodic paralysis
734 Hyperkeratotic cutaneous capillary-venous malformations
780 Hypoparathyroidism-retardation-dysmorphism syndrome
785 Hypoplastic enamel pitting, localized
792 Hystrix-like ichthyosis with deafness
803 Immunodysregulation, polyendocrinopathy, and enteropathy, X-linked
809 Infundibular hypoplasia and hypopituitarism
830 Jervell and Lange-Nielsen syndrome
833 Juvenile polyposis/hereditary hemorrhagic telangiectasia syndrome
843 Keratitis-ichthyosis-deafness syndrome
845 Keratoderma, palmoplantar, with deafness
847 Keratosis palmoplantaria striata
868 Laryngoonychocutaneous syndrome
891 Leukoencephalopathy with vanishing white matter
913 Lower motor neuron disease, progressive, without sensory symptoms
930 Lynch cancer family syndrome II
942 Malignant hyperthermia susceptibility
945 Mandibuloacral dysplasia with type B lipodystrophy
959 Mastocytosis with associated hematologic disorder
969 Medullary cystic kidney disease
982 Melorheostosis with osteopoikilosis
1001 Methionine adenosyltransferase deficiency, autosomal recessive
1002 Methylcobalamin deficiency, cblG type
1016 Mitochondrial complex deficiency
1050 Myelomonocytic leukemia, chronic
1056 Myoglobinuria/hemolysis due to PGK deficiency
1057 Myokymia with neonatal epilepsy
1080 Nephrogenic syndrome of inappropriate antidiuresis
1090 Neural tube defects, maternal risk of
1096 Neurofibromatosis-Noonan syndrome
1104 Nevus, epidermal, epidermolytic hyperkeratotic type
1105 Newfoundland rod-cone dystrophy
1113 Noncompaction of left ventricular myocardium
1119 Norwalk virus infection, resistance to
1133 Oculofaciocardiodental syndrome
1140 Oligodontia-colorectal cancer syndrome
1153 Ossification of the posterior longitudinal spinal ligaments
1164 Osteoporosis-pseudoglioma syndrome
1174 Pallidopontonigral degeneration
1183 Papillary serous carcinoma of the peritoneum
1227 Pigmentation of hair, skin, and eyes, variation in
1229 Pigmented paravenous chorioretinal atrophy
1232 Pituitary ACTH-secreting adenoma
1238 Pneumonitis, desquamative interstitial
1239 Pneumothorax, primary spontaneous
1263 Prion disease with protracted course
1265 Progressive external ophthalmoplegia with mitochondrial DNA deletions
1267 Prolactinoma, hyperparathyroidism, carcinoid syndrome
1297 Pyruvate dehydrogenase deficiency
1325 Rhizomelic chondrodysplasia punctata
1335 Robinow syndrome, autosomal recessive
1347 Sandhoff disease, infantile, juvenile, and adult forms
1361 Schwartz-Jampel syndrome, type 1
1376 Sensory ataxic neuropathy, dysarthria, and ophthalmoparesis
1383 Severe combined immunodeficiency
1396 Silver spastic paraplegia syndrome
1401 Skin fragility-woolly hair syndrome
1414 Solitary median maxillary central incisor
1432 Spondylocarpotarsal synostosis syndrome
1438 Stapes ankylosis syndrome without symphalangism
1446 Stevens-Johnson syndrome, carbamazepine-induced
1456 Subcortical laminar heterotopia
1466 Sweat chloride elevation without CF
1475 Tarsal-carpal coalition syndrome
1476 Tauopathy and respiratory failure
1490 Thanatophoric dysplasia, types I and II
1518 Transient bullous of the newborn
1519 Transposition of great arteries, dextro-looped
1526 Trifunctional protein deficiency
1528 Trismus-pseudocomptodactyly syndrome
1542 Ullrich congenital muscular dystrophy
1545 Unna-Thost disease, nonepidermolytic
1555 VATER association with hydrocephalus
1565 Vitamin K-dependent coagulation defect
1580 Warfarin resistance/sensitivity
1586 Weissenbacher-Zweymuller syndrome
1611 XLA and isolated growth hormone deficiency
1614 Yemenite deaf-blind hypopigmentation syndrome
2327 Chronic infections, due to opsonin defect
2354 Congenital bilateral absence of vas deferens
2385 Creatine deficiency syndrome, X-linked
2785 Hypoplastic left heart syndrome
3037 Multiple cutaneous and uterine leiomyomata
3144 Optic nerve coloboma with renal disease
3212 Persistent hyperinsulinemic hypoglycemia of infancy
3229 Pigmented adrenocortical disease, primary isolated
3260 Premature chromosome condensation w/ microcephaly, mental retardation
3512 Total iodide organification defect
3558 Ventricular fibrillation, idiopathic
4291 Cerebral cavernous malformations
5170 Ovarian hyperstimulation syndrome
5233 Placental steroid sulfatase deficiency

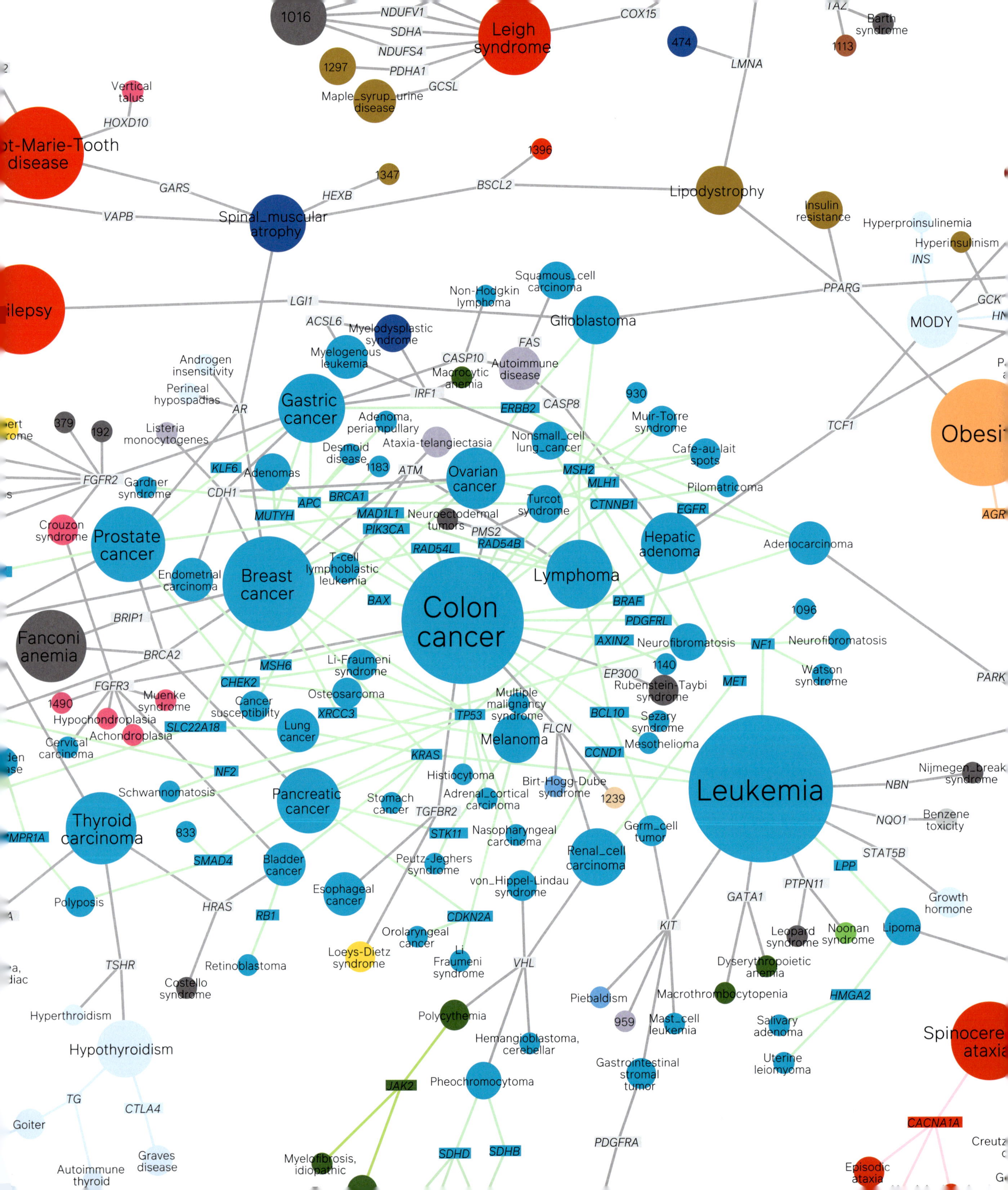

1016
NDUFV1
SDHA
NDUFS4
PDHA1
GCSL
1297
Maple_syrup_urine disease
Leigh syndrome
COX15
474
LMNA
Barth syndrome
1113
Vertical talus
HOXD10
Charcot-Marie-Tooth disease
GARS
VAPB
HEXB
1347
1396
BSCL2
Spinal_muscular atrophy
Lipodystrophy
Insulin resistance
Hyperproinsulinemia
Hyperinsulinism
INS
PPARG
GCK
MODY
LGI1
Epilepsy
Squamous_cell carcinoma
Non-Hodgkin lymphoma
Glioblastoma
ACSL6
Myelodysplastic syndrome
Myelogenous leukemia
FAS
CASP10
Autoimmune disease
Macrocytic anemia
Androgen insensitivity
Perineal hypospadias
AR
Gastric cancer
IRF1
ERBB2
CASP8
930
Muir-Torre syndrome
TCF1
Obesity
379
192
Listeria monocytogenes
Adenoma, periampullary
Ataxia-telangiectasia
Nonsmall_cell lung_cancer
Cafe-au-lait spots
Desmoid disease
1183
ATM
KLF6
Adenomas
FGFR2
Gardner syndrome
CDH1
Ovarian cancer
MSH2
MLH1
Pilomatricoma
APC
BRCA1
MUTYH
MAD1L1
Neuroectodermal tumors
Turcot syndrome
CTNNB1
EGFR
AGR
Crouzon syndrome
Prostate cancer
PIK3CA
PMS2
RAD54B
Hepatic adenoma
Adenocarcinoma
RAD54L
T-cell lymphoblastic leukemia
Lymphoma
Endometrial carcinoma
Breast cancer
Colon cancer
BAX
BRAF
PDGFRL
1096
Fanconi anemia
BRIP1
BRCA2
AXIN2
Neurofibromatosis
NF1
Neurofibromatosis
1140
Li-Fraumeni syndrome
MSH6
EP300
Rubenstein-Taybi syndrome
MET
Watson syndrome
PARK
FGFR3
CHEK2
Osteosarcoma
Multiple malignancy syndrome
1490
Muenke syndrome
Cancer susceptibility
XRCC3
TP53
BCL10
Sezary syndrome
Hypochondroplasia
Achondroplasia
SLC22A18
Lung cancer
FLCN
Melanoma
Mesothelioma
Cervical carcinoma
KRAS
CCND1
Leukemia
Nijmegen_breakage syndrome
NF2
Histiocytoma
Birt-Hogg-Dube syndrome
NBN
Schwannomatosis
Pancreatic cancer
Stomach cancer
Adrenal_cortical carcinoma
1239
TGFBR2
NQO1
Benzene toxicity
Thyroid carcinoma
833
STK11
Nasopharyngeal carcinoma
Germ_cell tumor
MPR1A
SMAD4
Bladder cancer
Peutz-Jeghers syndrome
Renal_cell carcinoma
STAT5B
LPP
PTPN11
von_Hippel-Lindau syndrome
Esophageal cancer
GATA1
Growth hormone
Polyposis
HRAS
RB1
CDKN2A
KIT
Leopard syndrome
Noonan syndrome
Lipoma
Oropharyngeal cancer
Dyserythropoietic anemia
TSHR
Retinoblastoma
Loeys-Dietz syndrome
Li Fraumeni syndrome
VHL
Costello syndrome
Piebaldism
Macrothrombocytopenia
HMGA2
Hyperthroidism
Polycythemia
959
Mast_cell leukemia
Salivary adenoma
Spinocerebellar ataxia
Hypothyroidism
Hemangioblastoma, cerebellar
Uterine leiomyoma
Gastrointestinal stromal tumor
JAK2
Pheochromocytoma
TG
CTLA4
Goiter
CACNA1A
SDHD
SDHB
PDGFRA
Myelofibrosis, idiopathic
Graves disease
Autoimmune thyroid
Episodic ataxia

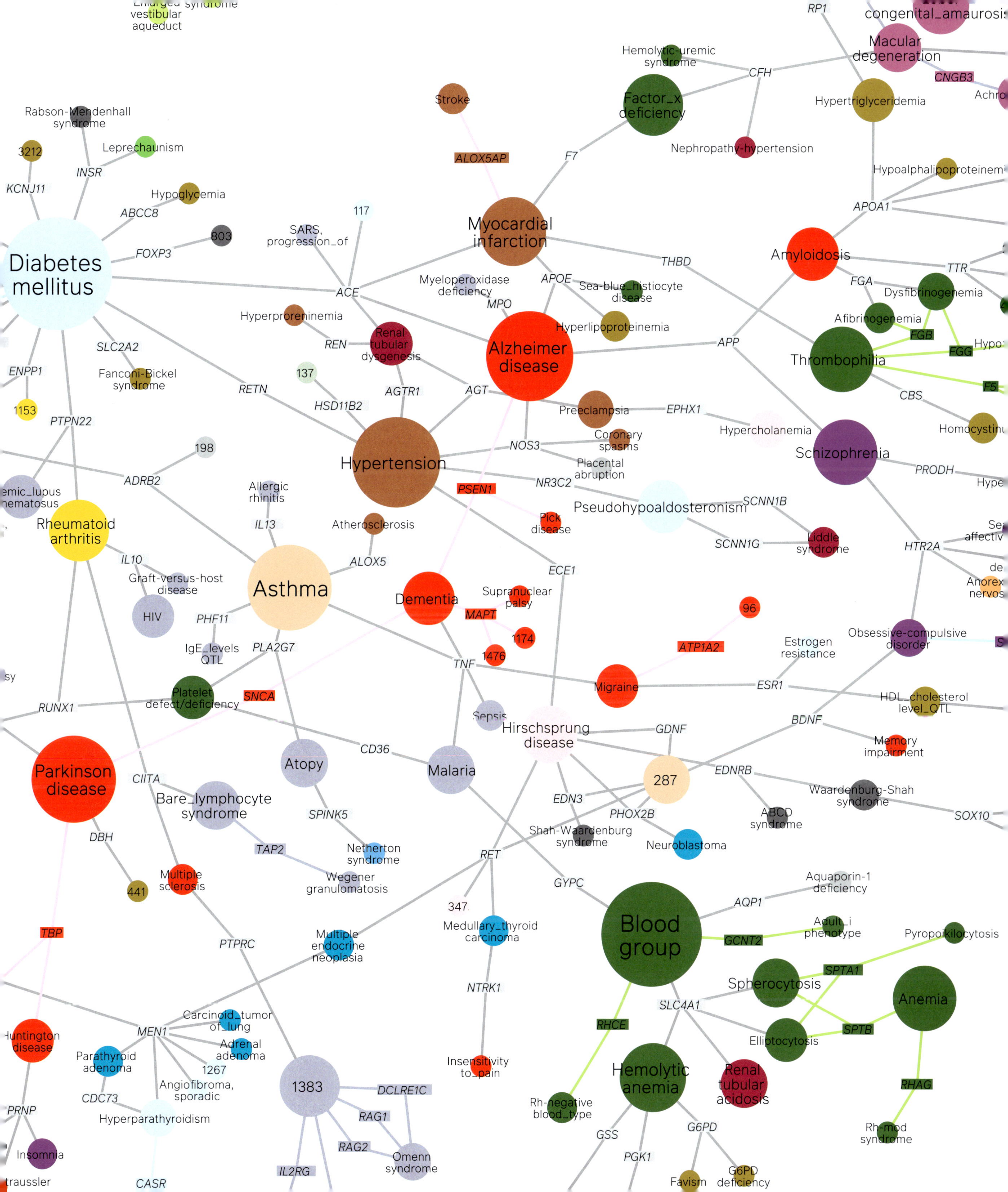

vestibular aqueduct
RP1
Macular degeneration
CNGB3
Hemolytic-uremic syndrome
CFH
Factor_x deficiency
Stroke
Hypertriglyceridemia
Rabson-Mendenhall syndrome
Leprechaunism
3212
INSR
ALOX5AP
F7
Nephropathy-hypertension
Hypoalphalipoproteinem
KCNJ11
Hypoglycemia
ABCC8
117
APOA1
803
SARS, progression_of
Myocardial infarction
FOXP3
Amyloidosis
Diabetes mellitus
THBD
TTR
Myeloperoxidase deficiency
APOE
Sea-blue_histiocyte disease
ACE
FGA
Dysfibrinogenemia
MPO
Hyperproreninemia
Renal tubular dysgenesis
Afibrinogenemia
SLC2A2
Hyperlipoproteinemia
REN
FGB
Alzheimer disease
APP
FGG
Thrombophilia
ENPP1
Fanconi-Bickel syndrome
137
F5
RETN
HSD11B2
AGTR1
AGT
CBS
1153
Preeclampsia
EPHX1
PTPN22
Homocystinu
Hypercholanemia
Coronary spasms
NOS3
198
Hypertension
Schizophrenia
Placental abruption
ADRB2
PRODH
NR3C2
Allergic rhinitis
PSEN1
SCNN1B
Pseudohypoaldosteronism
Rheumatoid arthritis
IL13
Atherosclerosis
Pick disease
SCNN1G
Liddle syndrome
HTR2A
IL10
ALOX5
ECE1
Graft-versus-host disease
Asthma
Dementia
Supranuclear palsy
96
MAPT
HIV
PHF11
Obsessive-compulsive disorder
1174
ATP1A2
Estrogen resistance
IgE_levels QTL
PLA2G7
1476
TNF
Migraine
ESR1
HDL_cholesterol level_QTL
Platelet defect/deficiency
SNCA
RUNX1
Sepsis
Hirschsprung disease
GDNF
BDNF
Memory impairment
CD36
Atopy
Malaria
EDNRB
Parkinson disease
CIITA
287
Bare_lymphocyte syndrome
Waardenburg-Shah syndrome
EDN3
PHOX2B
ABCD syndrome
SOX10
DBH
SPINK5
Shah-Waardenburg syndrome
TAP2
Netherton syndrome
Neuroblastoma
RET
Multiple sclerosis
Wegener granulomatosis
GYPC
441
Aquaporin-1 deficiency
347
AQP1
Medullary_thyroid carcinoma
Blood group
TBP
Adult_i phenotype
GCNT2
PTPRC
Multiple endocrine neoplasia
Pyropoikilocytosis
SPTA1
Spherocytosis
NTRK1
Anemia
Carcinoid_tumor of_lung
SLC4A1
MEN1
RHCE
SPTB
Elliptocytosis
Adrenal adenoma
Parathyroid adenoma
1267
Insensitivity to_pain
Hemolytic anemia
Renal tubular acidosis
Angiofibroma, sporadic
1383
DCLRE1C
RHAG
CDC73
PRNP
Hyperparathyroidism
RAG1
Rh-negative blood_type
GSS
G6PD
Rh-mod syndrome
RAG2
Omenn syndrome
Insomnia
PGK1
G6PD deficiency
IL2RG
CASR
Favism

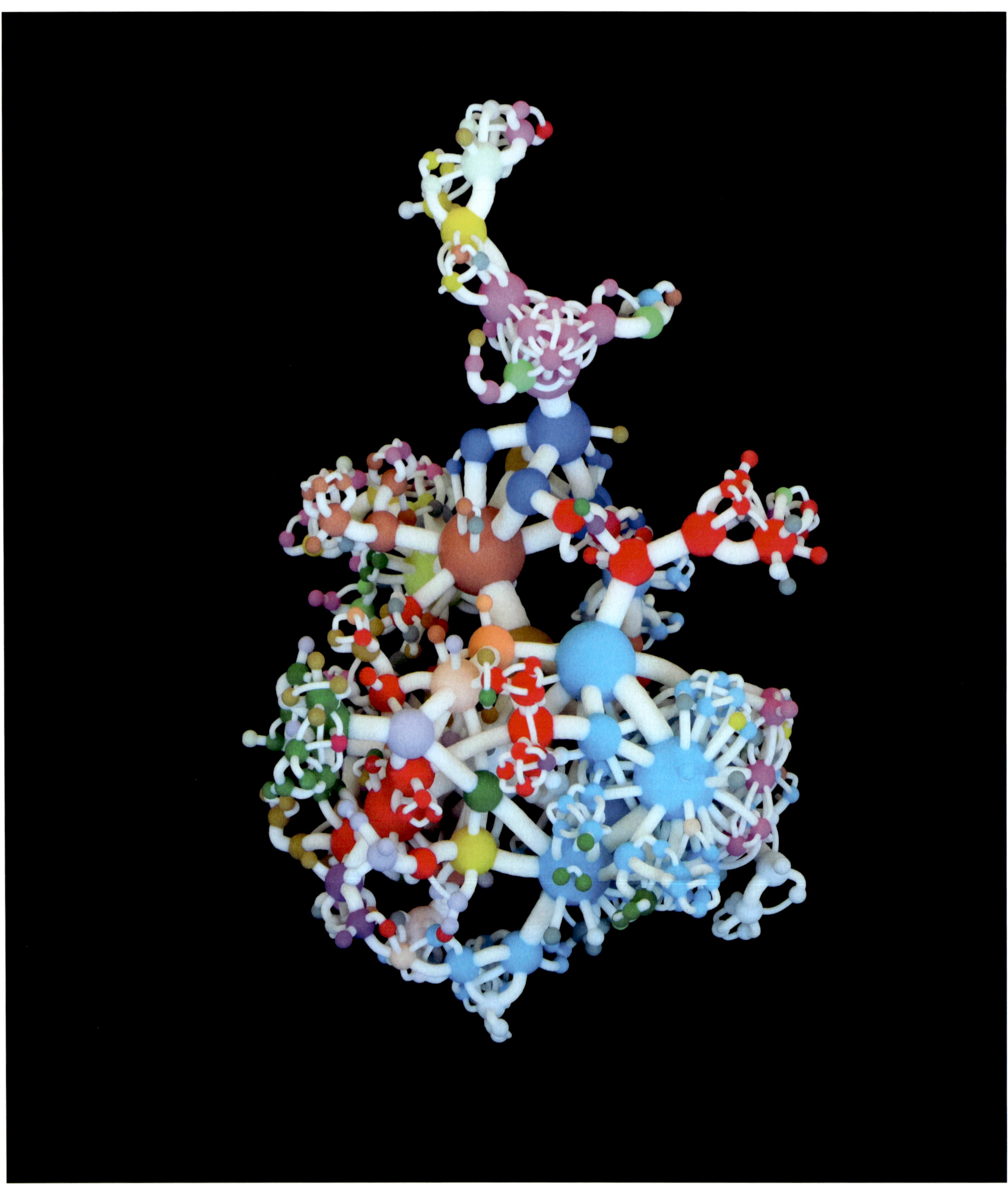

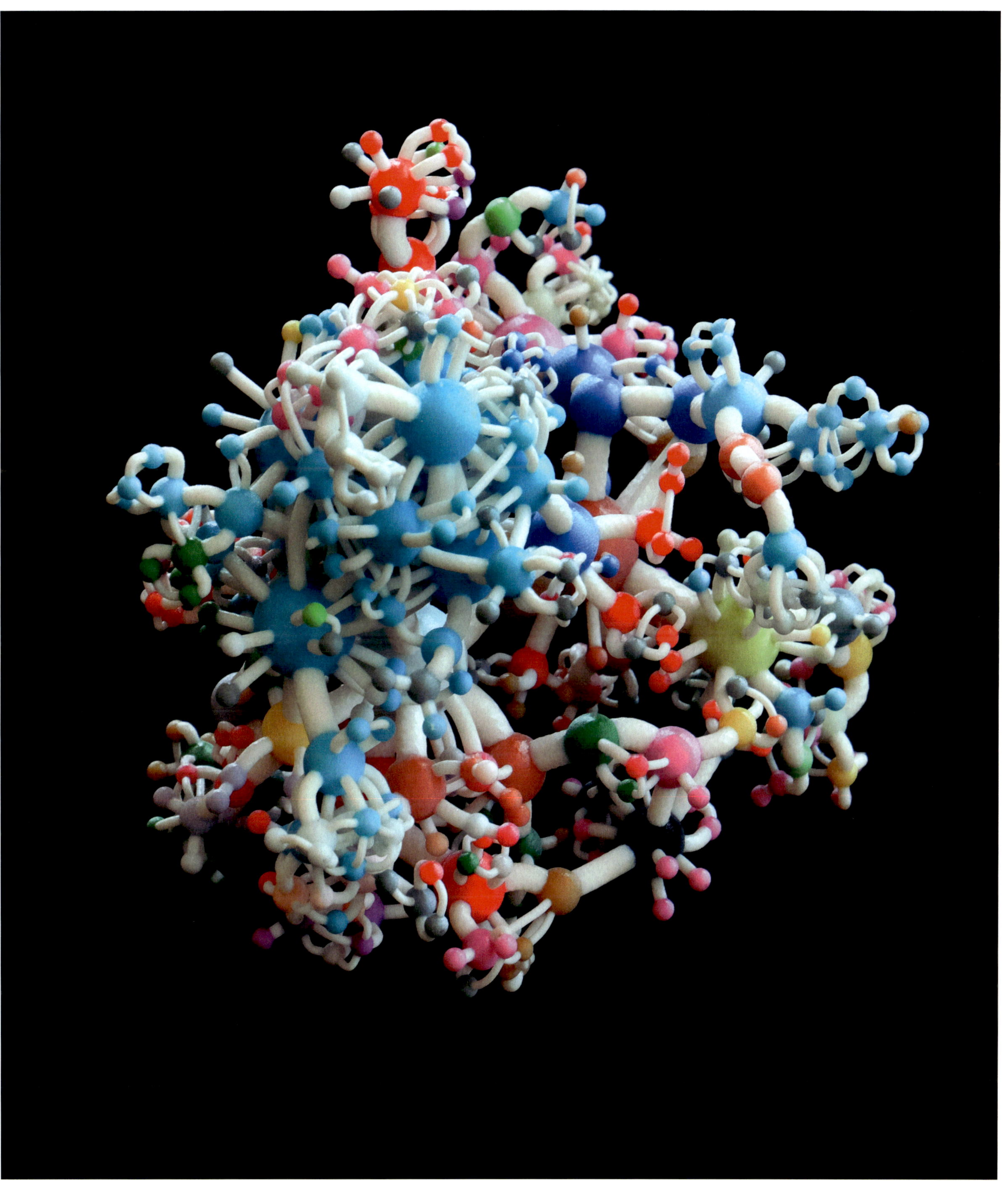

INTERACTOME, 2012

In 2014, Barabási was invited to speak at TEDMED about network medicine, an emerging subfield at the interface of medicine and network science. He asked Mauro Martino, the first full-time designer in the BarabásiLab, to help develop a visual narrative for the talk. Martino produced videos to show the human interactome, a network of 13,000 human proteins connected by 141,000 protein interactions. But visualizing such an exceptional number of nodes and links was not possible in a single map. The videos display only a small fraction of all links at any time, their occasional flickerings merely hinting at the many, largely invisible links. The images showing dark blue spectral fields with a light-colored core, pages 70 and 71, are stills from the TEDMED videos, while the dark-core image, opposite, was rendered in 2016 as a candidate for the cover of *Network Medicine*, a book co-edited by Barabási and published by Harvard University Press. By highlighting the genes involved in asthma, indicated by the purple cluster, and COPD, shown in yellow, this image illustrates how the proteins linked to the same disease cluster in the same vicinity of the network. This image also traces the slightly different perspectives of the asthma disease module within the interactome. The variations are hard to spot, as are the imperceptibly minute molecular differences between asthma patients. At the molecular level, each patient has her own unique manifestation of the disease. Yet all have the same painful experience—they can't breathe. In the still image there's a feeling of suspended animation that lends the maps an appropriately asthmatic undertone. It reminds us that breath itself is stuck in the web of the disease.

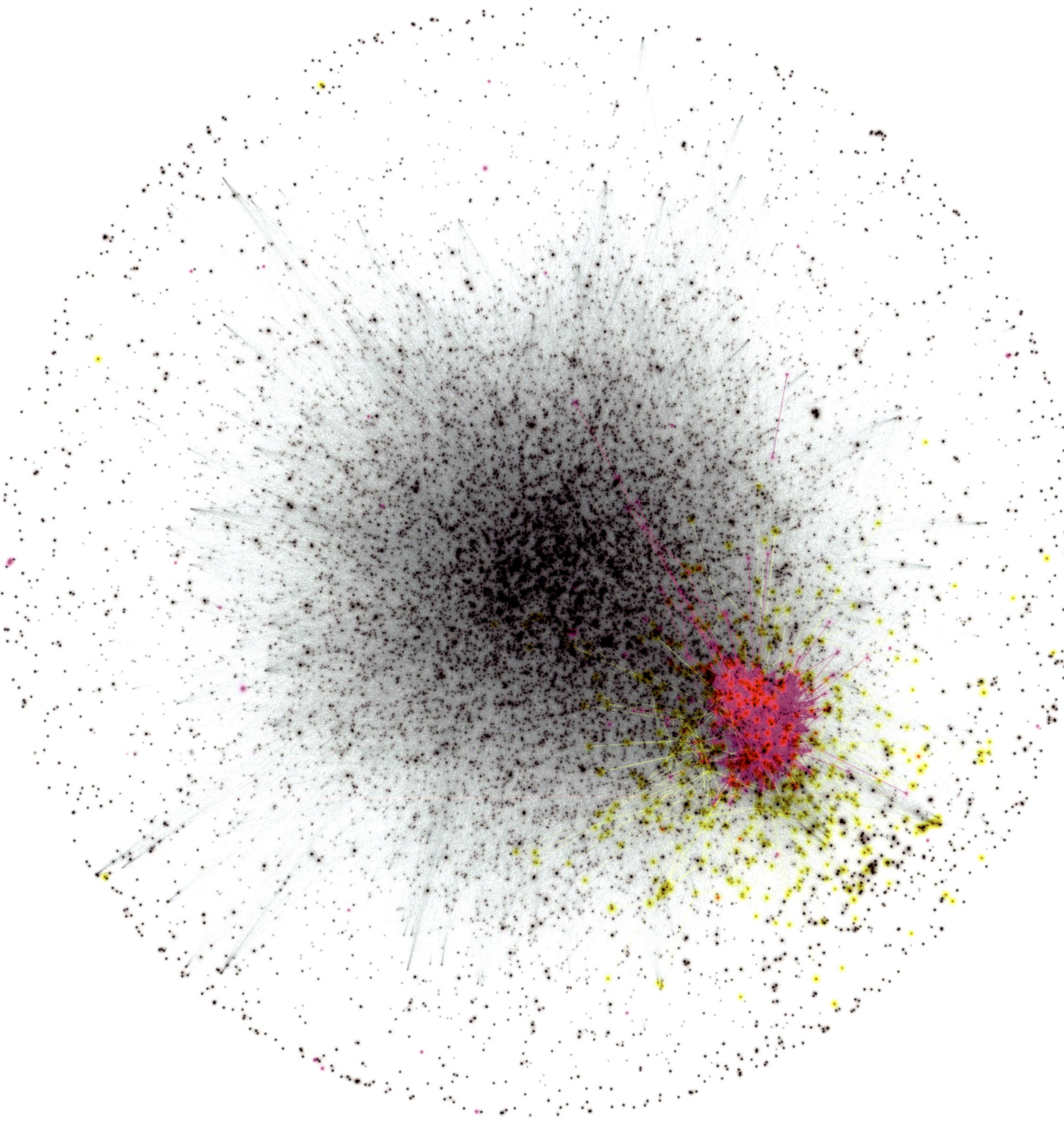

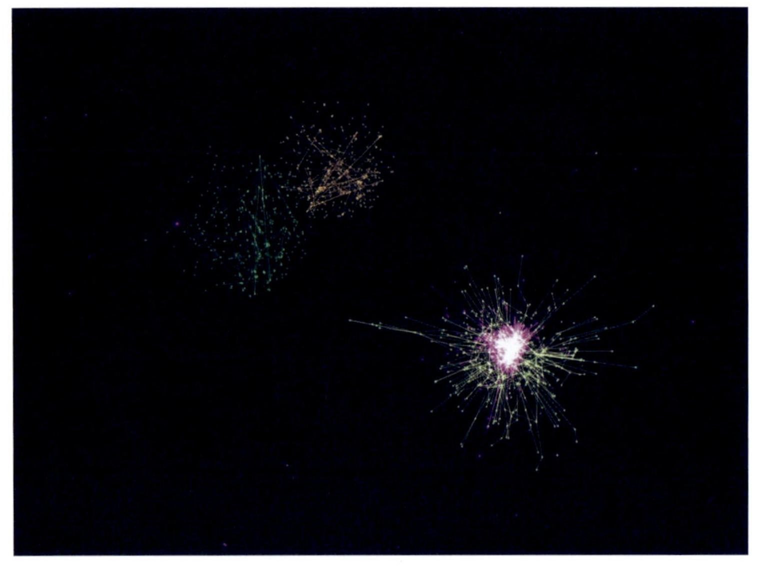

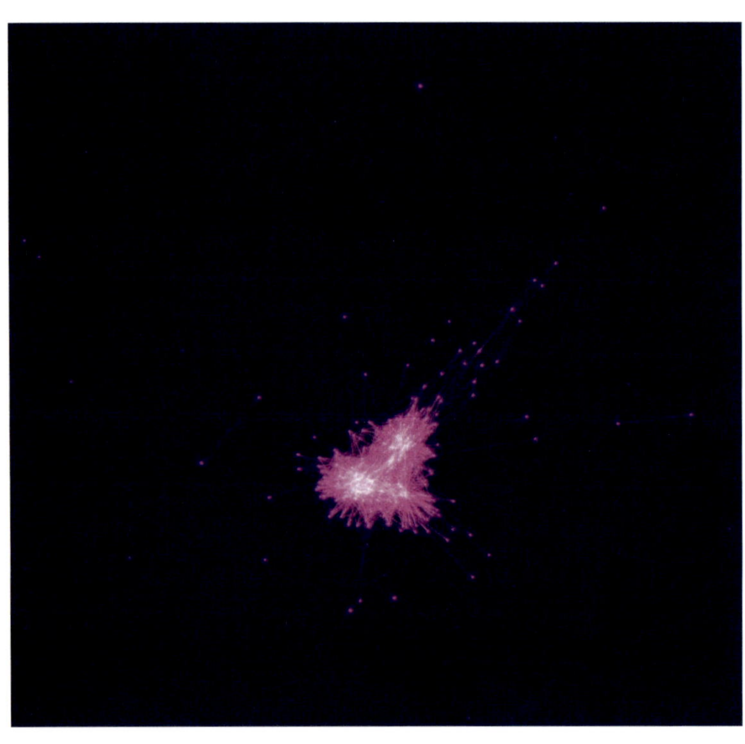

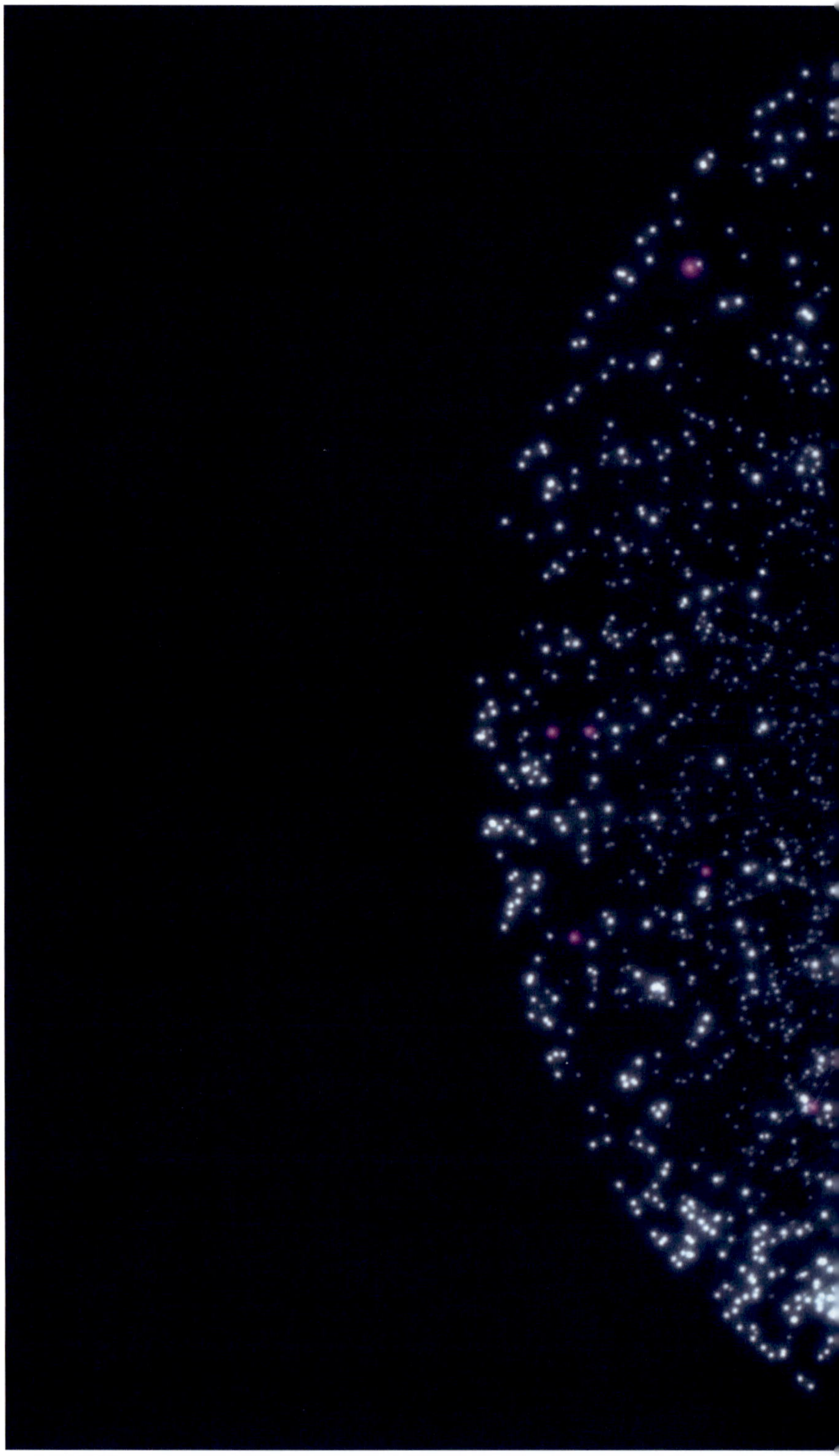

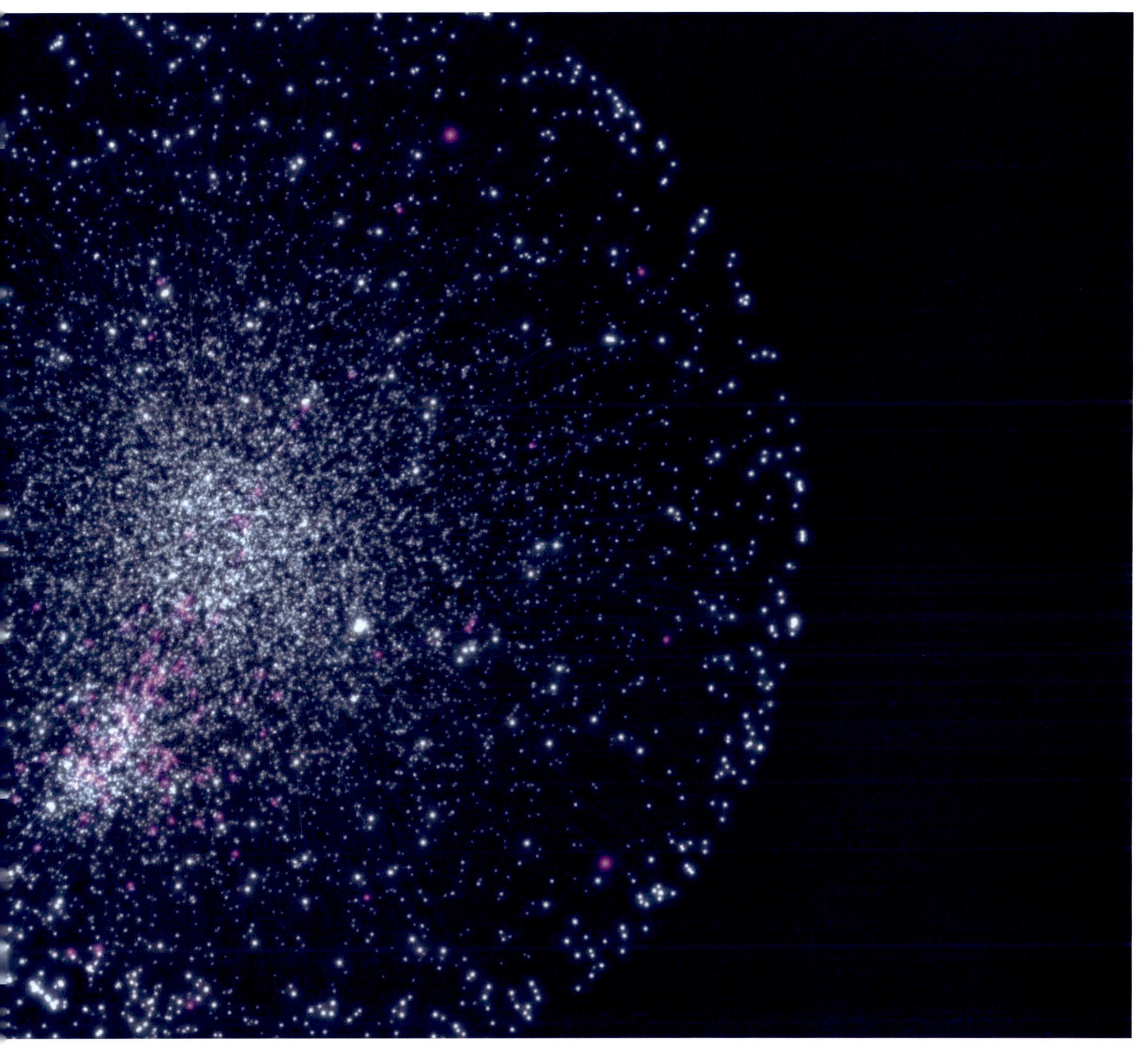

CHRONOGRAMS, 2007

While on sabbatical at Harvard Medical School's Dana-Farber Cancer Institute in 2005–06, Barabási joined an experimental project that was looking at how a small group of genes could control a much larger one. Specifically, the research focused on how 900 genes in the roundworm could turn on and off the creature's remaining 20,000 genes, thereby determining the purpose of each cell. The experiments resulted in a massive data set about when in the worm's life span and where in its body certain genes are activated. This spatiotemporal information called for a visual representation that would elucidate the data's underlying patterns. The resulting images, which the team called "chronograms" because they represent the chronology of when genes get turned on, use various visual techniques to combine and parse this data. The images, which were generated in different color palettes as candidates for the cover of *Nature Biotechnology,* the journal in which the research was published, distill genetic activity in a worm's development, from early larva to the adult worm. By capturing the full life history of a living organism, these visualizations illuminate the dynamics of the genes that enable it. In each chronogram, which represents data from thousands of worms, the short lines at the top correspond to the young animals, and longer lines at the bottom track older worms. The vertical axis is developmental time, or the age of the worms; the horizontal is space along the body of the animal. The colors, which capture the expression of one single set of genes, indicate gene activity. Blue signifies that the gene is turned off; red indicates it is highly active. This color code allows us to see when during development (i.e., in young animals on the top, or the older ones at the bottom) and where (in the head of the animal, to the left, or their tail, to the right) the gene is turned on.

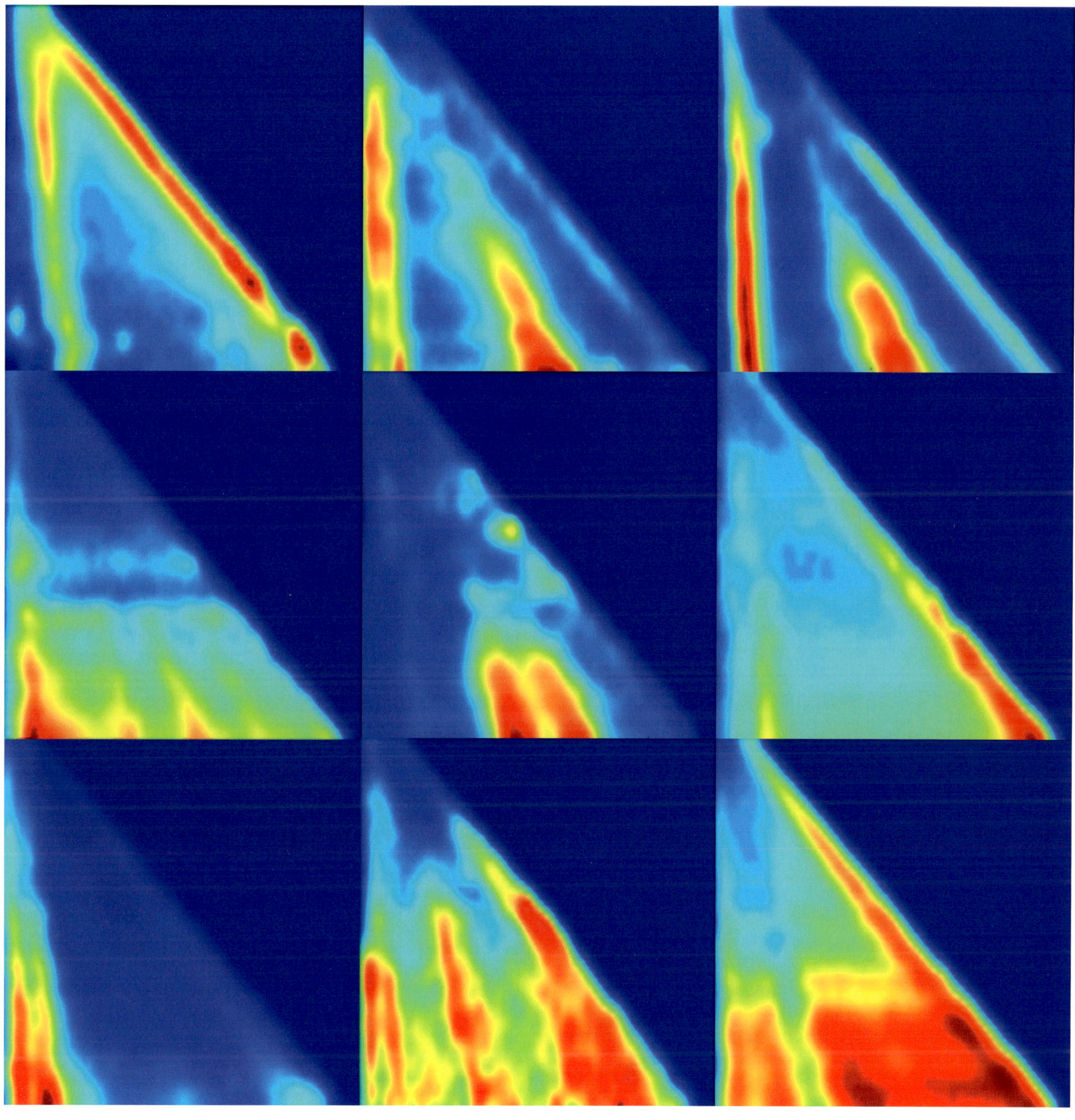

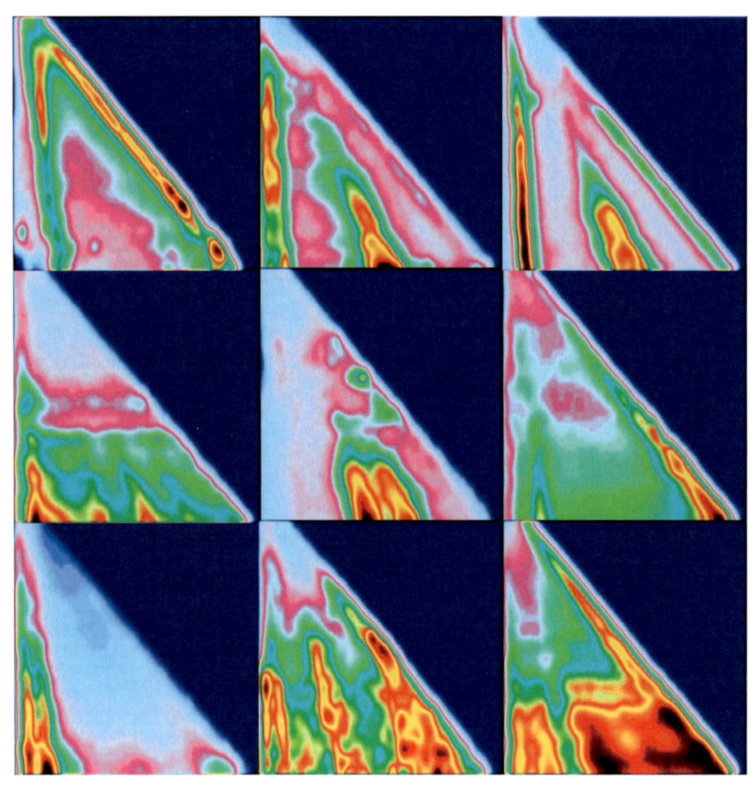

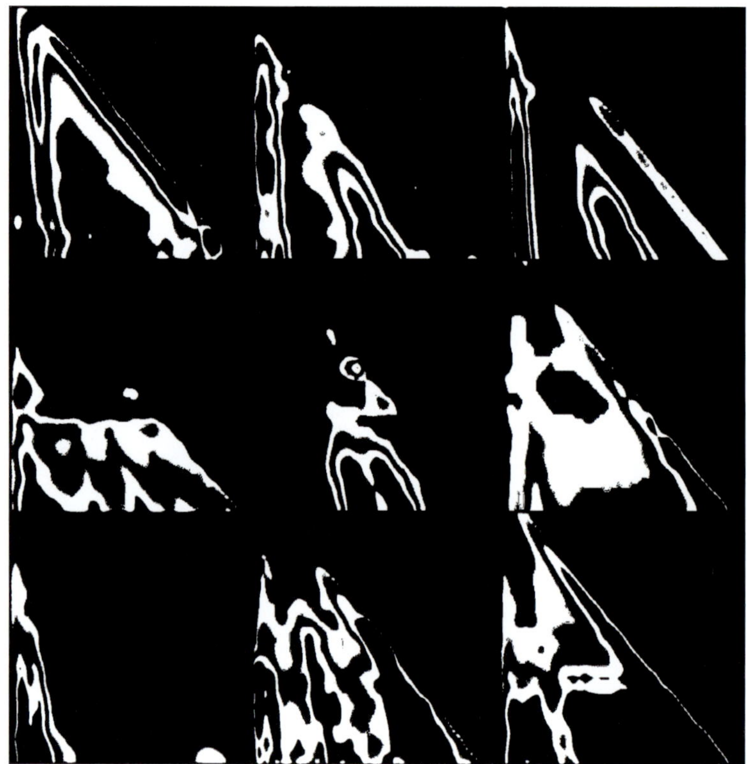

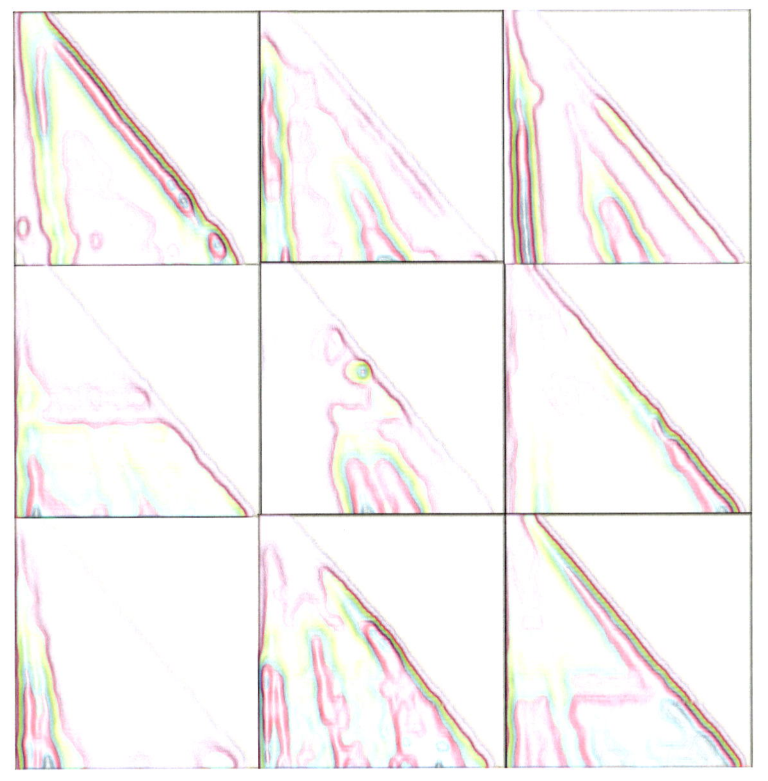

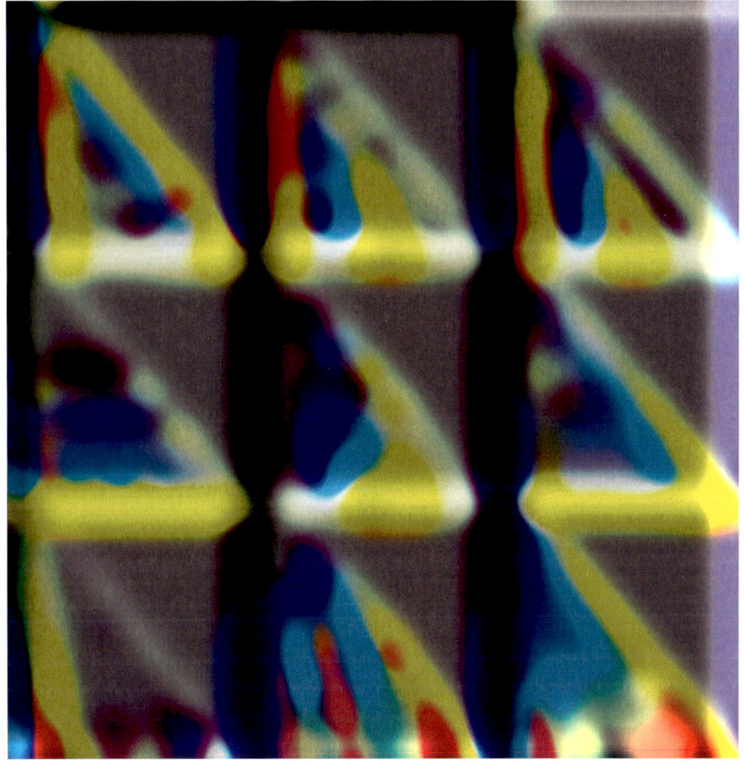

Laocoön and the Network

BY MATTHEW RITCHIE

Network theory shows us both how nature can be understood as information, and how information can be understood as part of nature. Information is humanly defined and humanly collected, to be sure. And, yes, it is codified and interpreted through computationally aided co-cognition. Yet, integrated inside a theory that applies equally to many nonhuman scales of being, information takes on new dimensions—and prompts the unnerving sense that we may be looking directly through a historical blind spot, with the viewer becoming beholder, reader, subject, and co-creator of this new interpretative state.

My first encounter with Barabási's work was the 2010 study "Limits of Predictability in Human Mobility," which used cell phone location data to show how terrifyingly predictable we are 93 percent of the time (see pages 84–85). On the bright side, an exhilarating 7 percent of the time, our trajectories remain, statistically, unknowable. Like most artists, I am intrigued by the emergence of any new visual language, so I was immediately struck by the novelty of these angled graphs, which represent mundane human activities as they stagger across a cellular frame. Descendants of the French physicist Jean Baptiste Perrin's late-nineteenth-and-early-twentieth-century observations of the "drunkard's walk" of atoms, these linear compositions seemed to me the very loom of fate, updated for the new millennium.

For the Hellenes, the loom and its operators, the *Moirae,* or Fates, personified how the tangled skeins of individual timelines can be understood as part of a larger and defined system. Their name means "portion" but also "ascertainment," or "proof." Just as the original loom was immediately understood as a mechanism for both storytelling and computation, weaving and reweaving the tapestry of individual lives, the scale-free data visualization is a machine for untangling chance, not eliminating it. Much later, the Spanish Jesuit Luis de Molina would argue that although an omniscient God could ascertain the result of all future possibilities, or "the true future," human beings can freely choose between those possibilities—a state of grace he called the "Middle Knowledge." It was understood, even in the sixteenth century when Molina was opining, that a free agent must operate in a continuously understood system—an unpunctuated space and time—to have real agency. What emerges from the BarabásiLab's images of human mobility is a more convincing characterization of this middle ground, because they illuminate the gray area between individual agency and systemic determination. This is the space where meaningful choice can be identified.

Human perceptual models always straddle the universal and the personal. By contrast, the radical transformations and scale shifts at the atomic scale cannot be easily understood "subjectively" or "objectively," no matter how we define those terms.

Which is why that first paper led me to a second, deeper dive into the principles behind Barabási's work. "Bose-Einstein Condensation in Complex Networks," which he published with Ginestra Bianconi in 2001, discusses the impact of the third law of thermodynamics on information, and specifically the process whereby the more entropy is introduced into any system, even one composed of pure information, the more homogeneous it will become. A mere four conditions are enough to stabilize any information system into a lockstep pattern where a Bose-Einstein superpositional state emerges. Translated to more relatable, contemporary terms, the World Wide Web becomes more and more self-similar as it approaches ever-higher levels of interconnectedness. The traditional subject—ourselves—previously examined retroactively through pictures, or stories, has become an infinitely recursive ghost story online, a wilderness of mirrors, continuously reconstituting itself as new data trails create new profiles. An infinity of such superposed reflections, which is generated for each citizen of what the Greeks called the *oikumene*, collectively sympathetic to forms of public theater, but ultimately subordinate to a mechanical perspective on the world and cumulatively indifferent to that citizen's human origin.

If there is a mythic template for this interpolation of image and information, it is not the loom of fate, but Indra's net, a Vedic thought experiment that posited our world as but one jewel in an infinite network of reflecting jewels. As the reflections in the Web are repeatedly and widely shared, accelerated by bandwidth, availability, and confirmation biases, the information complex becomes more and more similar overall.

For artists whose practices are increasingly based in the digital realm, this chain of consequences is significant. "Meaning" in this context can no longer be anything like the subjective or objective meaning we traditionally expect from a work of art, or of science, for that matter. Instead, meaning dissolves in a flow of exchanges mediated by, and dependent on, digitality. The ensuing boundary collapse fuses information with its source, the physical world, at every scale. The term "middle ground" suddenly seems both much larger and more dynamically integrated with the universe than we might have surmised.

Given this novel perspective on meaning, it is not so curious that the BarabásiLab decided to explore the structures and predilections of the art world. Visual art, a field with loose internal criteria, has long fetishized a regressive and poorly theorized model of pioneering exceptionalism, random encounters, and individual free will. As such, it makes a perfect target for the free-ranging intelligence of the lab to aim at with papers such as "Quantifying Reputation and Success in Art" (2018), which confirmed that the art world consists of preferential attachments, gatekeepers, and hubs that create a "rich club" of success, just as they do in other social realms. We all intuit that powerful institutions exhibit and collect based on the biases of their richest supporters. This has been true since the time of Ashurbanipal's library. That nearly 59 percent of artists are more likely to advance to success by forming early preferential attachments close to those centers of power is therefore also no surprise. But the fact that even 10 percent manage to survive on the fringes says something arguably even more interesting. Remember the unpredictable 7 percent from "Limits of Predictability"?

While the aforementioned informational aesthetic collapse might be generically co-opted by the related argument that for the contemporary art world, depersonalized aesthetic and informational compliance is part of its hidden appeal, this argument gets more complicated at the moment of visual encounter with specifically informational objects, such as these networks. These visualizations are not simply formal exercises. They are informational forms. Not quite, or not simply, diagrams, but not exactly drawings either, their visual sprawl, proliferating branches, intertwined coils, and fuzzy branches seem to be sketching an emerging informational understanding of nature, which may reflect a cultural shift toward seeing and understanding the post-Euclidian surfaces beneath our empirical observations of the world. The relationship between this new combination of programming, thinking, and seeing on the one hand, and how the human neurovisual system already processes connections between information, orthographic space, and complexity broadly speaking on the other, hints at the likelihood that we are developing visual forms derived from and inherently mutual with the informational society that sustains them—an event architecture more complex than the digital wilderness, and one that raises new questions about informational agency.

If there is a final visual myth, or *Sehrform*, that comes to mind, it is *Laocoön and His Sons*. The famous Hellenistic statue depicts the Homeric story of a priest who vigorously expressed his logical suspicion of the large horse that had suddenly appeared outside the ancient city of Troy. In the sculpture, Laocoön and his young children contend with a nest of murderous serpents sent by Athena to silence them on behalf of her clients, the Achaeans, who are hiding inside the horse. An icon of craftsmanship, agony, and antagonism, the sculpture is equally famous for the endless debate over its meaning conducted by, among others, Pliny, Michelangelo, Raphael, Titian, Napoleon, Goethe, Blake, Ruskin, Lessing, Babbit, and Greenberg. The assassination of Laocoön takes place on the beach, that ever-shifting middle ground between certainty and chaos. The figures struggle within a coiled group of nonhuman entities, a sort of network. But so complex and intricate is this intertwining of truth and falsehood, formal composition and ambivalent narrative, that over the vast span of time since its making, the artwork has come to represent an intergenerational discussion about the fundamental terms and divisions of how we think about art and truth, and seeing and meaning. No single image, or system, can ever tell the whole story of how we experience and interact with the full complexities of nature and ourselves. But like the struggling Laocoön, the BarabásiLab's studies and data images prompt us to imagine that possibility together. At this particular moment, in the spring of 2020, when humans, nature, information, and distribution networks are intertwined more intimately and critically than at any time in our brief shared history, such possibilities seem more valuable than ever.

RHYTHM, 2008

Barabási's 2008 paper on human mobility caused the biggest uproar in his professional career. Featured on the cover of *Nature,* it relied on data recorded by a European cell-phone company to track and plot individual cell-phone users' physical locations and trajectory in time. Its publication was the first time the broad public learned that their every move was being traced just by virtue of making a phone call, sending a text, or looking at something on the Internet—a rather upsetting realization for many people. The research captured thousands of individuals' geographic movements by stringing together their real-time locations. The BarabásiLab explored these anonymized data sets and revealed the exceptional predictability of our daily routine. Using algorithms, the team could forecast a person's future location with 93 percent accuracy. The visualizations opposite shows individual movements over time. The diagram on pages 82–83 shows the trajectories of several people whose collective movements span the vicinity of a whole country. Pages 86 and 87 show collective movements spanning a major city.

The images on pages 84 and 85, by contrast, trace the trajectories of three individuals, each with a different degree of predictability, as they move around a major city. In the same time period, one person visits four locations, a second visits about a dozen, and the third about a hundred. The space is partitioned into a Voronoi grid that captures the reception areas of each mobile-phone tower, the silent spy of our current era. These partitions illustrate the way space constrains our movement. In addition, the data reflects that just as our daily patterns are confined by the roads we travel, our socioeconomic existence is yoked to invisible structures.

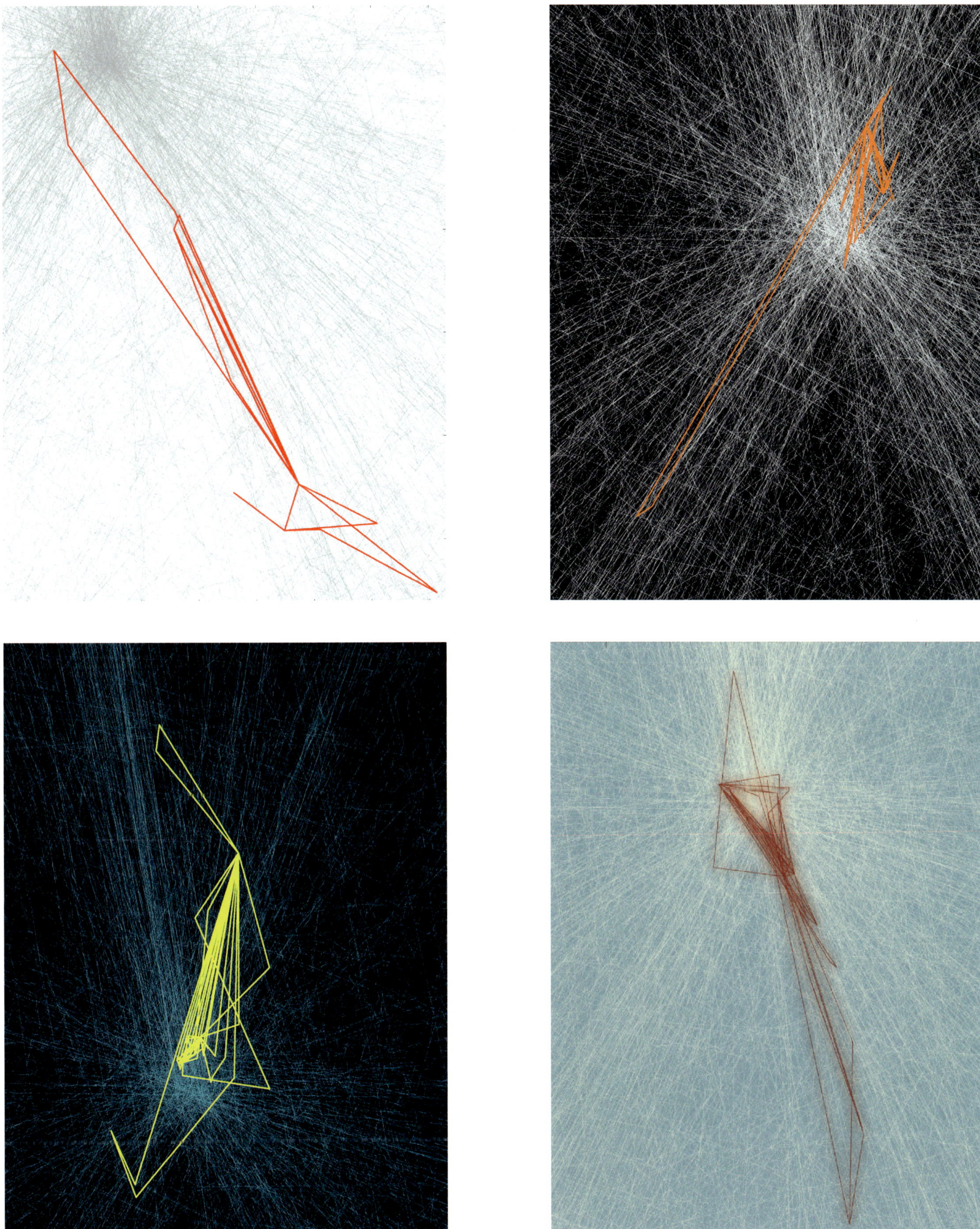

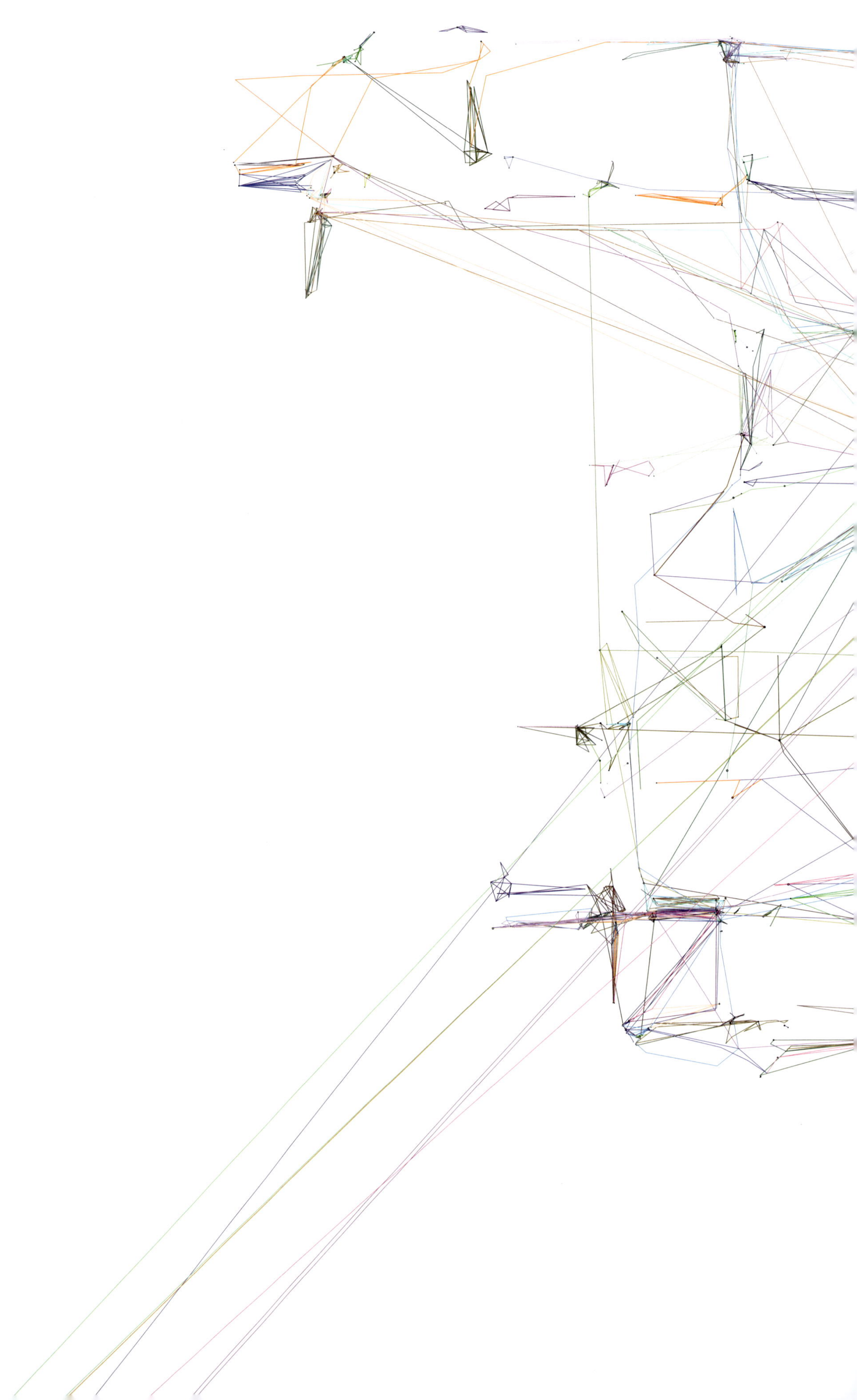

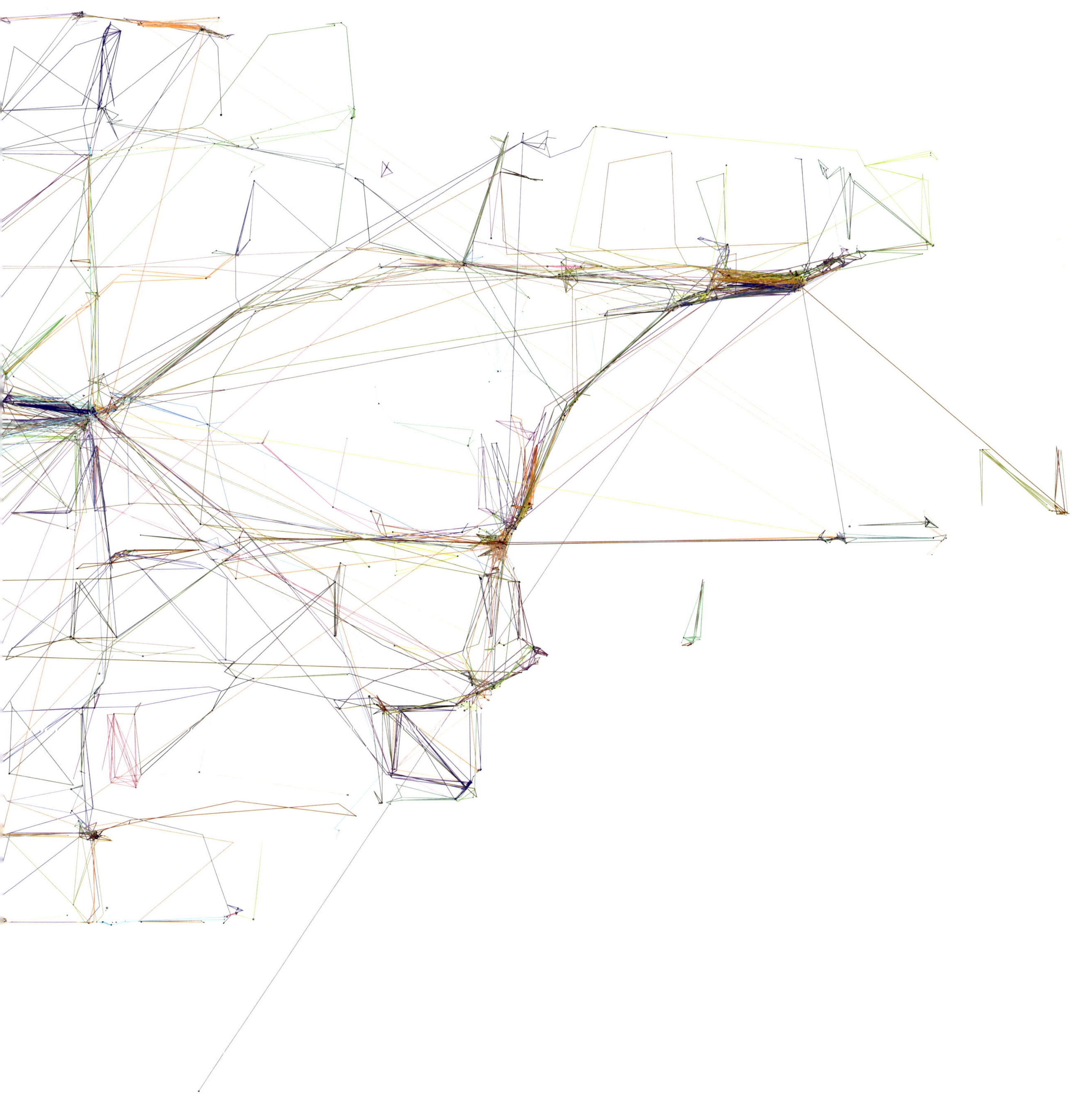

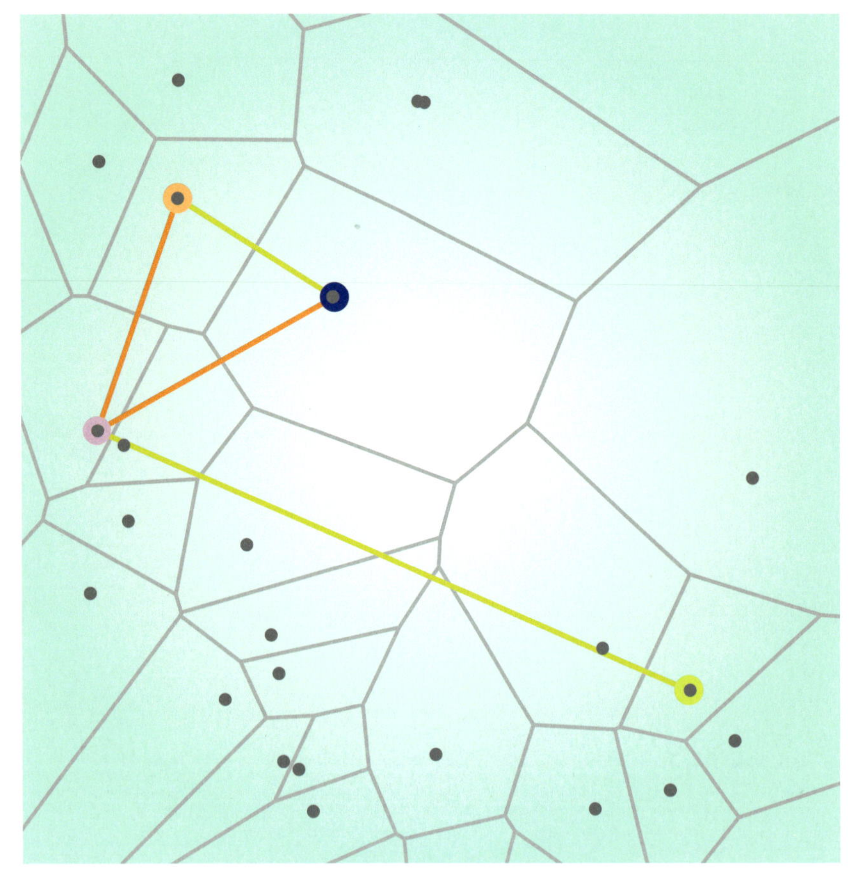

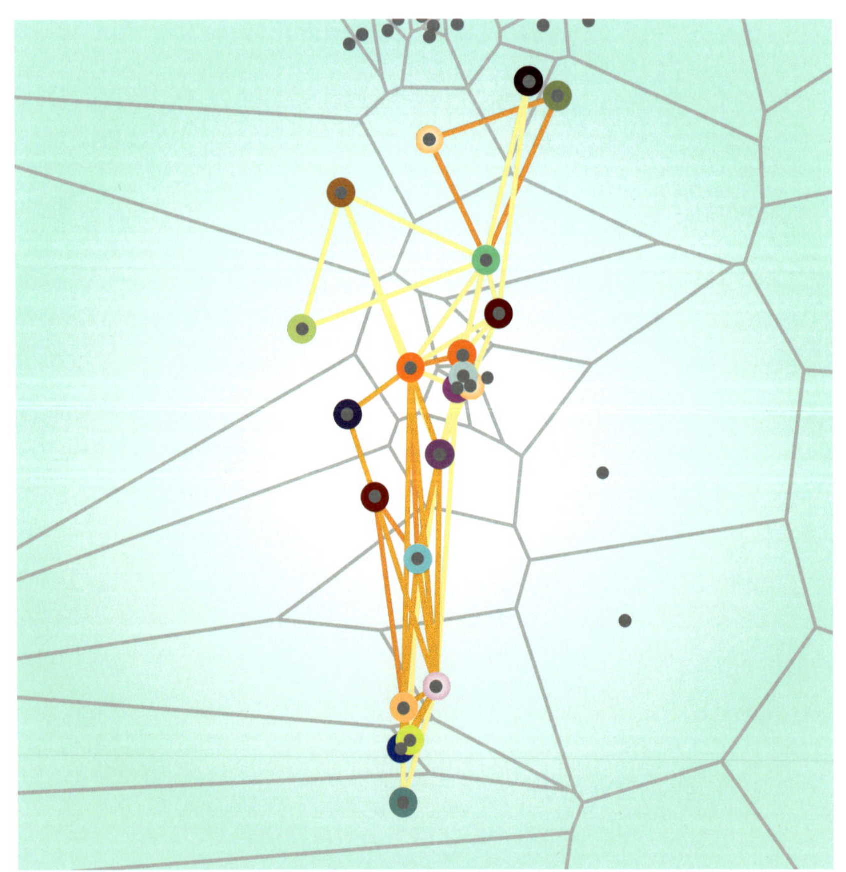

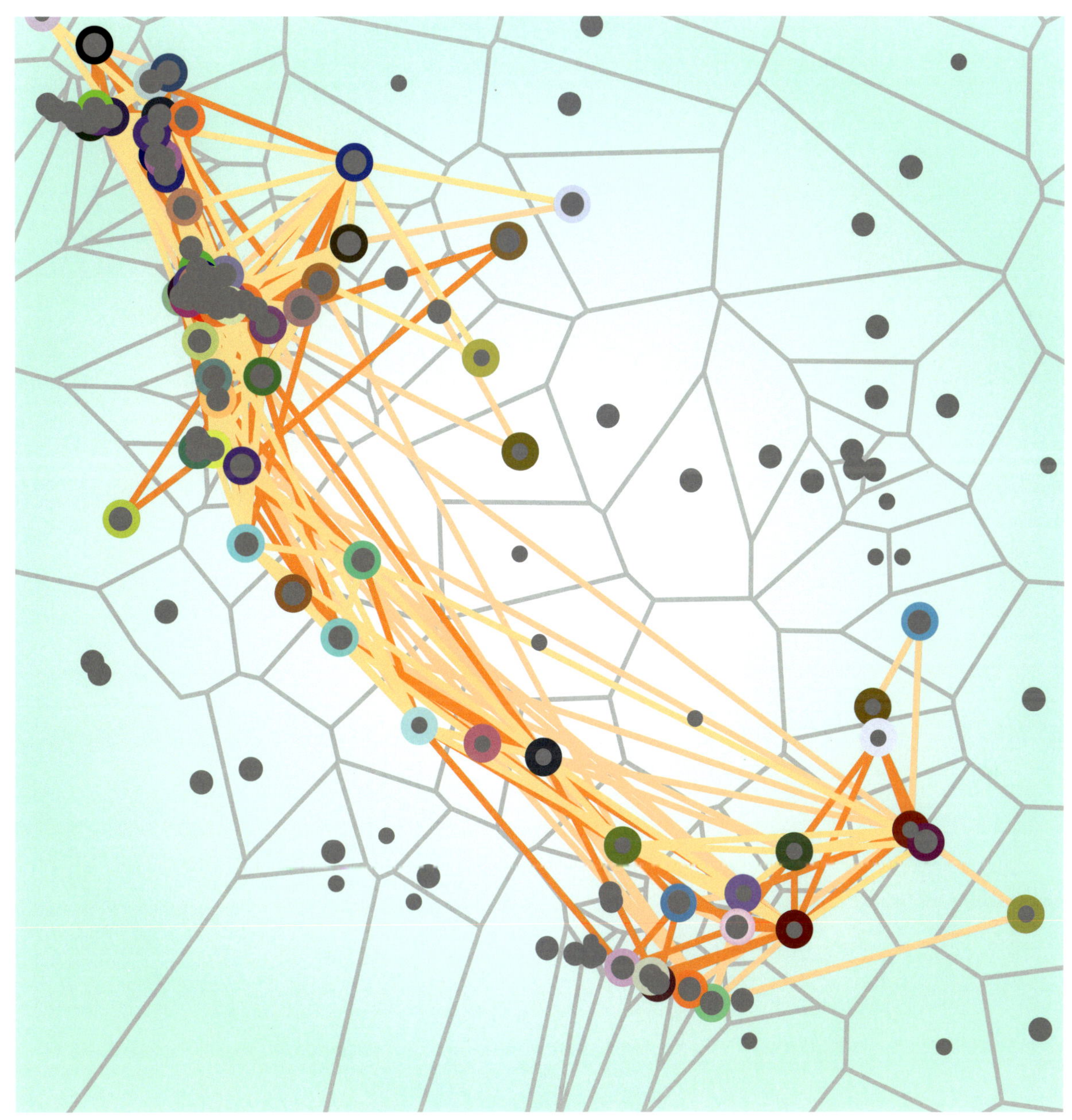

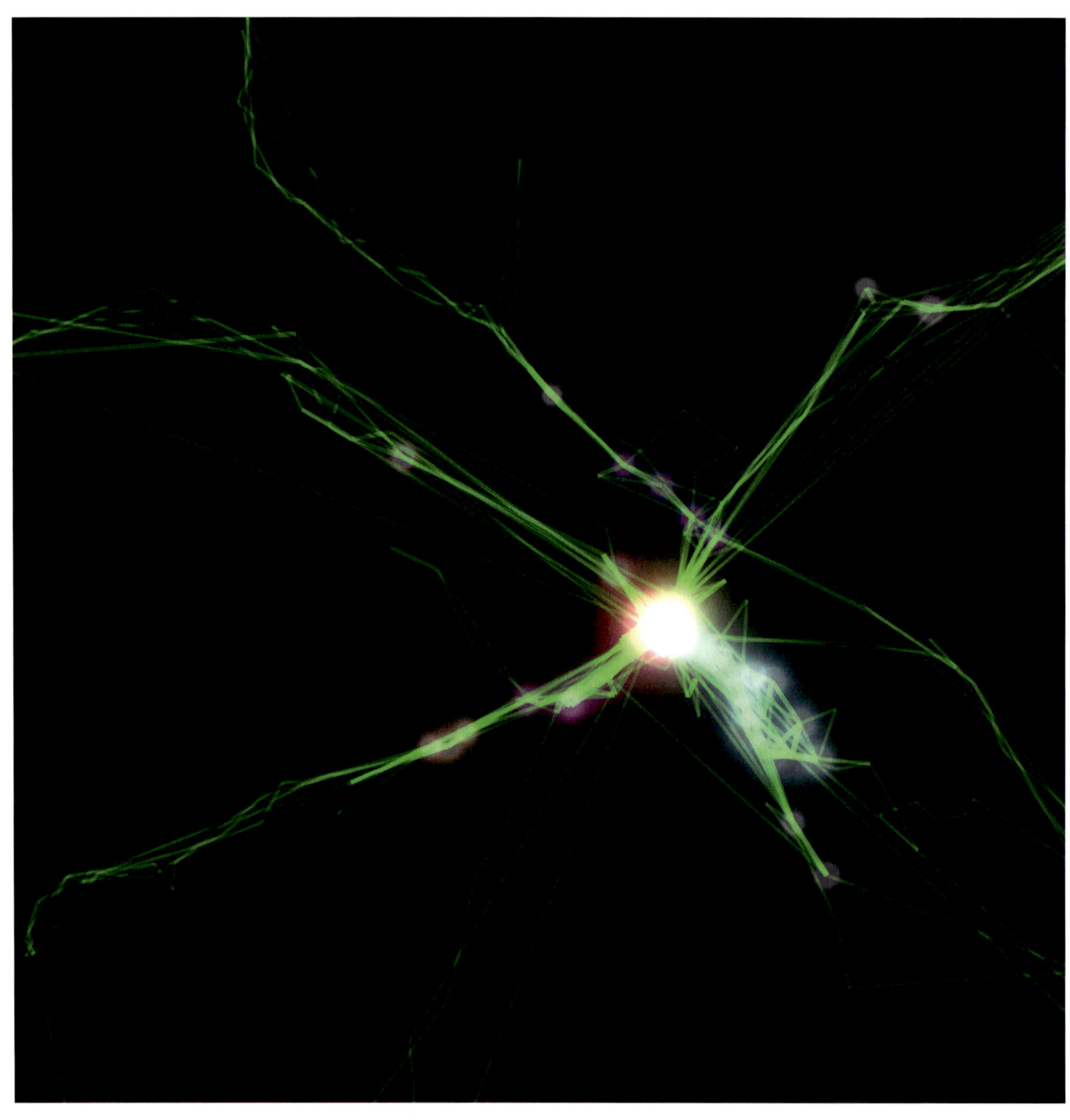

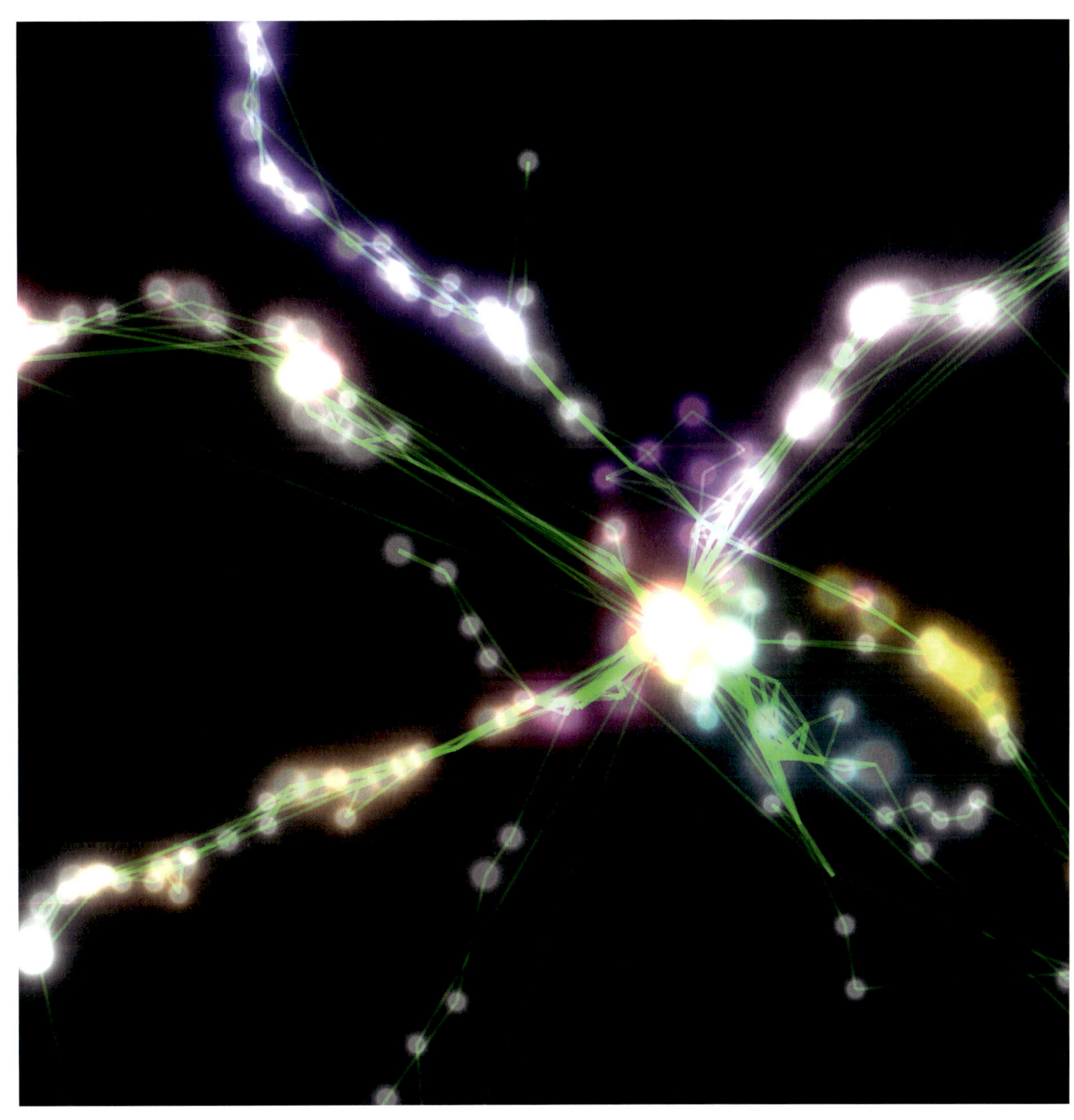

VIRUSES, 2009

A decade before the Covid-19 pandemic, the BarabásiLab was using mobile-phone data to map the spread of newly emerging mobile-phone viruses and predict their hidden transmission patterns. The pattern unveiled by the lab's work is strikingly similar to what's been observed during the asymptomatic spread of the Covid-19 virus.

The images opposite document the infection hot spots in a certain area in Europe. Each of the Voronoi-cell partitions captures the area of reception of a mobile-phone tower. The colors of the cells—red signifying the most prevalent spread, and dark blue the lack of infections—correspond to the percentage of infection in that region and foreshadow the viral-prevalence maps we have grown familiar with during the Covid-19 pandemic. The variation among the four is a reflection of enhancing or suppressing the visibility of the Voronoi lattice. The plates on pages 90 and 91 show the spread of a cell-phone virus in space and time. Starting with the first image on the left, the sequence reveals how the virus, beginning in a rural area, goes on to infect densely populated regions first, and then spreads back from urban to rural areas. The plates on pages 92 and 93 illustrate the contact network of two super-spreaders, each of whom appears as a giant red node in the middle of their network, with their node size being proportional to the number of infections caused. Both super-spreaders are connected to all of the individuals they infected, who in turn are linked to the people they infected, reflecting the cascade of infections that supports the virus in the society.

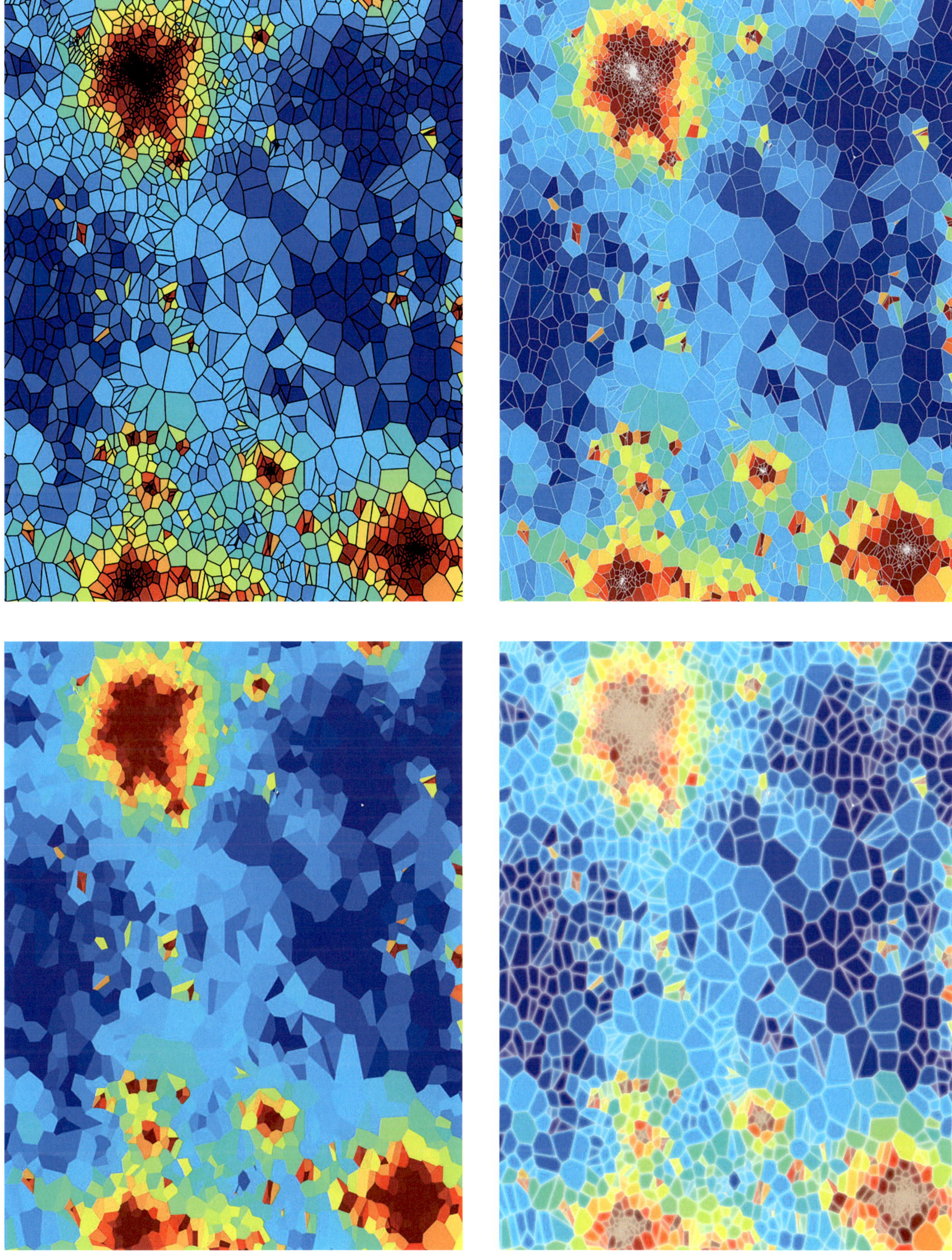

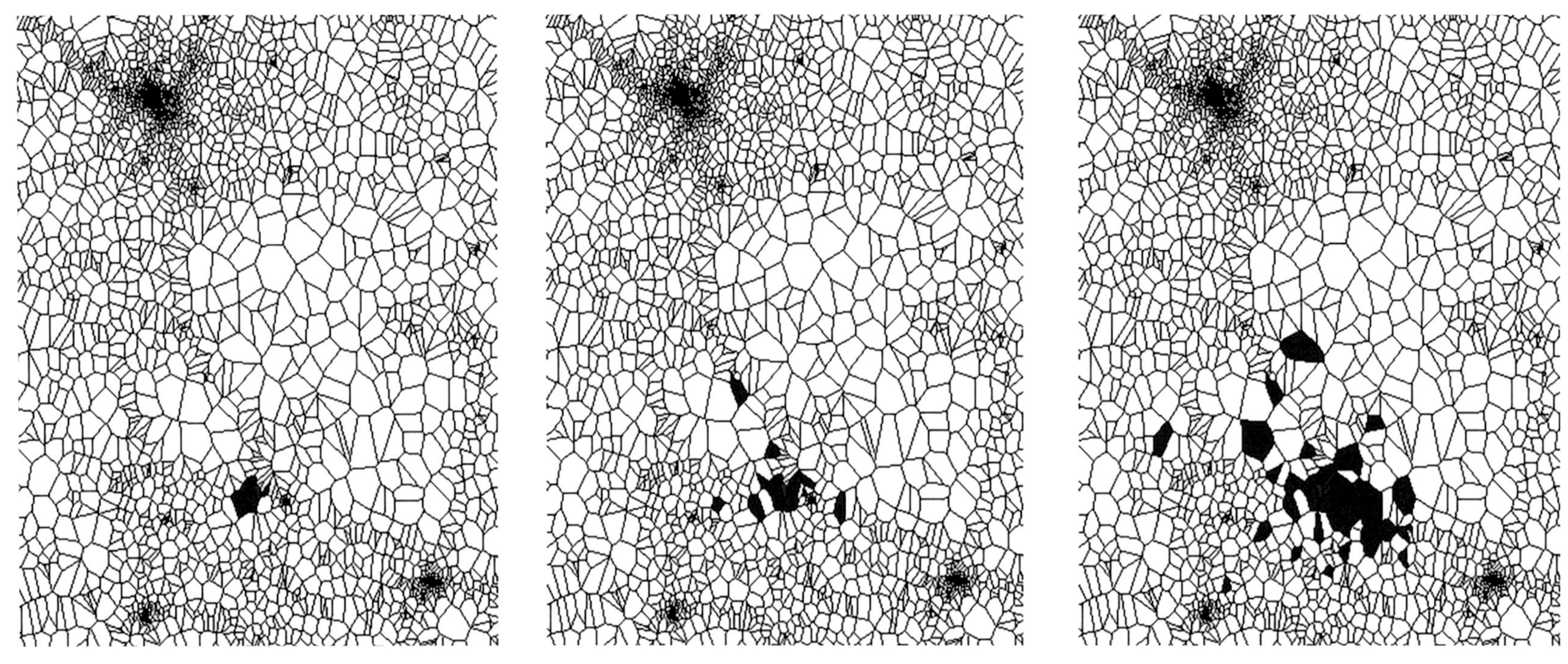

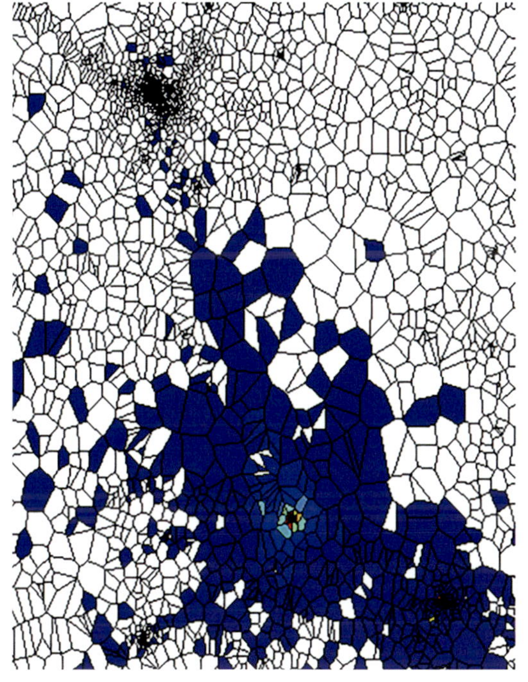
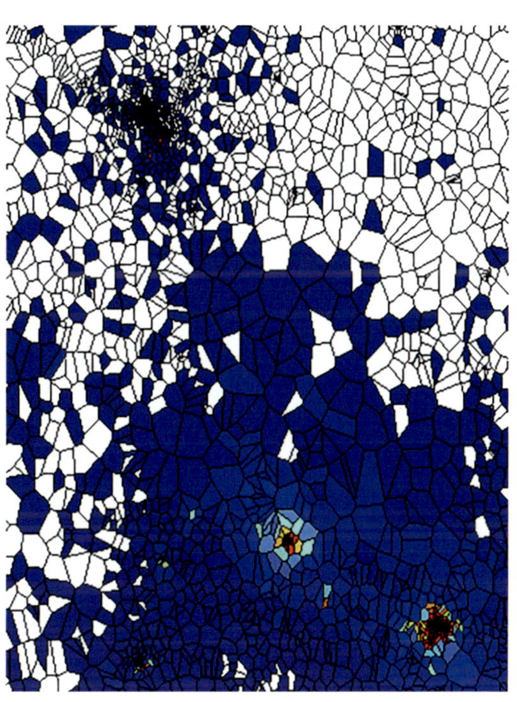
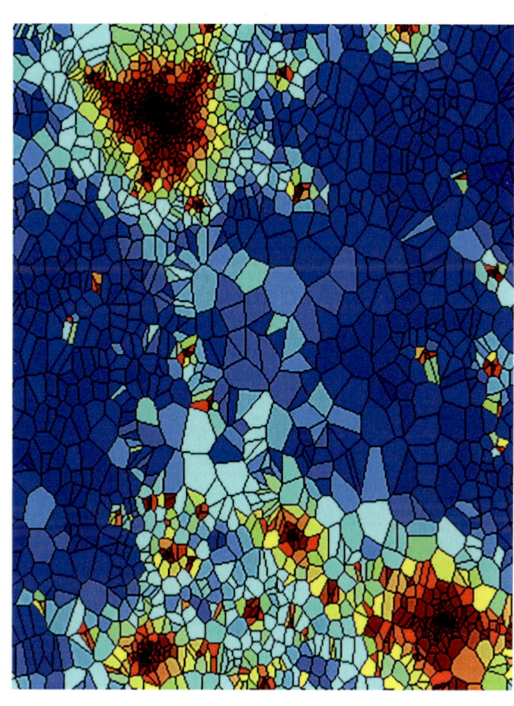

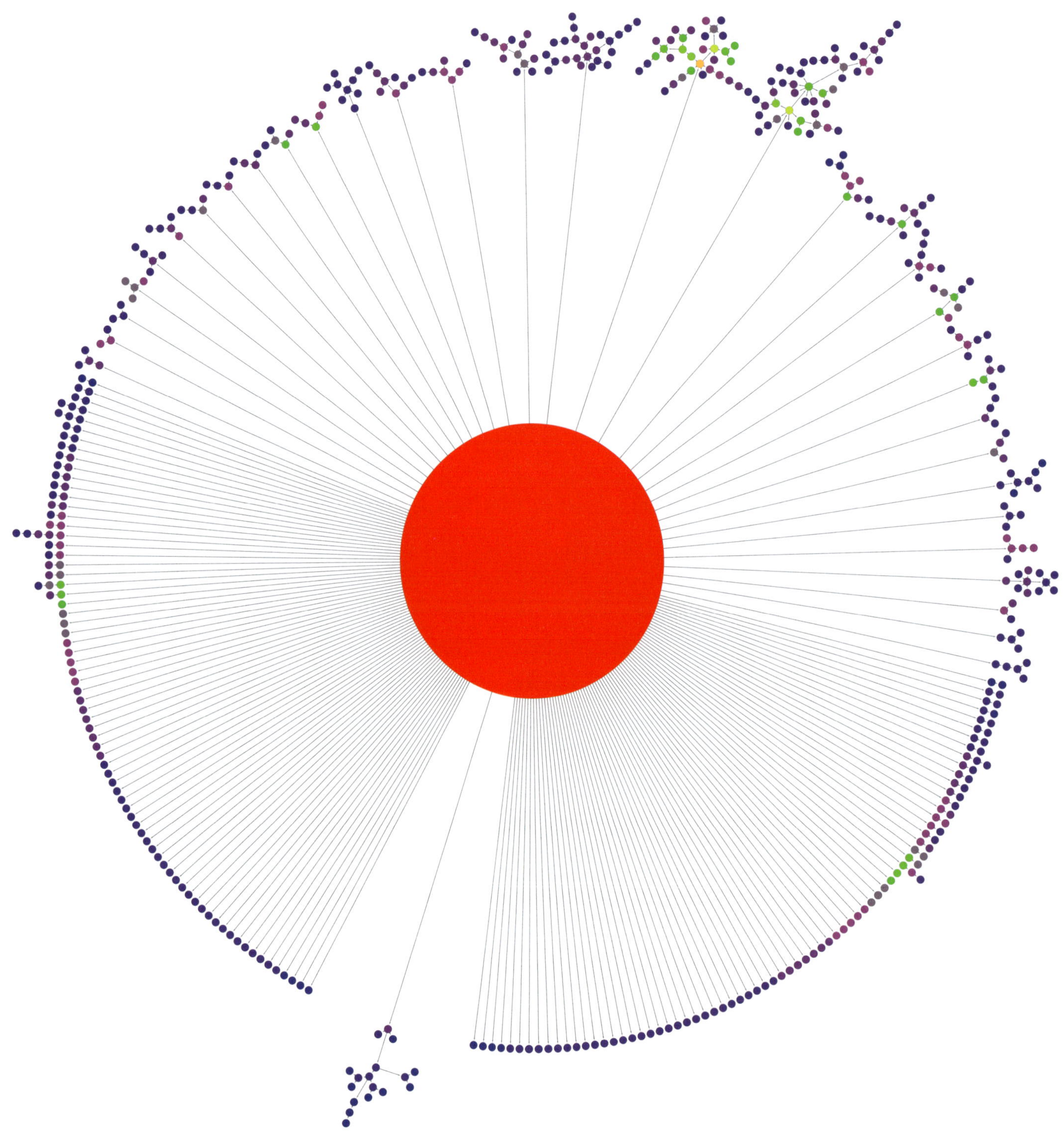

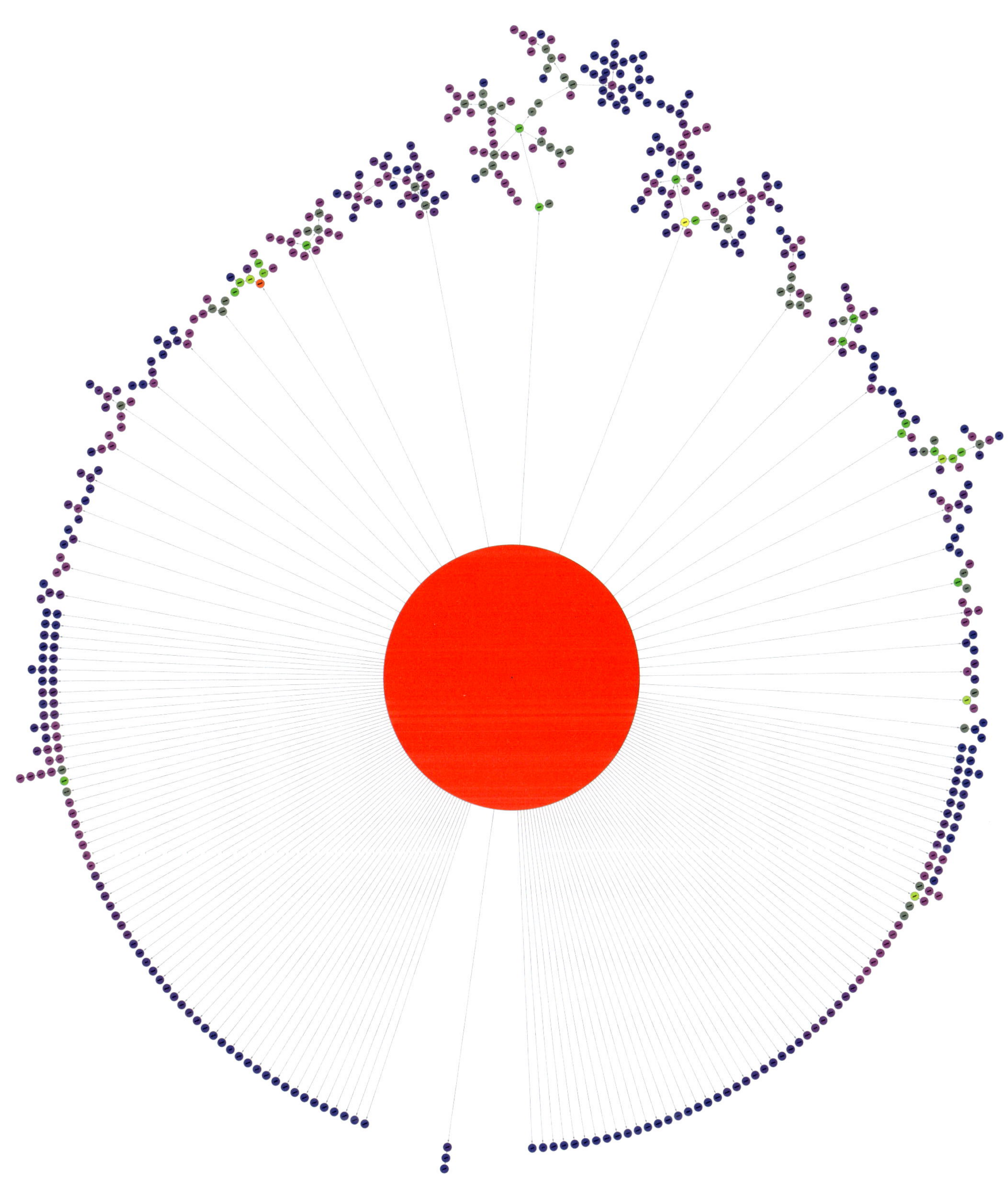

EMERGENCIES, 2011

From hurricanes to terrorist attacks, wildfires to mass shootings, life-threatening emergencies have dominated the twenty-first-century news cycle. Mobile phones increasingly act as personal broadcasting devices in a crisis. They enable individuals to raise awareness of unfolding events through their personal networks and social media. Between January 2007 and January 2009, the BarabásiLab used mobile-phone data to detect human reactions to a whole slew of life-threatening events, from bomb explosions to riots. The team began by scanning media reports to identify social, technological, and natural emergencies. The next step was combing through national mobile-phone records to identify the individuals who experienced these events and analyze their reactions, in the form of whom those individuals called and when they made calls. This form of contact tracing presaged by a decade the tools authorities have been using to track potential infections during Covid-19.

To illustrate their findings, Barabási's team mapped the cascade of calls tearing through the social networks of the witnesses of two emergencies, a bombing, opposite, and a riot, pages 96 and 97. The links of the network capture calls that the witnesses, shown as red squares, made immediately following the event and the subsequent calls their acquaintances, shown as circles, made upon hearing the news. Colors capture time—the increasingly blue nodes represent individuals to whom the news arrives later, as they are at the end of the chain of calls. These visualizations describe how the sensitive fabric of the social network springs into action in the face of an emergency through a series of events that flare up like independent forest fires. They also show that while most news will dead-end in small pockets of the social network, a very few witnesses will create global awareness by triggering the engagement of hundreds of individuals.

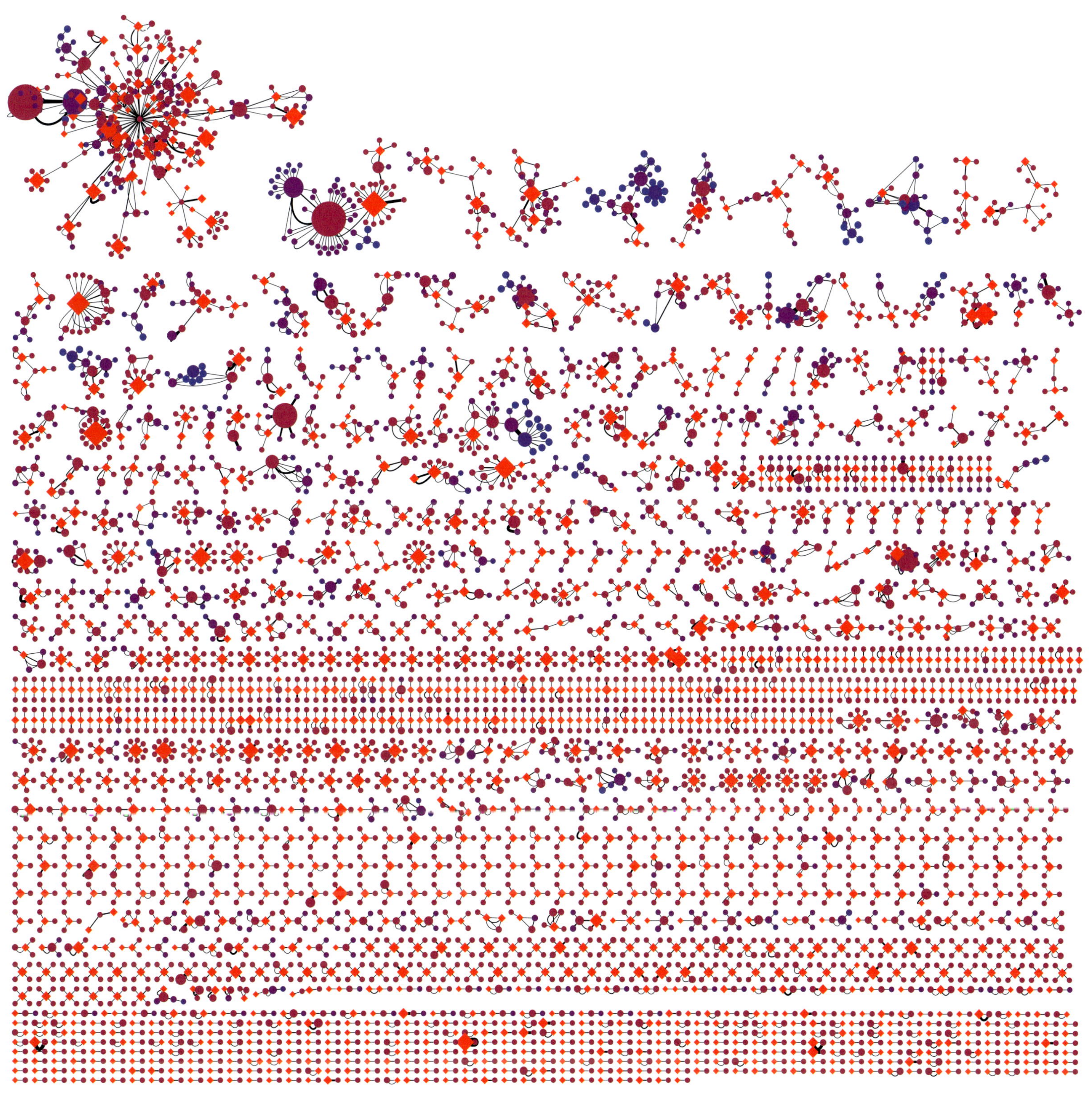

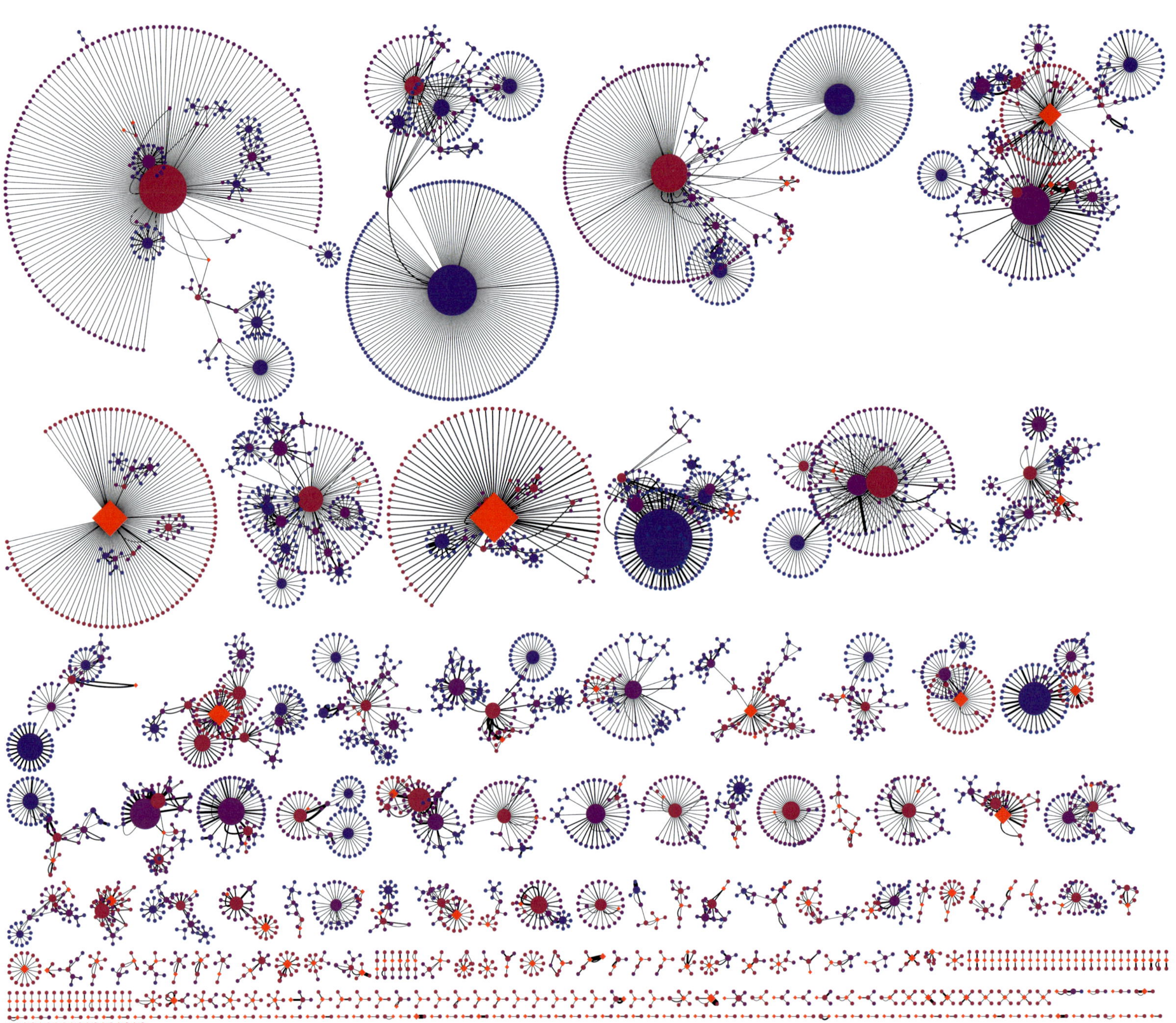

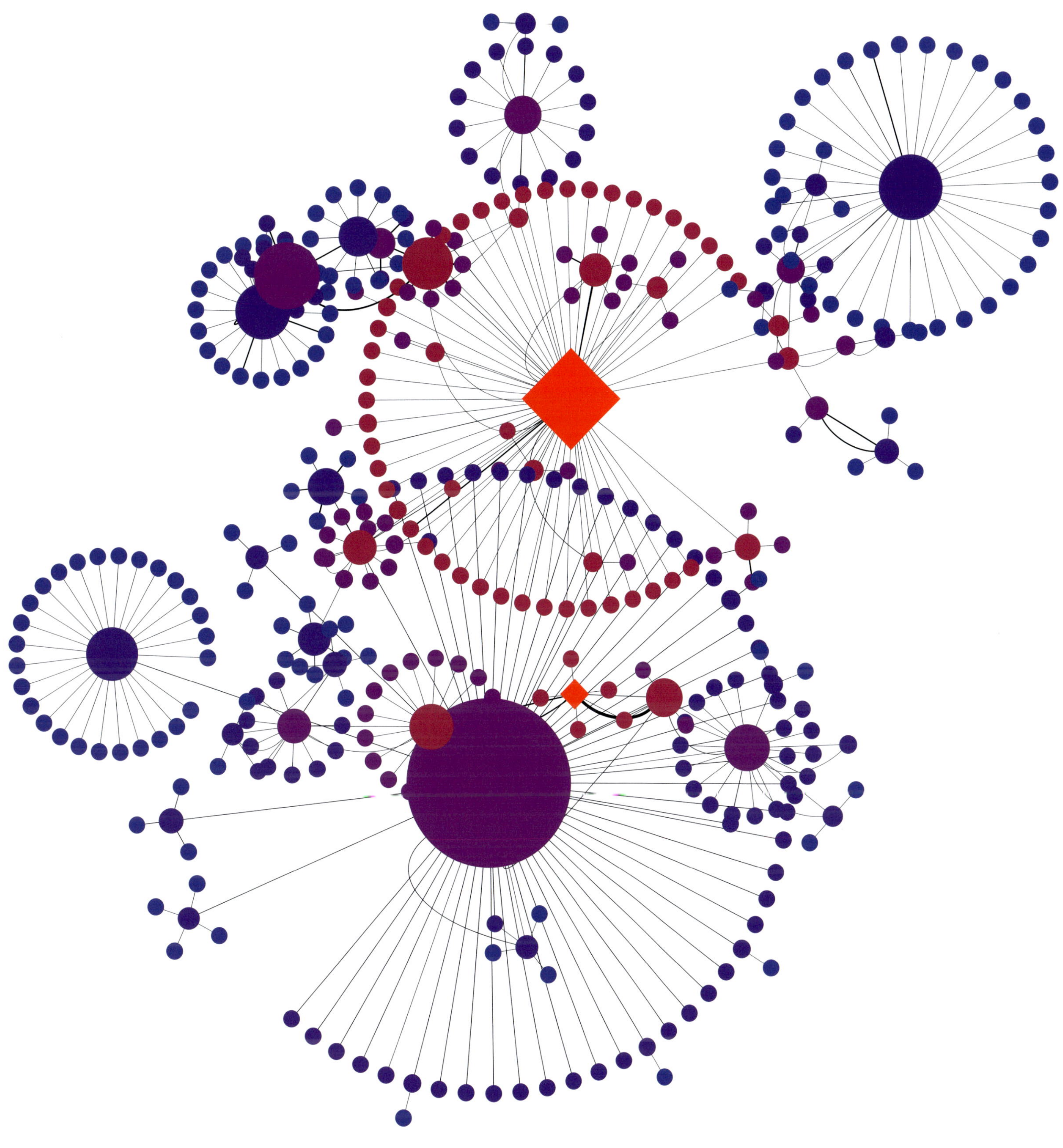

The Road from Rome

BY CARLO RATTI

When Italian architect and surveyor Giambattista Nolli created his famous 1748 *Map of Rome* (*Pianta grande di Roma*), he knew that the age-old dream of an accurate urban representation would require engraving more than just stones and streets. Somehow, a true map should capture the social dimension of a city. Which is why his iconic document encoded information about public and private access—buildings are rendered as dark, solid figures, while streets and public spaces are light.

A few decades later, the idea of mapping human activity resurfaced with Charles Joseph Minard's graphic representations of aggregate flows of physical material. Minard, a French civil engineer, pioneered the field of concise data visualization, rendering subjects such as production, immigration, shipping and trade, disease outbreak, and—most famously—Napoleon's fatal march to Moscow. Yale University statistician and political-science professor Edward Tufte, one of today's most notable data-visualization researchers, calls Minard's Napoleonic invasion map "probably the best statistical graphic ever drawn,"[1] citing it as the birth of the modern infographic.

Minard had found a way to represent large-scale flows in the nineteenth century. But it was not until the twentieth century that resolution increased from the aggregate to the individual. In 1957, Paul-Henry Chombart de Lauwe, a French urban sociologist who had studied sculpture at the École des beaux-arts, approached cartography from the perspective of sociology, creating such documents as *Journeys During a Year in the Life of a Young Woman from the 16th Arrondissement* ("Trajects pendant un an d'une jeune fille du XVIe arrondissement"). The map charted the movements of a single person, showing her characteristic paths from home to university to piano teacher, as well as anomalies and diversions.

In Chombart de Lauwe's footsteps, the Situationists, a group of avant-garde creatives who coalesced in the 1960s, developed the theory and practice of "*urban dérive*," an emotional and intuitive wandering or drifting through the city to elucidate personal "psychogeographies." Some well-known examples of such *dérives* are French philosopher Guy Debord's *Guide Psychogéographique de Paris*, a map showing the links and flows between non-contiguous locations in Paris, and Dutch artist Constant Nieuwenhuys's New Babylon, a Dériville or "drift city" that would span the globe and become the infinite context for a neo-nomadic humanity.

At the turn of the twenty-first century, the introduction of the Internet, the miniaturization of computing, and the ubiquity of telecommunications networks opened a new dimension of physical space. Nearly every material movement—whether of people, vehicles, or goods—could suddenly be tracked and tagged in real time. What took Chombart de Lauwe a painstaking year to record with analog tools can now be generated instantaneously and on a massive scale. Individual traces are recorded in real time, and their aggregate sum becomes urban big data. To put the scale of this revolution in perspective, approximately 90 percent of the data in the world was generated in the past two years alone.

Early experiments in mobility mapping, such as *You Are Here,* a 1995 installation for the opening of the Museu d'Art Contemporani Barcelona (MACBA), or, later, the Waag Society's 2015 map showing bicycle movement in Amsterdam, were built on a deployment of GPS trackers released into public space. Now that the diffusion of cell phones has placed a high-resolution sensor in virtually every pocket, millions of people can be tracked simultaneously, revealing the natural behavior of a new urban cyborg. In 2005, at the Massachusetts Institute of Technology's Senseable City Lab, my colleagues and I produced one of the first maps of individual mobility on a massive scale, using real-time data sets for the cities of Graz and Rome. Our project illustrated the relationships between different dimensions of urban inhabitation through data.

Around the same time, Barabási arrived at mobility mapping from the direction of network science. Initially interested in the social network of mobile-phone users, he soon started unveiling the fundamental mathematical laws that govern individual mobility and predictability. These discoveries led to several pioneering works on human mobility (see pages 80–87) and to our collaborations on other projects exploring the boundaries between data visualization and analytics. What we have learned is that, as computation becomes ubiquitous and sensing tags disperse in the environment, data visualization and analytics are becoming increasingly integrated. More and more, geospatial data points flicker across the planet, allowing for the possibility that all human and material flow can be tracked. The progeny of Nolli's *Map of Rome* is a real-time digital twin, an amalgamation of personal and public information that opens up a new, multifaceted exploration of reality in between mapping and analytics.

---

1 Edward Tufte, Poster of Napoleon's March, edwardtufte.com/tufte/posters.

CONTROL, 2011

Having grown up in Transylvania during the darkest years of Ceaușescu's communist regime, Barabási witnessed the extraordinary role control plays in a dictatorship. In the context of political power dynamics, control seems like a uniquely human concept. Yet control is ubiquitous—and essential—in the physical and biological realms. A brain must continually control its neural circuits to maintain its alertness. Our planet must constantly regulate multiple environmental variables, from temperature to humidity to oxygen content. Each of our cells must persistently regulate the concentration of its molecules and proteins to stay alive and maintain its function. The seeming contradiction between the way control is wielded by humans and exploited by nature inspired Barabási to explore how complex, self-organized networks control themselves. His resulting theory predicted that full control does not require authority over each individual element, but that a few elements—called driver nodes—can guide the dynamics of the whole system.

When this theory was accepted for publication by *Nature,* BarabásiLab designer Mauro Martino set out to illustrate it in all its complexity. The theory predicted that each driver node controls a "cactus," a mathematics term that describes a connected subgraph that represents the elementary units of control. Martino depicted these cacti and their area of control as small, tree-like network neighborhoods forming a forest, which represented the larger network. In the images, the explanatory power and the visual narrative are divorced. Pages 101–03 depict the field of cacti that determines the controllability of specific networks. Pages 104 and 105 represent the controllability of a network capturing trust and an intra-organizational social network, respectively. While none of these visualizations explain how one specific part of the image exerts control over the system, the information they display makes the hidden order behind control visible by capturing the forces necessary to command the respective network.

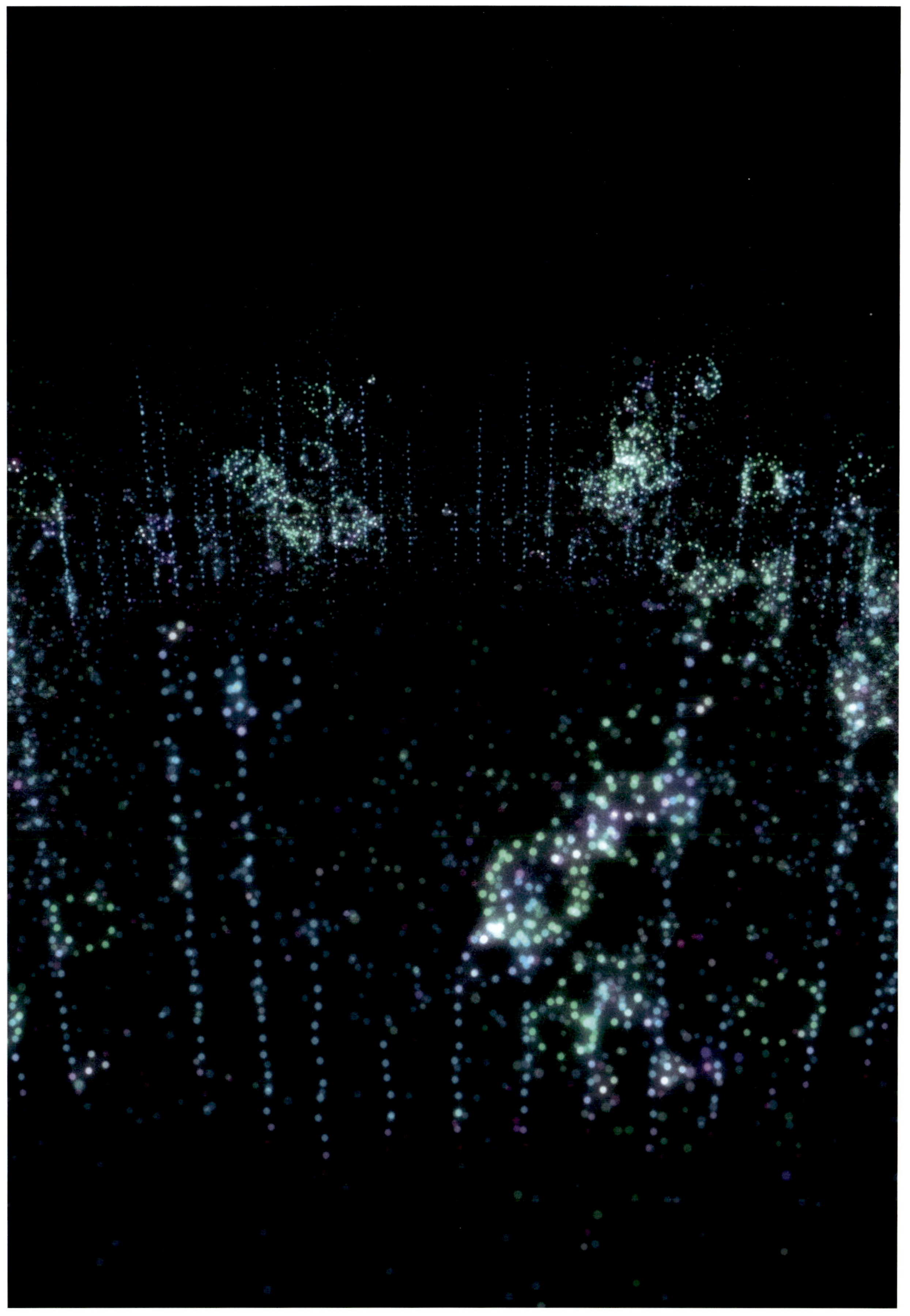

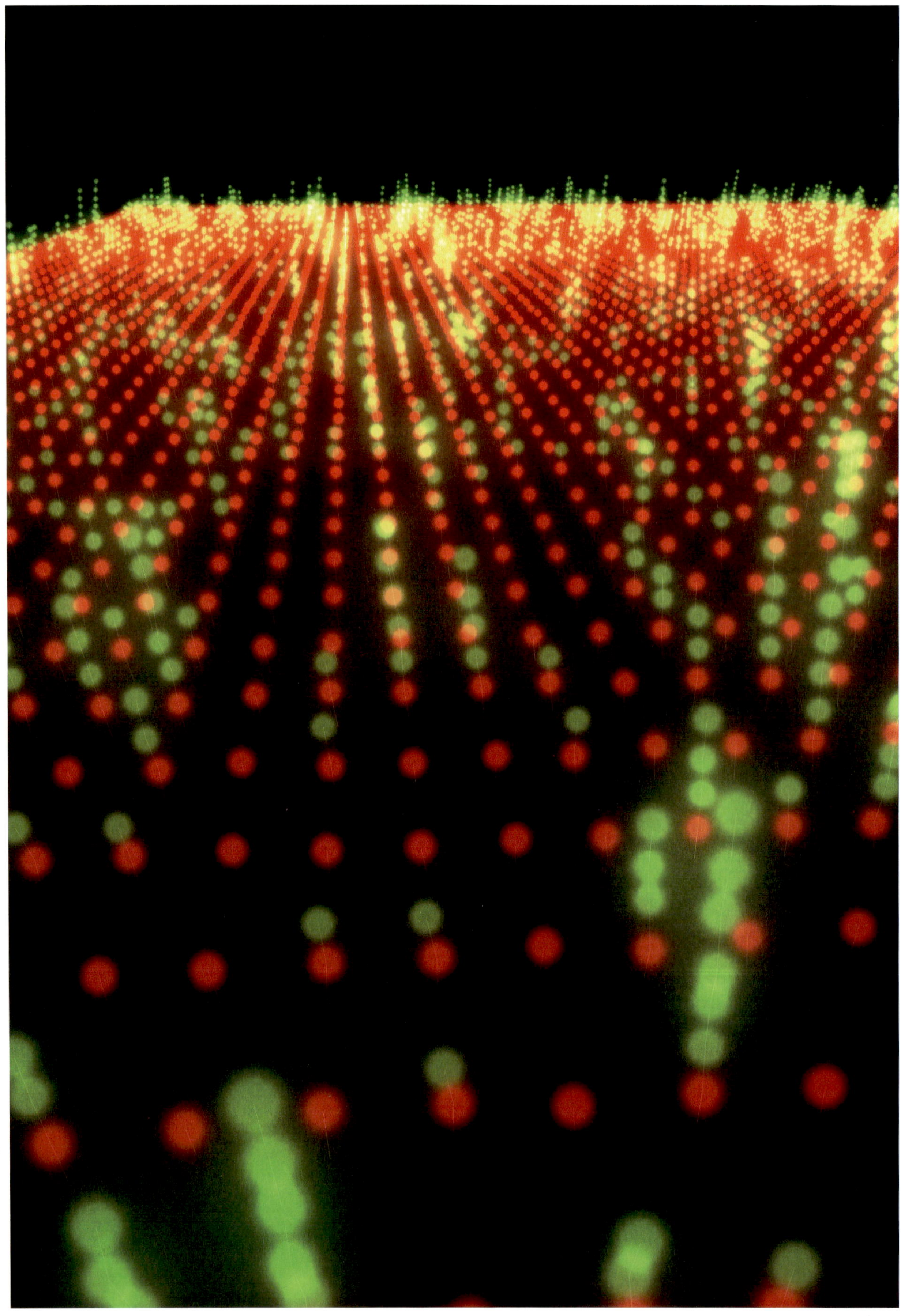

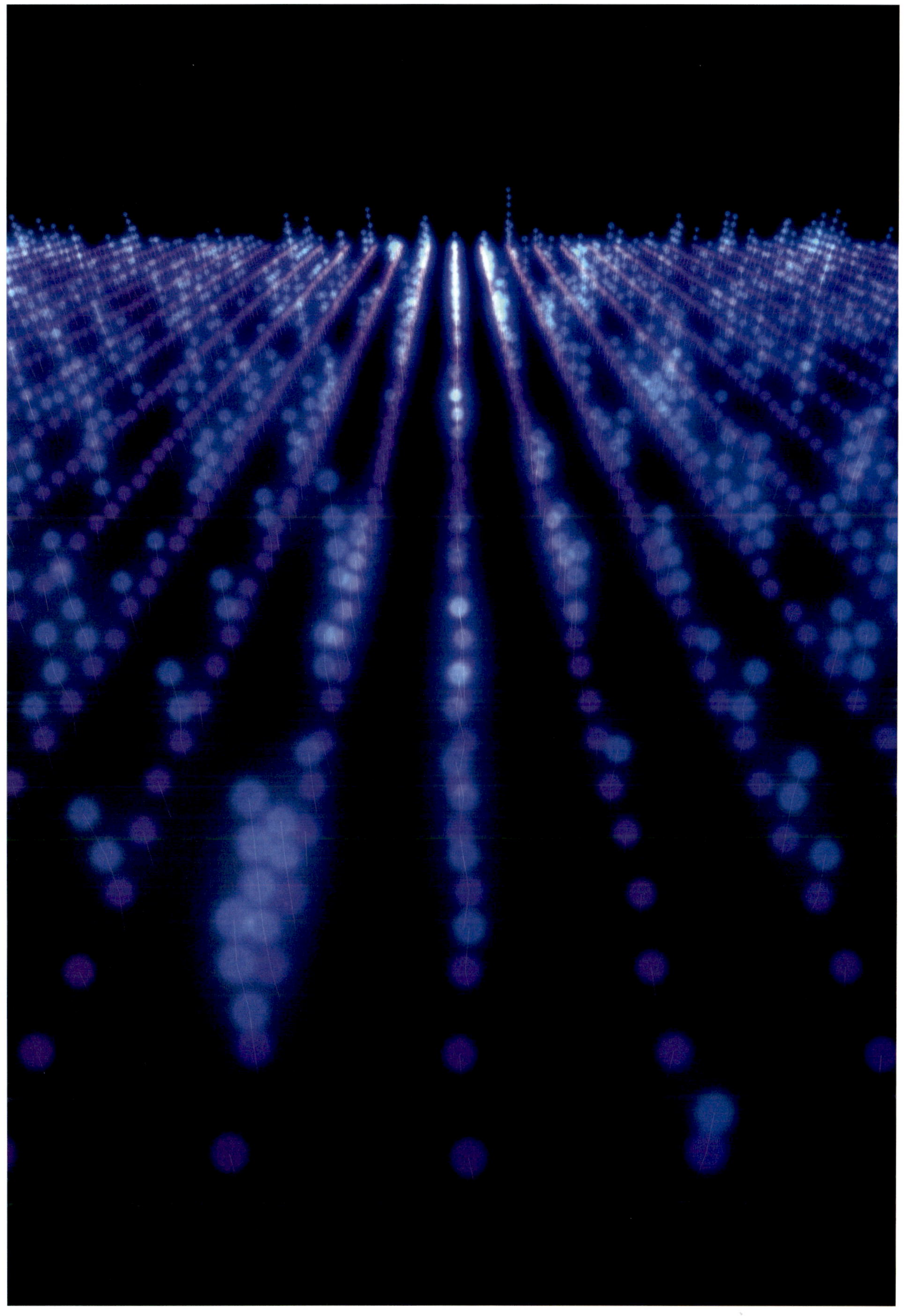

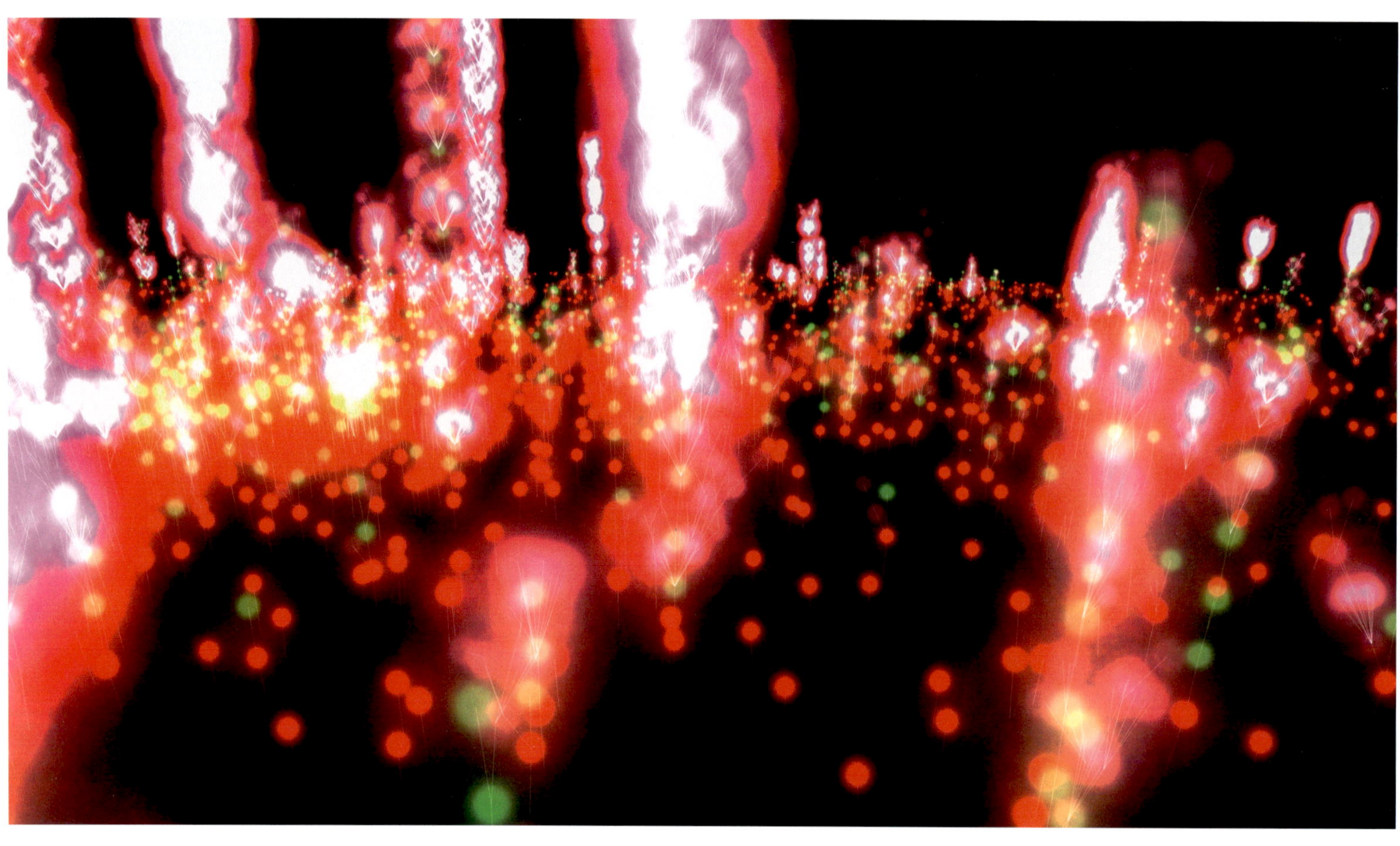

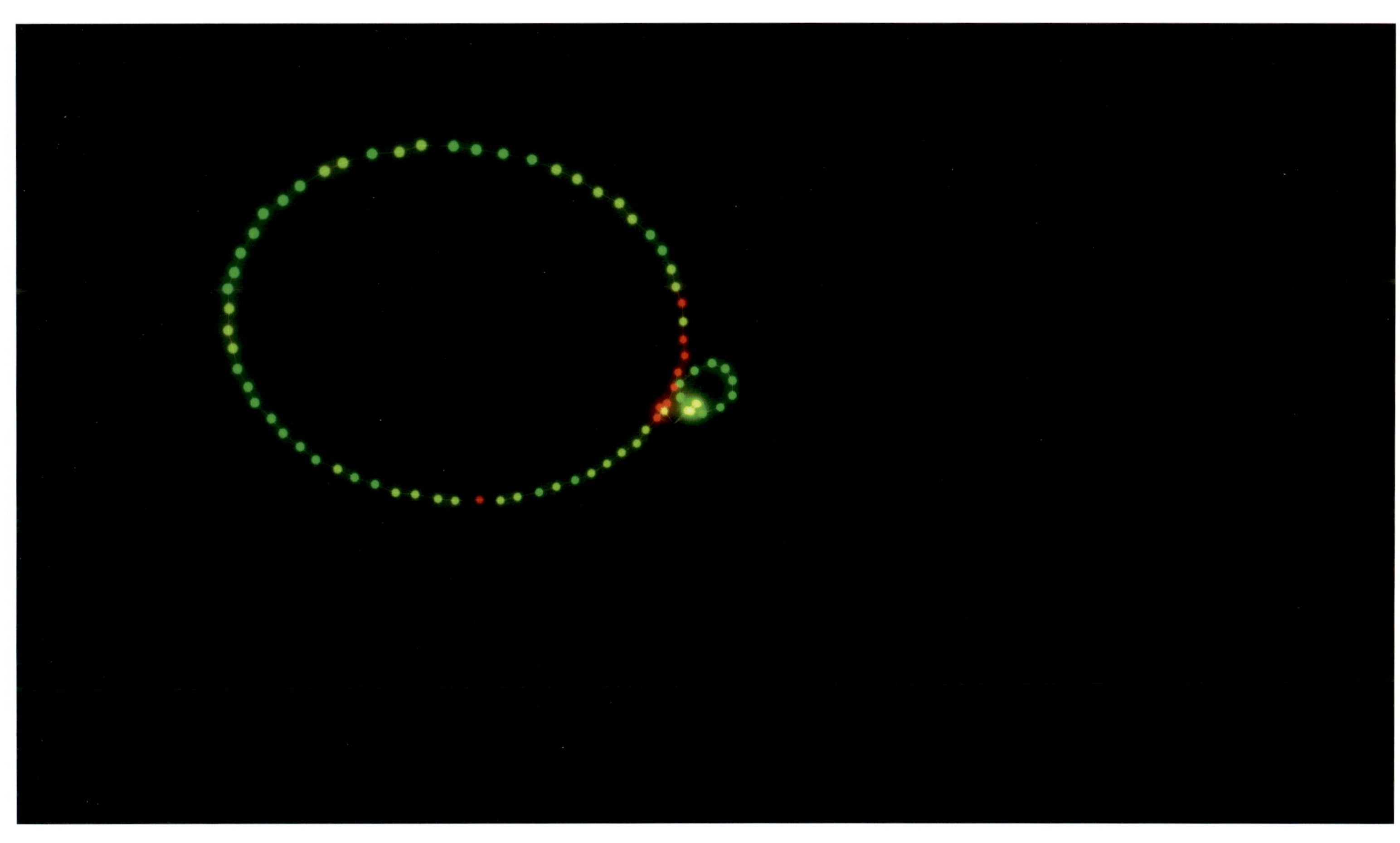

A CENTURY OF PHYSICS, 2015

Starting in 2012, the Lab turned its research focus on the science of science, using big data to explore how impact emerges in science. For the ten-year anniversary of *Nature Physics*, the most prestigious physics journal, the team used publication data going back to 1900 to explore the history of physics. As part of this project, the BarabásiLab generated an image representing all the papers published by *Nature Physics* in the previous decade. The information was organized clockwise based on the publication date. In the visualization, font size, color, and distance from the center signify the impact of each paper, with the large green titles corresponding to the most influential scientific discoveries. The background and the center show the citation network that connects these papers. The image simultaneously captures the temporal evolution of the journal, and the exceptional diversity of impact their individual published papers have had. Page 108 shows an alternative depiction of the central citation matrix connecting these papers. Page 109 shows an alternative organization of the information.

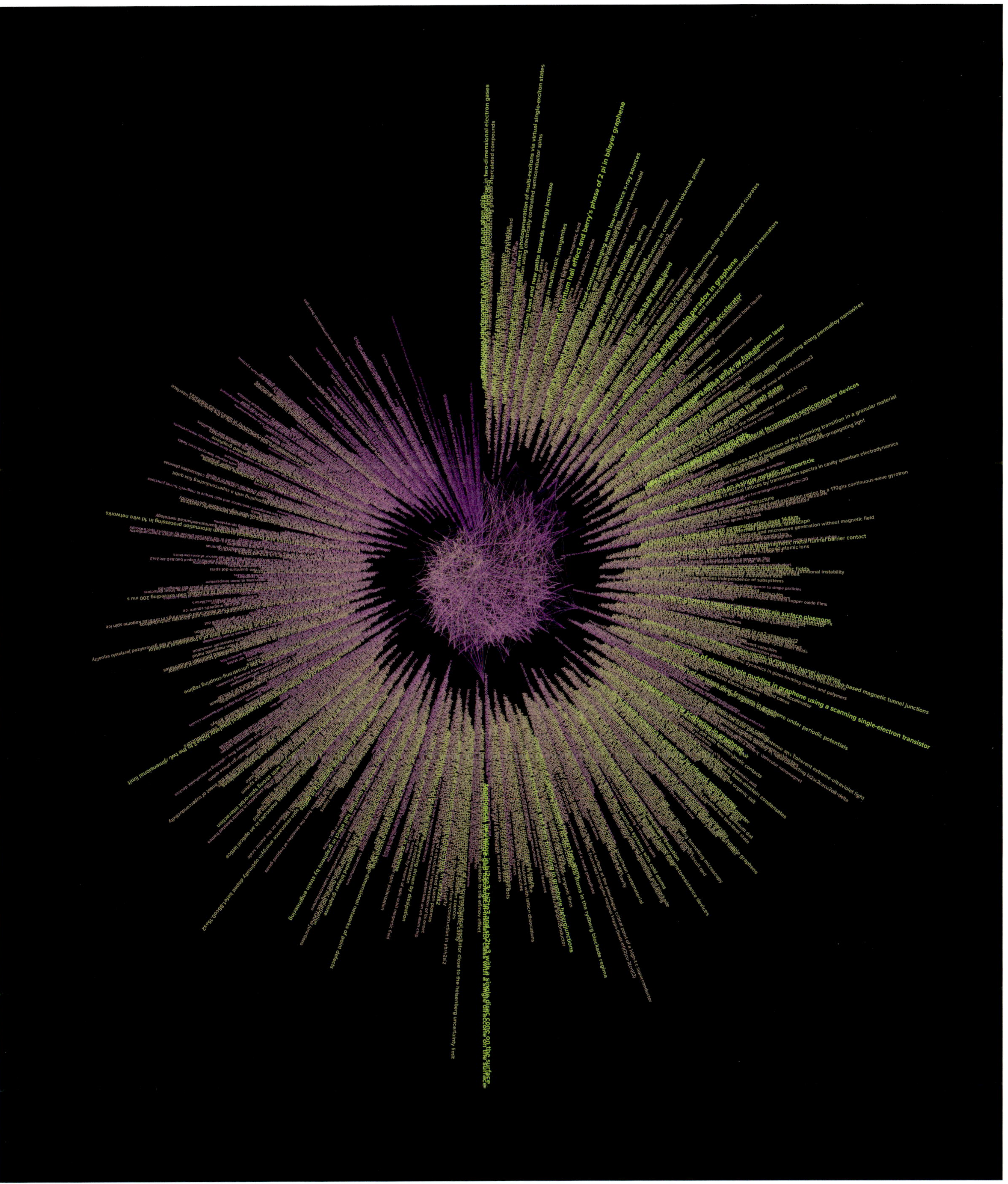
quantum hall effect and berry's phase of 2 pi in bilayer graphene
observation of electron-hole puddles in graphene using a scanning single-electron transistor

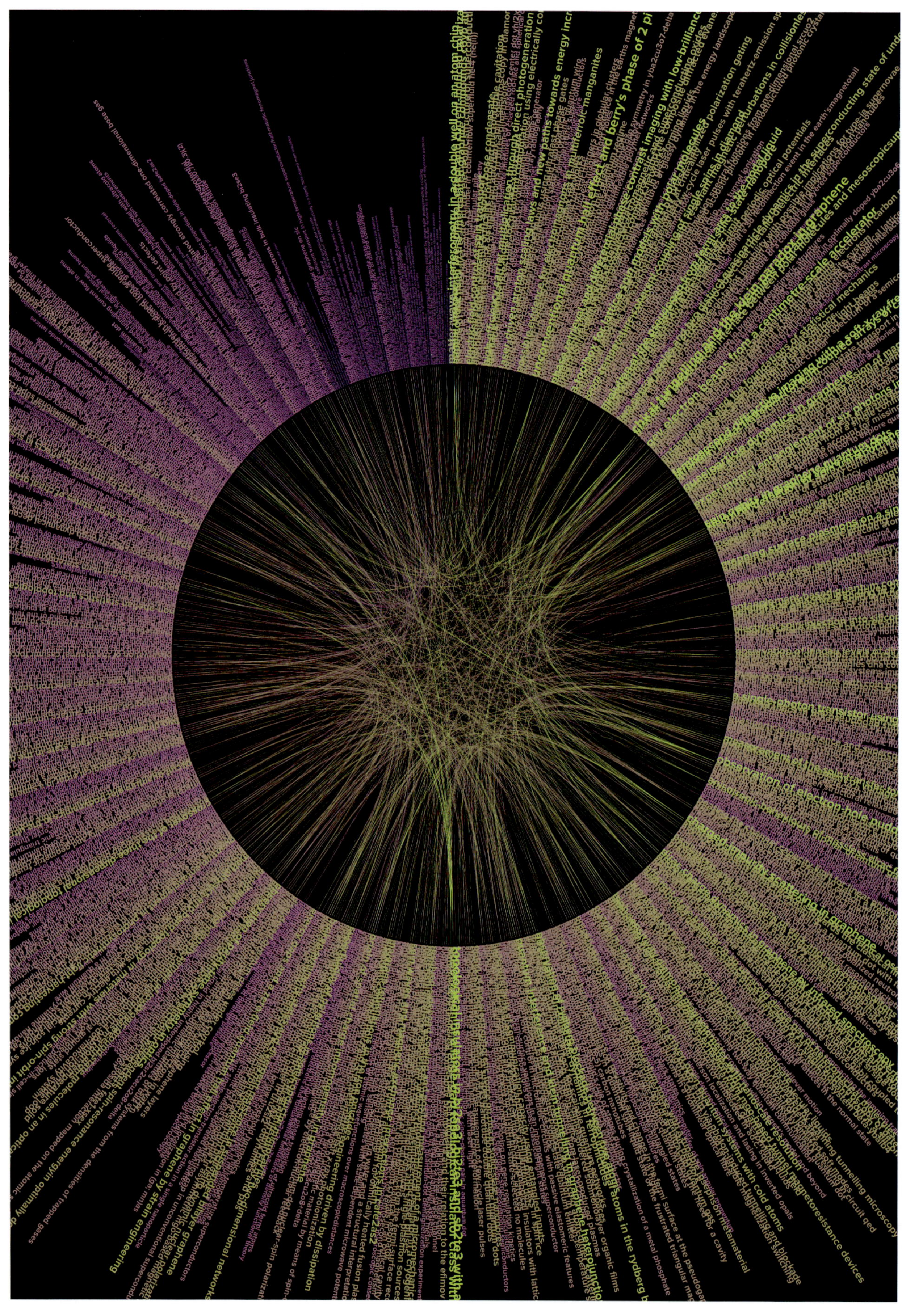

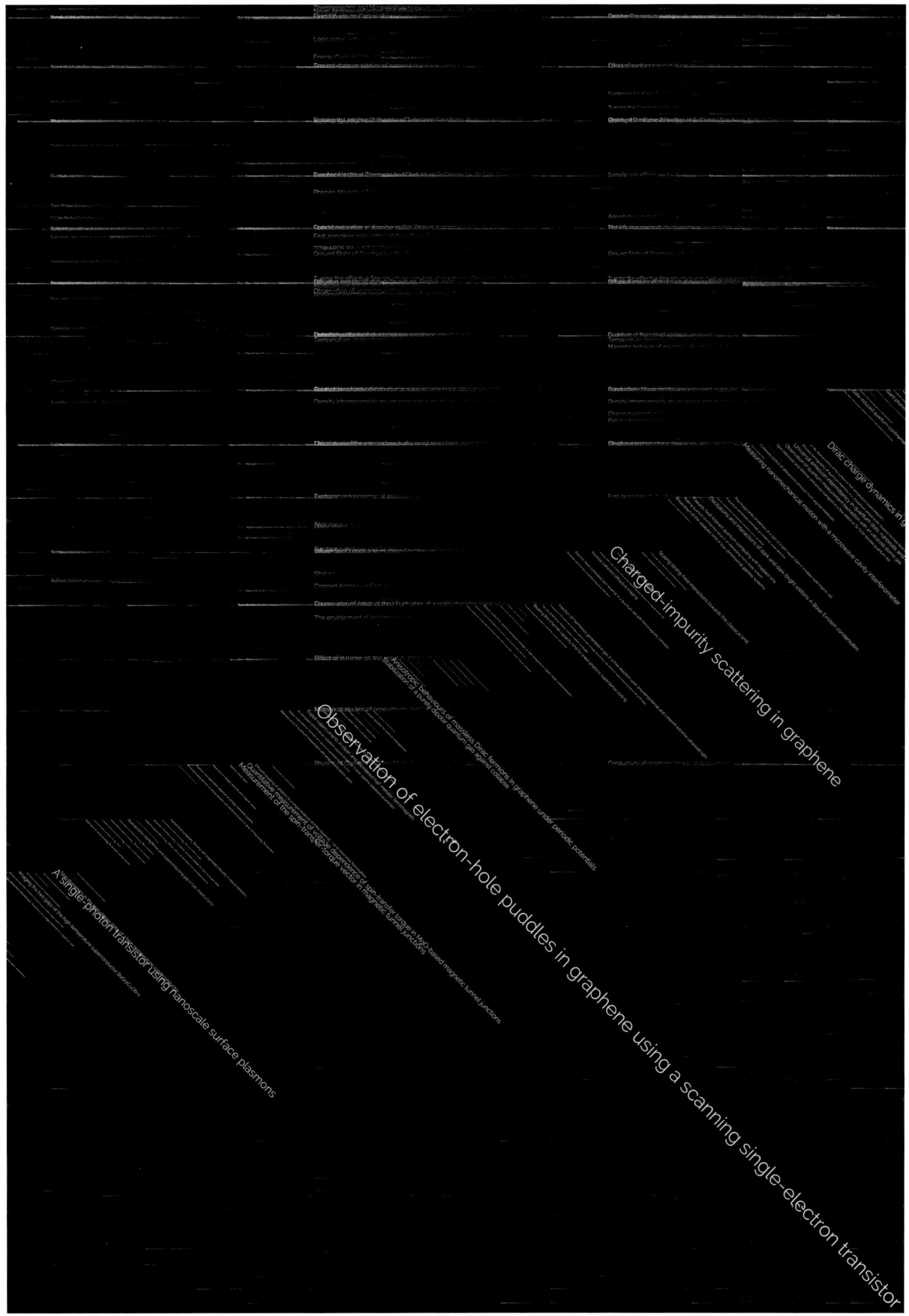
Observation of electron-hole puddles in graphene using a scanning single-electron transistor
Charged-impurity scattering in graphene
A single-photon transistor using nanoscale surface plasmons
Dirac charge dynamics in g

RESILIENCE, 2016

Resilience is a fundamental property of many complex systems. Its presence or absence indicates how well or poorly a system will cope when confronted with environmental changes or failures. Events leading to loss of resilience—from mass extinctions to cascading failures—are rarely predictable, are often irreversible, and have lasting consequences. In January 2013, "Resilient Dynamism" was the theme of the World Economic Forum in Davos, Switzerland. The presentations and discussions helped Barabási appreciate the important role networks play in resilience, inspiring a new research program in the lab.

The outcome of his investigation, which was published three years later, introduced the theory of network resilience. The paper was accompanied by a video entitled *Network Earth,* co-produced by the BarabásiLab and *Nature,* that illustrates the globe-spanning networks—bees and plants are two examples—that ensure our planet's resilience. "To live on Earth is to live as part of a network," proclaims the opening statement of the video, for which Mauro Martino generated the images shown here as stills. Page 111 illustrates the time line of multiple networks. Each horizontal line corresponds to the history of a different ecosystem and indicates the gradual and random loss of species due to human intervention. The break in each line captures the respective network's sudden collapse. These lines telegraph the fact that while species loss is a gradual process, the loss of resilience and the resulting collapse of an ecosystem are sudden events. Pages 112 and 113 show the symbiotic, globe-spanning relationships between plants and pollinator species that result in the invisible ecologic network that is essential for ensuring ecosystem resilience. These networks were the starting point of the BarabásiLab's ongoing exploration of resilience.

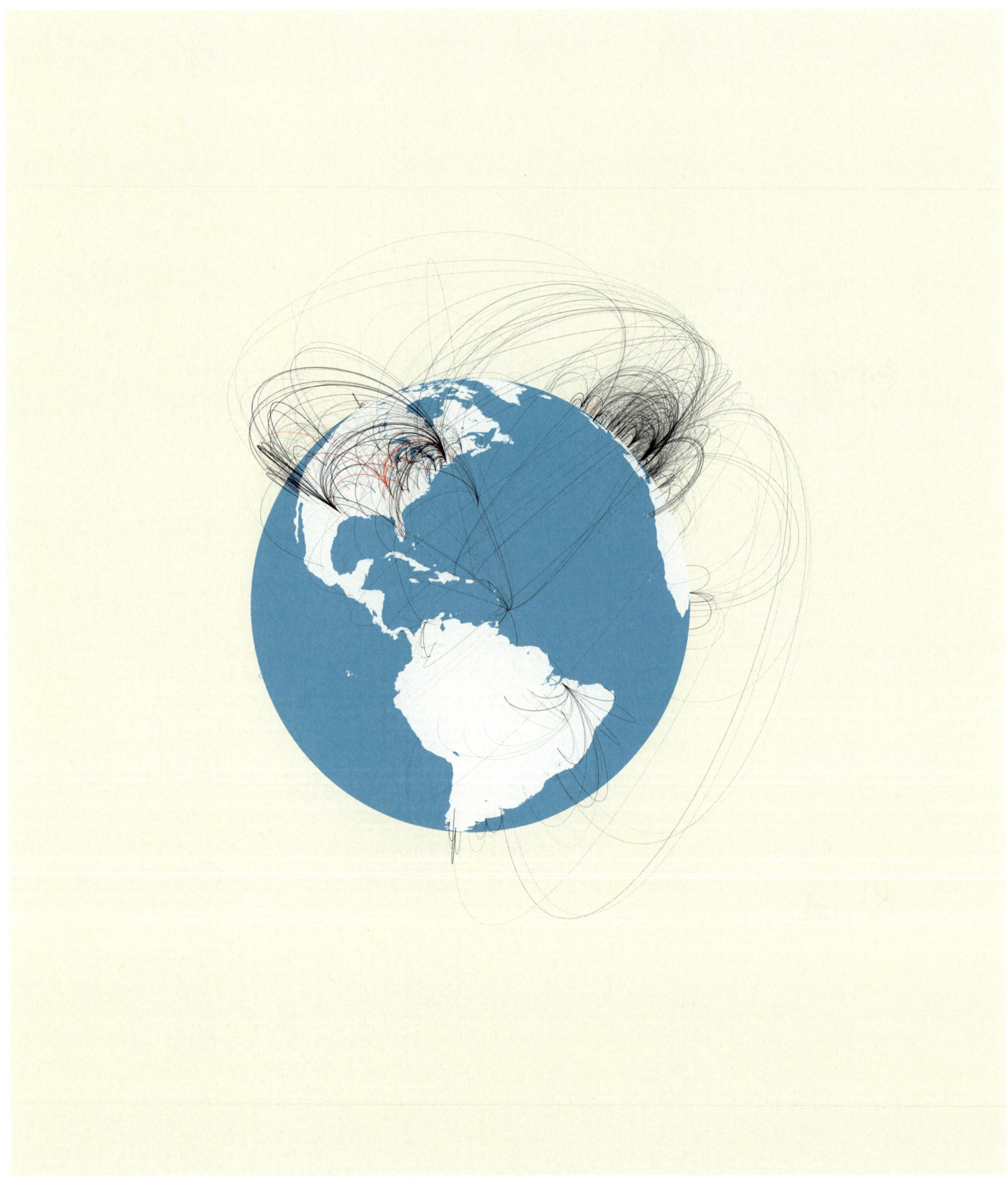

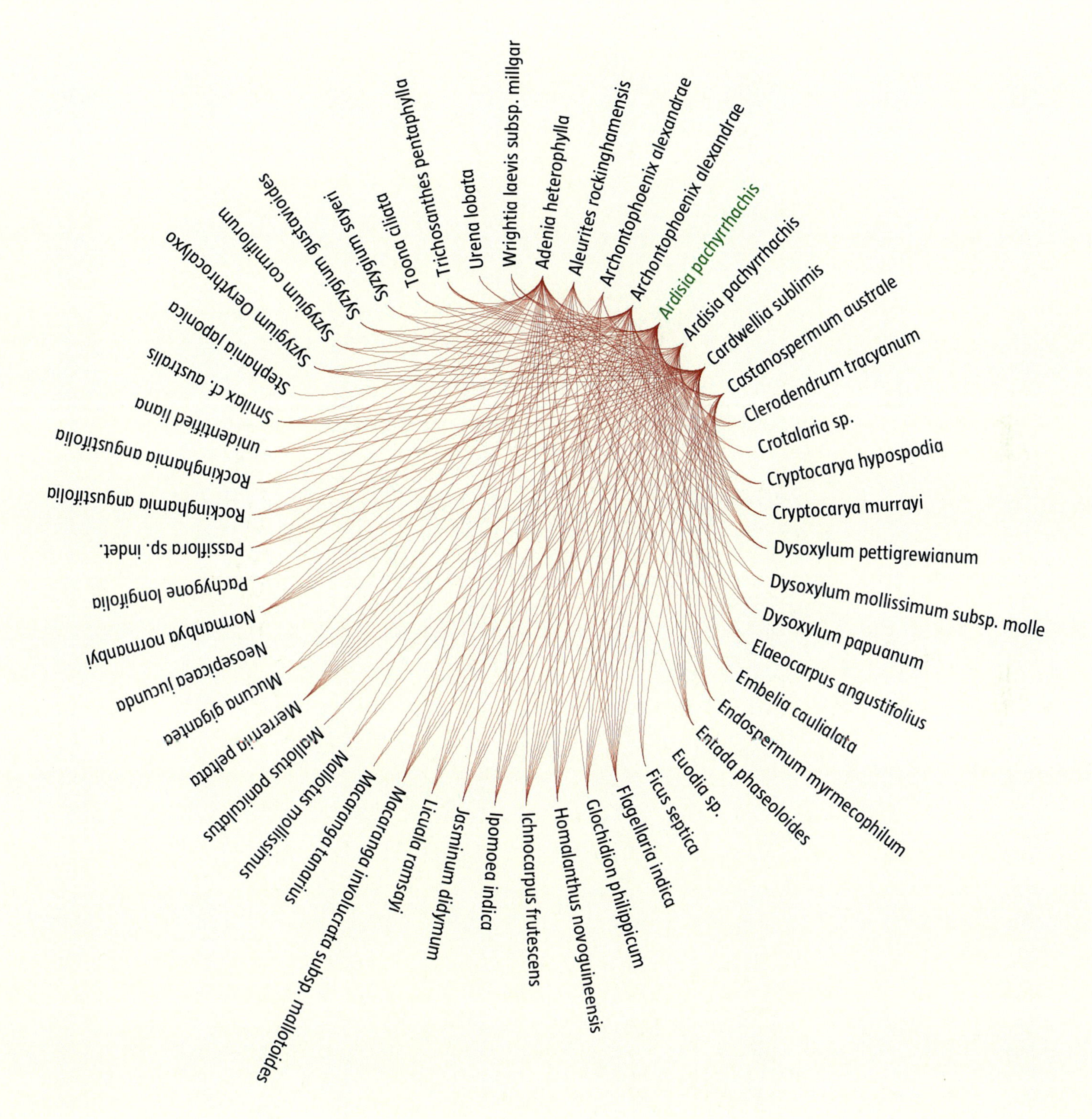
Adenia heterophylla
Aleurites rockinghamensis
Archontophoenix alexandrae
Archontophoenix alexandrae
Ardisia pachyrrhachis
Ardisia pachyrrhachis
Cardwellia sublimis
Castanospermum australe
Clerodendrum tracyanum
Crotalaria sp.
Cryptocarya hypospodia
Cryptocarya murrayi
Dysoxylum pettigrewianum
Dysoxylum mollissimum subsp. molle
Dysoxylum papuanum
Elaeocarpus angustifolius
Embelia caulialata
Endospermum myrmecophilum
Entada phaseoloides
Euodia sp.
Ficus septica
Flagellaria indica
Glochidion philippicum
Homalanthus novoguineensis
Ichnocarpus frutescens
Ipomoea indica
Jasminum didymum
Licuala ramsayi
Macaranga involucrata subsp. mallotoides
Macaranga tanarius
Mallotus mollissimus
Mallotus paniculatus
Merremia peltata
Mucuna gigantea
Neosepicaea jucunda
Normanbya normanbyi
Pachygone longifolia
Passiflora sp. indet.
Rockinghamia angustifolia
Rockinghamia angustifolia
unidentified liana
Smilax cf. australis
Stephania japonica
Syzygium Oerythrocalyxo
Syzygium cormiflorum
Syzygium gustavioides
Syzygium sayeri
Toona ciliata
Trichosanthes pentaphylla
Urena lobata
Wrightia laevis subsp. millgar

SUCCESS IN SCIENCE, 2016

Success is not about you, it's about us. That's the thesis of Barabási's 2019 book *The Formula,* which explores the role community plays in embracing a high-performance individual and aiding her success. The book, built on years of previous research in the lab, reconstructed the professional careers of thousands of artists and scientists in the course of distilling the five universal laws of success. For one line of research, the BarabásiLab relied on data drawn from the massive record of all scientific publications published since 1900 to identify the quantitative patterns that drive individual success in science. During the course of the study, the team developed multiple tools and visualizations to capture the evolution of a scientific career and explore the conditions necessary for the emergence of a high-impact discovery. The resulting visualizations show the careers of hundreds of scientists, depicting their patterns of creativity over time. Each line corresponds to the publishing career of a single scientist. In the image opposite, and on pages 120–21, the publications of one scientist are shown as concentric circles. In the images on pages 116–19, the careers are laid out along a straight line. Deviations from the line capture the impact of each work within a scientist's career. Large deviations correspond to the coveted, high-impact career-defining publications. Some of the excessively wavy lines highlight the few scientists who have changed the course of science. The images illustrate not only the exceptional disparity of impact, but also just how rare career-defining breakthroughs actually are.

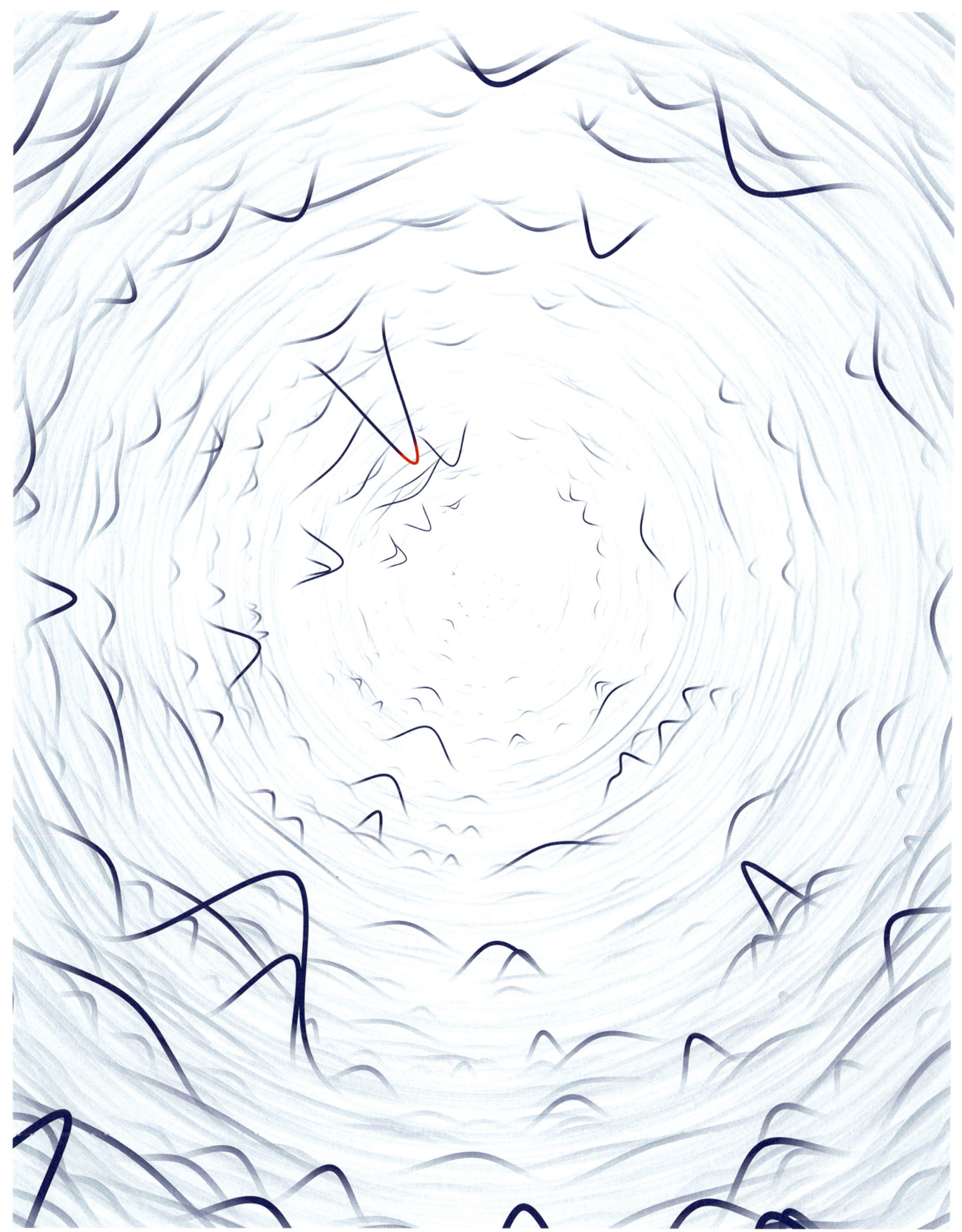

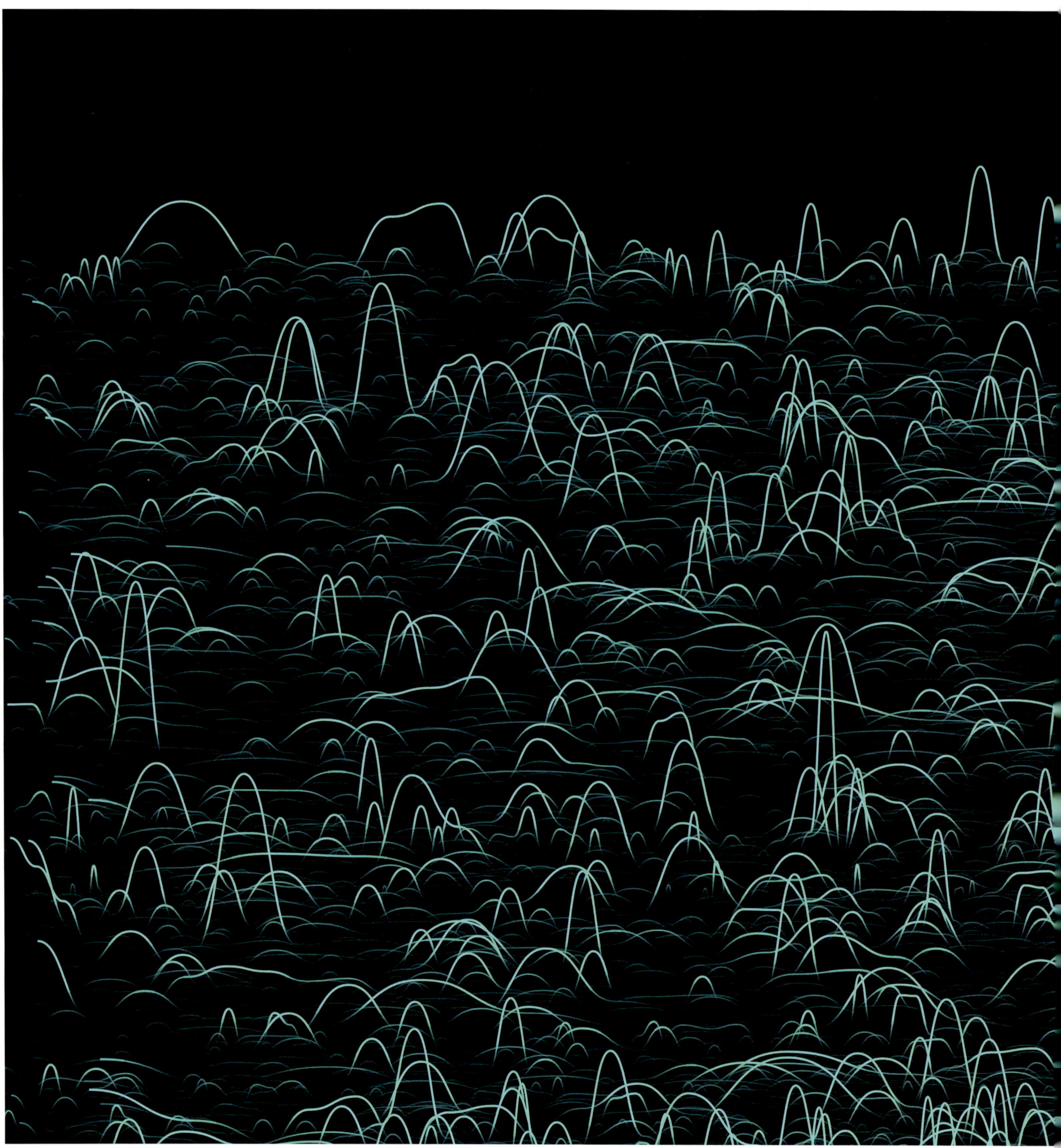

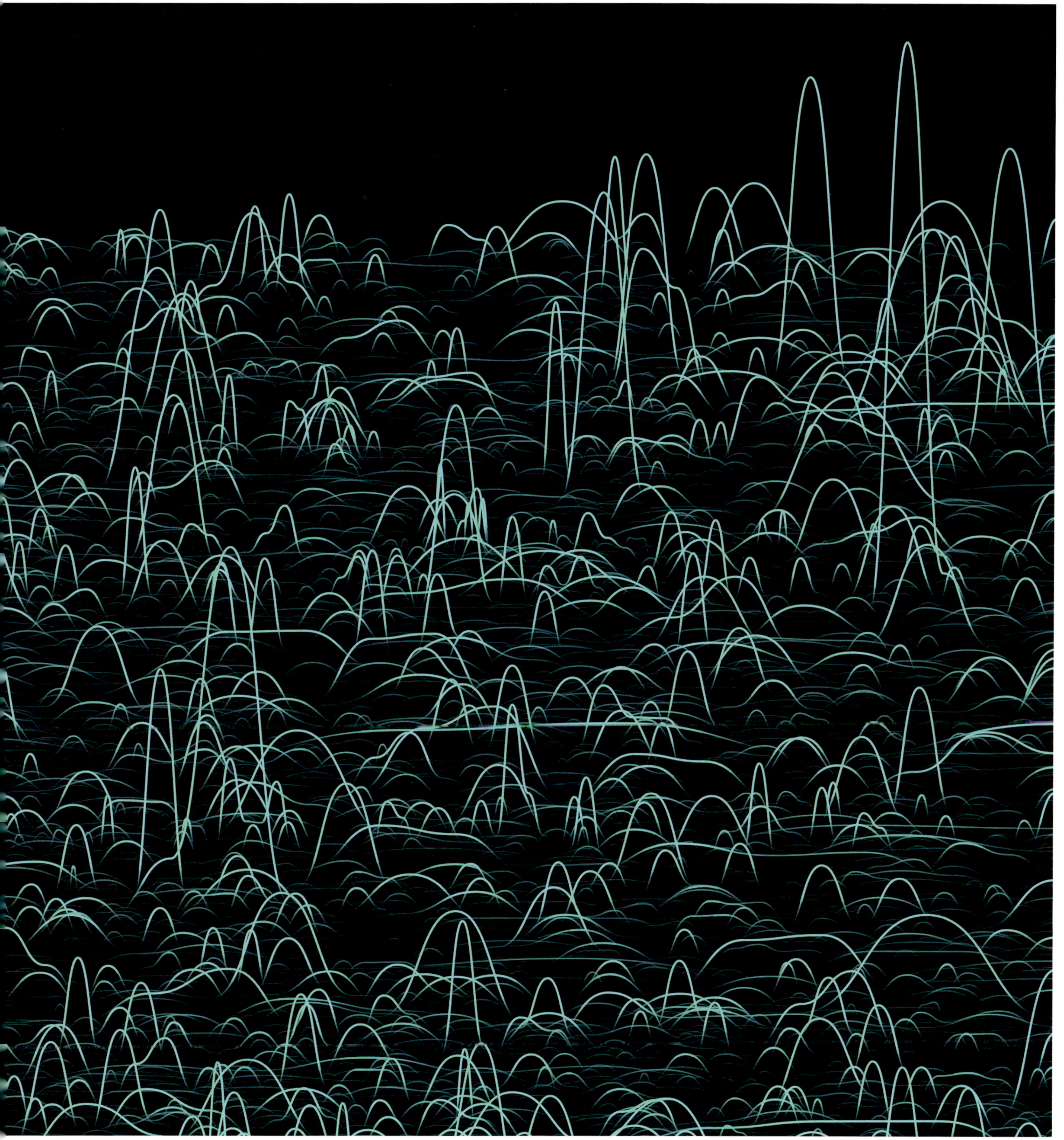

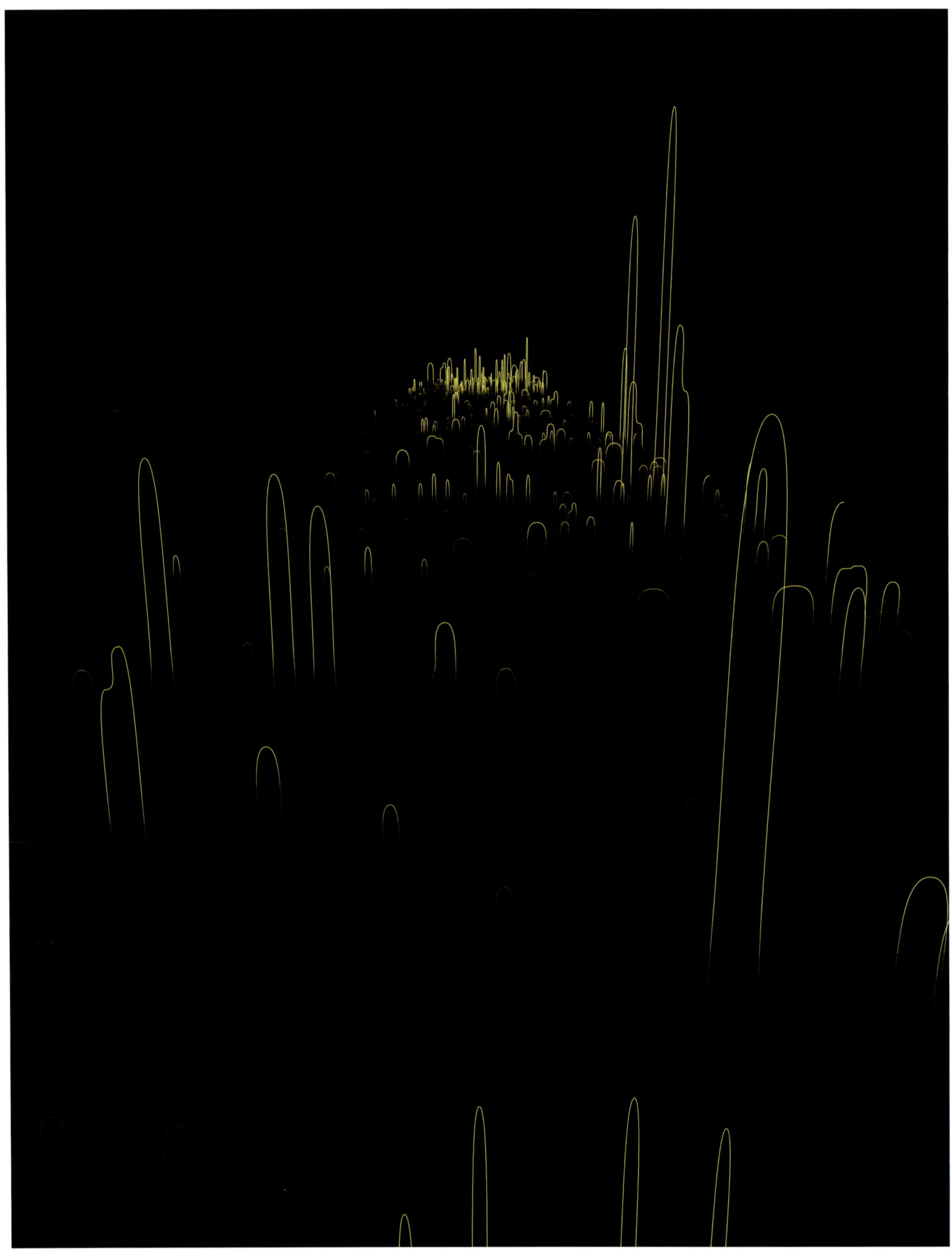

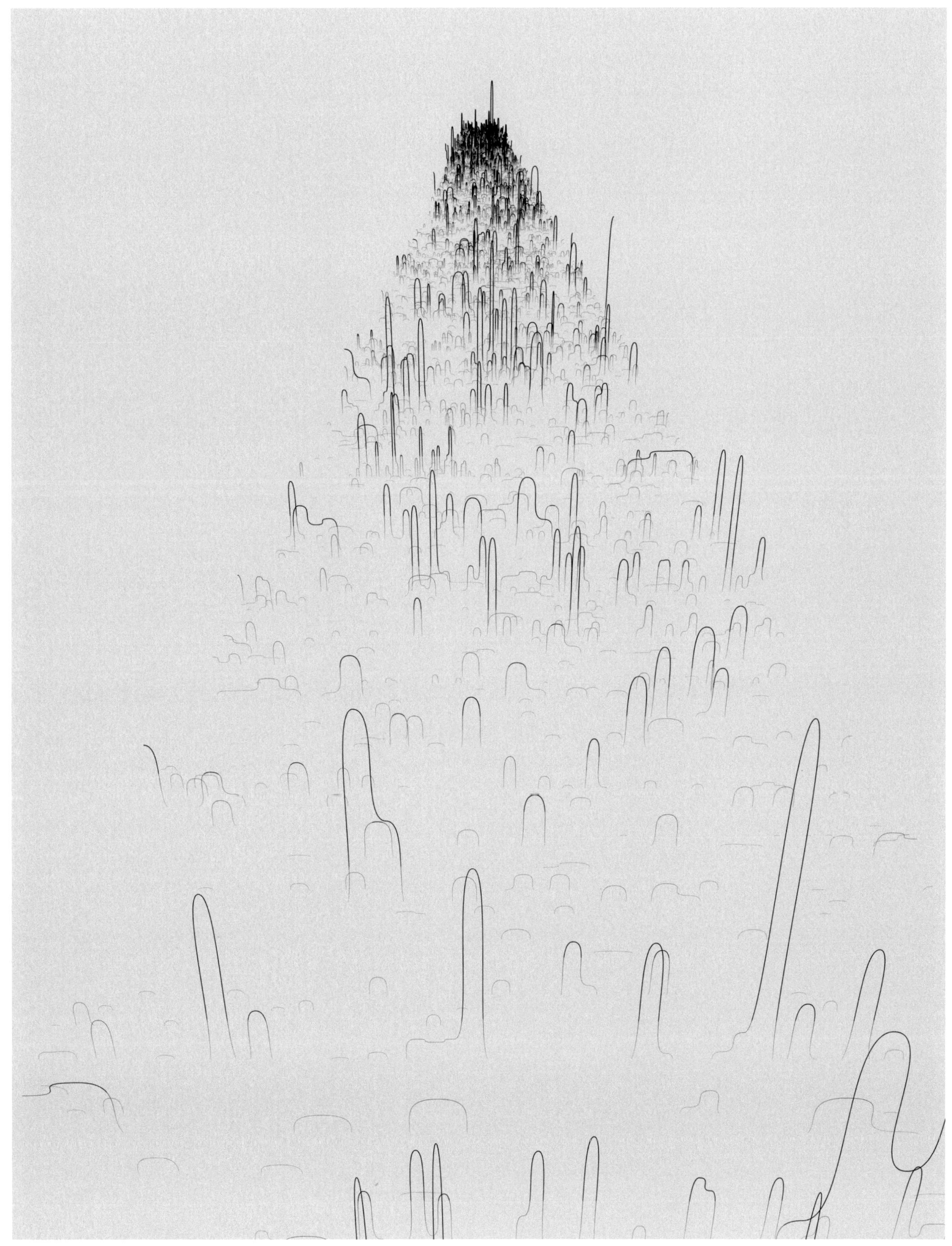

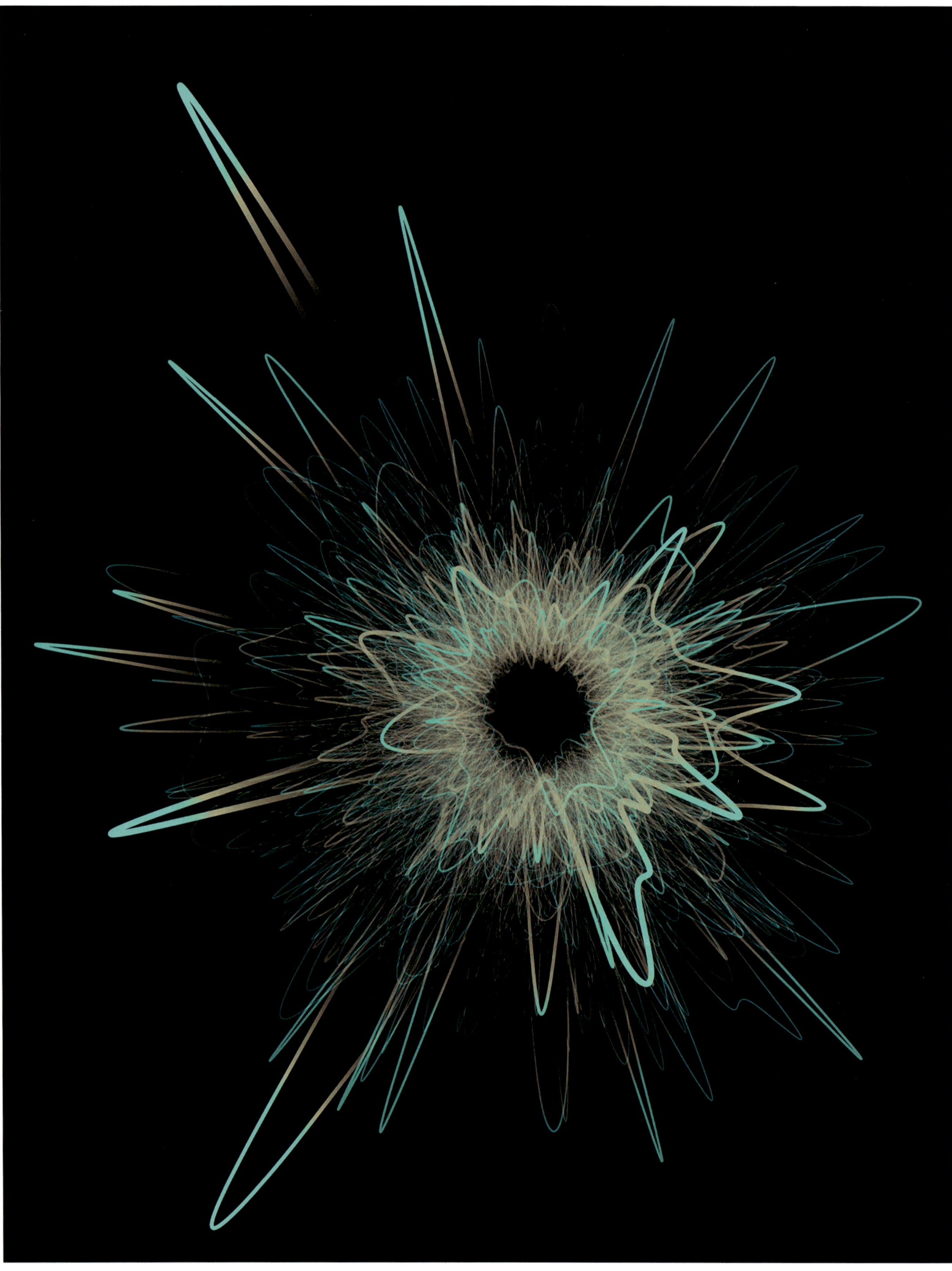

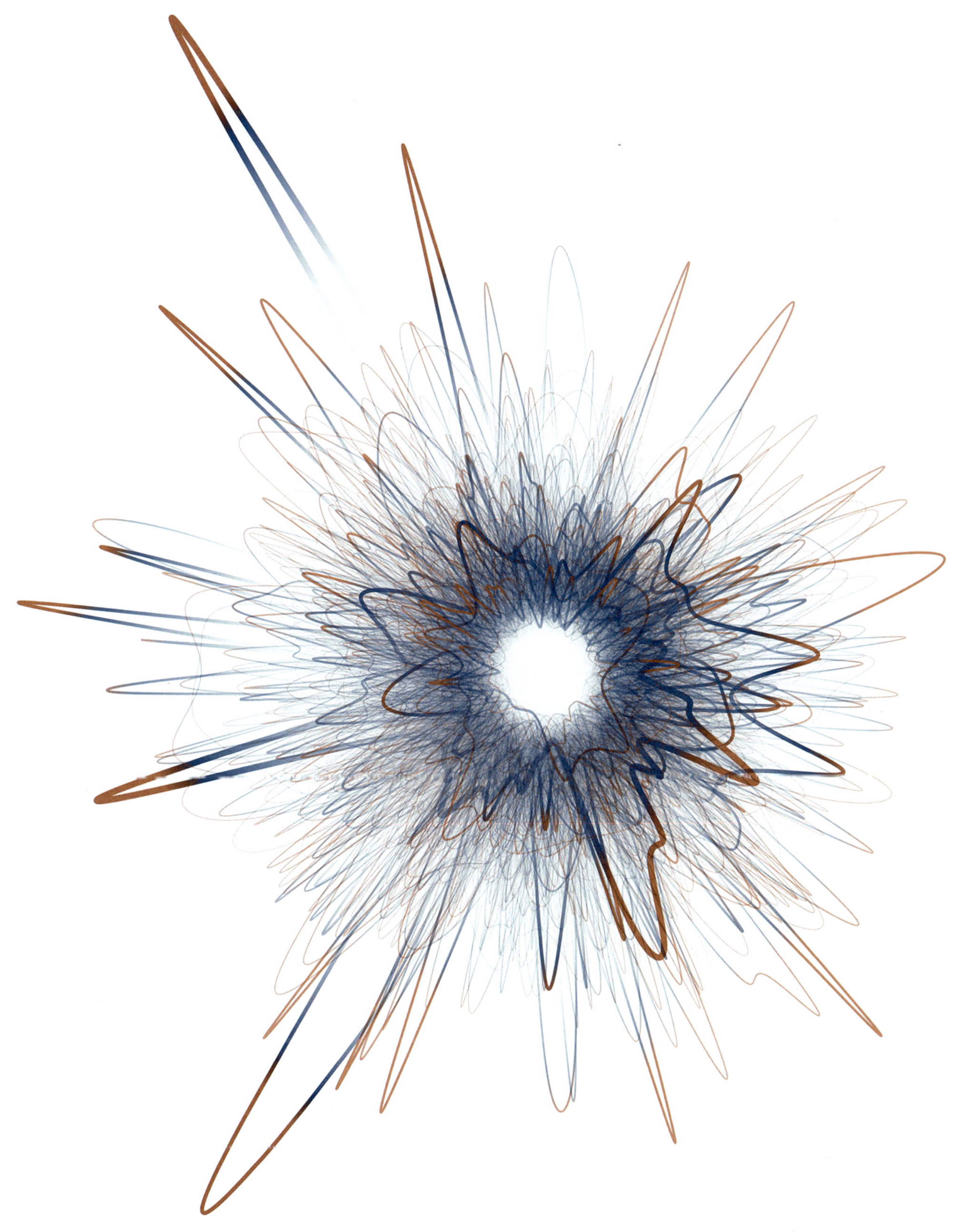

Artists and the Age of Interconnectivity

BY MÓNICA BELLO

Art and science have always looked with different registers at nature's unseen structures through observation and analysis. What they have in common is a set of complex yet discrete networks that bind together and connect the plethora of phenomena that describe the natural world and its agents. In recent times, we have witnessed the rapid development of network and complexity theories, which have been applied to a range of problems across disciplines. Responses to these developments have been seen across the fields of both science and art, each maximizing the potential of its different approaches. In the work of Albert-László Barabási, a convergence between approaches to artistic and scientific visualization techniques has become highly apparent. His extraordinary, pioneering way of bringing complex data science to life employs the tools of a society powered by the visual. And while his work displays many characteristics of experimental art, his approach is definitely based in scientific methods.

Since the moment that the theory of networks and complexity united with the World Wide Web—it was in the late 1980s that the demand for a system of automated information sharing between scientists and researchers around the world led CERN software-engineer consultant Tim Berners-Lee to develop the first proposal of the Web—artists have eagerly explored the new possibilities it offered. The Web's connectivity enabled new ways for artists to access and manipulate data, while its global platform offered them hitherto unseen possibilities for dissemination. At the same time, its participatory nature allowed audiences to interact with the artworks the Web was engendering in novel and experimental ways.

In 1995, artist Jane Prophet, in collaboration with computer-graphics programmer Gordon Selley, created the online project TechnoSphere, a three-dimensional, real-time world populated by artificial life-forms. This "digital ecology"—a groundbreaking term at that time—enabled users to devise their own artificial life-forms from kits of parts and release them into the virtual environment, where they would interact with others according to complex sets of rules and algorithms that determined how the ecosystem reacted. That same year, in a speech at the UK's National Photography Conference, Prophet asserted that "the excitement caused by interactivity and interconnection can be seen as part of a larger cultural development." Just as chaos theory had illuminated the importance and power of interaction, she said, "the Internet provides a rich environment for more than browsing information: it has the potential to provide us with an environment in which to collaborate on a global scale on both research and artistic projects."

Many other artists and collectives who subsequently began to occupy the Internet took advantage of the way its vastly linked complex infrastructure amplified its capacity for untold and unexpected phenomena. By the mid-to-late 1990s, certain artists were actively subverting and challenging the very structure that was becoming established. JODI, Joan Leandre, Vuk Ćosíc, Alexei Shulgin, 0100101110101101.org, and irational.org were among the Net Art pioneers who radically exploited the hidden information pathways of these burgeoning complex networks to comment on the rising online behaviors and agencies. What drove many of these artists was an interest in exploiting the code and mechanics of the Web—specifically the ASCII and HTML that were usually invisible to the end user—to create new worlds and anarchic visualizations that simultaneously revealed and commented on its hidden structures. The narratives they developed vary. Eva and Franco Mattes of 0100101110101101.org make work that highlights the ethical and political issues arising from the inception of the Internet. The work of irational.org is based around the democracy (or lack thereof) of communications technologies and the perception of physical and online borders. In 1995, irational.org created a dummy site for CERN, titled *European Lab for Network Collision*, which connected to the sites and projects of irational.org's Net Art colleagues in a *Participant Accelerator Ring*. As network technologies develop and become ubiquitous, artists continue to exploit them as an effective narrative tool.

In 2001, in his book *The Language of New Media,* digital culture professor Lev Manovich explained that the dramatic rise in use of the Web and the protocol of linking to other sites has turned each website into a database, and therefore each website owner into a data indexer. "The map [of the Internet]," he writes, "has become larger than the territory. Sometimes, much larger." Within this map, the world is reduced to data structures and algorithms that exploit their symbiotic relationships and interactions. Artist Ryoji Ikeda has been particularly interested in the esoteric and entrancing processes enacted by these agents. His installations *micro macro,* developed through his residency at Arts at CERN in 2014, and *data-verse*, a trilogy presented at the Venice Biennale in 2019, use massive open-source scientific data sets from CERN, NASA, and the Human Genome Project to reflect on the progressive digitalization of our society. Processed and expressed in visual and sound forms, the data is formed into multimedia experiential sculptures that capture hidden facets of nature and the vast scientific knowledge underpinning our existence.

Other artists have been interested in elaborating topographies and maps that explore the strangeness and information density of ostensibly invisible networked spaces. In 2005, Eric Fischer began mapping out demographic and transport networks, using publicly available data—*2013 NYC Taxi Trips* is one of his works—and social media content to reveal surprising patterns and relationships in the data visualizations. Around the same time, Aaron Koblin created *Flight Patterns,* a data visualization of airplane traffic over North America during a twenty-four-hour period that reveals the immaterial and intangible networks generated through social interaction and mobility.

Many of these artistic projects have been unfolding in parallel with Barabási's scientific research and visualization of networks. His scientific publications, and in particular his book, *Linked: How Everything Is Connected to Everything Else and What It Means for Business, Science, and Everyday Life*, have brought the language of networks to a wide audience, creating an awareness of the subject that has shaped a dialogue between art and science. For example, artist Tomás Saraceno, who has collaborated with Barabási and whose work also explores interconnectivity, has taken another approach. Rather than visualize and explore existing complex data networks, he deploys notions from meteorology, climatology, and biology to investigate the fundamental properties of systems as a natural and universal phenomenon. His 2012 work *Hybrid Webs* draws on the analogies between the cosmic filaments in the universe and a spider web, subtly connecting the mathematics behind complex emergent infrastructures and the spider webs themselves. Via a pioneering process of preserving and scanning the webs in three dimensions, Saraceno offers a tangible form of these structures through which we can observe and understand the complexities of nodes and connections in networks of various scales, from the microscopic to the planetary and cosmic.

The notion of the web as a metaphor for complex networks in both natural and technological ecosystems has proved resilient. Yet in some respects, it creates a misleading impression of how these phenomena behave. We should see the Web—any web—as a snapshot of a network, a still moment in an ongoing evolutionary and emergent process. As Barabási makes clear in *Linked*, networks have mathematical properties that describe them as expanding and growing, evolving and adapting, establishing new nodes and new connections as unseen interactions take place. This unforeseen emergence is what creates such a rich territory for both scientific and artistic investigation and expression. The study, navigation, and development of novel, complex, and interconnected systems will surely be an ongoing source of expression within artistic practice, especially as inspired, inventive thinkers continue to discover new ways to bring the arts and the sciences into productive contact.

THE ART NETWORK, 2018

In 2016, Barabási began turning the tools of network and data science, which his lab had been honing for two decades already, on the art world. He started with a massive number of data points about the exhibition history of half a million artists in galleries and museums worldwide that had been collected by Magnus Resch, an economist and entrepreneur who studies the art market. The data enabled the BarabásiLab to unveil the invisible connections that shape artists' careers.

In *The Art Network*, opposite, two institutions—for example, a museum and a gallery—are connected if an artist whose work was exhibited at the museum is also exhibited next at the gallery, or vice versa. The image captures the largely invisible network of influence and trust between thousands of institutions worldwide. At its core is a dense community of major European and North American institutions with uninhibited access to a common pool of artistic talent. These institutions are represented as large nodes. And it will come as no surprise to anyone who follows the art world that the largest among them are New York's Museum of Modern Art (MoMA), the Centre Pompidou in Paris, the Tate in London, and the Gagosian gallery. The colors, which indicate the countries where each institution is based, telegraph how the dense regional communities of institutions in eastern Europe (green) or Australia and Oceania (yellow), for example, are largely isolated from the American (red) and European (blue) hubs at the heart of the art world. The network demonstrates how institutional prestige and hidden connections of influence determine access to opportunities for artists. The detailed image on pages 128–29 reveals the identity of key museums and galleries and the connections between them. The plates on pages 130 and 131, which show 3-D renderings of *The Art Network*, are among the first of the lab's ongoing attempts to represent this constellation as a data sculpture.

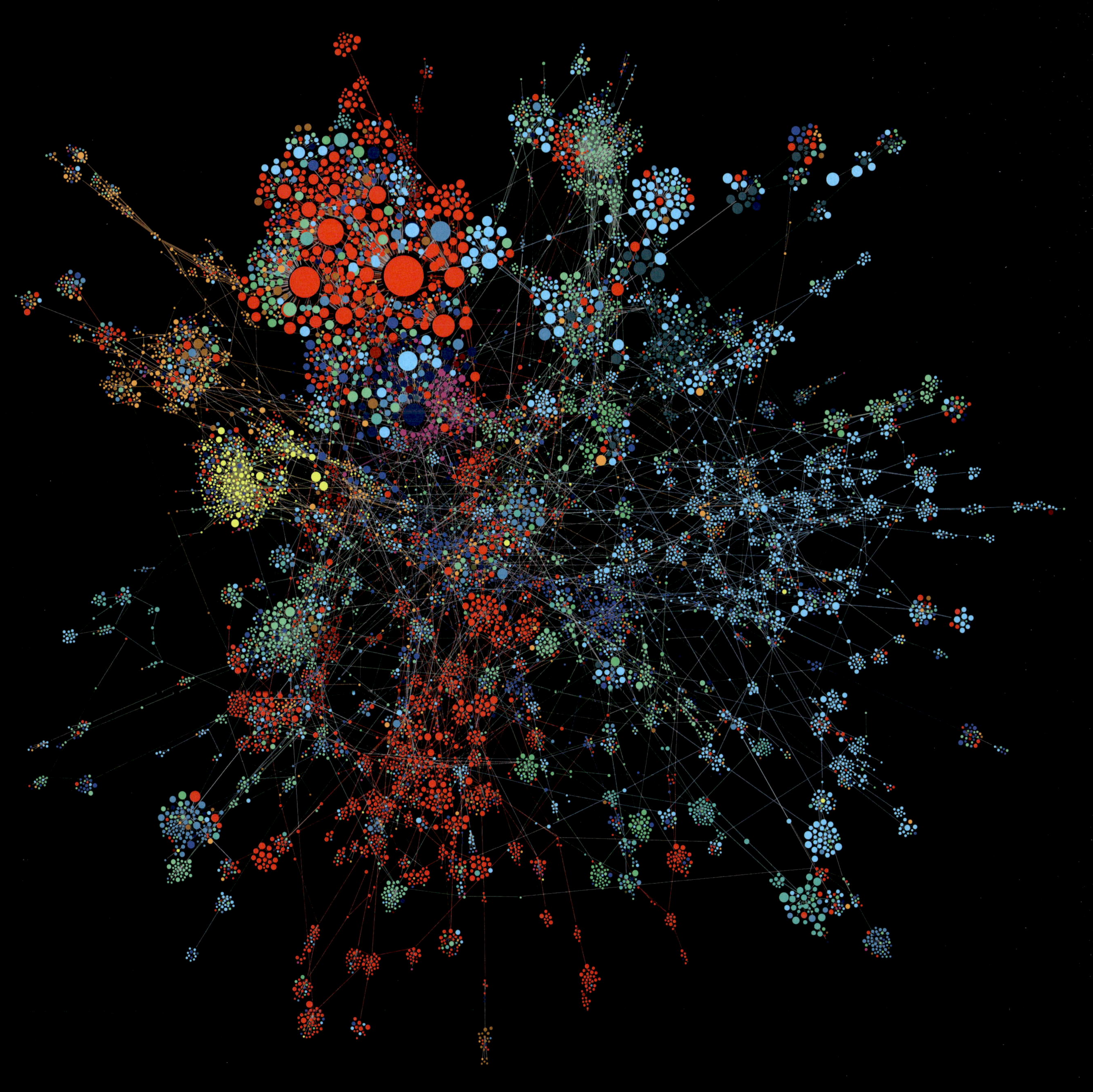

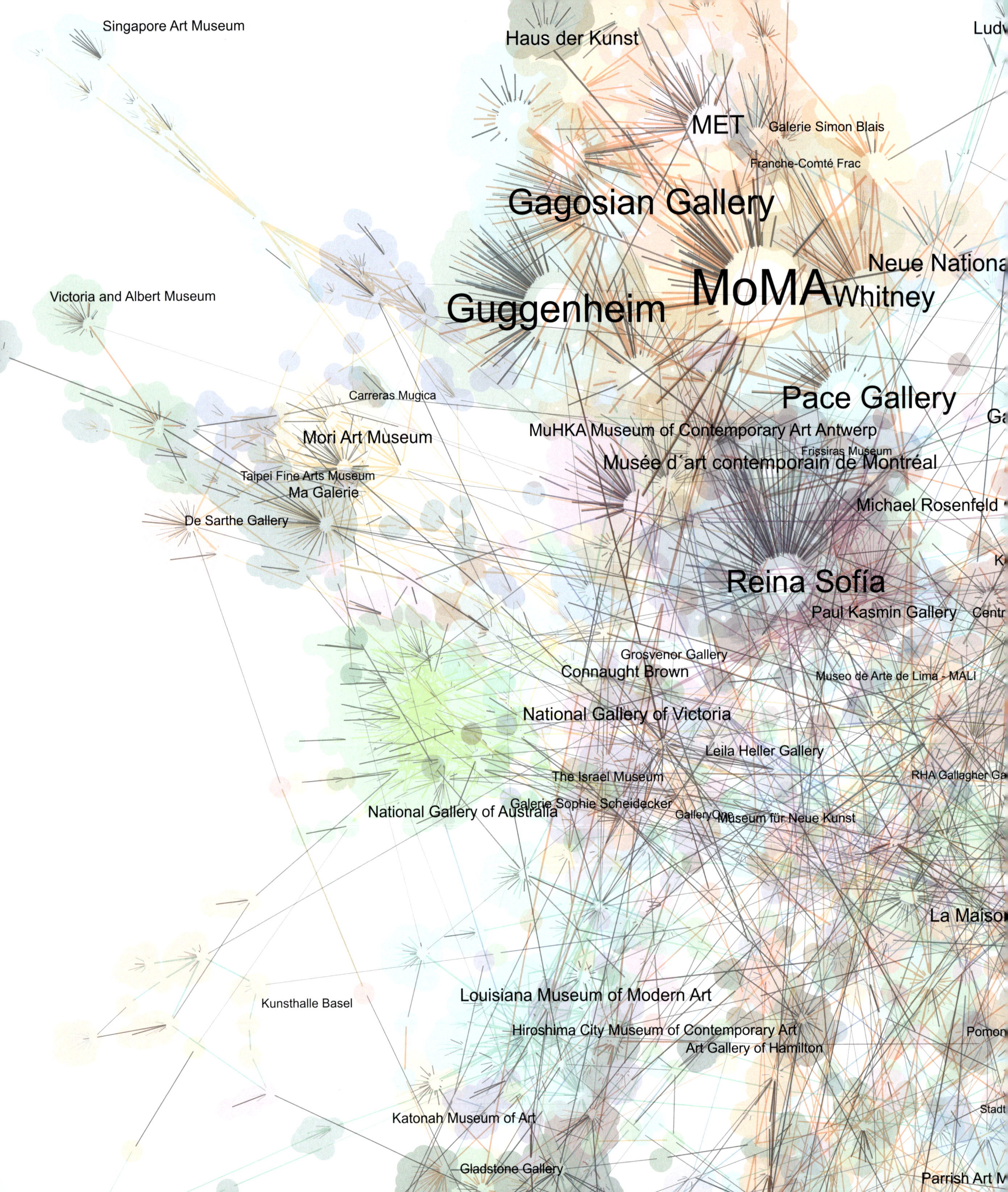
Singapore Art Museum
Haus der Kunst
MET
Galerie Simon Blais
Franche-Comté Frac
Gagosian Gallery
Victoria and Albert Museum
Guggenheim
MoMA
Whitney
Carreras Mugica
Pace Gallery
Mori Art Museum
MuHKA Museum of Contemporary Art Antwerp
Frissiras Museum
Musée d´art contemporain de Montréal
Taipei Fine Arts Museum
Ma Galerie
De Sarthe Gallery
Michael Rosenfeld
Reina Sofía
Paul Kasmin Gallery
Grosvenor Gallery
Connaught Brown
Museo de Arte de Lima - MALI
National Gallery of Victoria
Leila Heller Gallery
The Israel Museum
RHA Gallagher Ga
Galerie Sophie Scheidecker
National Gallery of Australia
Gallery One
Museum für Neue Kunst
Louisiana Museum of Modern Art
Kunsthalle Basel
Hiroshima City Museum of Contemporary Art
Art Gallery of Hamilton
Katonah Museum of Art
Gladstone Gallery
Parrish Art M

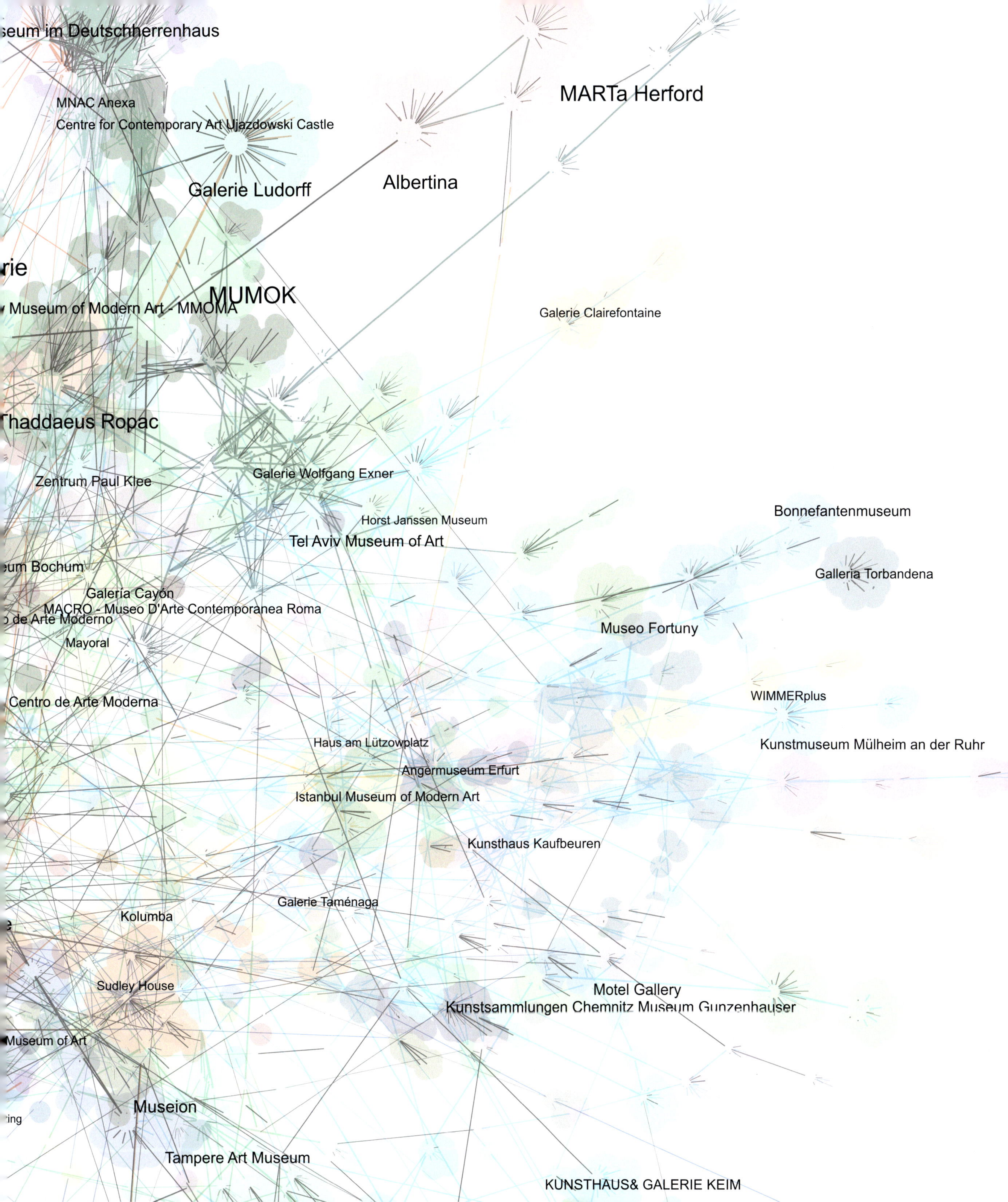
seum im Deutschherrenhaus
MNAC Anexa
Centre for Contemporary Art Ujazdowski Castle
MARTa Herford
Galerie Ludorff
Albertina
rie
MUMOK
Museum of Modern Art - MMOMA
Galerie Clairefontaine
Thaddaeus Ropac
Zentrum Paul Klee
Galerie Wolfgang Exner
Horst Janssen Museum
Tel Aviv Museum of Art
Bonnefantenmuseum
Galleria Torbandena
eum Bochum
Galería Cayón
MACRO - Museo D'Arte Contemporanea Roma
o de Arte Moderno
Museo Fortuny
Mayoral
Centro de Arte Moderna
WIMMERplus
Kunstmuseum Mülheim an der Ruhr
Haus am Lützowplatz
Angermuseum Erfurt
Istanbul Museum of Modern Art
Kunsthaus Kaufbeuren
Galerie Taménaga
Kolumba
Sudley House
Motel Gallery
Kunstsammlungen Chemnitz Museum Gunzenhauser
Museum of Art
Museion
ing
Tampere Art Museum
KUNSTHAUS& GALERIE KEIM

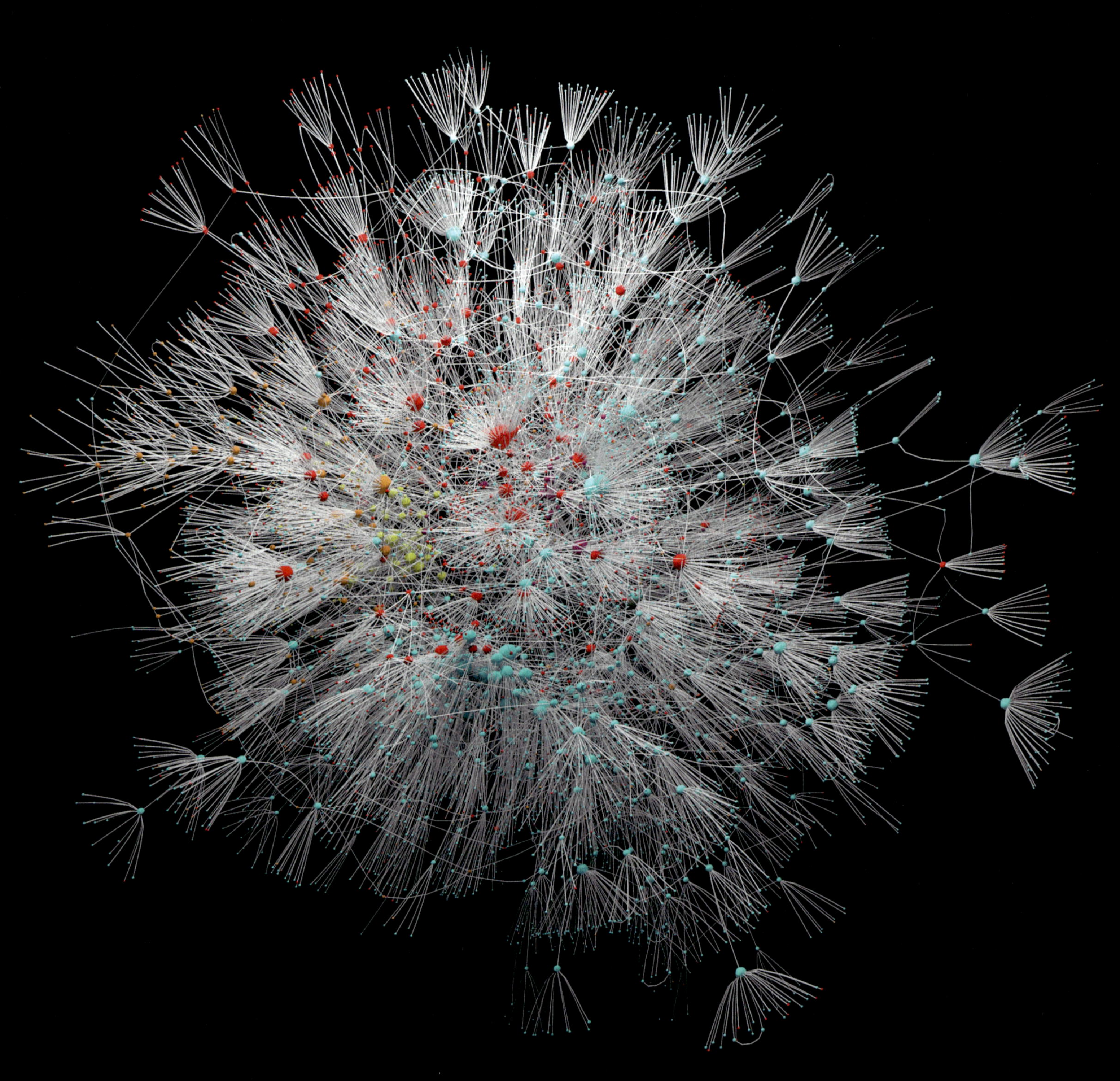

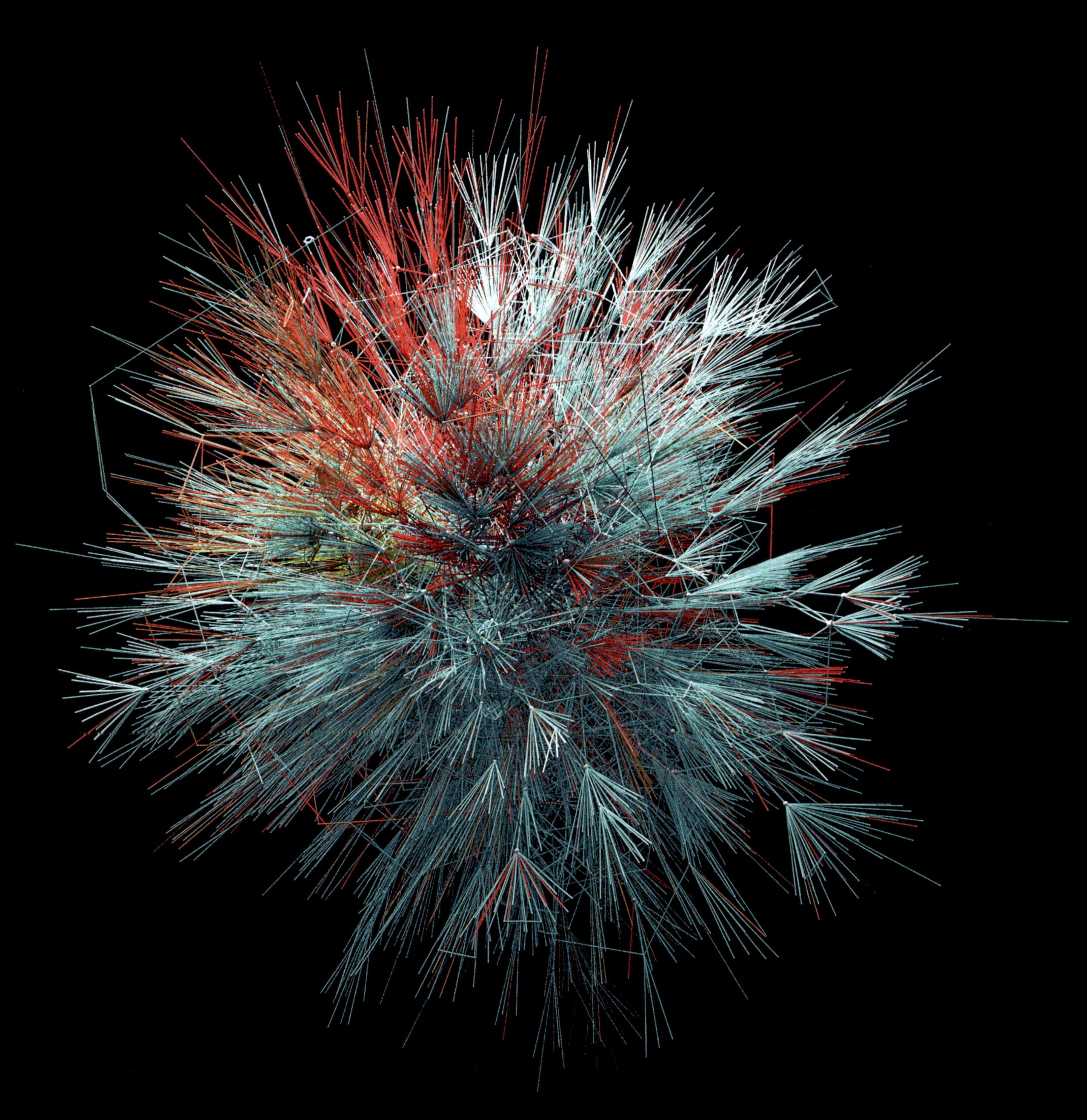

THE COSMIC WEB, 2016

The cosmic web—the idea that the universe is a largely invisible web of galaxies held together by gravity—is deeply ingrained in cosmology. Yet our ability to see this web is hindered by a fundamental limitation: thanks to gravity, everything attracts everything else. With *The Cosmic Web* project, the BarabásiLab aimed to deepen our perspective on the origins of the cosmic web, bringing alive this hard-to-fathom network behind the universe. To construct its map, the team used data on 24,000 galaxies, provided by a cosmological simulation that traces the evolution of all galaxies since the Big Bang. It then tested multiple types of links to connect individual galaxies, capturing dependencies grounded in physics and cosmology. Kim Albrecht, the lab's designer at the time, was embedded in a team of network scientists and cosmologists to generate a series of images and videos that bring alive the cosmic web's structure. While grasping the enormity of the universe remains a challenging undertaking, the BarabásiLab's visualizations of it gesture at the overwhelming intricacy of this network, tracing the relationships between galaxies in almost microscopic detail.

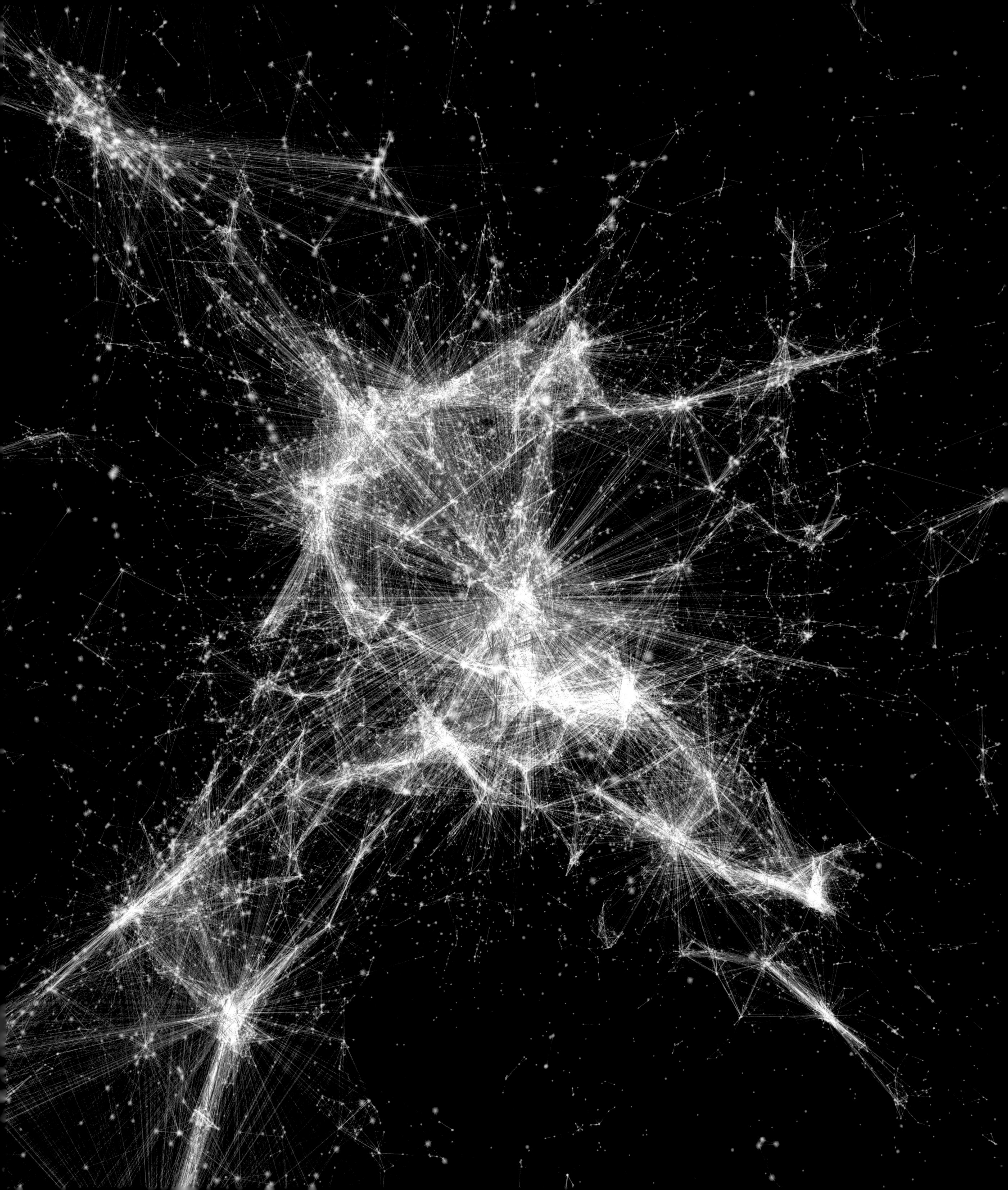

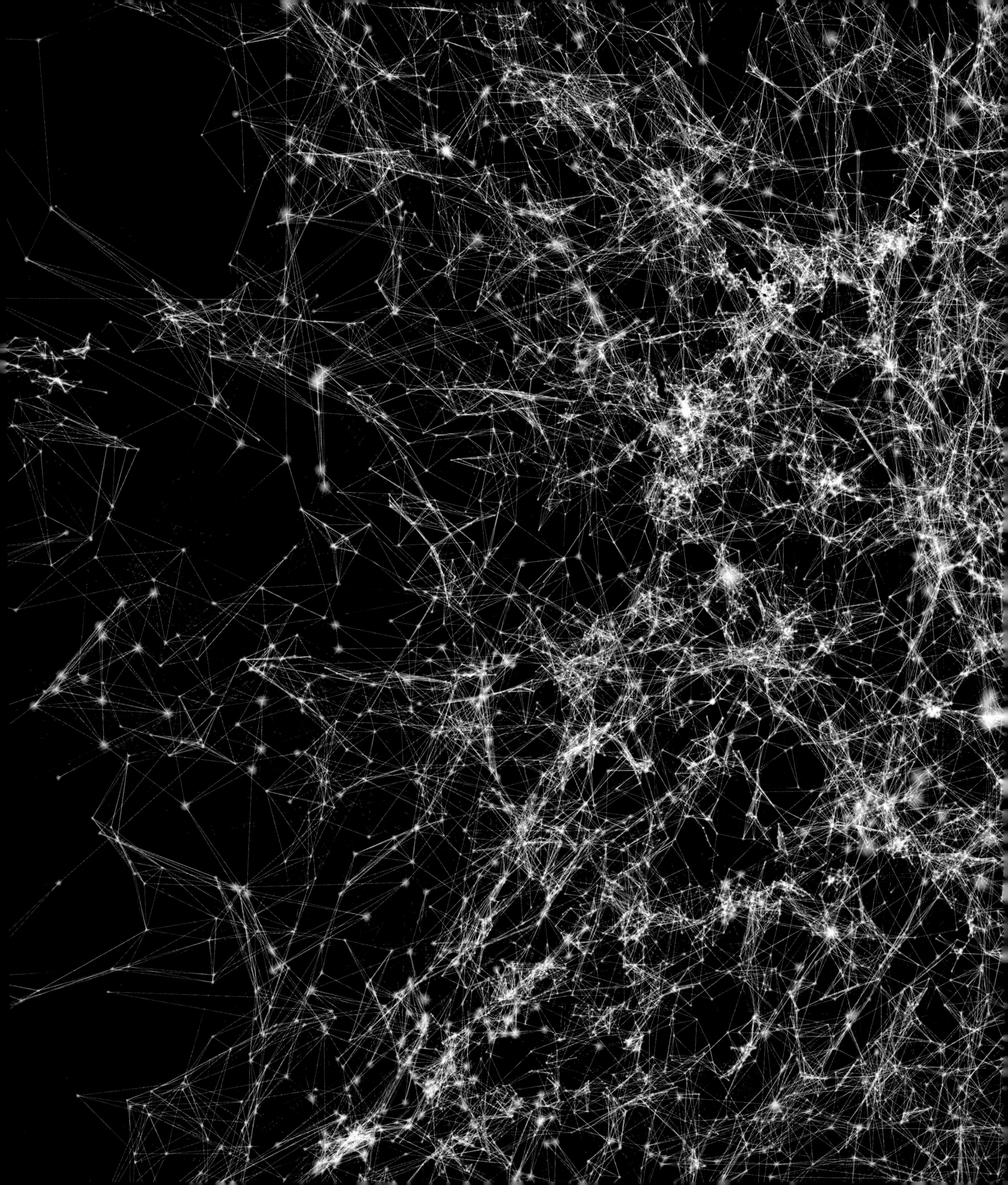

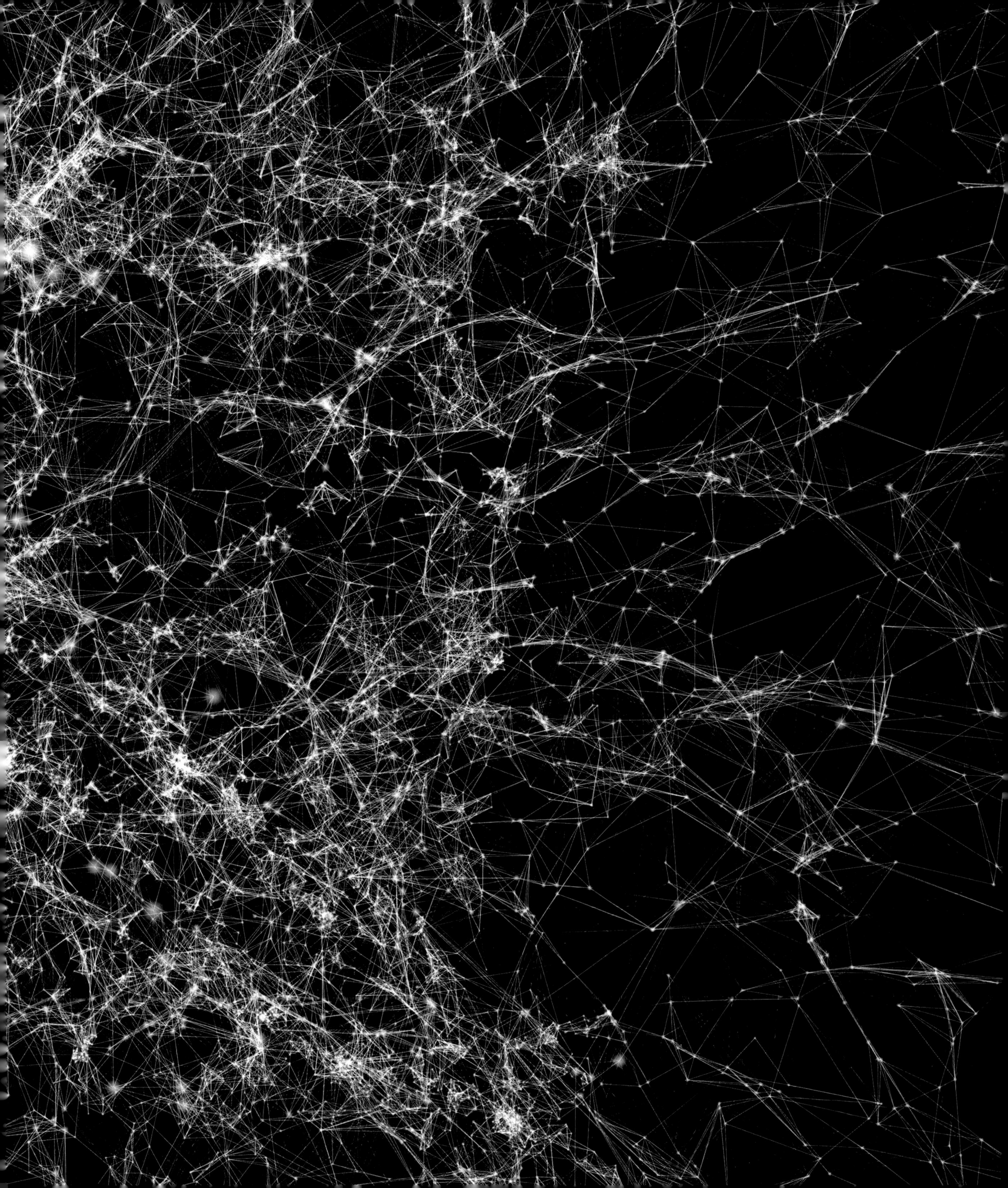

DATA SCULPTURES, 2018

For years, Barabási had been exasperated by the fact that network visualization seemed to be stuck in two dimensions. But, in 2017, the emergence of accessible 3-D printing gave him the opportunity to get closer to his dream of giving sculptural form to his visualizations. First, though, there was the hurdle of creating software that would suit his needs. The existing network-layout algorithms perceived the links as virtual and bodyless objects, which meant they were allowed to cross each other. Such crossings not only violate the viewer's sense of physicality, they are forbidden in many physical networks, such as the brain, where the neurons avoid other neurons, except when they synapse together. The BarabásiLab developed a new mathematical and algorithmic framework inspired by actual physical and biological patterns for laying out networks in three dimensions without link-crossings. This software, combined with the newly emerging powder printing, a technology that allows for the printing of intricate data sculptures, enabled Barabási to turn 3-D printing into the lab's medium of choice.

Barabási began by testing the 3-D network-layout methodology on *The Flavor Network*, which encodes how ingredients in our food connect to one another through shared flavor chemicals and was originally mapped and published in 2011 (see page 33). In contrast with the colorful 2-D map, this initial 3-D map, opposite, was monochromatic. Color 3-D powder printing was not ready yet. But even in a single solid hue, this sculptural diagram presents a clear separation of the different flavor communities and unveils previously hidden relationships between groups of foods.

The next 3-D visualization challenge the BarabásiLab took on was to represent the very real obstructions that occur in dense networks. If links are sufficiently thick, the paths connecting the nodes are often obstructed, forcing the links to follow convoluted routes to their destination. Such curving can be extreme, so extreme that very dense physical networks enter a new phase of their existence—this process happens in much the same way that cooling water freezes into a rigid organization that we perceive as ice. The dense bundles shown on pages 138–41 exemplify this new condition. Barabási calls these objects *Gurgas*, the Latin word for "gorge," because their twisting, interweaving form resembles constrained water as it struggles to find an outlet in the landscape. Thanks to their compact shape and absence of loose links, these *Gurgas* became the lab's testing ground for new 3-D printing materials, such as bronze and plastic, as shown on page 139. The plates on pages 140 and 141 contrast the computer-generated 3-D rendering with the sculptural physicality of the final 3-D print; those on pages 142 and 143 reveal the *Gurgas's* inner structure.

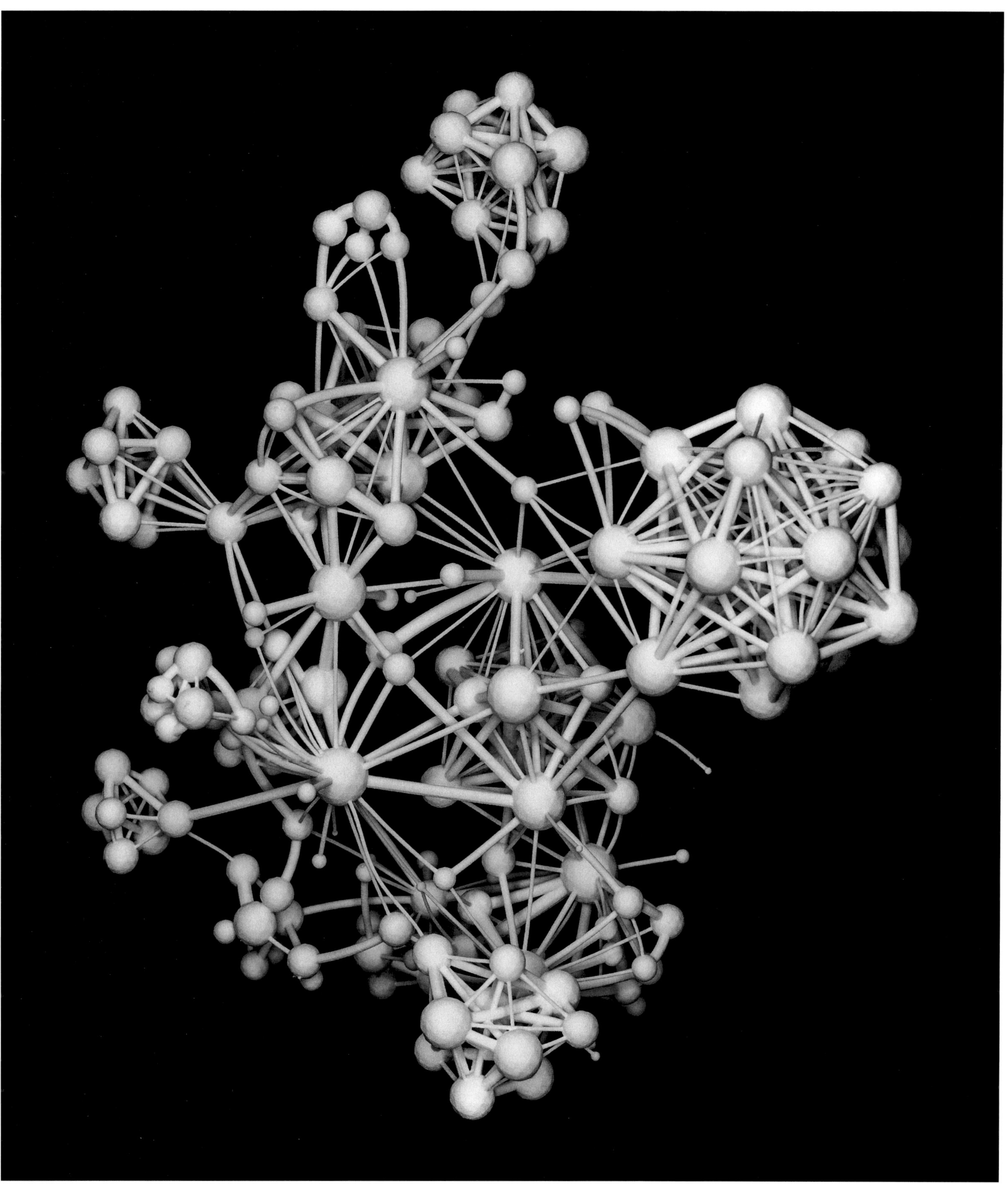

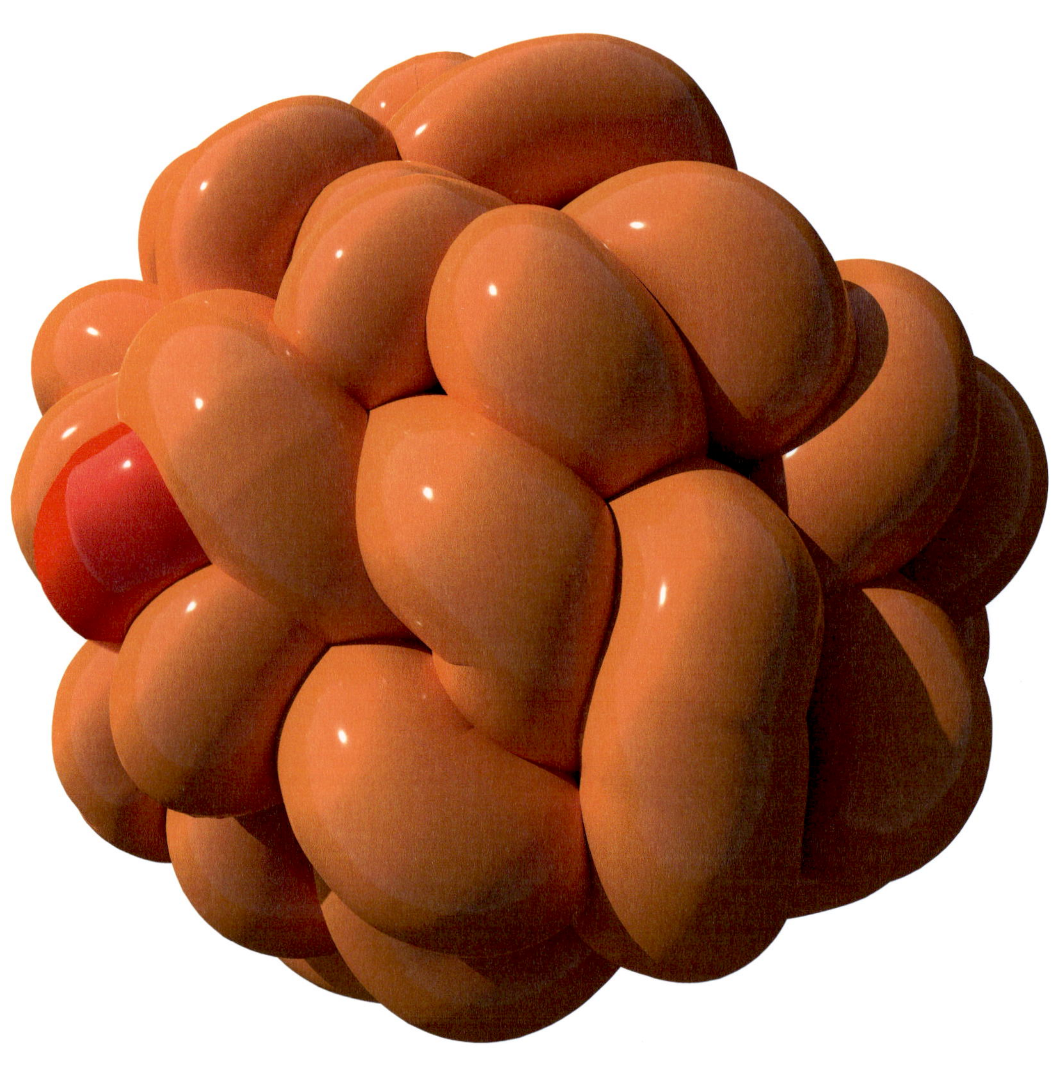

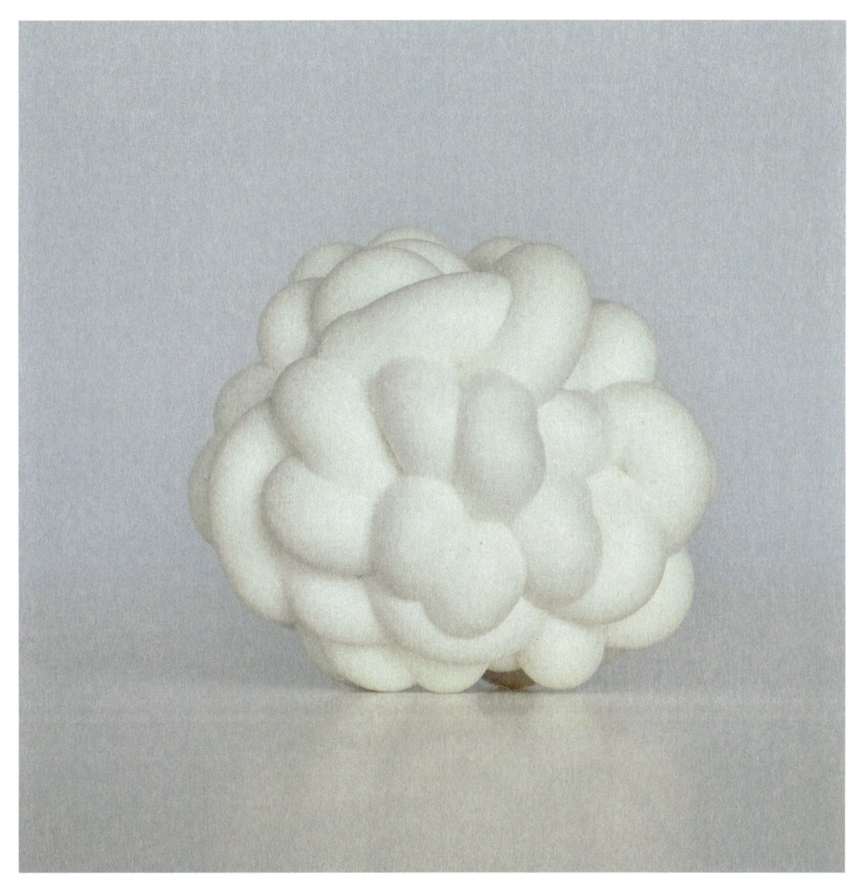

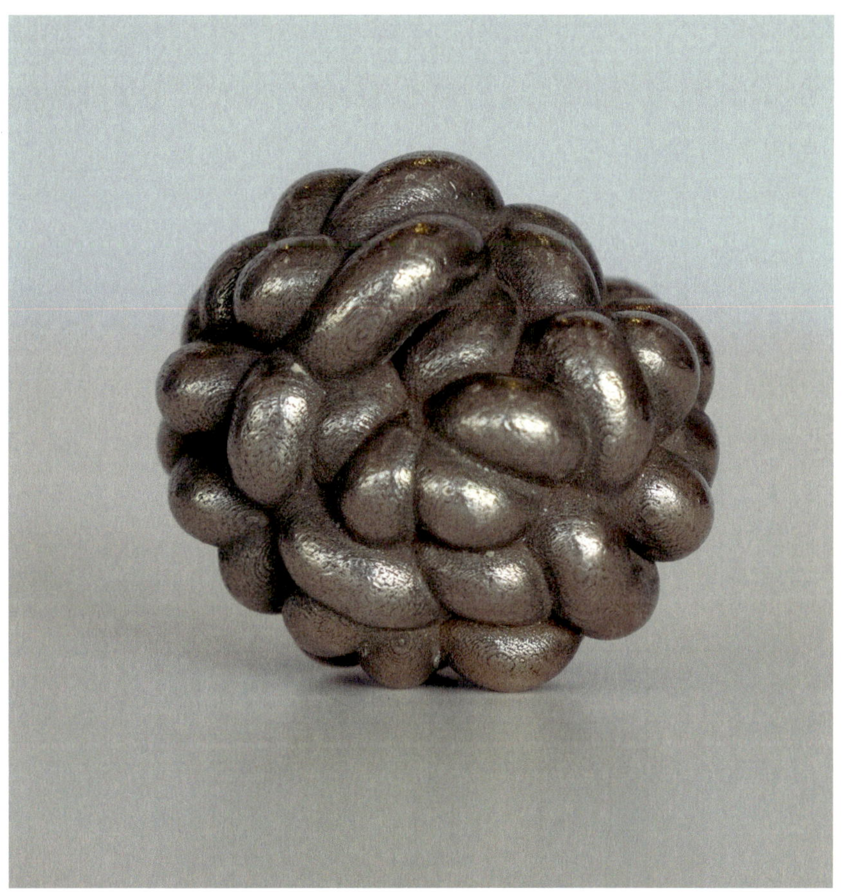

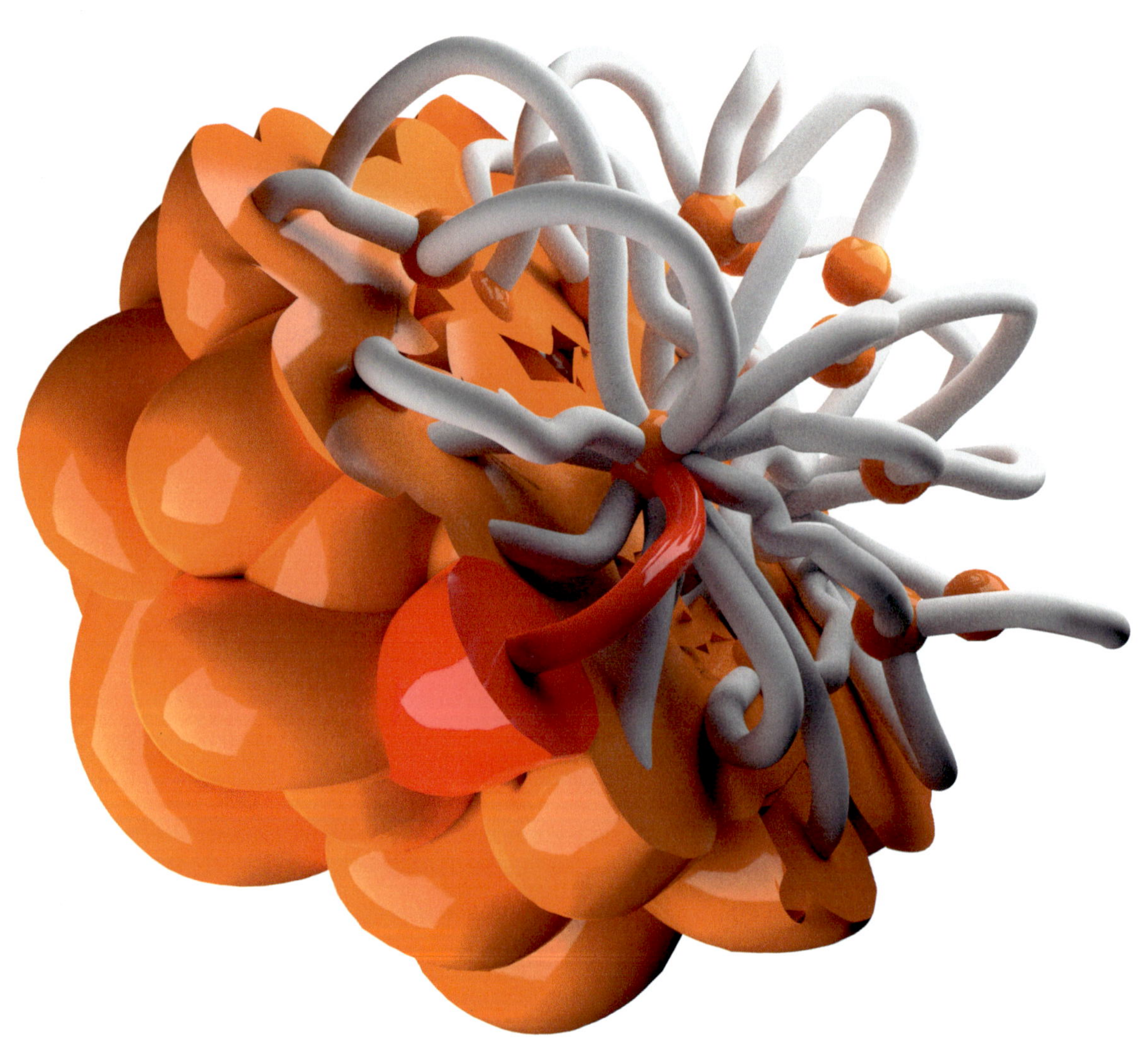

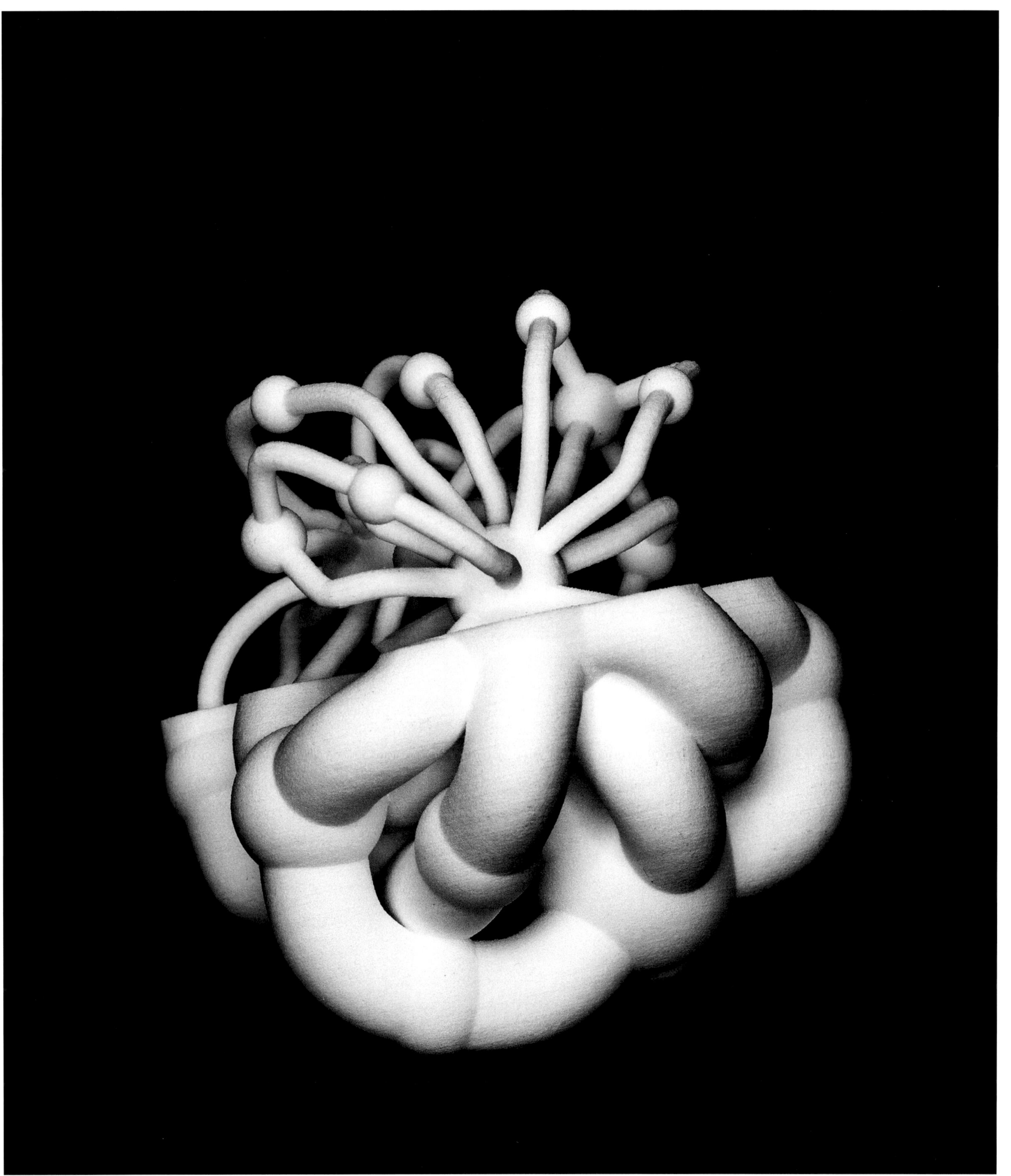

THE NETWORK CANON, 2018

Soon after developing the mathematical tool set for data sculptures, Barabási returned to the project of illustrating the canonical network models, which he had begun in 2000. With a 3-D printer and a refined layout by BarabásiLab designer Alice Grishchenko, it was now possible to render the structural differences between the two highly studied networks, known as the Erdős-Rényi and Barabási-Albert networks, that contrast randomness with the scale-free architecture of real networks (see page 31, top). The plates on pages 144–45 show the first successful attempt to turn the random and scale-free network models, respectively, into data sculptures. In 2019, after the models had been successfully 3-D printed, Barabási and lab designer Mauro Martino visited the Fonderia Artistica Battaglia in Milan, and had them both cast in bronze, as shown on pages 146 and 147. The plates on pages 148 and 149 are details of the original plastic and bronze data sculptures. The image opposite shows the results of the lab's attempt to scale up the tools in order to print a large scale-free network generated by the Barabási-Albert model with hundreds of nodes.

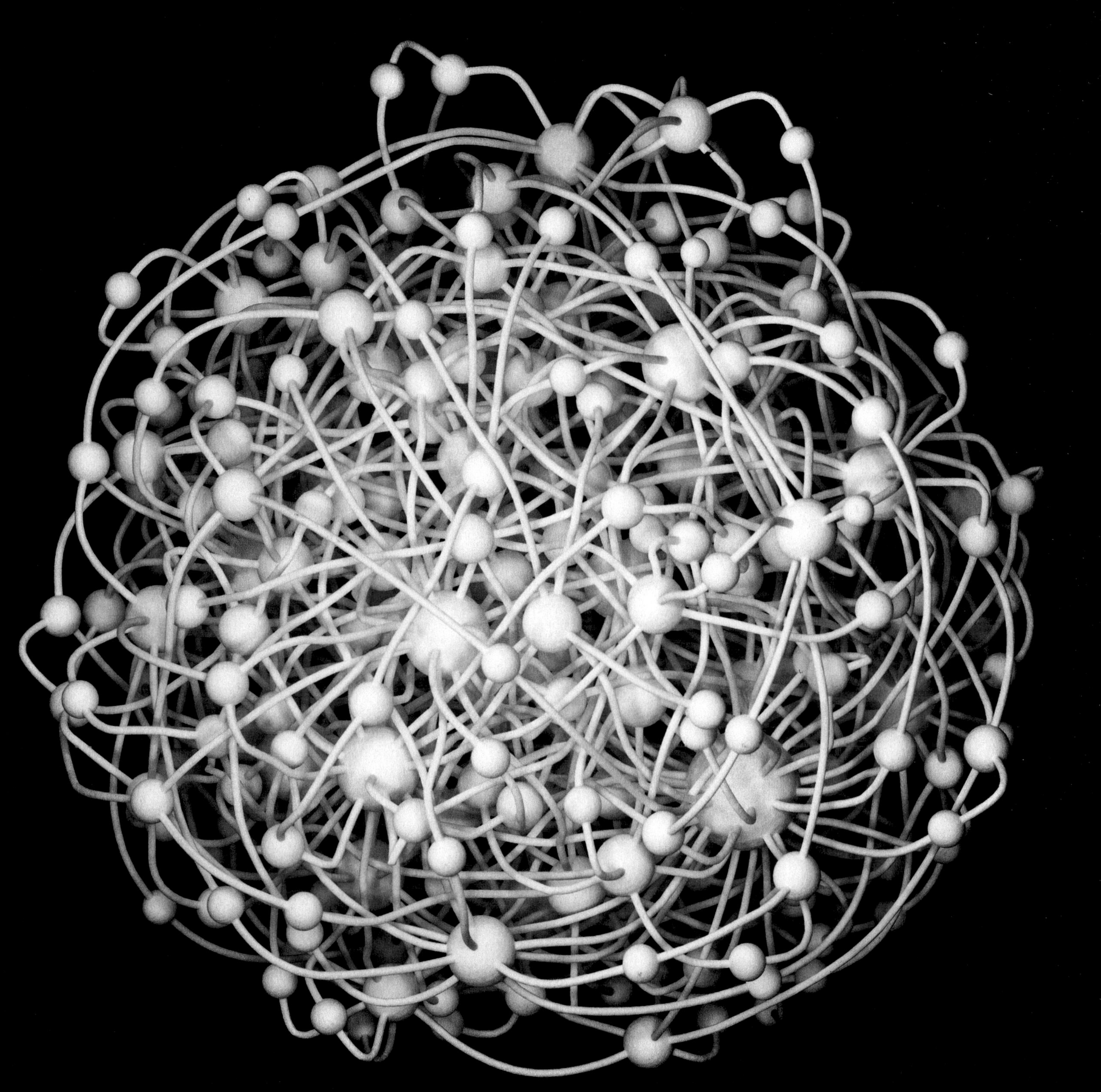

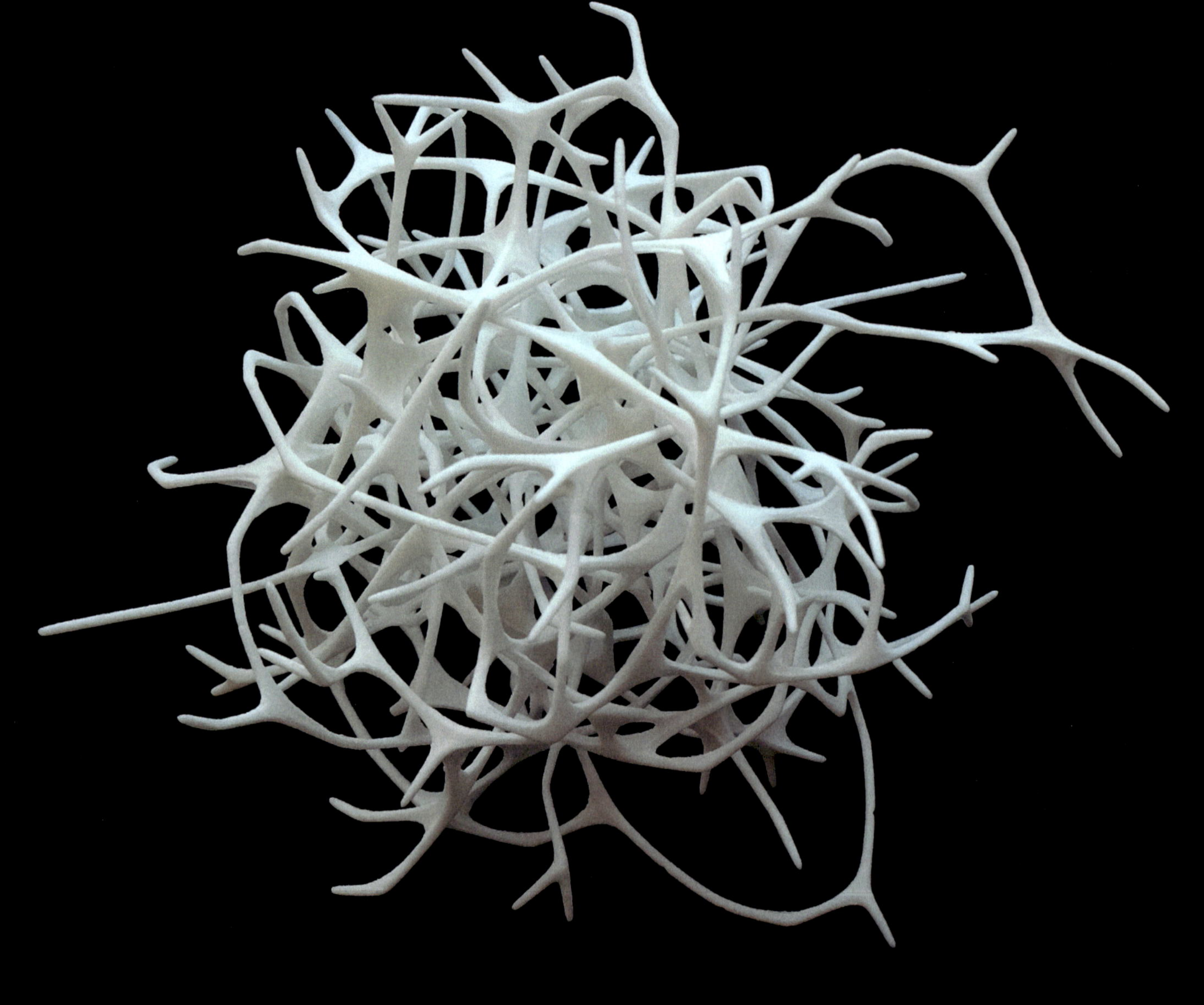

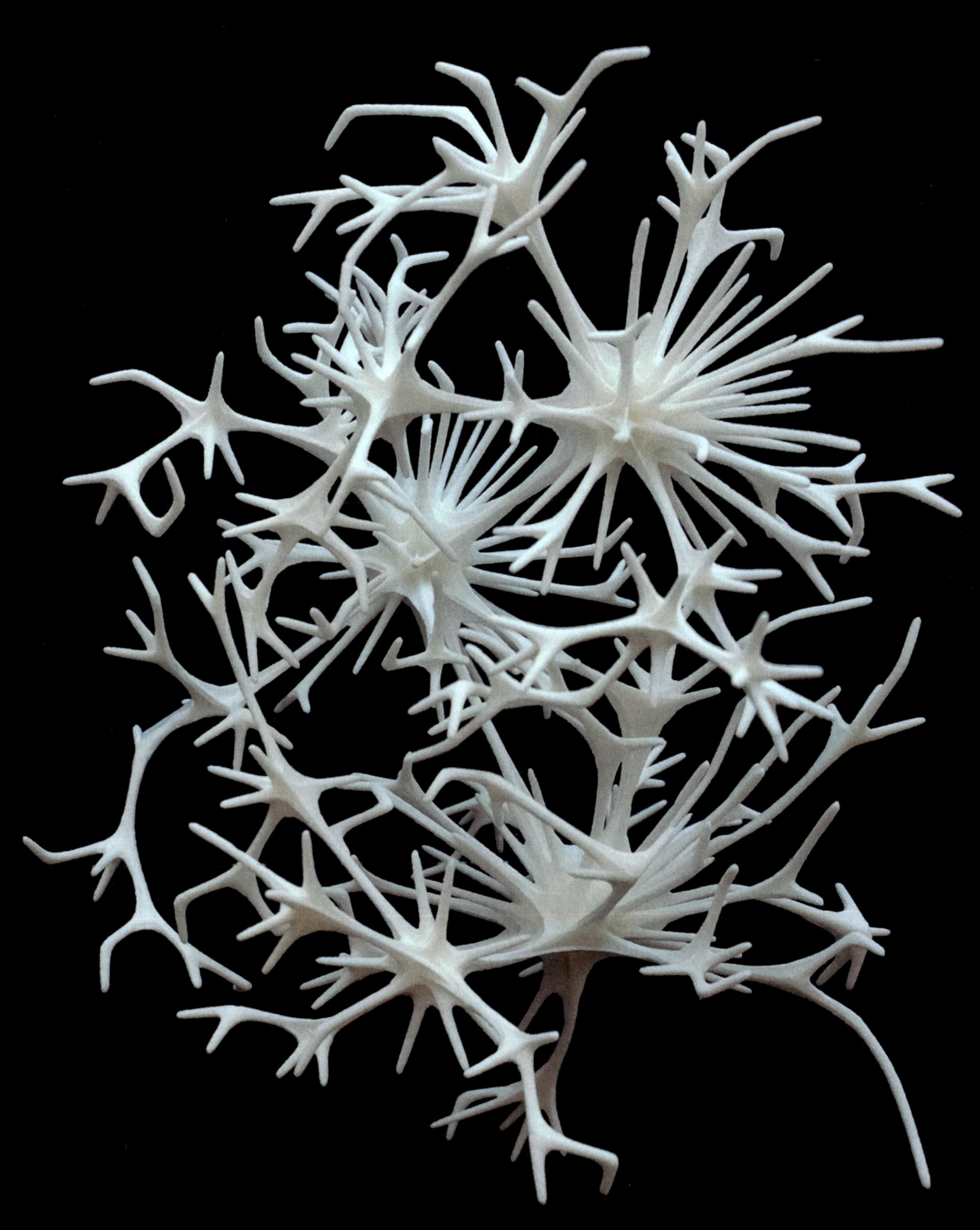

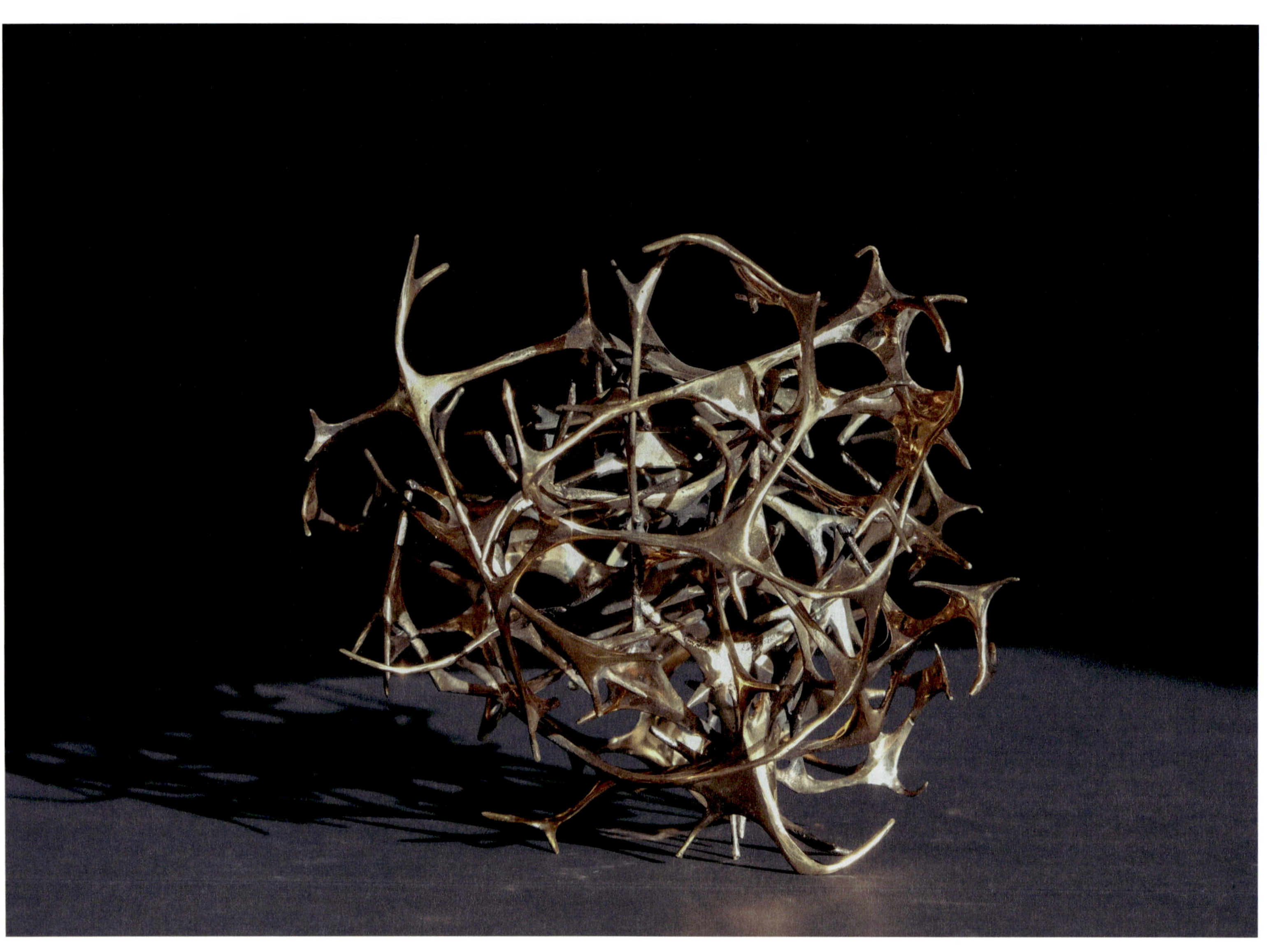

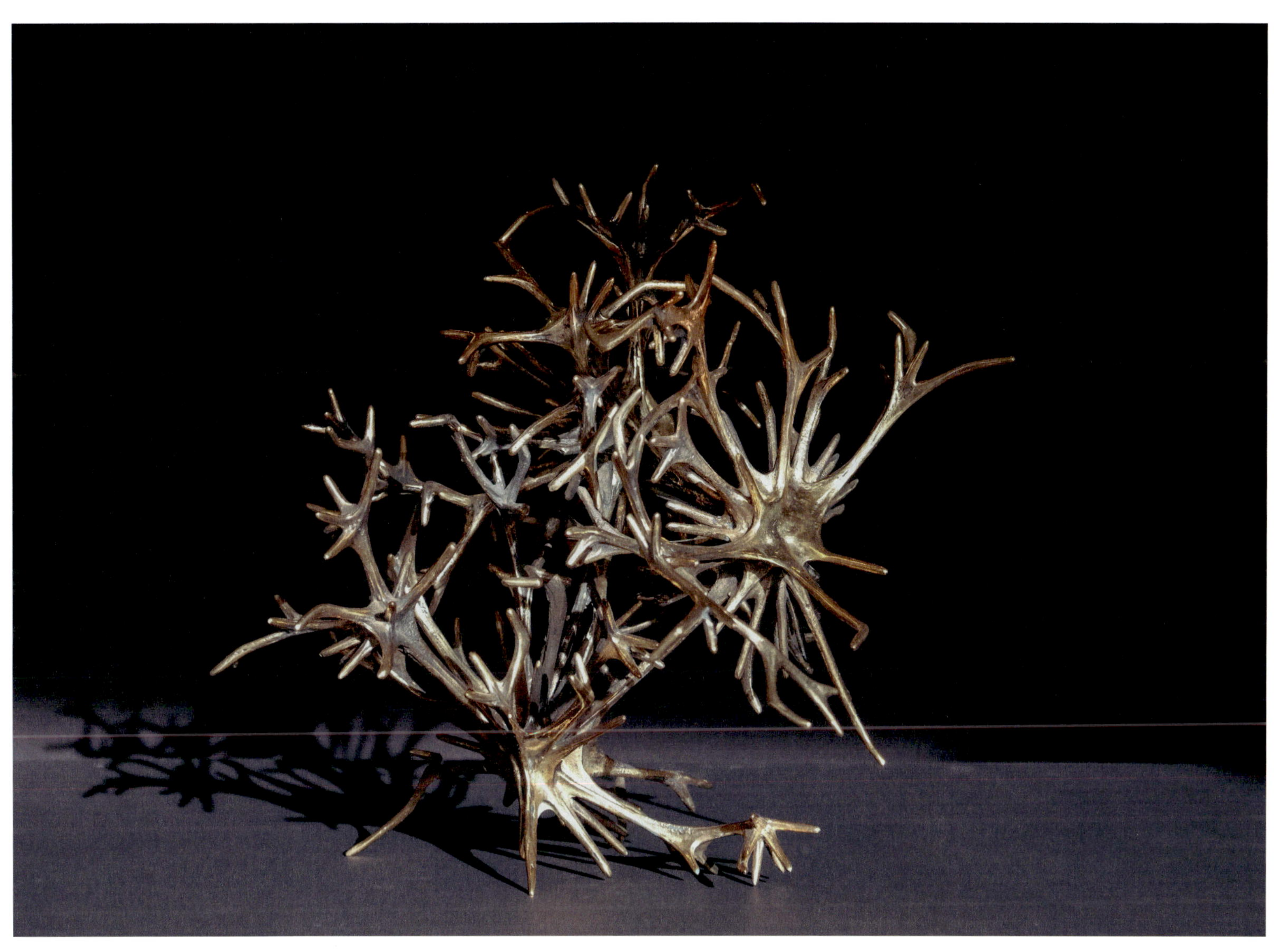

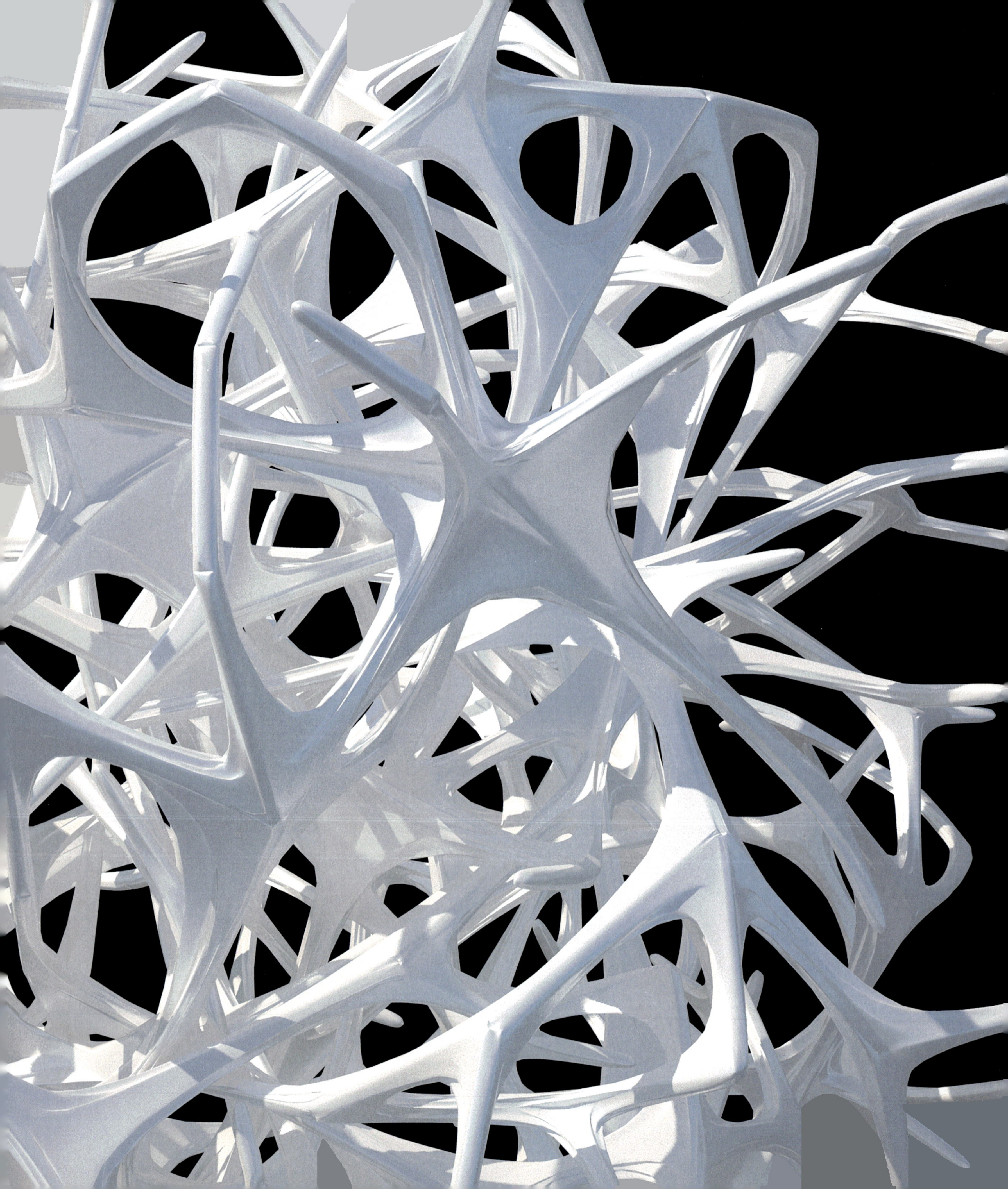

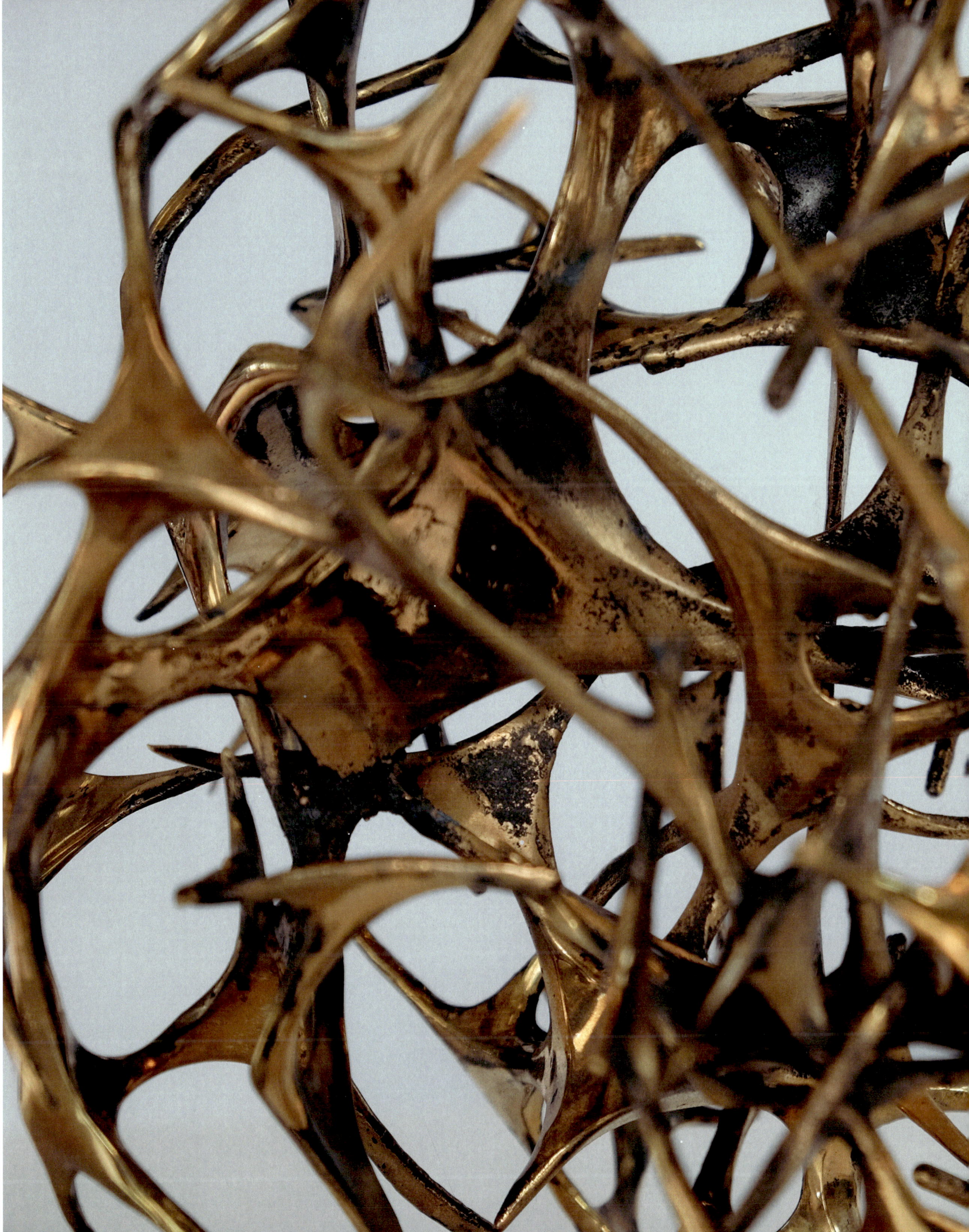

How to Assemble a Watch: The Art of Network Science

BY KATHLEEN FORDE

If you disassemble a watch and lay the parts out on a table, they will not tell the time the way an assembled watch does. The watch, when whole and functional, is a set of structures—connected and interdependent. Those internal structures communicate a visualization of time and enable us to grasp time endlessly passing, from back then to now to the future.

For Albert-László Barabási, network science tells the story of invisible time rendered visible. Consciousness results from networked parts of the brain that communicate with one another. We communicate as a culture via telephone, e-mail, and social networks. Our economy functions as a vast network of buyers, producers, and sellers. These collaborations can be mapped into a series of connected nodes, with the size and relative centrality of each node dictated by the frequency and significance of interactions. Three-dimensional visualizations of networks are generally static, though what their structures represent is anything but inanimate. Network scientists develop models that represent the actions of networks as they move through time—as time passes. Those models propose that in a representation of the fourth dimension the true nature and viability—as well as the universality—of networks will be revealed.

Barabási speaks about our dependence on networks, the way in which our individual interactions with the networks of technology, communication, or the economy shape our lives. But we could apply this concept to how we perceive the shape itself—our personal lives, the memories and the stories that we tell ourselves and others about our life's path. Essentially, this subjective narrative is a way of creating a network model of our own existence, one in which particular events are connected and perceived as being causal or interdependent, thus becoming a coherent story rather than a set of sheer moments in isolation.

It is the interplay between—and sum of—moments that construct a lifetime of impact. As time passes and our individual network of memories grows, our personal story acquires a depth and a complexity. In other words, our past colors our present and informs our future. Like the mechanisms underneath the face of the watch, a life of meaning cannot be seen, but it is felt as it is built. A lifetime, an individual's story, is an invisible structure crafted from the memories that we keep.

Artists, as storytellers, are also driven by a desire to expose those shrouded structures. They create visualizations of subjective experience to render visible the unique unseen in a way that is seemingly at odds with the premise of universality that network science offers. But the artist's agenda is not to negate the objective or universal nature of a network. Rather, it is to express our perception of it, to offer evidence that in that perception is the truth of our existence: our subjective experience is the very thing that constructs the memory network that defines our personal narrative. The nodes are those moments that have affected us most deeply, emotionally or intellectually—they are the memories that we keep rather than the memories that fade. In the eyes of the artist, consciousness constructs the network, rather than being constructed by it.

The paradox of network scientists, in their quest to map networks four-dimensionally, is that the network model only coheres with the element of time as an innate characteristic: each interaction, each connection between nodes, is a causal relationship that can only be defined—or identified—as one thing preceding the other. It may be impossible to determine whether consciousness creates the network or is created by it; both models are generated by the concept of time itself.

THE CONNECTOME, 2019

With over 100 billion nodes, the human brain is perhaps the most complex network known to science. Neuroscientists call whole brain networks "the connectome," and until recently they were unmappable. Yet given the important role the connectome plays in brain function and consciousness, Barabási has had a long-standing interest in trying to understand its structure. The BarabásiLab's first attempt to visualize the structure of the brain took form as a 3-D rendition of the connectome of the mouse brain. The configuration is based on data collected over the course of a multiyear project at the Allen Institute, a bioscience research center in Seattle. *The Mouse Connectome* was laid out using the same algorithm that generated *The Flavor Network*. Its arrangement unveils the exceptional complexity of the brain's wiring patterns. The plates opposite and on pages 156–57 capture images of the full connectome, while the plate on pages 154–55 zooms into one densely packed section—or local neighborhood—of the mouse brain's wiring.

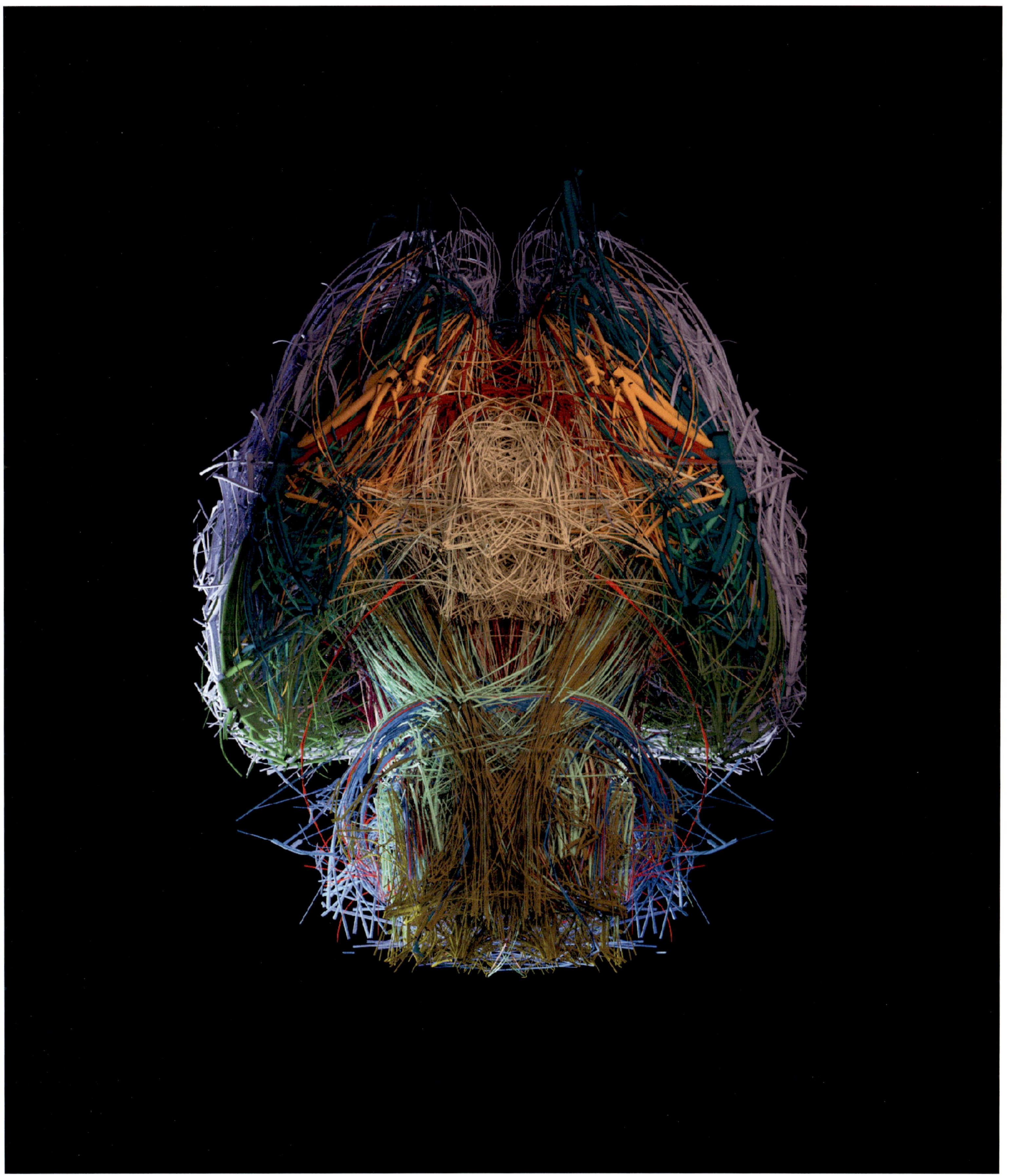

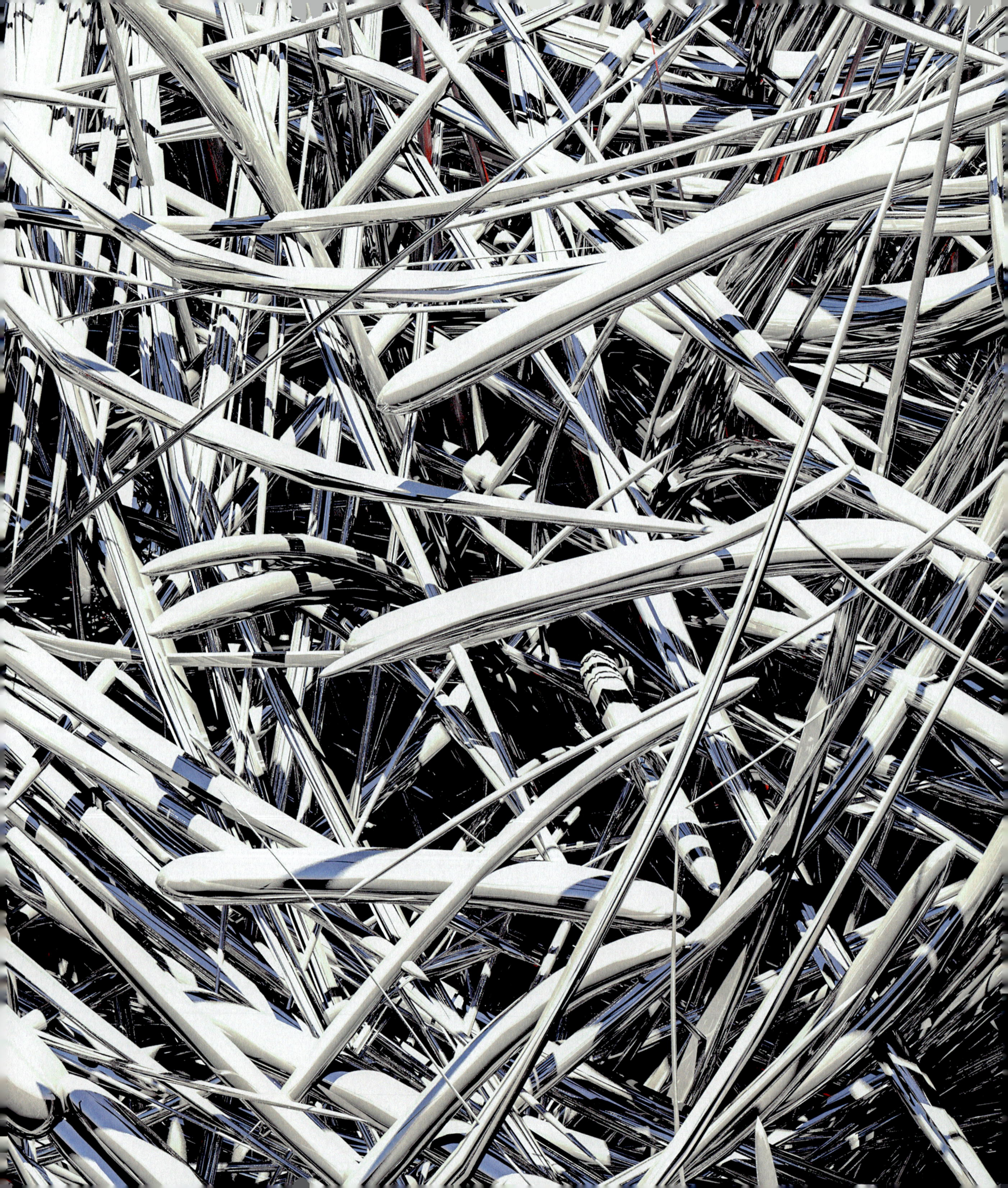

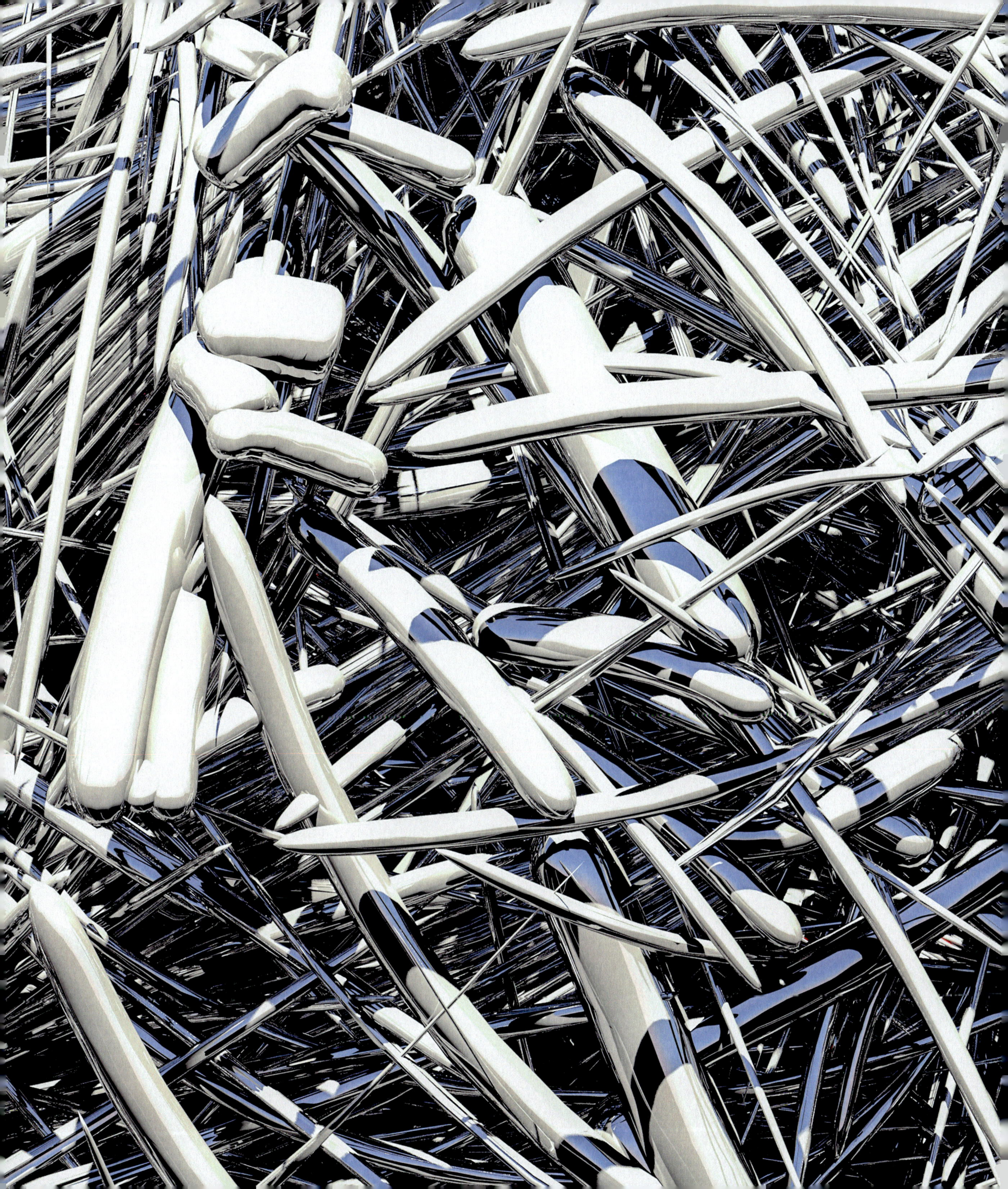

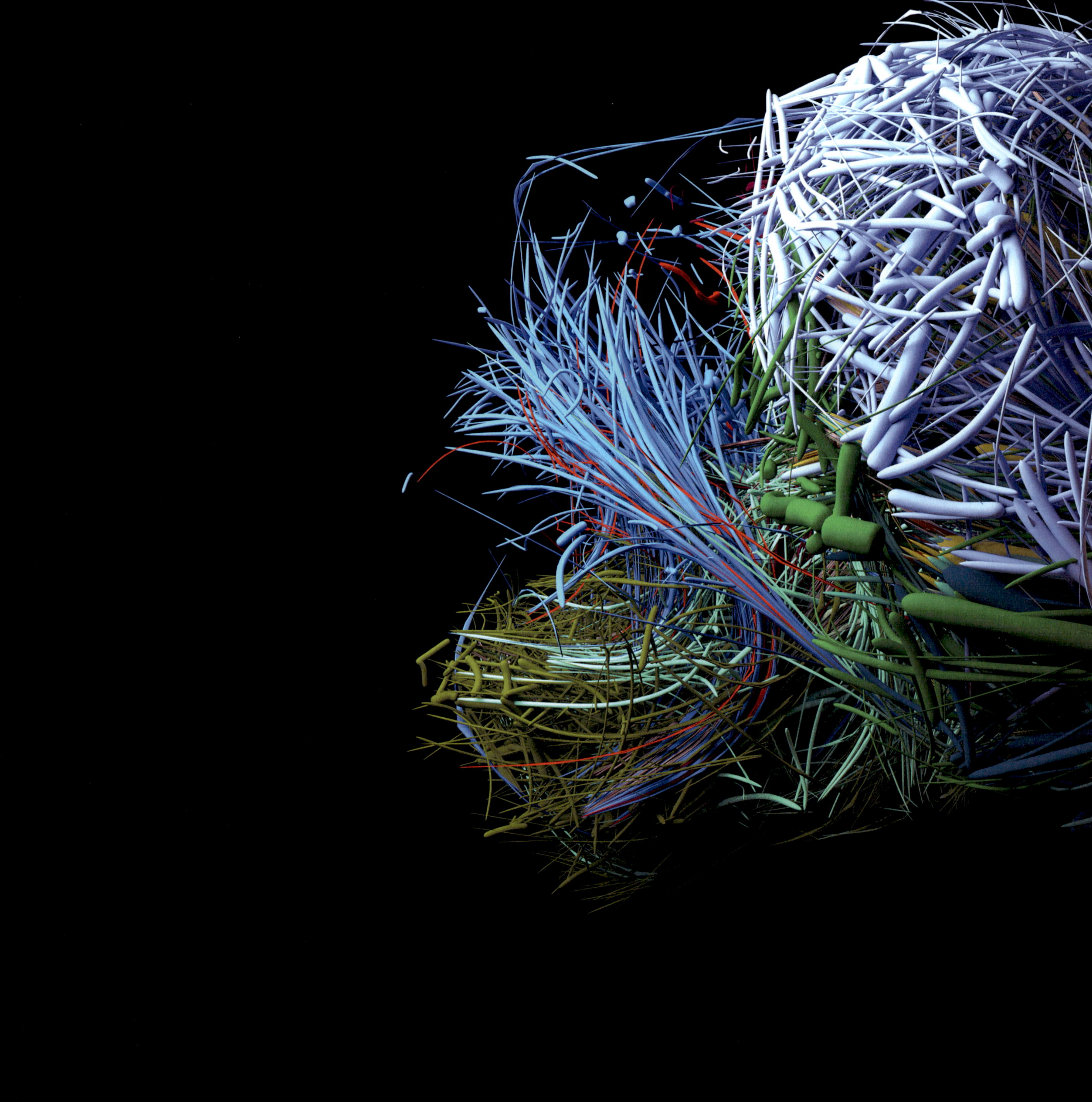

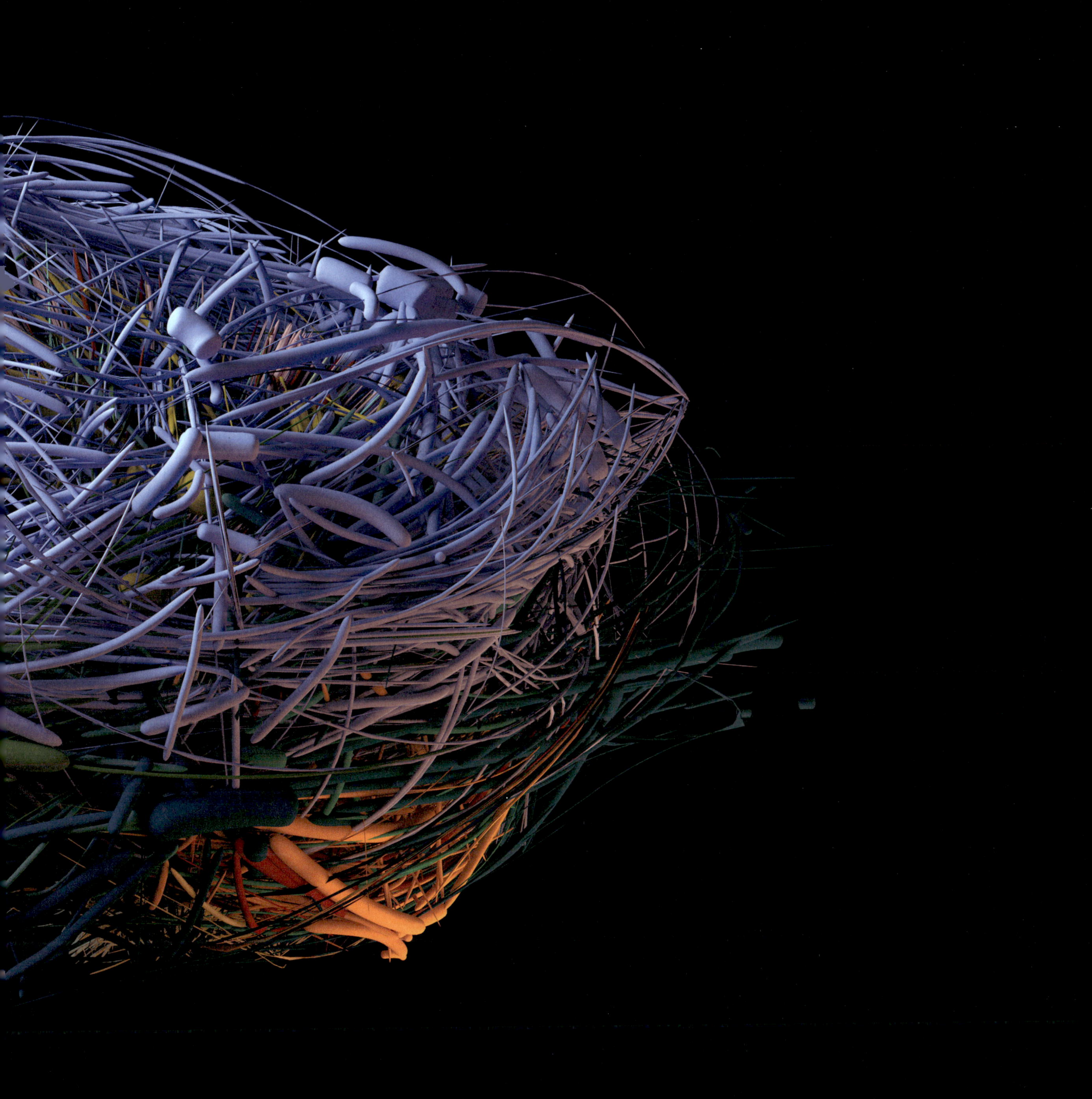

FAKE NEWS, 2018

The spread of fake news is enabled by social networks empowered by social media. One person posts a bogus story alleging that several high-ranking Democratic Party officials are running a sex-trafficking ring in the basement of a Washington, DC pizza parlor on a few sites, and suddenly everybody knows about it. The BarábasiLab chose to map the spread of the Pizzagate scandal because it was the first well-documented fake news event—the debunked right-wing conspiracy theory was traced to right-wing conspiracy website Infowars—that affected the 2016 US election landscape. What the *Fake News* network depicts is the spread of tweets sharing the *#pizzagate* hashtag on Twitter. By 2016, a substantial amount of activity on Twitter was generated by bots, program-driven accounts that pose as humans. To show the important role such bots play in the propagation of fake news, the team evaluated each Twitter account that retweeted *#pizzagate* using a Botometer, an artificial-intelligence tool that separates humans from bots. The number of bot tweets versus human tweets in spreading Pizzagate are represented on the map shown opposite, and in detail on the following pages, by node color—the bots are shown in ocher-colored nodes, the humans in teal.

The *Fake News* network was conceived as a data sculpture and created as part of the Wonder Net project (netwonder.net), the first public release of several data sculptures. At the time, however, the 3-D-printing technology lacked the resolution to sufficiently articulate the structure's fine details. Instead, the BarabásiLab produced this map in two other mediums, first as a 2-D monochromatic print, page 162, and then as a laser-engraved glass etching, page 163, a medium used by the BarabásiLab to represent 3-D networks with exceptional complexity.

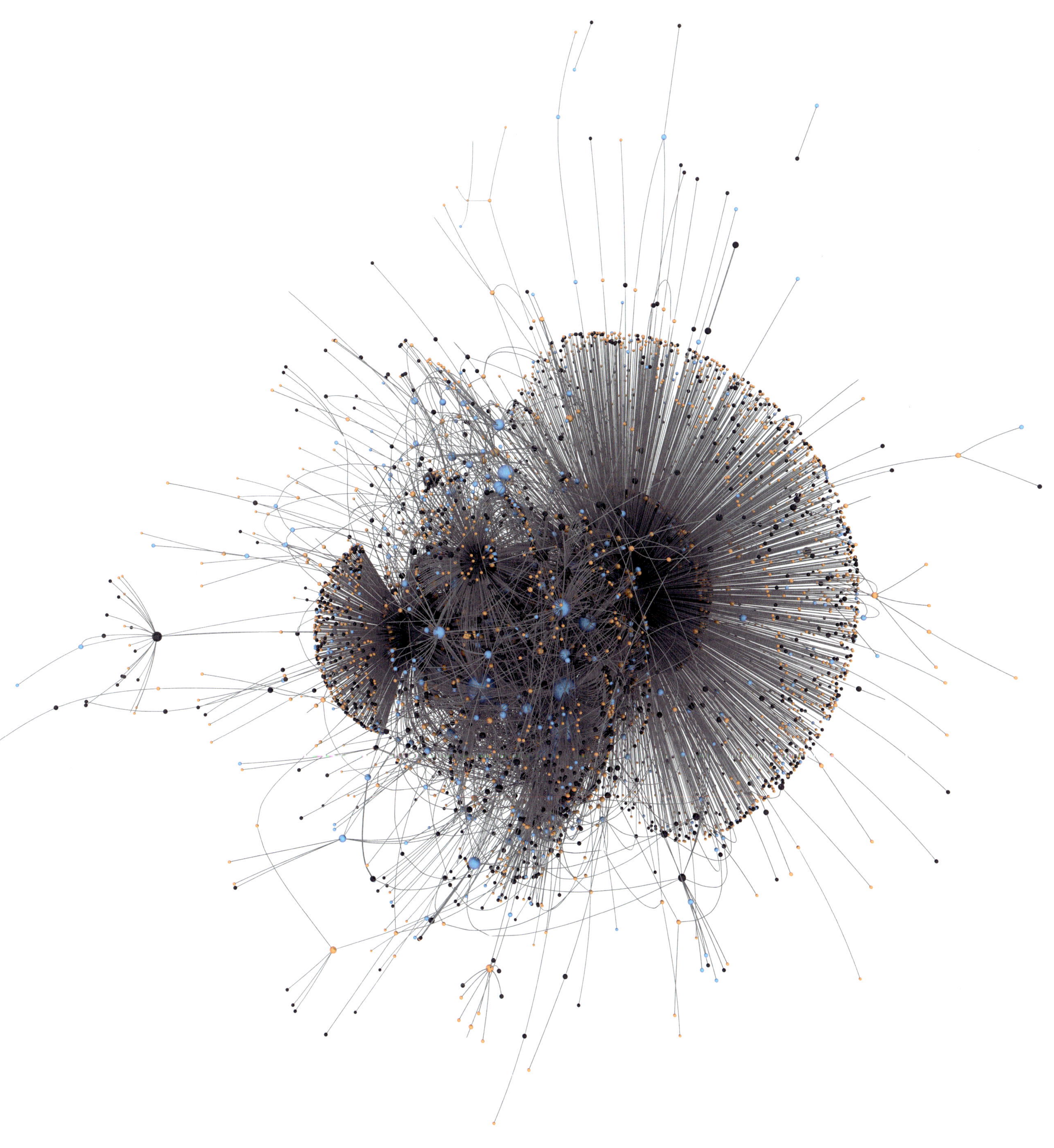

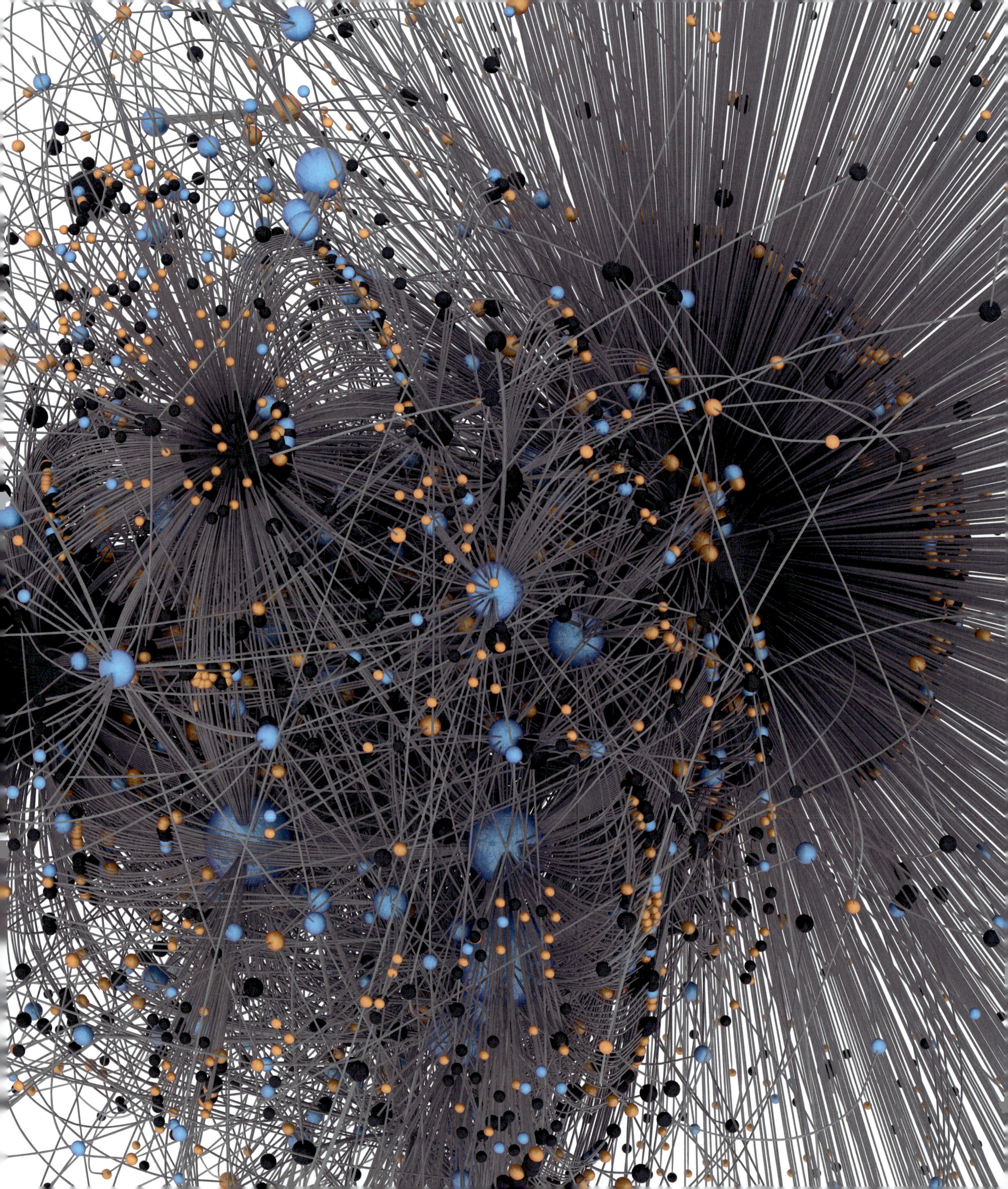

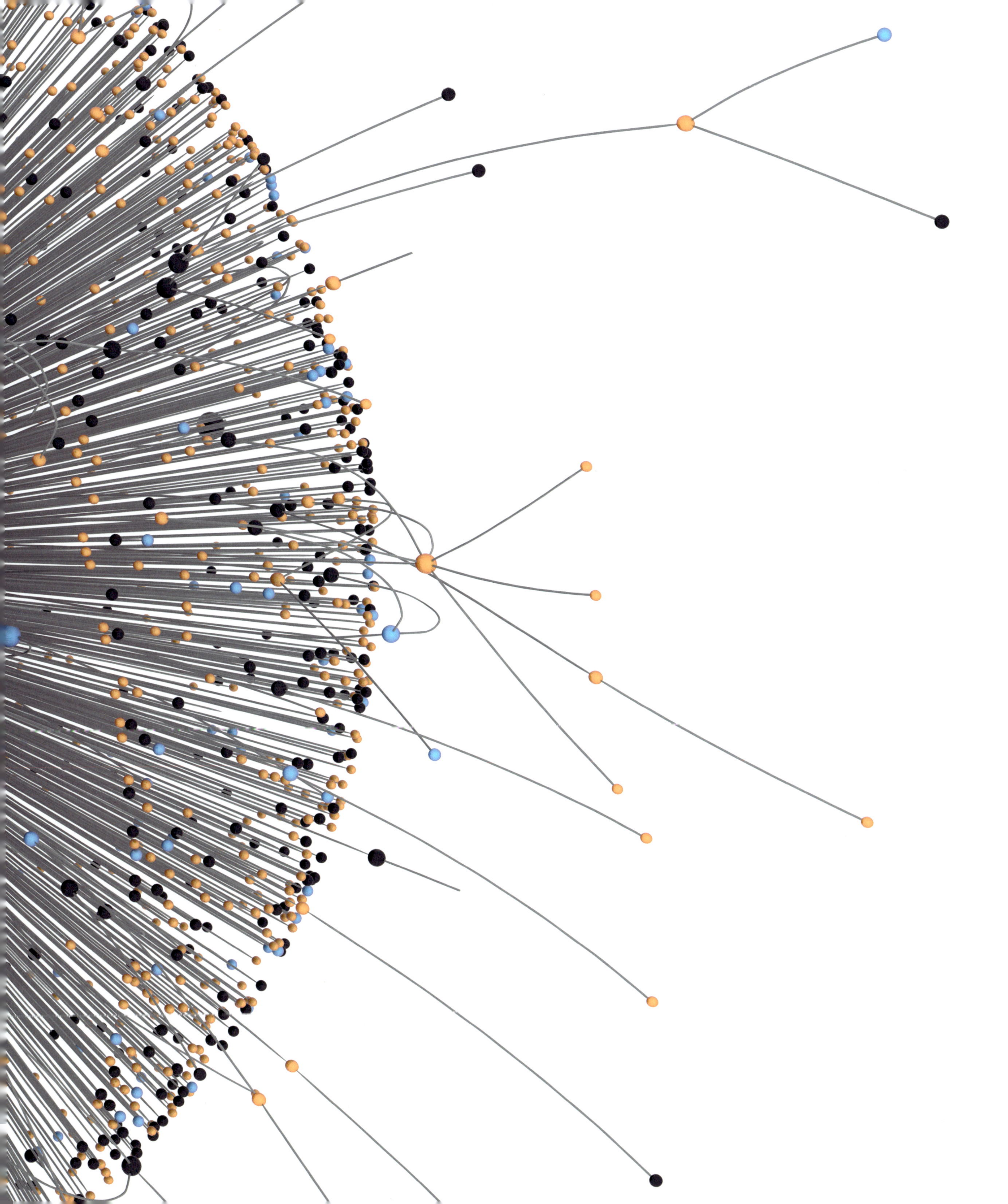

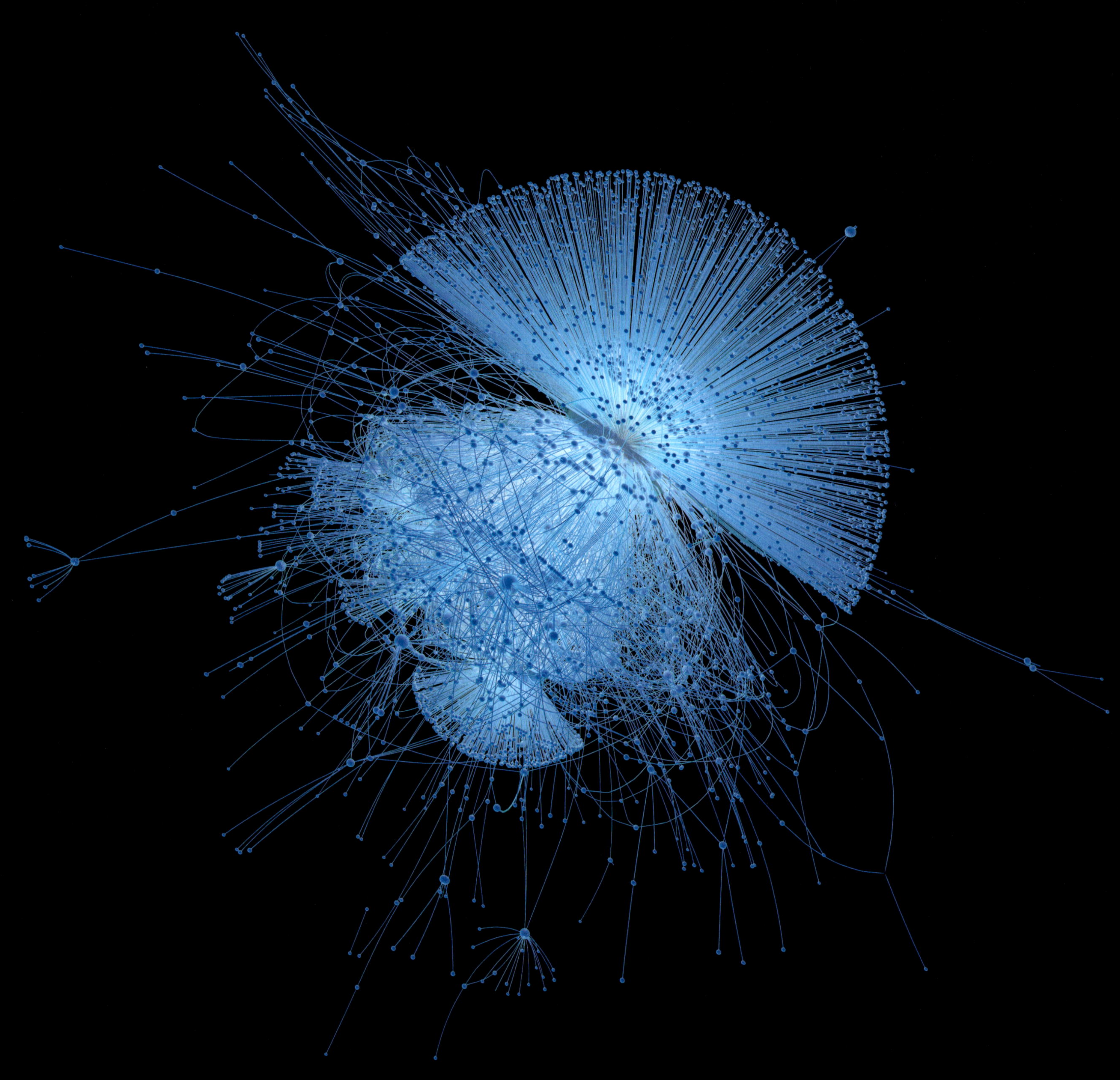

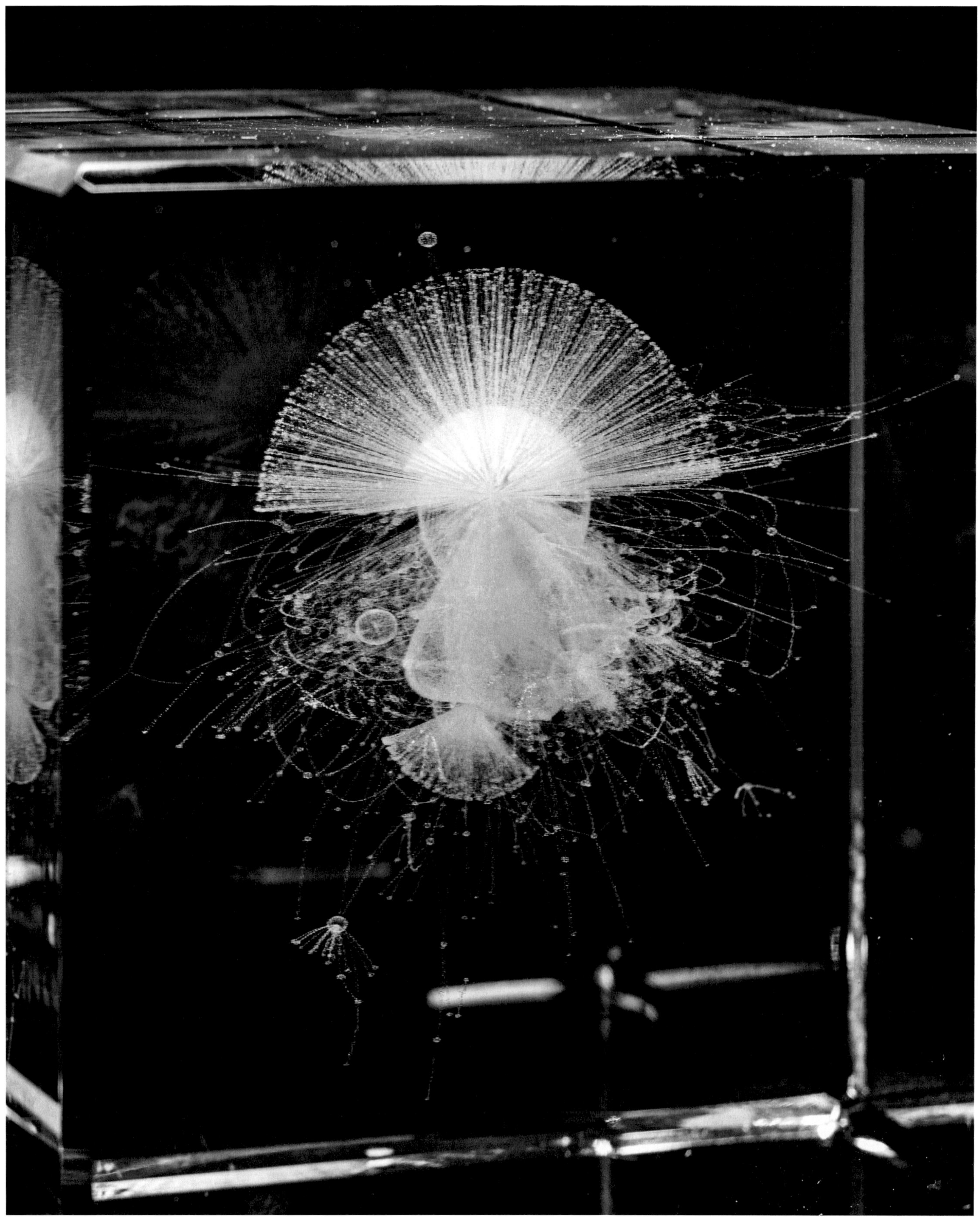

150 YEARS OF NATURE, 2019

In early 2019, Barabási got an unexpected request from the creative director of the venerable scientific journal *Nature,* asking if he would design the cover of the 150th-anniversary issue. Barabási's work had been featured on *Nature*'s cover many times before, but always as an accompaniment to the publication of one of his papers. This request, a commission, was different. The BarabásiLab began the process with a data-driven analysis of the whole history of the journal. The team then mapped out the massive co-citation network connecting the 88,000 papers *Nature* had published since 1900. Two papers were linked if another scientific publication had cited them both. The visualization of the network reveals the highly multidisciplinary scope of the journal and illuminates how various disciplines, which appear in different colors, are co-cited.

The original plan of a single cover image turned into a multimedia project consisting of a foldout cover of the co-citation network, and a three-page image illustrating the impact of several iconic *Nature* publications, opposite. The project was also accompanied by a video, stills from which are shown in the plates on pages 169–71, and an interactive website. The plates on pages 166 and 167 show black-and-white renderings of the co-citation network generated during the design process. While this map represents data specific to one journal, its bigger takeaways are about how discovery informs and alters our thinking, how ideas are born when disciplines collide, and how the knowledge that leads to the emergence of schools of thought is itself an enlightening and vibrant topic of inquiry.

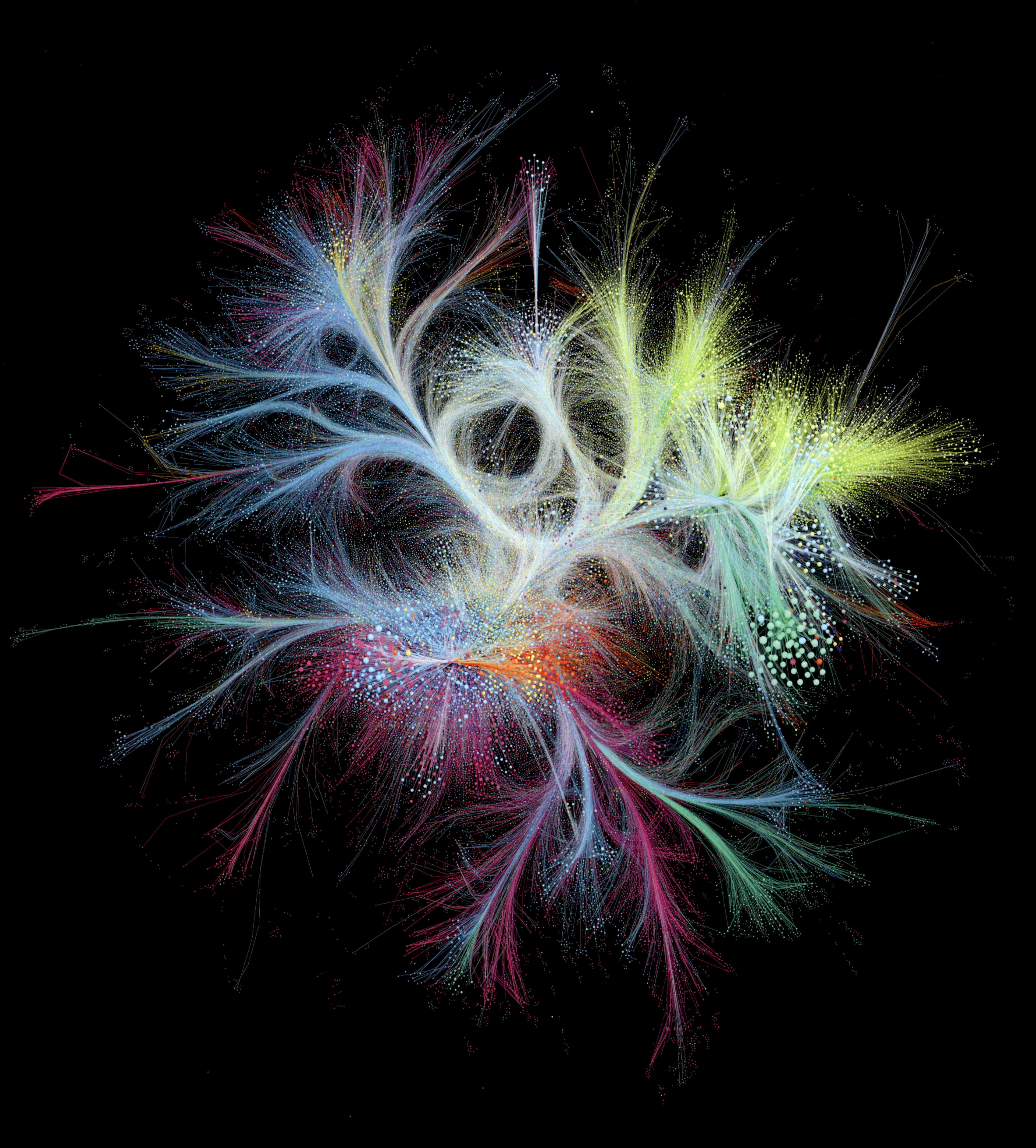

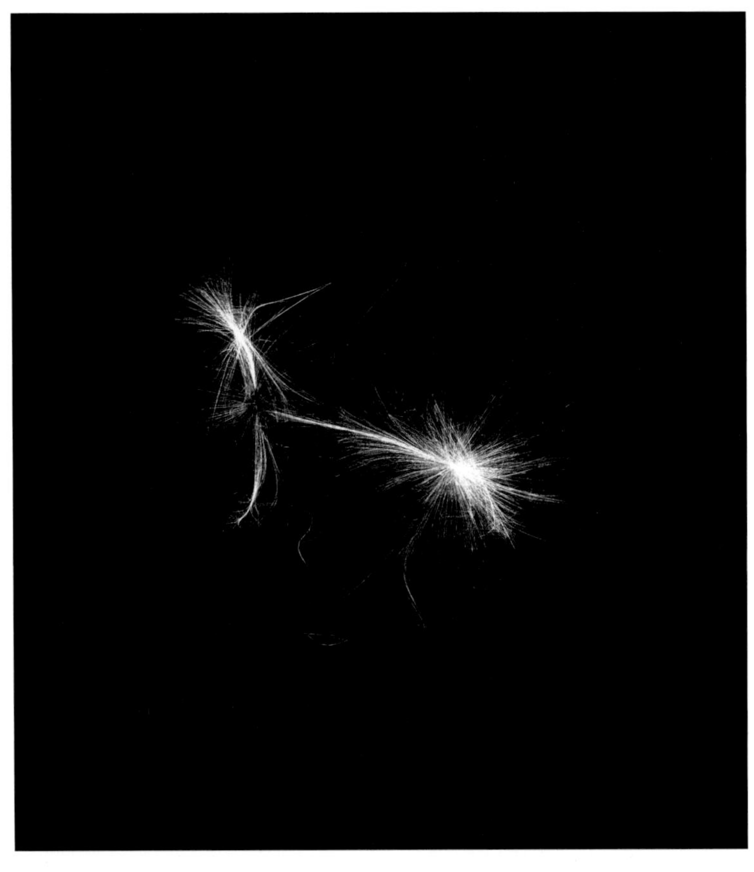

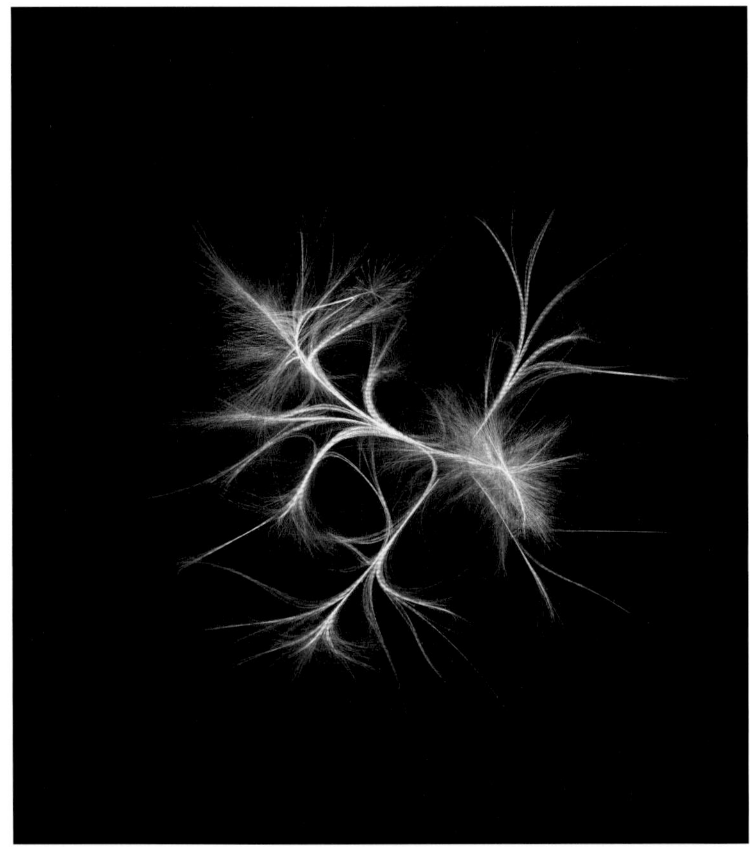

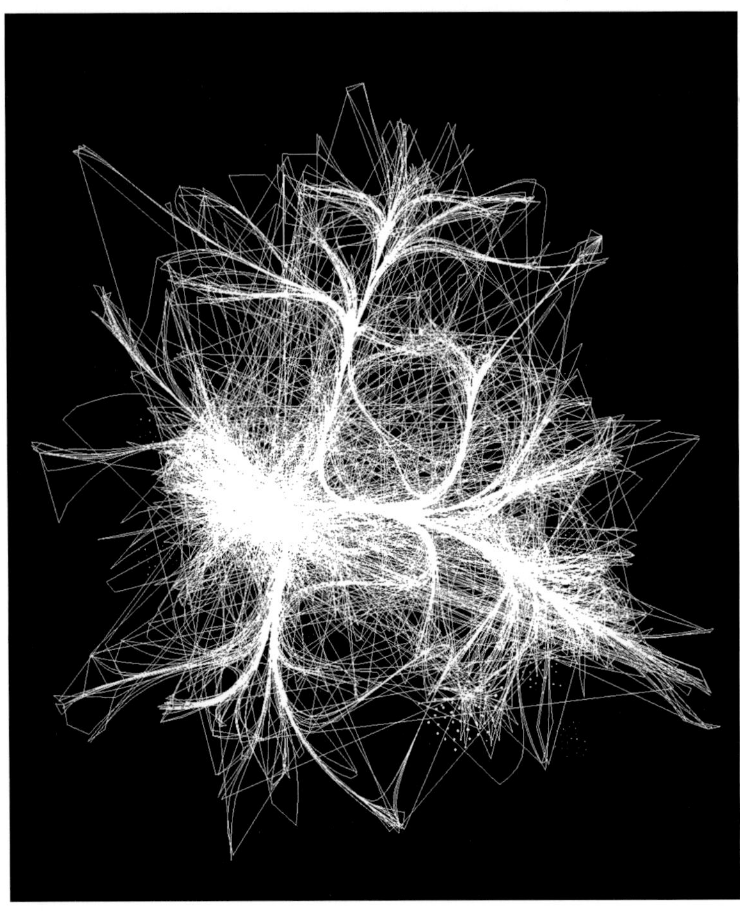

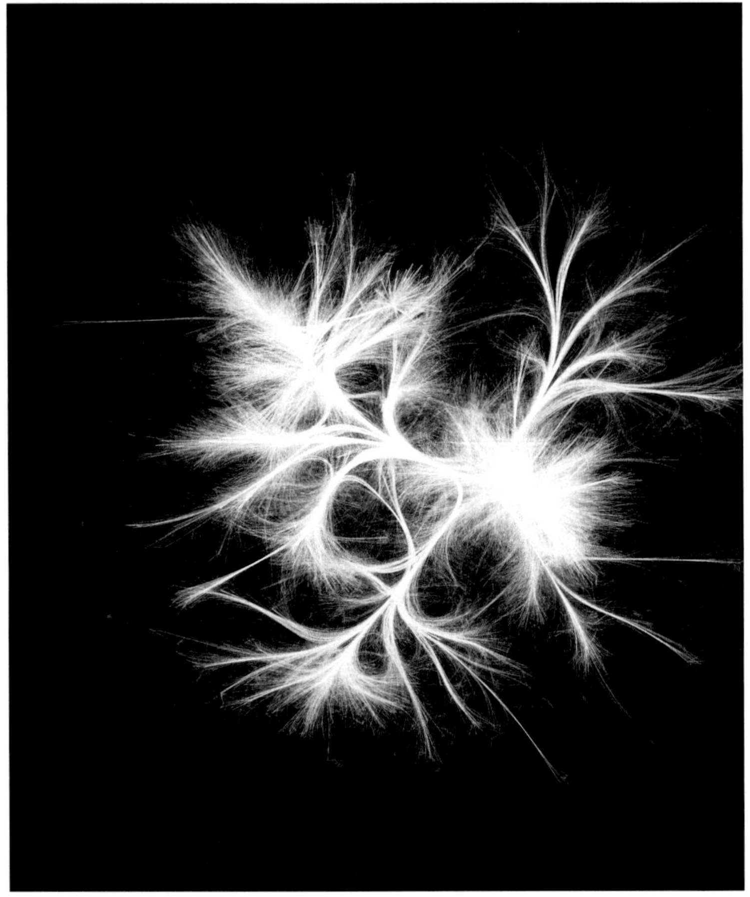

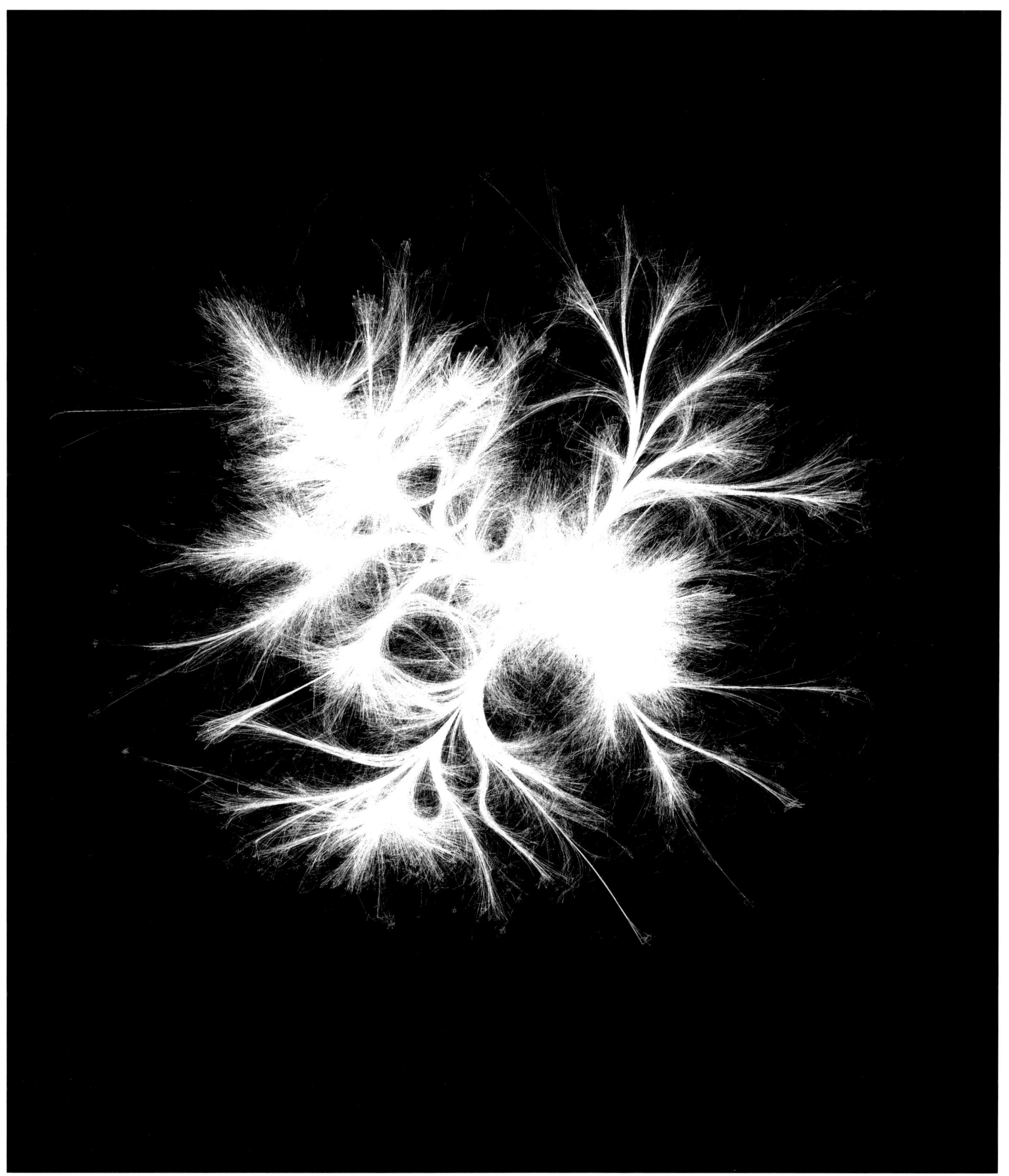

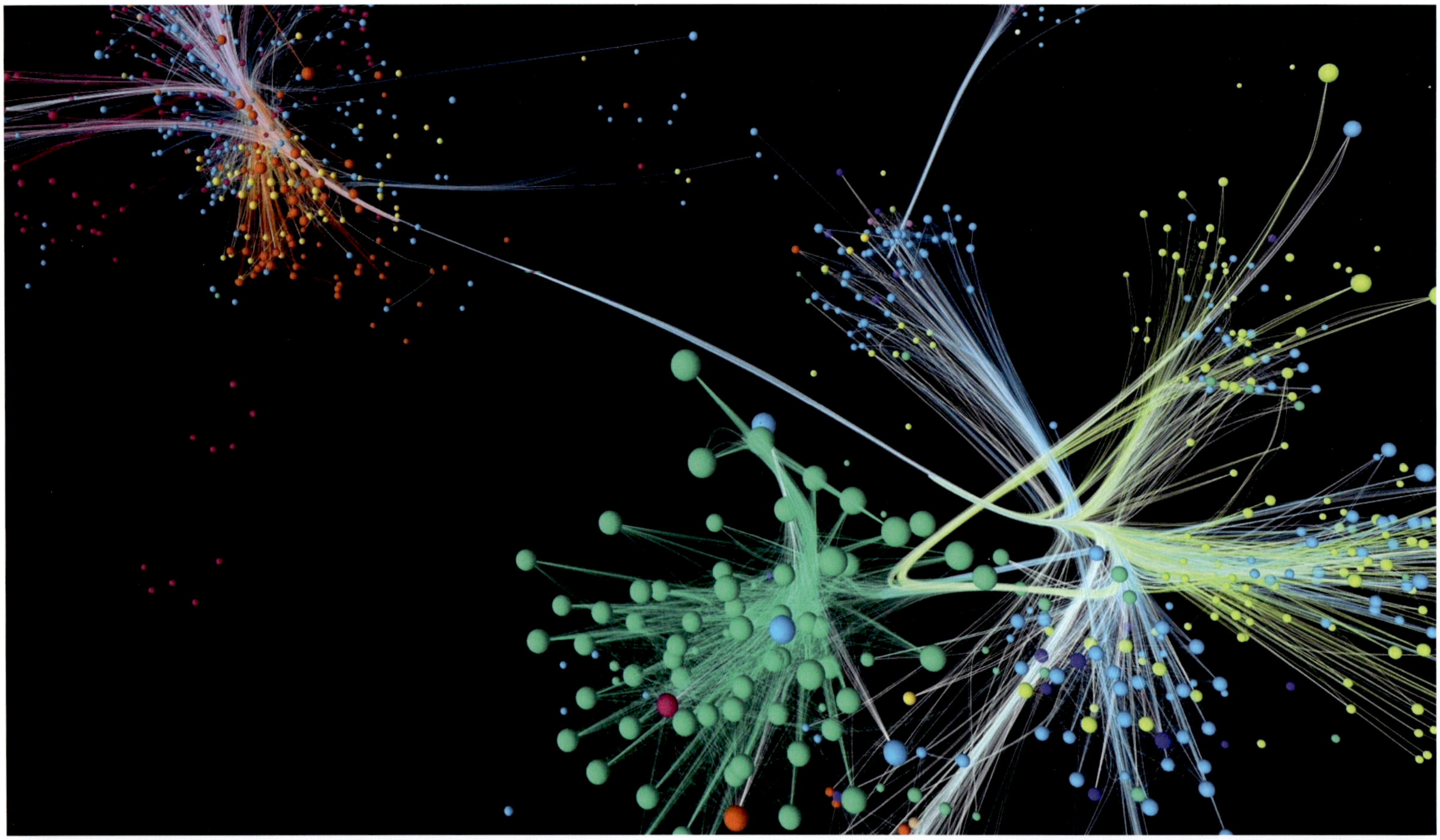

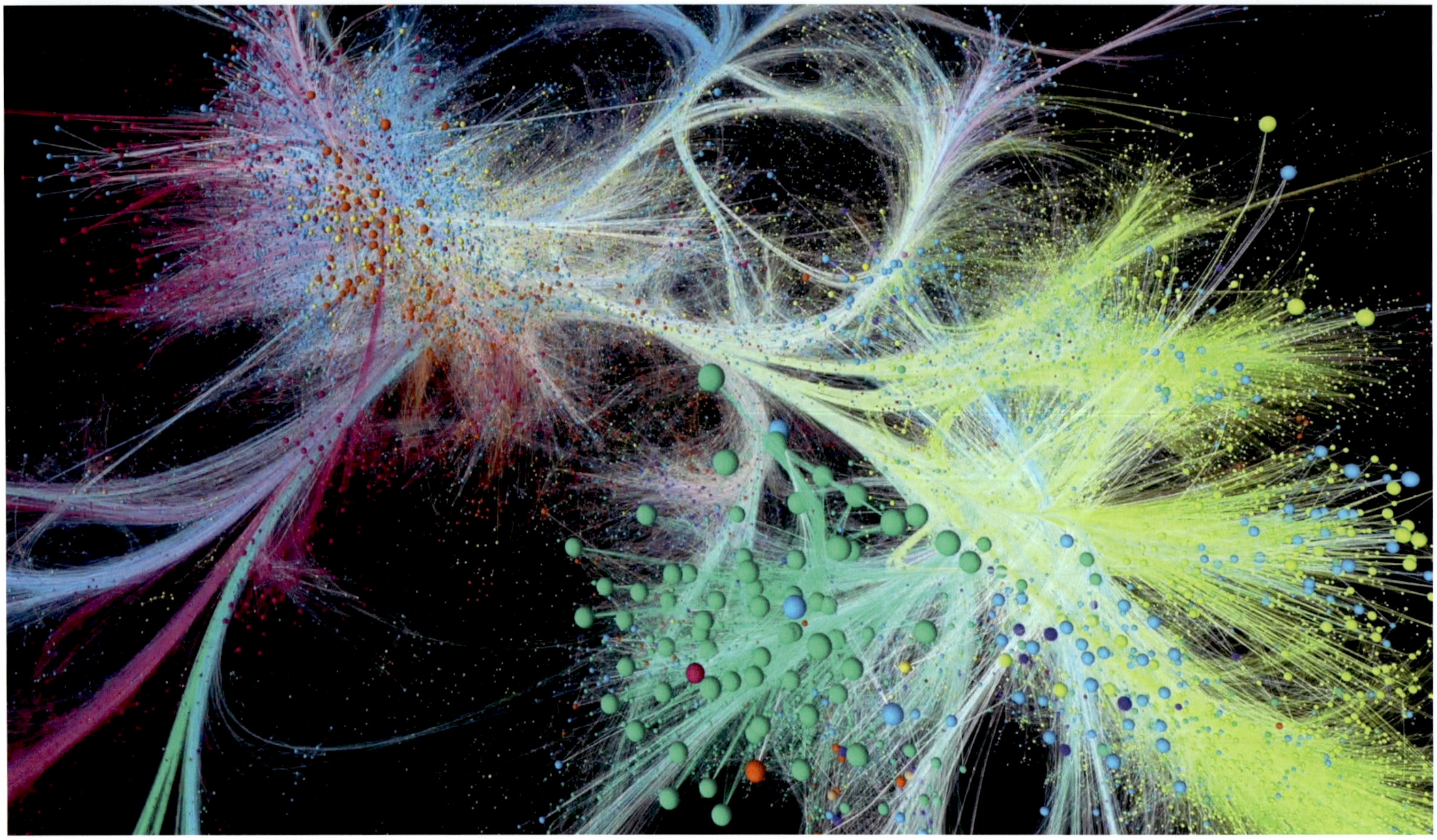

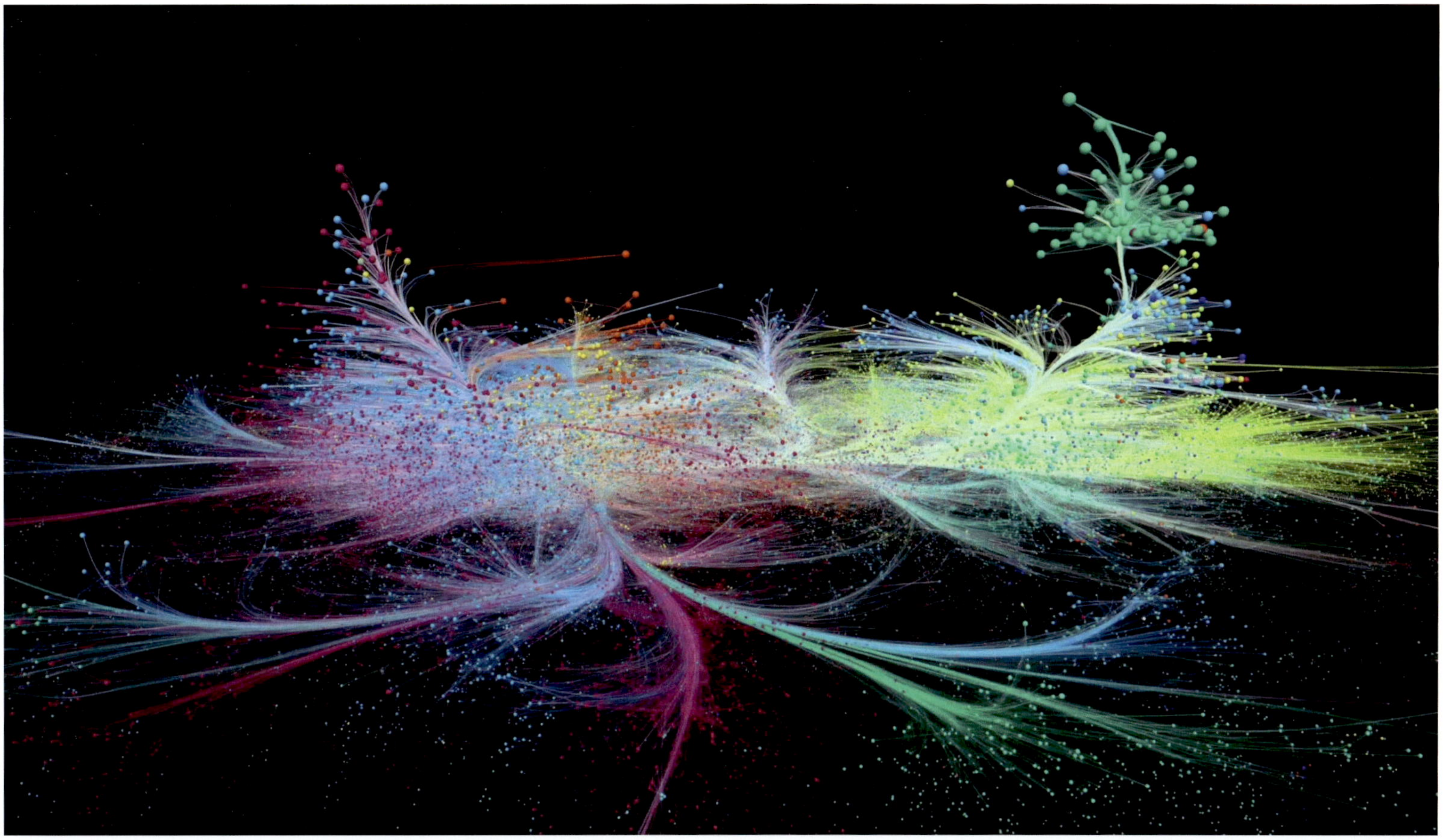

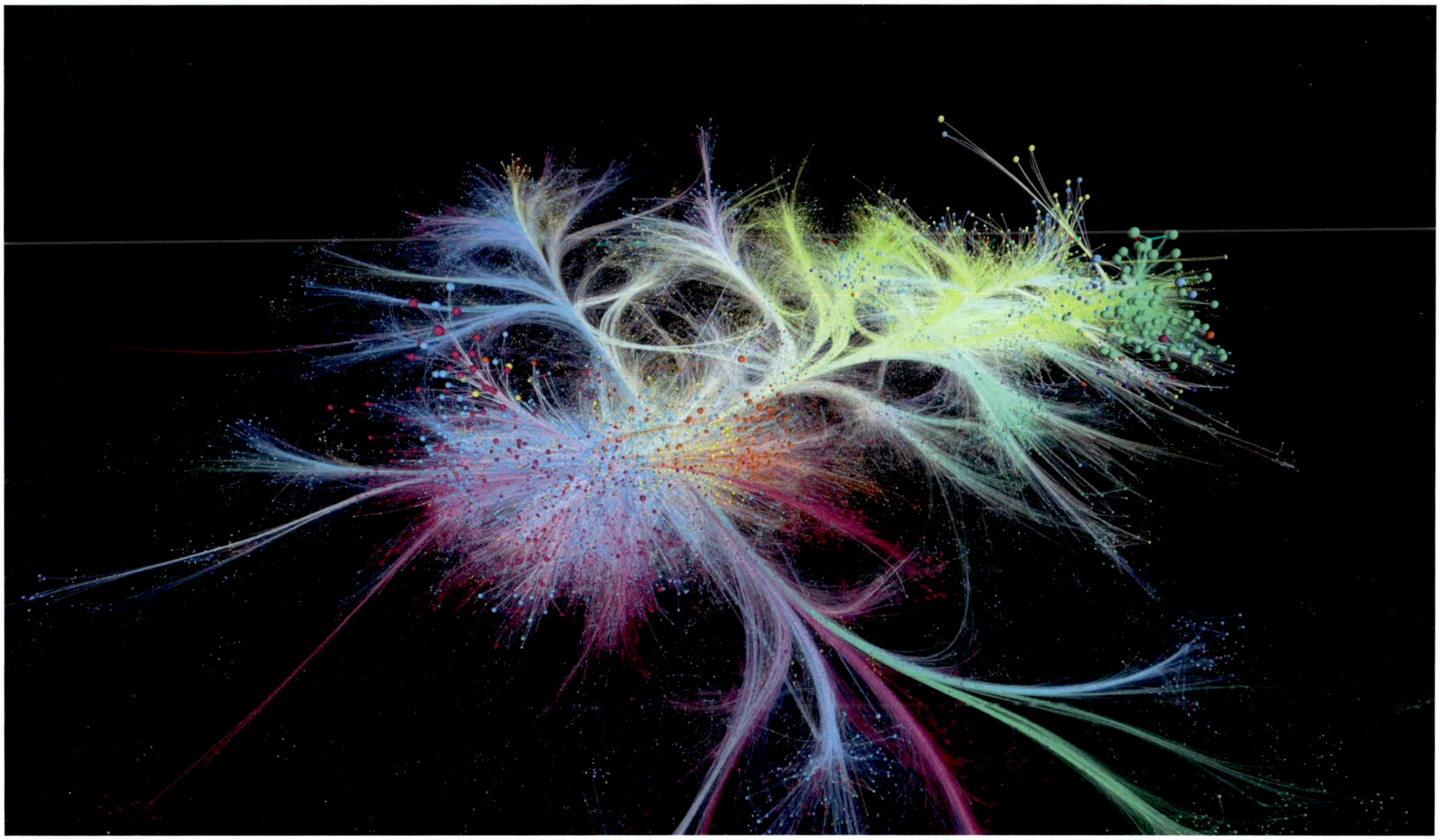

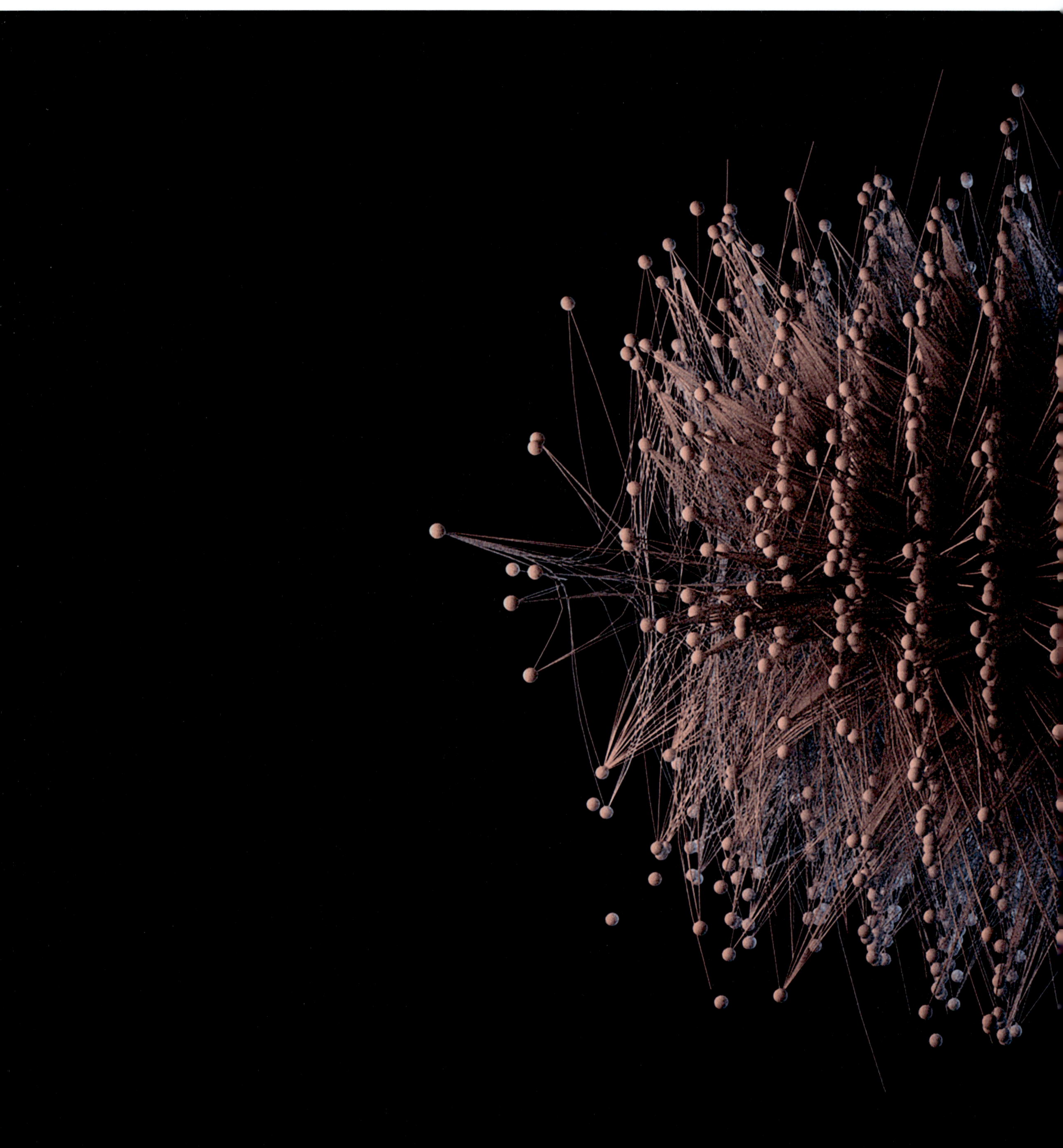

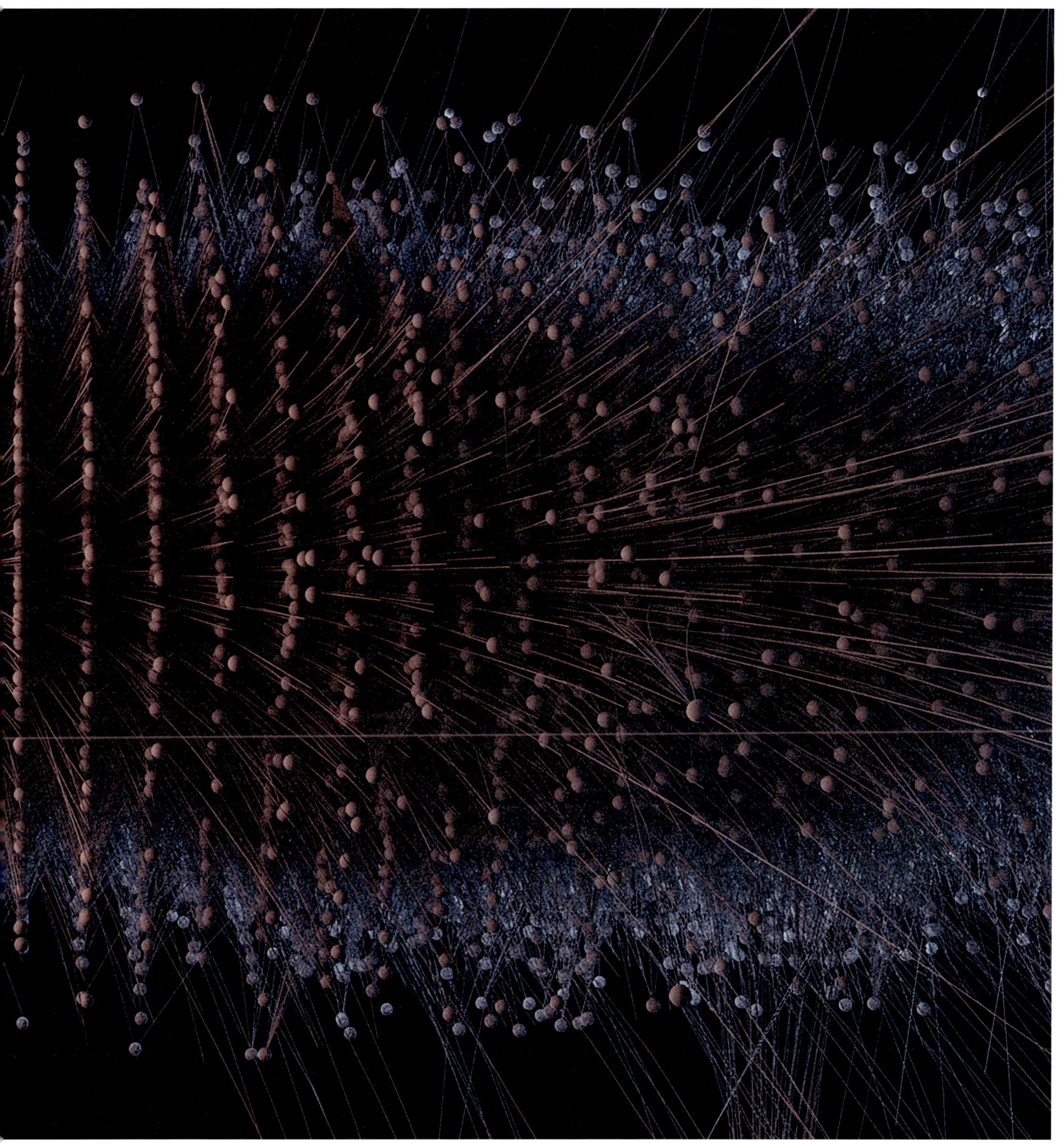

HEAT, 2019–20

The physicality of a network often forces its links to deviate from a straight line as they struggle to find a path to their destination. The need to quantify these deviations inspired the BarabásiLab's development of the "network temperature" concept. Just as air temperature captures the randomness of the air's molecular trajectories in the gas, the temperature of a network describes the degree to which individual links wander in space. A zero-temperature network has only straight links. The links of a "hot network," by contrast, swerve and curve as they reach their destination. The image opposite shows a "hot lattice," the temperature of which increases toward the center of the plane. The plates on pages 174 and 175 show projections of three-dimensional cubic lattices, whose temperature is elevated at the center of the network. Page 176 shows renderings of what happens to networks when the temperature of all its links is increased. While these hot networks were intended to exist as data sculptures, many could not yet be printed with the spatial resolution offered by existing 3-D-printing technologies. The plate on page 177 shows the hot network the BarabásiLab printed successfully.

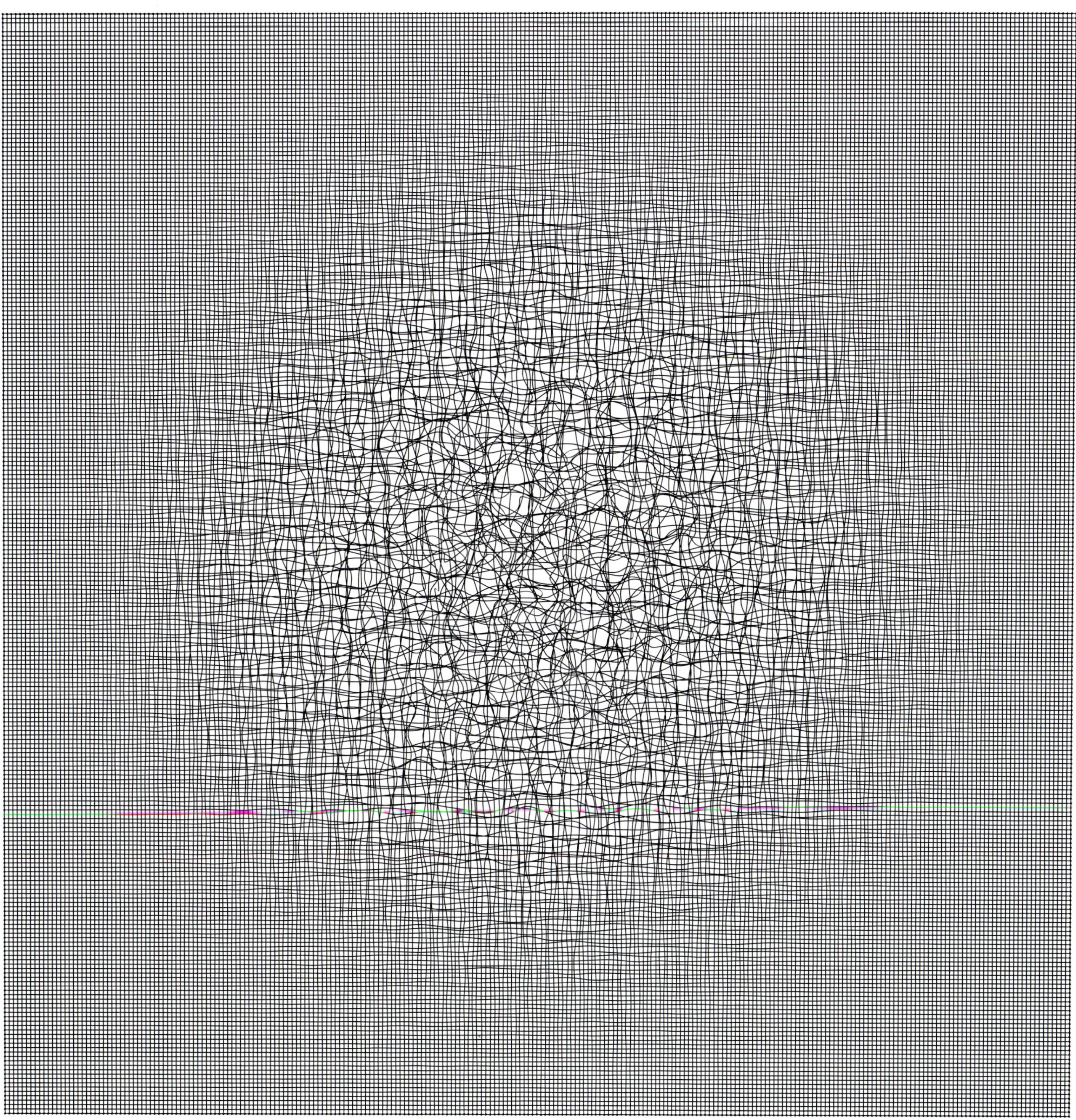

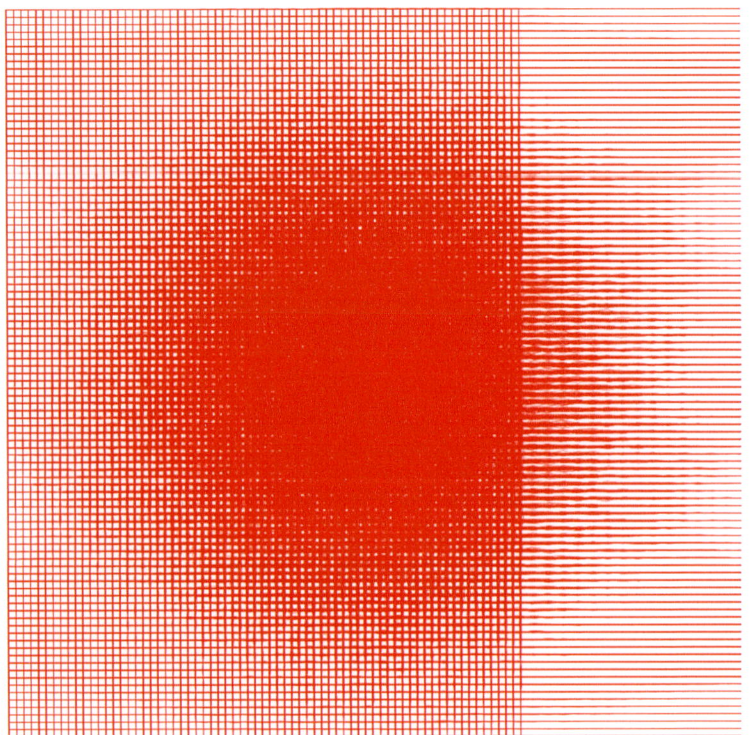

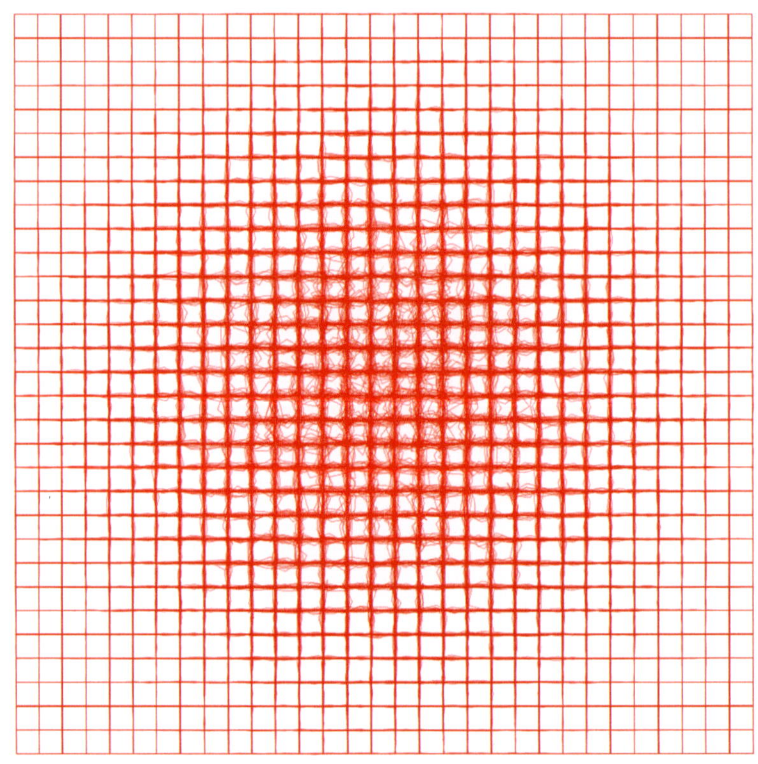

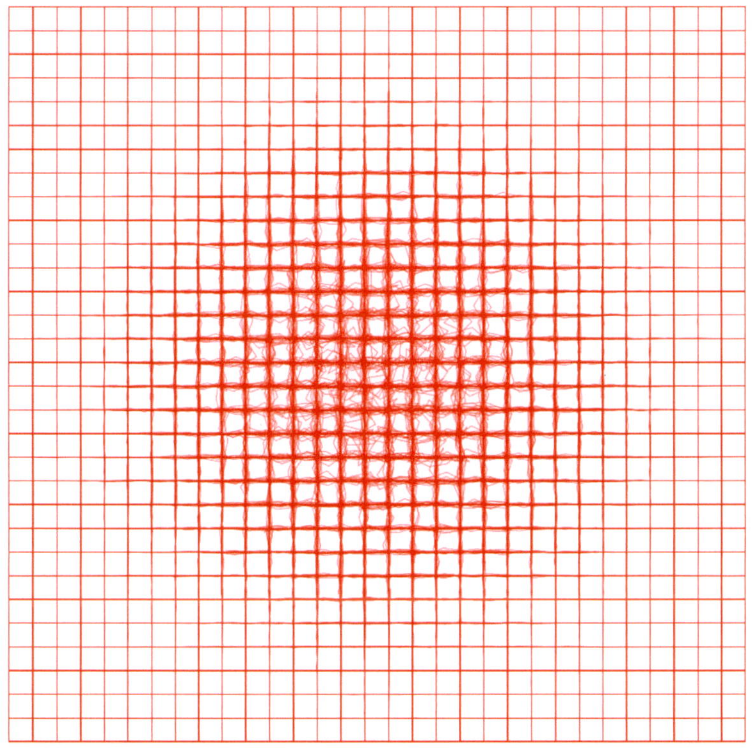

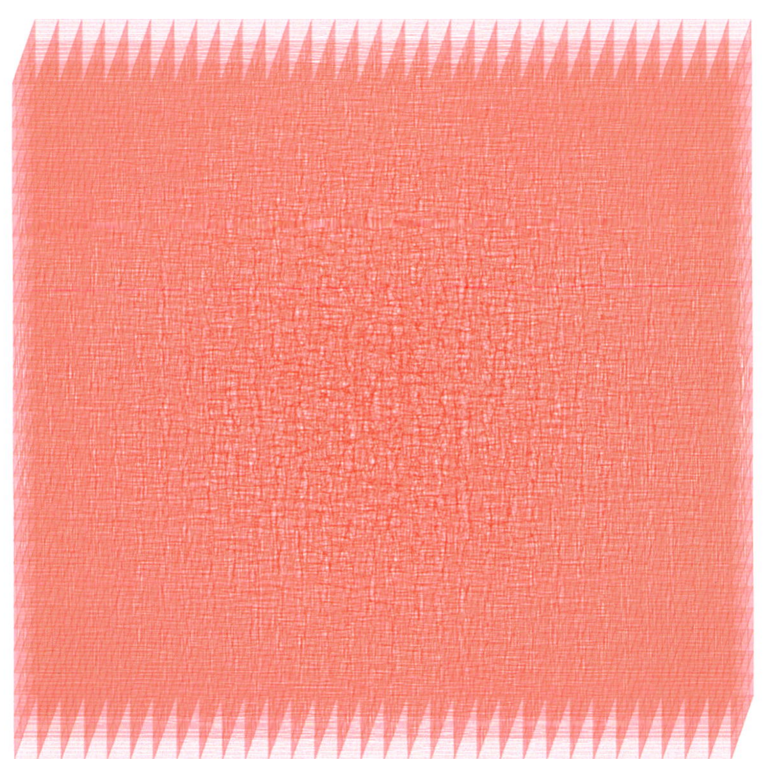

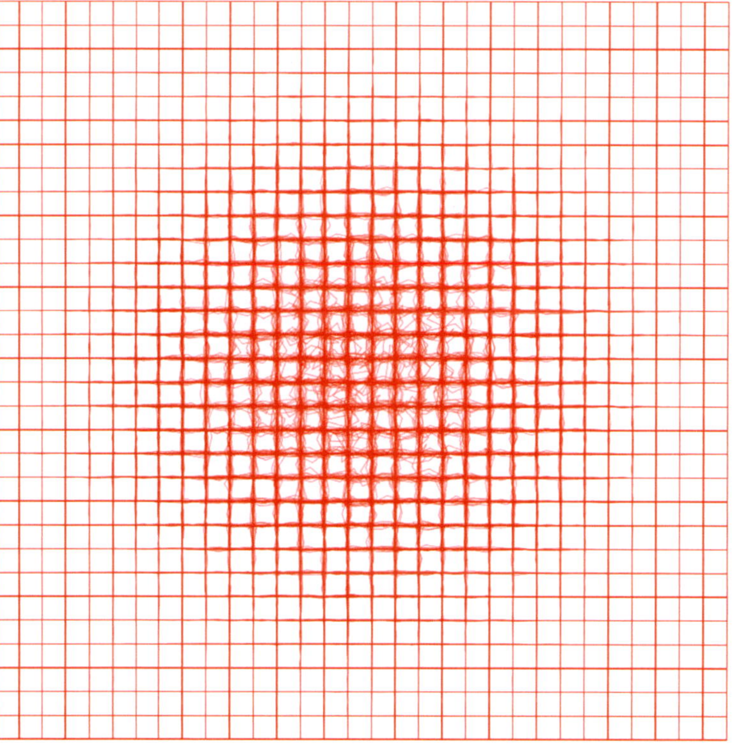

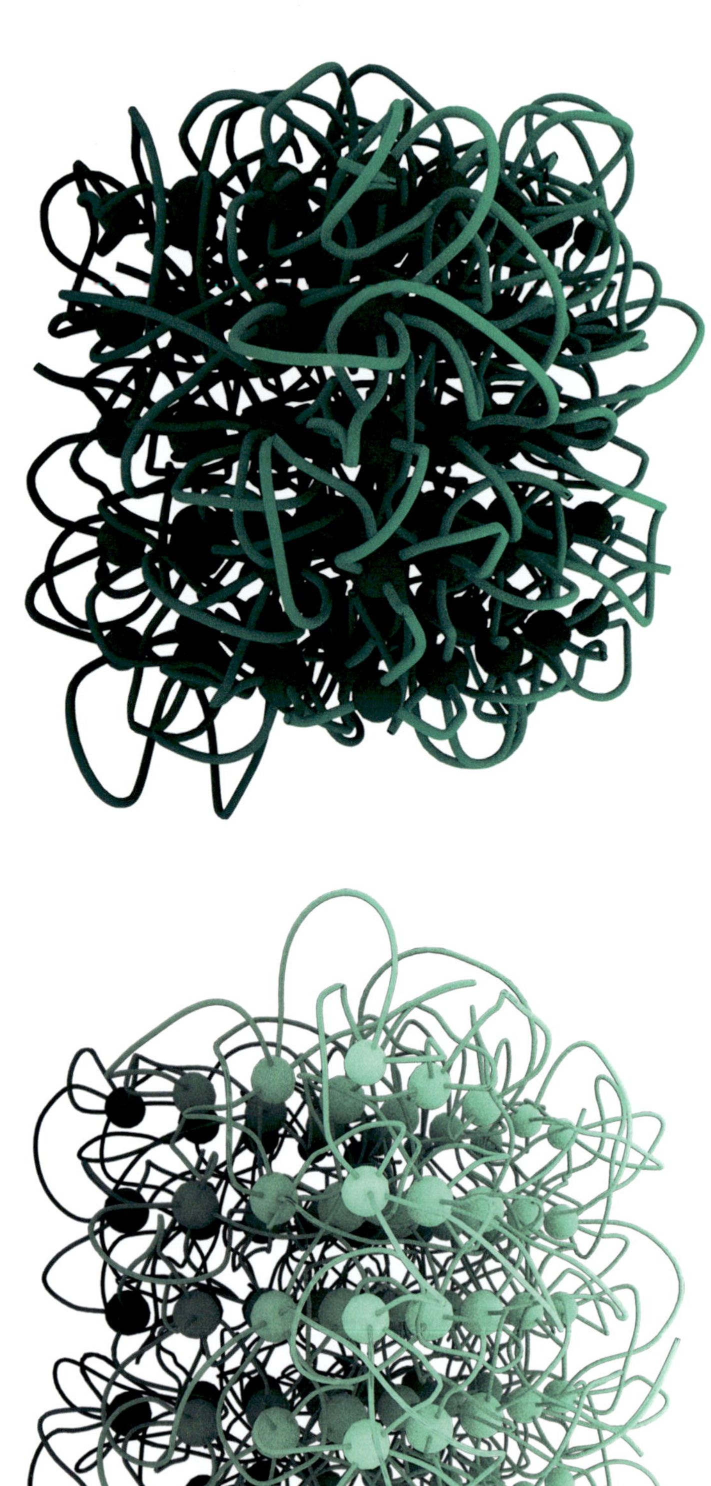

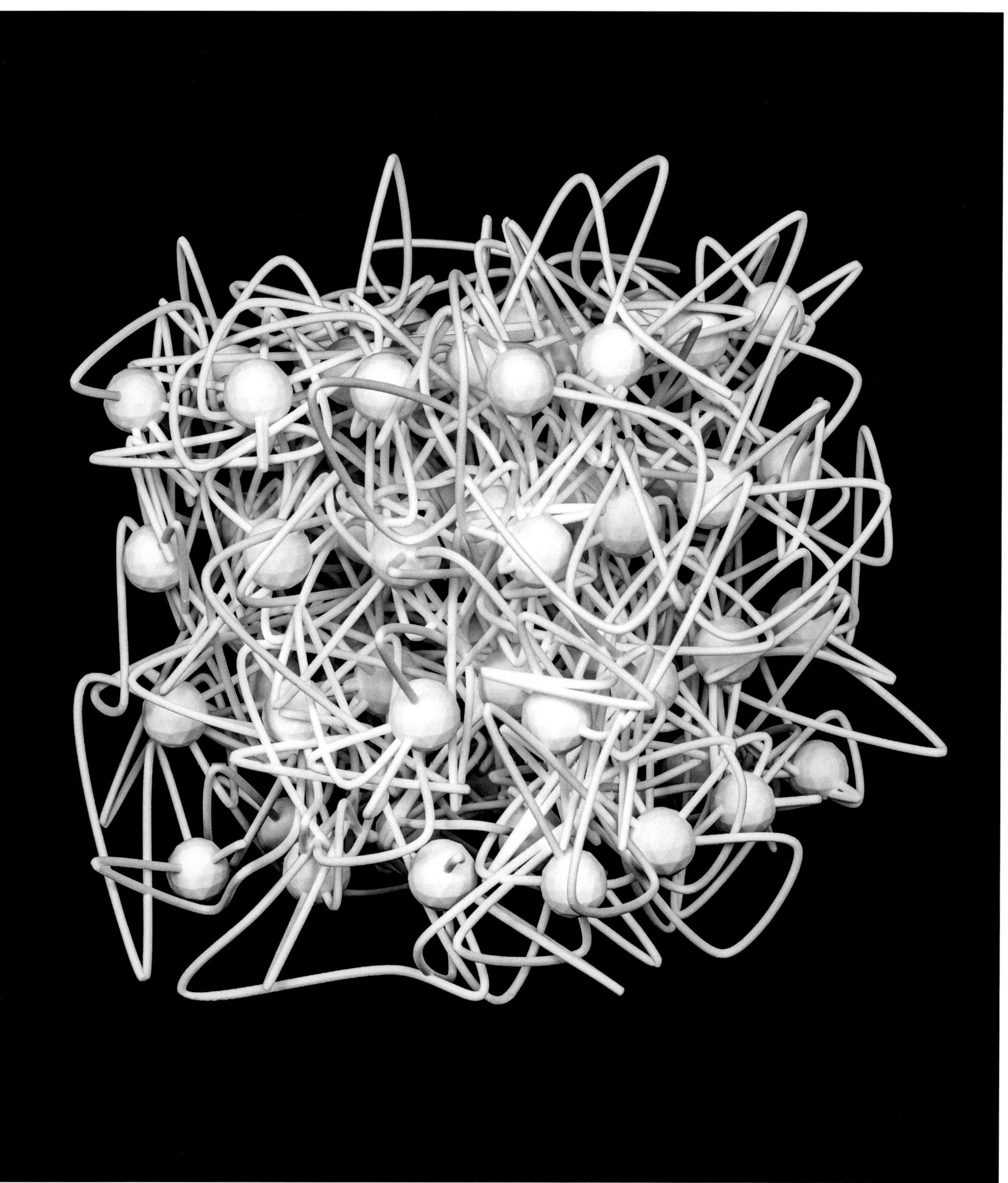

MUSEUM GOVERNANCE, 2019–20

The Art Board project is a data-driven look at the governance of art institutions. Who should sit on a museum board has become an increasingly complicated issue in the art world, as long-standing conversations about wealth concentration and influence in patronage have become focused on the hot-button topics of gender and racial equity, and of whether donors with problematic sources of wealth should have a seat at the table. To look at who is currently controlling our art institutions, the BarabásiLab obtained the tax forms filed by all US nonprofits, which enabled it to identify the board members active in the art space. By ascertaining which board members sit on multiple boards, the team was able to turn the data into a map that charts the joint governance of seemingly independent institutions. The plate on pages 180–81 shows the labeled map, the nodes of which are art institutions and the links the individuals who sit on their boards. The visualization illustrates that a few individuals who sit on multiple boards play outsize roles in the insular world of high-profile art. The data sculpture of this network, opposite, which displays the same information while obscuring the identity of institutions and board members, reinforces the role of connectedness of the art ecosystem. *The Art Board* is an ongoing project and just one of the many ways the BarabásiLab is continuing to quantify the forces that shape the art world.

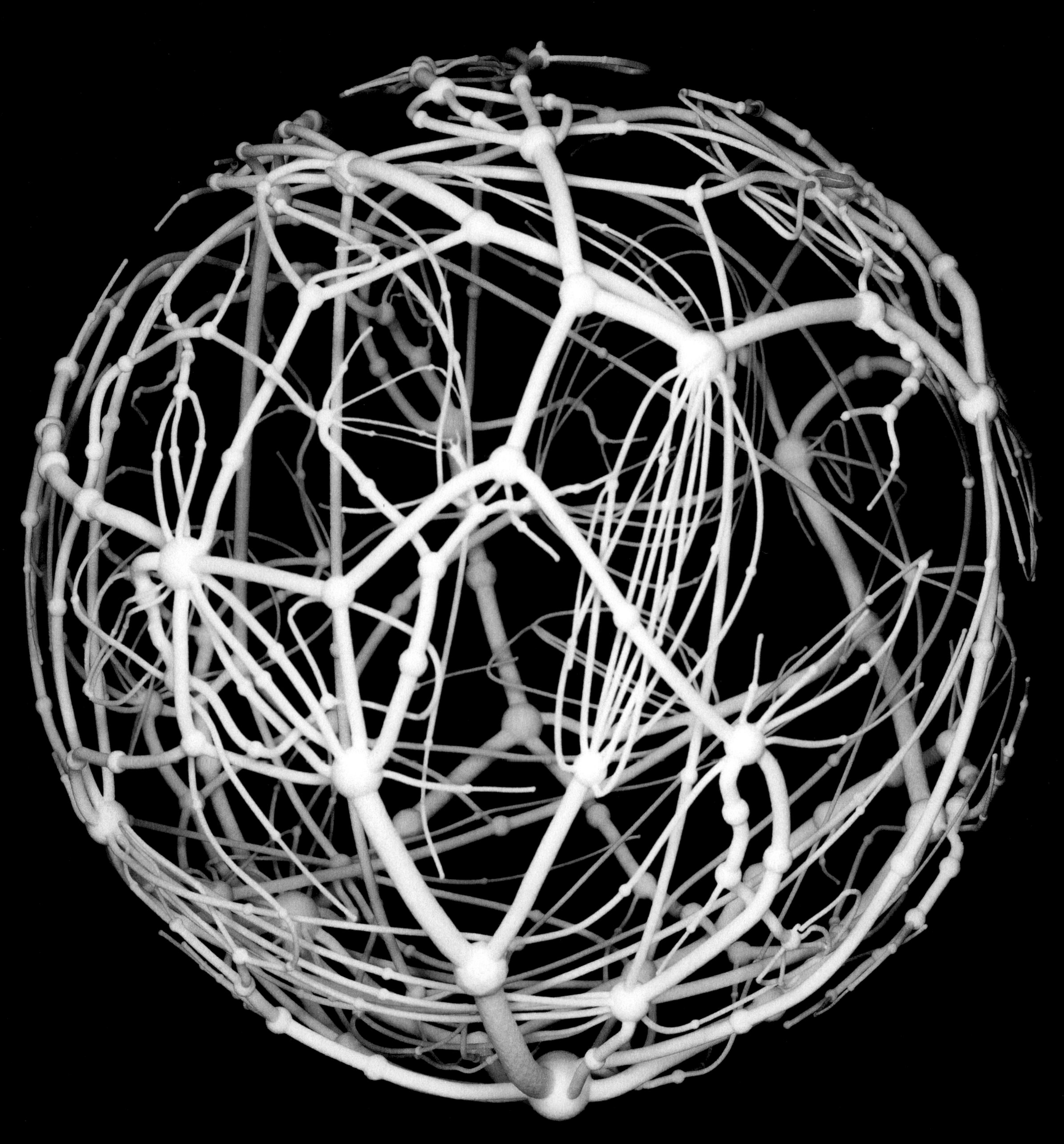

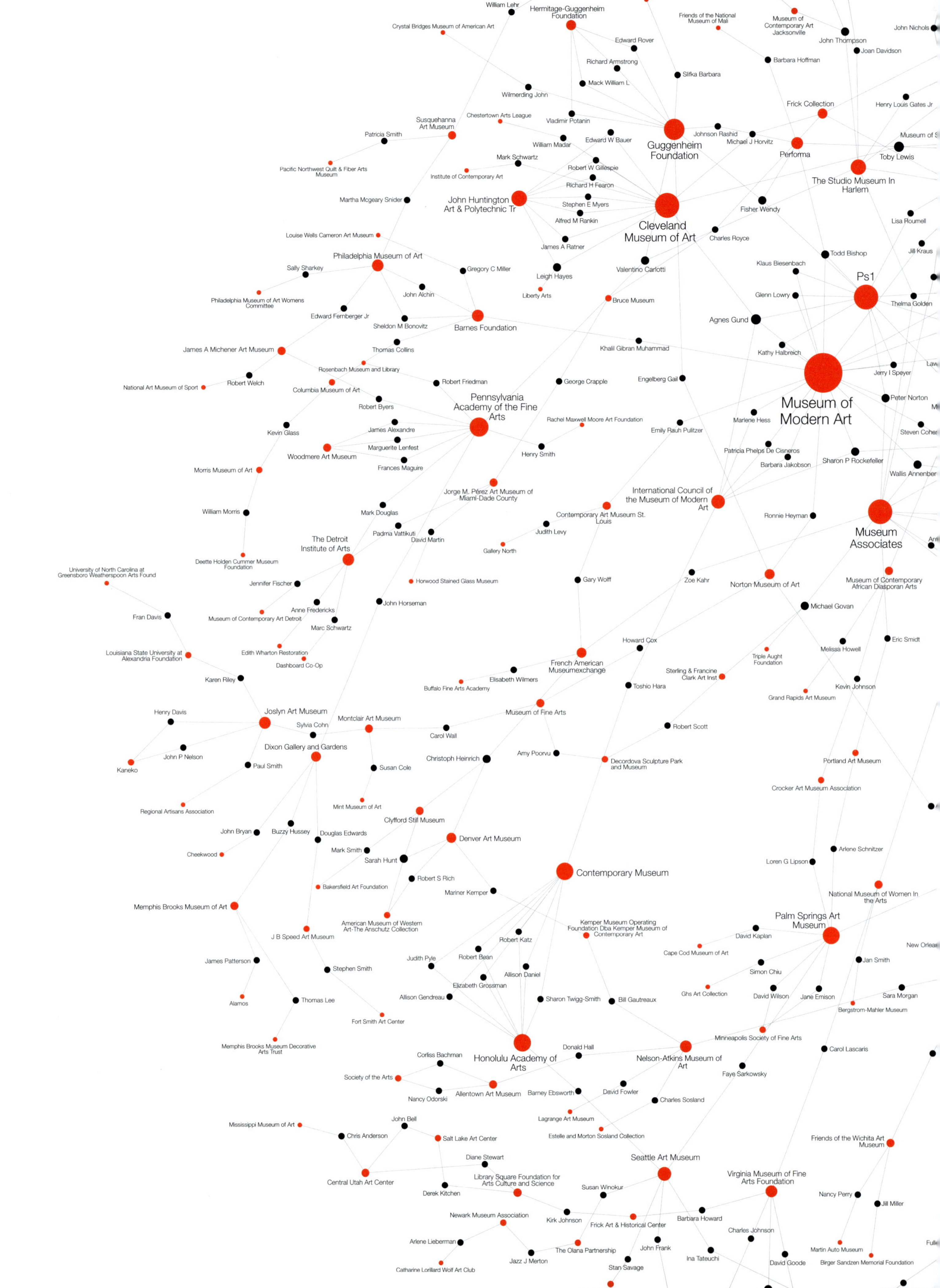

William Lehr
Hermitage-Guggenheim Foundation
Crystal Bridges Museum of American Art
Friends of the National Museum of Mall
Museum of Contemporary Art Jacksonville
John Nichols
John Thompson
Joan Davidson
Edward Rover
Richard Armstrong
Barbara Hoffman
Mack William L
Slifka Barbara
Wilmerding John
Frick Collection
Henry Louis Gates Jr
Susquehanna Art Museum
Chestertown Arts League
Vladimir Potanin
Patricia Smith
Johnson Rashid
Michael J Horvitz
William Madar
Edward W Bauer
Guggenheim Foundation
Performa
Toby Lewis
Mark Schwartz
Robert W Gillespie
The Studio Museum In Harlem
Pacific Northwest Quilt & Fiber Arts Museum
Institute of Contemporary Art
Richard H Fearon
Martha Mcgeary Snider
John Huntington Art & Polytechnic Tr
Stephen E Myers
Cleveland Museum of Art
Fisher Wendy
Alfred M Rankin
Lisa Roumell
Louise Wells Cameron Art Museum
Charles Royce
James A Ratner
Jill Kraus
Todd Bishop
Philadelphia Museum of Art
Klaus Biesenbach
Sally Sharkey
Gregory C Miller
Leigh Hayes
Valentino Carlotti
Ps1
John Alchin
Liberty Arts
Glenn Lowry
Thelma Golden
Philadelphia Museum of Art Womens Committee
Bruce Museum
Edward Fernberger Jr
Agnes Gund
Sheldon M Bonovitz
Barnes Foundation
Khalil Gibran Muhammad
Kathy Halbreich
James A Michener Art Museum
Thomas Collins
Rosenbach Museum and Library
Jerry I Speyer
Robert Welch
Robert Friedman
George Crapple
Engelberg Gail
National Art Museum of Sport
Columbia Museum of Art
Peter Norton
Pennsylvania Academy of the Fine Arts
Robert Byers
Museum of Modern Art
Rachel Maxwell Moore Art Foundation
Kevin Glass
Marlene Hess
James Alexandre
Emily Rauh Pulitzer
Steven Cohen
Marguerite Lenfest
Woodmere Art Museum
Henry Smith
Patricia Phelps De Cisneros
Sharon P Rockefeller
Frances Maguire
Barbara Jakobson
Wallis Annenberg
Morris Museum of Art
Jorge M. Pérez Art Museum of Miami-Dade County
International Council of the Museum of Modern Art
William Morris
Mark Douglas
Contemporary Art Museum St. Louis
Ronnie Heyman
Padma Vattikuti
Judith Levy
Museum Associates
The Detroit Institute of Arts
David Martin
Gallery North
Deette Holden Cummer Museum Foundation
University of North Carolina at Greensboro Weatherspoon Arts Found
Zoe Kahr
Norton Museum of Art
Museum of Contemporary African Diasporan Arts
Jennifer Fischer
Horwood Stained Glass Museum
Gary Wolff
John Horseman
Michael Govan
Anne Fredericks
Fran Davis
Museum of Contemporary Art Detroit
Marc Schwartz
Eric Smidt
Howard Cox
Melissa Howell
Edith Wharton Restoration
Louisiana State University at Alexandria Foundation
Triple Aught Foundation
Dashboard Co-Op
French American Museumexchange
Sterling & Francine Clark Art Inst
Karen Riley
Elisabeth Wilmers
Buffalo Fine Arts Academy
Toshio Hara
Kevin Johnson
Grand Rapids Art Museum
Henry Davis
Joslyn Art Museum
Museum of Fine Arts
Montclair Art Museum
Sylvia Cohn
Robert Scott
Carol Wall
Dixon Gallery and Gardens
John P Nelson
Amy Poorvu
Christoph Heinrich
Decordova Sculpture Park and Museum
Portland Art Museum
Kaneko
Paul Smith
Susan Cole
Crocker Art Museum Association
Regional Artisans Association
Mint Museum of Art
Clyfford Still Museum
John Bryan
Buzzy Hussey
Douglas Edwards
Denver Art Museum
Arlene Schnitzer
Cheekwood
Mark Smith
Sarah Hunt
Loren G Lipson
Contemporary Museum
Robert S Rich
Bakersfield Art Foundation
Mariner Kemper
National Museum of Women In the Arts
Memphis Brooks Museum of Art
American Museum of Western Art-The Anschutz Collection
Kemper Museum Operating Foundation Dba Kemper Museum of Contemporary Art
Palm Springs Art Museum
J B Speed Art Museum
Robert Katz
David Kaplan
Cape Cod Museum of Art
James Patterson
Judith Pyle
Robert Bean
Jan Smith
Stephen Smith
Allison Daniel
Simon Chiu
Elizabeth Grossman
Alamos
Thomas Lee
Allison Gendreau
Sharon Twigg-Smith
Bill Gautreaux
Ghs Art Collection
David Wilson
Jane Emison
Sara Morgan
Bergstrom-Mahler Museum
Fort Smith Art Center
Minneapolis Society of Fine Arts
Memphis Brooks Museum Decorative Arts Trust
Corliss Bachman
Honolulu Academy of Arts
Donald Hall
Nelson-Atkins Museum of Art
Carol Lascaris
Faye Sarkowsky
Society of the Arts
Nancy Odorski
Allentown Art Museum
Barney Ebsworth
David Fowler
Charles Sosland
Lagrange Art Museum
John Bell
Mississippi Museum of Art
Chris Anderson
Salt Lake Art Center
Estelle and Morton Sosland Collection
Friends of the Wichita Art Museum
Diane Stewart
Seattle Art Museum
Central Utah Art Center
Library Square Foundation for Arts Culture and Science
Virginia Museum of Fine Arts Foundation
Derek Kitchen
Susan Winokur
Nancy Perry
Jill Miller
Newark Museum Association
Kirk Johnson
Frick Art & Historical Center
Barbara Howard
Charles Johnson
Arlene Lieberman
The Olana Partnership
John Frank
Martin Auto Museum
Jazz J Merton
Stan Savage
Ina Tateuchi
David Goode
Birger Sandzen Memorial Foundation
Catharine Lorillard Wolf Art Club

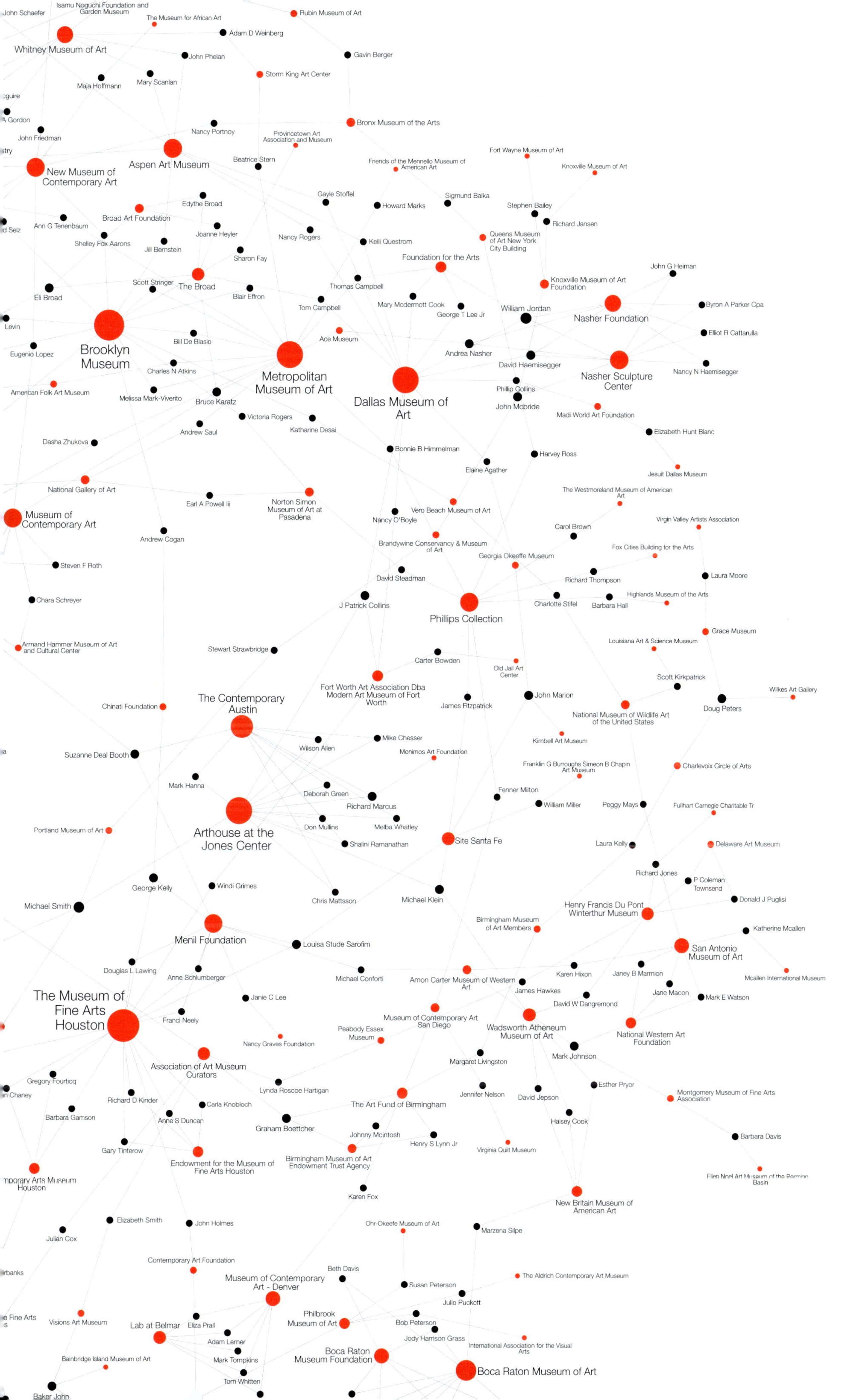

John Schaefer
Isamu Noguchi Foundation and Garden Museum
The Museum for African Art
Rubin Museum of Art
Adam D Weinberg
Whitney Museum of Art
John Phelan
Gavin Berger
Maja Hoffmann
Mary Scanlan
Storm King Art Center
John Friedman
Nancy Portnoy
Bronx Museum of the Arts
Provincetown Art Association and Museum
Aspen Art Museum
Beatrice Stern
New Museum of Contemporary Art
Fort Wayne Museum of Art
Friends of the Mennello Museum of American Art
Knoxville Museum of Art
Gayle Stoffel
Sigmund Balka
Edythe Broad
Howard Marks
Stephen Bailey
Broad Art Foundation
Ann G Tenenbaum
Joanne Heyler
Nancy Rogers
Richard Jansen
Kelli Questrom
Queens Museum of Art New York City Building
Shelley Fox Aarons
Jill Bernstein
Sharon Fay
Foundation for the Arts
John G Heiman
Scott Stringer
The Broad
Thomas Campbell
Knoxville Museum of Art Foundation
Eli Broad
Blair Effron
Tom Campbell
Mary Mcdermott Cook
George T Lee Jr
William Jordan
Nasher Foundation
Byron A Parker Cpa
Brooklyn Museum
Ace Museum
Bill De Blasio
Elliot R Cattarulla
Andrea Nasher
Eugenio Lopez
Charles N Atkins
Metropolitan Museum of Art
David Haemisegger
Nasher Sculpture Center
Nancy N Haemisegger
Dallas Museum of Art
Phillip Collins
American Folk Art Museum
Melissa Mark-Viverito
Bruce Karatz
John Mcbride
Madi World Art Foundation
Victoria Rogers
Katharine Desai
Elizabeth Hunt Blanc
Andrew Saul
Dasha Zhukova
Bonnie B Himmelman
Harvey Ross
Elaine Agather
Jesuit Dallas Museum
National Gallery of Art
The Westmoreland Museum of American Art
Earl A Powell Iii
Norton Simon Museum of Art at Pasadena
Vero Beach Museum of Art
Nancy O'Boyle
Museum of Contemporary Art
Virgin Valley Artists Association
Carol Brown
Andrew Cogan
Brandywine Conservancy & Museum of Art
Fox Cities Building for the Arts
Georgia Okeeffe Museum
Steven F Roth
David Steadman
Richard Thompson
Laura Moore
Highlands Museum of the Arts
Chara Schreyer
J Patrick Collins
Charlotte Stifel
Barbara Hall
Phillips Collection
Grace Museum
Armand Hammer Museum of Art and Cultural Center
Stewart Strawbridge
Louisiana Art & Science Museum
Carter Bowden
Old Jail Art Center
Scott Kirkpatrick
Fort Worth Art Association Dba Modern Art Museum of Fort Worth
Wilkes Art Gallery
The Contemporary Austin
John Marion
Doug Peters
James Fitzpatrick
Chinati Foundation
National Museum of Wildlife Art of the United States
Mike Chesser
Wilson Allen
Kimbell Art Museum
Suzanne Deal Booth
Monimos Art Foundation
Franklin G Burroughs Simeon B Chapin Art Museum
Charlevoix Circle of Arts
Mark Hanna
Fenner Milton
Deborah Green
Richard Marcus
William Miller
Peggy Mays
Fullhart Carnegie Charitable Tr
Arthouse at the Jones Center
Don Mullins
Melba Whatley
Site Santa Fe
Laura Kelly
Delaware Art Museum
Shalini Ramanathan
Portland Museum of Art
Richard Jones
P Coleman Townsend
George Kelly
Windi Grimes
Chris Mattsson
Michael Klein
Donald J Puglisi
Michael Smith
Henry Francis Du Pont Winterthur Museum
Birmingham Museum of Art Members
Katherine Mcallen
Menil Foundation
Louisa Stude Sarofim
San Antonio Museum of Art
Douglas L Lawing
Anne Schlumberger
Michael Conforti
Amon Carter Museum of Western Art
Karen Hixon
Janey B Marmion
Mcallen International Museum
James Hawkes
Jane Macon
Janie C Lee
Mark E Watson
The Museum of Fine Arts Houston
David W Dangremond
Franci Neely
Museum of Contemporary Art San Diego
Peabody Essex Museum
Wadsworth Atheneum Museum of Art
National Western Art Foundation
Nancy Graves Foundation
Mark Johnson
Association of Art Museum Curators
Margaret Livingston
Gregory Fourticq
Lynda Roscoe Hartigan
Esther Pryor
Richard D Kinder
Jennifer Nelson
David Jepson
Montgomery Museum of Fine Arts Association
Carla Knobloch
The Art Fund of Birmingham
Barbara Gamson
Anne S Duncan
Graham Boettcher
Halsey Cook
Johnny Mcintosh
Henry S Lynn Jr
Barbara Davis
Gary Tinterow
Birmingham Museum of Art Endowment Trust Agency
Virginia Quilt Museum
Endowment for the Museum of Fine Arts Houston
Ellen Noel Art Museum of the Permian Basin
Karen Fox
New Britain Museum of American Art
Elizabeth Smith
John Holmes
Ohr-Okeefe Museum of Art
Marzena Silpe
Julian Cox
Contemporary Art Foundation
Beth Davis
Museum of Contemporary Art - Denver
Susan Peterson
The Aldrich Contemporary Art Museum
Julio Puckett
Philbrook Museum of Art
Visions Art Museum
Lab at Belmar
Eliza Prall
Bob Peterson
Jody Harrison Grass
Adam Lerner
International Association for the Visual Arts
Boca Raton Museum Foundation
Bainbridge Island Museum of Art
Mark Tompkins
Boca Raton Museum of Art
Tom Whitten
Baker John

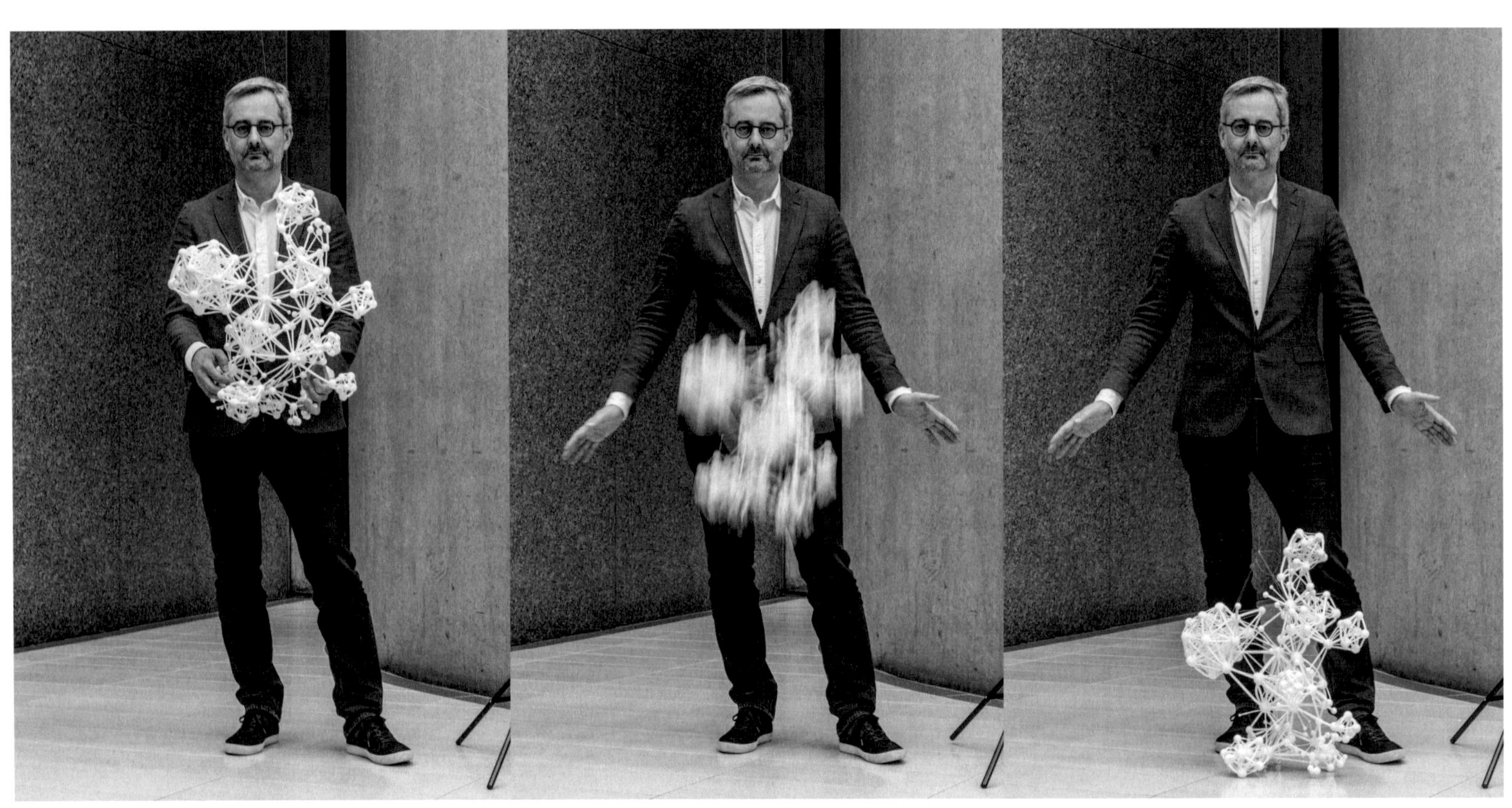

ABOUT ALBERT-LÁSZLÓ BARABÁSI

ALBERT-LÁSZLÓ BARABÁSI (b. 1967), a Romanian-born Hungarian-American physicist, is the Robert Gray Dodge Professor of Network Science, a Distinguished University Professor of Physics, and the director of the Center for Complex Network Research at Northeastern University. He also holds an appointment in the Department of Medicine at Harvard University and runs a European Research Council project at Central European University, in Budapest, Hungary.

In 1999, Barabási changed the course of modern science with his discovery of scale-free networks. Having mapped the World Wide Web, Barabási found—contrary to the mainstream thinking about network theory in mathematics—that network growth is not random but certain nodes within a network are more vital than others, and, most importantly, that it is possible to determine which hubs are crucial to the health of a network. With subsequent studies, Barabási would go on to prove that nearly all real networks follow his scale-free model.

The Center for Complex Network Research (CCNR) at Northeastern University, known as the BarabásiLab, which Barabási established in 2007, is a thirty-person lab dedicated to a deeper understanding of networks—how they emerge and evolve, what they look like, and how they impact our understanding of complex systems. CCNR's research spans a wide range of subjects, from protein interactions within a cell to how distant galaxies interact in the cosmic web to what blend of access and performance leads to success in art.

In addition to his theoretical breakthroughs in network science, Barabási and his lab are renowned for producing highly creative visualizations that depict the research findings in often colorful 2-D and 3-D models. Since 1995, when he presented a paper that included illustrations of an invasion network, Barabási has made the high-definition and highly interpretive visualization of his research central to his work. Examples of his visualizations have been shown at the Serpentine Gallery in London and the Cooper Hewitt, Smithsonian Design Museum in New York City.

Barabási is the recipient of the 2018 Moholy-Nagy Prize, for his humanistic approach to technology, and of numerous science awards, including Italy's Lagrange-CRT Foundation Prize for outstanding interdisciplinary research, and the US National Academy of Sciences's Cozzarelli Prize for papers that reflect scientific excellence and originality. He has written several popular books—*The Formula* (2018), *Bursts* (2010), and *Linked* (2002)—and is the author of the award-winning textbooks *Network Science* (2016) and *Fractal Concepts in Surface Growth* (1995). Additionally, Barabási co-edited *Network Medicine* (2017) and *The Structure and Dynamics of Networks* (2006). His books have been translated into more than twenty languages.

Barabási has been a member of the World Economic Forum's Global Agenda Council on Complex Networks since 2012, and is a frequent speaker at the organization's annual meeting in Davos, Switzerland. His 2019 TEDx Talk, "The Real Relationship Between Your Age and Your Chance of Success," has had more than 1.3 million views.

He lives in Brookline, Massachusetts, and Budapest, Hungary, with his wife and three children.

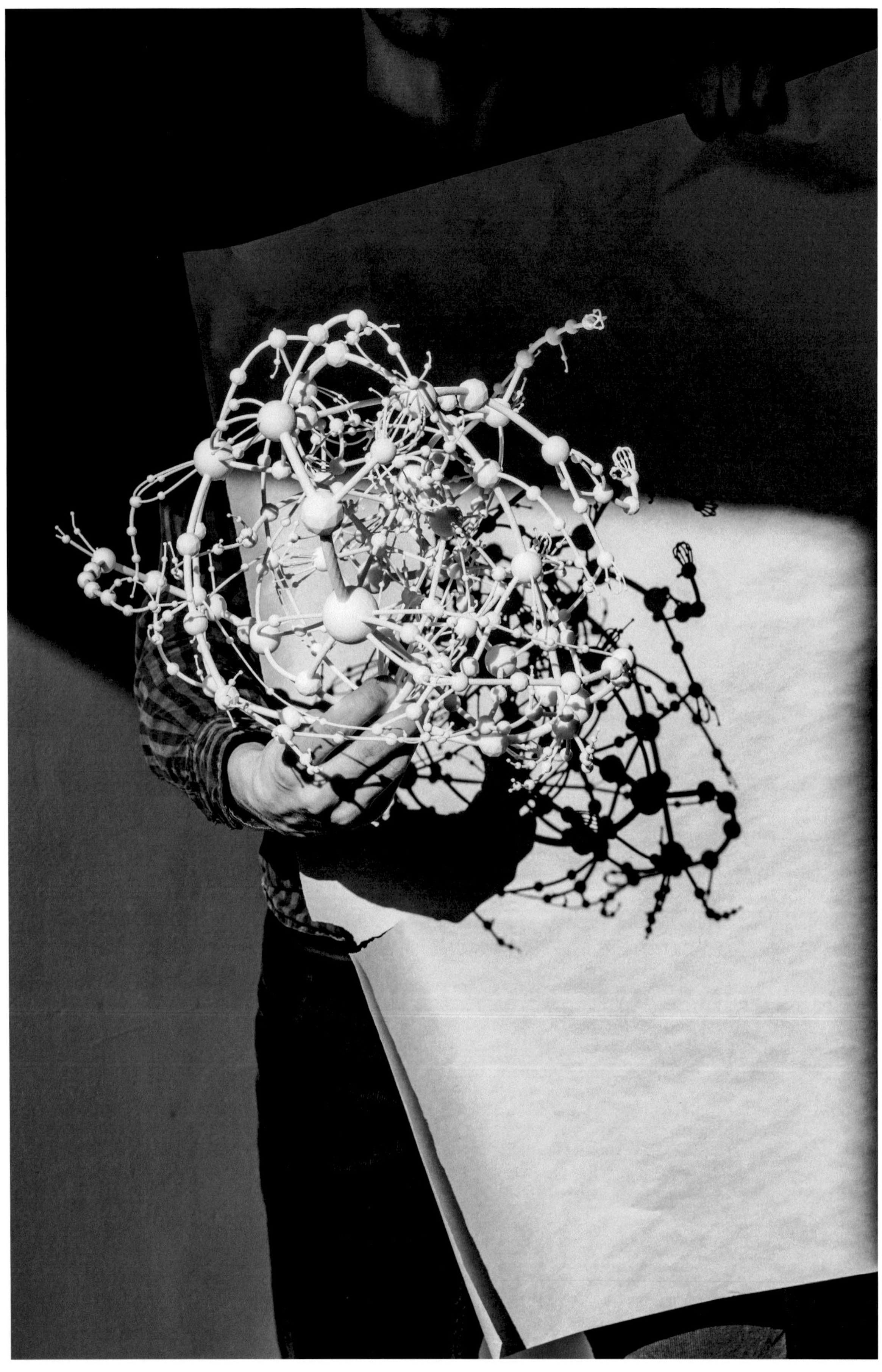

CONTRIBUTORS

MÓNICA BELLO is a curator and art historian who works internationally, organizing projects and events that examine the way artists instigate new conversations around the role of science and technology and its impact in society. In 2015, Bello became the first-ever head of Arts at the European Organization for Nuclear Research (CERN), in Geneva, where she has focused on promoting a dialogue between the arts and particle physics. In addition to fostering the creation of new expert knowledge in the arts by extending artists' practice in connection with fundamental research, she has strengthened synergies between the laboratory and international cultural organizations by supporting numerous artist residencies, art commissions, and the involvement of scientists in art initiatives. Between 2010 and 2015, Bello was artistic director of the VIDA Art and Artificial Life International Awards, which were founded by Fundación Telefónica in Madrid to foster cross-cultural expressions around the notion of life. Previously, she established and ran the Department of Education at LaBoral Centro de Arte y Creación Industrial, in Gijón, Spain; and Capsula, a curatorial platform that focused on intersections of art, science, and nature. In 2003, Bello received the Inéditos emergent curators award at La Casa Encendida, Madrid.

Art historian JULIA FABÉNYI has been director of the Ludwig Museum in Budapest since 2013. After earning a PhD in art history and archaeology from Leipzig University in Germany, Fabényi went on to teach there and in the applied-arts department at Burg Giebichenstein University of Arts and Design in Halle, Germany. In 1990, she returned to her native Hungary as curator of the Műcsarnok, Budapest's *Kunsthalle*. From 1996 to 2000, she directed the *Kunsthalle* in Szombathely, Hungary, and then she returned to the Műcsarnok as director from 2000 to 2005. Between 2006 and 2013, she directed the Janus Pannonius Museum in Pécs, Hungary. Fabényi's research focuses on the history of exhibitions and contemporary exhibition development, specifically how to integrate traditional art with culturally important non-academic art forms. She has curated more than 110 exhibitions over the course of her career, including numerous international shows. Between 2000 to 2005 and again since 2017, Fabényi has served as national commissioner for the Hungarian Pavilion at the Venice Biennale.

KATHLEEN FORDE is the inaugural curator for PaceX in New York, an initiative spearheaded by Pace Gallery dedicated to art, technology, and the meaningful presentation of experiential art. Previously, she was artistic director at large for Borusan Contemporary, a collection-based space for media-arts exhibitions and commissions in Istanbul, where she curated and toured numerous solo exhibitions and collaborated with such institutions as the San Francisco Museum of Modern Art; Espacio Fundación Telefónica Madrid; LaBoral Centro de Arte y Creación Industrial, in Gijón, Spain; and the *Kunsthalle* Darmstadt, in Darmstadt, Germany. Forde has worked as an independent curator with such institutions as the University of Michigan Museum of Art; the Frye Art Museum, in Seattle; and Audemars Piguet, on its annual art commission in collaboration with Art Basel Miami Beach. From 2005 to 2012 she served as curator of time-based visual arts at the Experimental Media and Performing Arts Center (EMPAC), in Troy, New York. In 2010, she was a fellow at the Center for Curatorial Leadership (CCL), and from 2002 to 2003 she held an Alexander von Humboldt research scholarship in Berlin. Forde earned an MA in post-1945 art and theory from Goldsmiths College, University of London.

Art historian JÓZSEF KÉSZMAN, who curated *Hidden Patterns,* is head of collection and of the exhibition department at the Ludwig Museum in Budapest. A graduate of Eötvös Lóránd University (ELTE), where he read art history and philosophy, he specializes in the phenomenological examination of contemporary art. Készman began his career at Várfok Gallery, a contemporary-art space in Budapest, where he worked from 1998 to 2002. He then went on to become chief curator of Műcsarnok, Budapest's *Kunsthalle,* between 2003 and 2014. From 2006 to 2008, he also served as Műcsarnok's deputy manager. Készman is active as an arts educator in Hungary. He has taught in the communication and media-studies program of the University of Pécs and is a former lecturer and research fellow at ELTE's visual art-program in Szombathely. He currently teaches courses in art theory at MOME, the Moholy-Nagy University of Art and Design, in Budapest. His articles on art have appeared in a variety of specialist journals, both in Hungary and internationally, including *Új Művészet, Műértő, Balkon, Artmagazin, Flash Art Hungary,* and *Spike Magazine.* Készman's numerous curatorial projects and exhibitions straddle topics in media art, art studies, and cultural anthropology.

ISABEL MEIRELLES is an information designer and educator whose intellectual curiosity lies in the relationships between visual thinking and visual representation. She is a professor in the faculty of design at Ontario College of Art and Design University (OCAD), in Toronto, and the recipient of the 2015/16 OCAD University Award for Distinguished Research, Scholarship and Creative Activity. From 2003 to 2014, she was on the faculty of Northeastern University's College of Arts, Media and Design in the department of art and design, where she helped create the MFA in information design and data visualization. In addition to writing widely on the technical problems as well as the role of data visualization in society, culture, and education, Meirelles is the author of *Design for Information:*

An Introduction to the Histories, Theories, and Best Practices Behind Effective Information Visualizations (2013). Her research focuses on the theoretical and experimental examination of the fundamentals underlying how information is structured, represented, and communicated in different media. Meirelles frequently teams up with colleagues on interdisciplinary projects involving visualization of information, and she has organized numerous conferences, initiatives, and exhibitions on the topic. In her creative practice, she collaborates with artists and curators to design print and digital publications of their work.

Budapest-based artist PETER PUKLUS studied photography at the Moholy-Nagy University of Art and Design, Budapest (MOME), and new-media design at the École nationale supérieure de création industrielle (ENSCI) in Paris. Currently enrolled in the doctoral school of MOME, Puklus produced two books of his photography in 2012, *One and a Half Meter* and *Handbook to the Stars*. In 2016, Puklus published a third photography book, *The Epic Love Story of a Warrior*, which was shortlisted for the Aperture/Paris Photo Photobook Award 2016. His recent solo exhibitions include *Life Is Techno* at Trafó Gallery, Budapest; *New Works* at Galerie Conrads, Düsseldorf; and *Unsafe to Dance* at C/O Berlin. Puklus's ongoing project, *The Hero Mother – How to Build a House*, won Images Vevey's Grand Prix Images Award for 2017/18. In addition to continuing his photographic work, Puklus has recently begun producing sculptures, objects, paintings, installations, drawings, and videos. Puklus is represented by the Glassyard Gallery in Budapest, the Robert Morat Gallery in Berlin and Hamburg, Galerie Conrads in Düsseldorf, and the Folia Gallery in Paris.

Architect and engineer CARLO RATTI, a founding partner of the international design and innovation office Carlo Ratti Associati, directs the Senseable City Lab at the Massachusetts Institute of Technology (MIT). A graduate of the Politecnico di Torino and the École nationale des ponts et chaussées, in Paris, Ratti earned his MPhil and PhD from Cambridge University. His work has been exhibited internationally, including at the Venice Biennale, the Museum of Modern Art in New York, the Science Museum in London, the Design Museum of Barcelona, and the the Shenzhen Bi-city Biennale of Urbanism\Architecture. Three of his projects—the Digital Water Pavilion, in Zaragoza, Spain; the Copenhagen Wheel; and Scribit—have been hailed by *Time* magazine as "Best Inventions of the Year." *Blueprint* magazine named Ratti among the "25 People Who Will Change the World of Design" and *Wired* magazine counted him as one of the "50 People Who Will Change the World." Ratti is currently serving as co-chair of the World Economic Forum's Global Council on the Future of Cities and Urbanization.

London-born, New York–based artist MATTHEW RITCHIE attended Boston University and received a BFA from the Camberwell College of Arts, London. Since the early 1990s, he has developed a practice drawing from the vocabularies of science, sociology, anthropology, mythology, and the history of art. In his paintings, installations, wall drawings, light boxes, sculptures, projections, artist's books, and performances, Ritchie describes the generation of systems, ideas, and their subsequent interpretations in a kind of cerebral web, concretizing ephemeral and intangible theories of information and time in a unique and recognizable gestural form that emphasizes the human trace. Ritchie's work has been shown in solo exhibitions at the Dallas Museum of Art; the Contemporary Arts Museum, Houston; Massachusetts Museum of Contemporary Art; San Francisco Museum of Modern Art; and the Museum of Contemporary Art, North Miami. It has been included in the Whitney Biennial (1997), the Sydney Biennale (2002), and the Bienal de São Paulo (2004); and is in the permanent collections of New York's Museum of Modern Art, Solomon R. Guggenheim Museum, and Whitney Museum of American Art, as well as in San Francisco's Museum of Modern Art and the MIT List Visual Arts Center in Boston, among others.

ALANNA STANG is an editor, writer, book packager, and content strategist. The cofounder of Brooklyn-based content consultancy Well Said NYC, Stang advises companies, organizations, and individuals on all aspects of content and communication. As an editorial executive for many years, she launched, revamped, and ran several magazines at Condé Nast and Martha Stewart Omnimedia, including *Whole Living, Martha Stewart Living,* and *Cookie*. Additionally, she has served as executive editor of *International Design* (*I.D.*) and *eDesign* magazines. Stang studied philosophy at Vassar College and is the co-author of two books: *The Green House: New Directions in Sustainable Architecture* (2005) and *Time for Dinner: Strategies, Inspiration, and Recipes for Family Meals Every Night of the Week* (2010).

ANDRÁS SZÁNTÓ is a Brooklyn-based cultural strategist and widely published author who advises museums, foundations, educational institutions, and corporations on cultural initiatives and program development worldwide. After studying economics in Budapest, where he was born and raised, he earned a PhD in sociology from Columbia University. His writings have appeared in the *New York Times, Artforum, Artnet,* and *The Art Newspaper,* among other publications. As a consultant, he advises some of the world's leading cultural institutions and corporate art programs. He has lectured on art business at the Sotheby's Institute of Art and directed the National Arts Journalism Program at Columbia

University. At the Metropolitan Museum of Art, he helped launch and oversee the Global Museum Leaders Colloquium, a series of ten-day seminars for international museum directors. Szántó is a frequent moderator of the Art Basel Conversations series, and he has curated exhibitions on Hungarian art of the 1960s and 70s in London and New York. His most recent book is *The Future of the Museum: 28 Dialogues* (2020).

PETER WEIBEL is chairman and CEO of ZKM | Center for Art and Media in Karlsruhe, Germany, and the director of the Peter Weibel Research Institute for Digital Cultures at the University of Applied Arts Vienna. A central figure in European media art on account of his various activities as artist, theoretician, and curator, Weibel publishes widely in the intersecting fields of art and science. His career took him from studying literature, medicine, logic, philosophy, and film in Paris and Vienna and working as an artist to head of the digital arts laboratory at the media department of the University at Buffalo in New York (1984 to 1989). Subsequently, he was founding director of the Institute for New Media at the Städelschule in Frankfurt (1989–94), professor of media theory at the University of Applied Arts Vienna (1984–2011), and artistic director of Ars Electronica in Linz, Austria (1986–95). Weibel served as artistic director of the Seville Biennial (BIACS3) in 2008 and the Moscow Biennale of Contemporary Art in 2011. He commissioned the Austrian Pavilions at the Venice Biennale from 1993 to 1999 and was chief curator of the Neue Galerie Graz between 1993 and 1998.

IMAGE CREDITS

Cover
Heat, by A.-L. Barabási, A. Grishchenko, and Y. Liu, 2020

Inside front cover
The Art Board, Version II, by A.-L. Barabási, Cs. Both, A. Grishchenko, A. Gates, and L. Shekhtman, 2019
Photographs courtesy of Peter Puklus

Pages 7, 11
Courtesy of Peter Puklus

Page 16
Fig. 1: *Invasion,* by A.-L. Barabási, a black-and-white version of which was published in "Invasion Percolation and Global Optimization," *Physical Review Letters* (May 13, 1996)

Page 18
Fig. 2: Detail of *Protein Interactions,* by A.-L. Barabási, H. Jeong, S. P. Mason, and Z. N. Oltvai, as published in "Lethality and Centrality in Protein Networks," *Nature* (May 3, 2001)

Fig. 3: Detail of *Flow,* by E. Almaas, A.-L. Barabási, B. Kovacs, Z.N. Oltvai, and T. Vicsek, as published in "Global Organization of Metabolic Fluxes in the Bacterium *Escherichia coli,*" *Nature* (February 27, 2004)

Fig. 4: Detail of *The Human Disease Network,* by A.-L. Barabási, B. Childs, M.E. Cusick, K.-I. Goh, D. Valle, and M. Vidal, created for "The Human Disease Network," *Proceedings of the National Academy of Sciences* (May 22, 2007)

Page 19
Fig. 5: Detail of *The Flavor Network,* by Y.-Y. Ahn, S. Ahnert, A.-L. Barabási, and J. Bagrow, as published in "Flavor Network and the Principles of Food Pairing," *Scientific Reports* (December 15, 2011)

Fig. 6: Detail of *The Flavor Network* as a 3-D data sculpture, by A.-L. Barabási, A. Grishchenko, N. Dehmami, and S. Milanlouei, as published in "A Structural Transition in Physical Networks," *Nature* (November 28, 2018)
Photograph courtesy of Peter Puklus

Fig. 7: Detail of *The Human Disease Network* as a color 3-D data sculpture, by A.-L. Barabási, N. Dehmami, and A. Grishchenko, 2018
Photograph by Alice Grishchenko

Page 22
Courtesy of Peter Puklus

Page 28–29
Fig. 1: Genealogy of Jupiter from *Genealogy of the Gods,* by Virgil and other authors, fifteenth century. The British Library Harley 2473, f. 3v. (ff. 1-4). The British Library

Fig. 2: First edition of the *Map of London's Underground Railways,* by Henry Charles Beck, 1933. London Transport. David Rumsey Map Collection, David Rumsey Map Center, Stanford Libraries

Fig. 3: Dust jacket with chart prepared by Alfred H. Barr, Jr., of the exhibition catalogue, *Cubism and Abstract Art,* by Alfred H. Barr, Jr., 1936. Offset, printed in color, 10 1/8 × 7 3/4 inches. The Museum of Modern Art Library, New York. Digital image courtesy of The Museum of Modern Art/ Licensed by SCALA/Art Resource, NY

Fig. 4: *Neuroglia of the Grey Central Region and Neighboring Portions of the White Substance of the Spinal Marrow of a Boy of Eight Days,* by Santiago Ramón y Cajal. From *Textura del Sistema Nervioso del Hombre y de Los Vertebrados Tomo,* 1899. Wellcome Library, the Wellcome Collection

Fig. 5: *Figurative and Approximate Map of Travelers' Movements on the Main Railroads of Europe (Carte figurative et approximative du mouvement des voyageurs sur les principaux chemins de fer de l'Europe en 1862),* by Charles Joseph Minard, 1865. Bibliothèque Nationale de France

Page 30
Fig. 6: *World Finance Corporation and Associates, c. 1970-84: Miami, Ajman, and Bogota-Caracas (Brigada 2506: Cuban Anti-Castro Bay of Pigs Veteran) (7th Version),* by Mark Lombardi, 1999. Colored pencil and graphite on paper, 69 1/8 x 84 inches. Courtesy of Pierogi Gallery and the Lombardi Family
Photograph by John Berens

Page 31
Fig. 7: *Random vs. Scale-free Networks,* by R. Albert, A.-L. Barabási, and H. Jeong, as published in "Error and Attack Tolerance of Complex Networks," *Nature* (July 27, 2000)

Fig. 8: Stills from *The Human Disease Network* digital video, by M. Martino and A.-L. Barabási for Barabási's 2012 TEDMED Talk

Page 32
Fig. 9: *Protein Interactions,* by A.-L. Barabási, H. Jeong, S. P. Mason, and Z. N. Oltvai, as published in "Lethality and Centrality in Protein Networks," *Nature* (May 3, 2001)

Page 33
Fig. 10: *The Flavor Network,* by Y.-Y. Ahn, S. E. Ahnert, J. P. Bagrow, and A.-L. Barabási, as published in "Flavor Network and the Principles of Food Pairing," *Scientific Reports* (December 15, 2011)

Page 35
Fig. 11: *The Birth of a Scale-free Network,* by A.-L. Barabási and H. Jeong, as published in A-L. Barabási's *Linked: How Everything Is Connected to Everything Else and What It Means for Business, Science, and Everyday Life* (2002)

Fig. 12: Photograph of scale-free and random network data sculptures with annotations, by A.-L. Barabási, as shown in Tomás Saraceno's Palais de Tokyo exhibition catalogue, *On Air* (2018)

Page 36
Fig. 13: *Hierarchical Network,* by A.-L. Barabási, D. A. Mongru, Z. N. Oltvai, and E. E. Ravasz, as published in "Hierarchical Organization of Modularity in Metabolic Networks," *Science* (August 30, 2002)

Page 39
Courtesy of Peter Puklus

Pages 42–55
Barabási's sketches and notes, 2019–20

Pages 59–61
Flow, by E. Almaas, A.-L. Barabási, B. Kovács, Z.N. Oltvai, and T. Vicsek, created as potential cover art for "Global Organization of Metabolic Fluxes in the Bacterium *Escherichia coli,*" *Nature* (February 27, 2004)

Pages 62–65
The Human Disease Network, by A.-L. Barabási, B. Childs, M.E. Cusick, K.-I. Goh, D. Valle, and M. Vidal, created for "The Human Disease Network," *Proceedings of the National Academy of Sciences* (May 22, 2007)

Pages 66–67
The Human Disease Network as a data sculpture, by A. Grishchenko, A.-L. Barabási, and N. Dehmami, 2018
Photograph by Alice Grishchenko

Pages 69–71
Stills from *The Human Disease Network* digital video, by M. Martino and A.-L. Barabási for Barabási's 2012 TEDMED Talk. Research for these visualizations was published by A.-L. Barabási, D. Ghiassian, M. Kitsak, J. Loscalzlo, J. Menche, A. Sharma, and M. Vidal in "Uncovering Disease-disease Relationships through the Incomplete Interactome," *Science* (February 20, 2015)

Pages 73–75
Chronograms, by C. A. Hidalgo and A.-L. Barabási, created for "Genome-scale Analysis of In Vivo Spatiotemporal Promoter Activity in *Caenorhabditis elegans,*" by D. Dupuy et al., *Nature Biotechnology* (June 2007)

Page 81
Mobility, by C. A. Hidalgo and A.-L. Barabási, created for "Understanding Individual Human Mobility Patterns," by A.-L. Barabási, M. C. González, and C. A. Hidalgo, *Nature* (June 5, 2008)

Pages 82–85
Rhythm, by A.-L. Barabási, N. Blumm, C. Song, and Z. Qu, created for "Limits of Predictability in Human Mobility," *Science* (February 19, 2010)

Pages 86–87
Mobility diagrams, by J. P. Bagrow and Y.-R. Lin, created for "Mesoscopic Structure and Social Aspects of Human Mobility," *PLOS ONE* (May 31, 2012)

Pages 89–93
Viruses, by A.-L. Barabási, M. Gonzalez, C. A. Hidalgo, and P. Wang, created for "Understanding the Spreading Patterns of Mobile Phone Viruses," *Science* (May 22, 2009)

Pages 95–97
Emergencies, by J. P. Bagrow, A.-L. Barabási, and D. Wang, created for "Collective Response of Human Populations to Large-scale Emergencies," *PLOS ONE* (March 30, 2011)

Pages 101–05
Control, by M. Martino and A.-L. Barabási, created as potential cover art for "Controllability of Complex Networks," by A.-L. Barabási, Y.-Y. Liu, and J.-J. Slotine, *Nature* (May 12, 2011)

Pages 107–09
A Century of Physics cover art (page 107) and studies, by A.-L. Barabási, P. Deville, M. Martino, R. Sinatra, M. Szell, and D. Wang, as published in "A Century of Physics," *Nature Physics* (October 1, 2015)

Page 111–13
Video stills from *Network Earth,* by M. Martino, A.-L. Barabási, B. Barzel, and J. Gao, created for the publication of "Universal Resilience Patterns in Complex Networks," *Nature* (February 17, 2016)

Pages 115–21
Success in Science, by K. Albrecht (pages 117, 122, 123), A.-L. Barabási, P. Deville, M. Martino (pages 118–119, 120, 121), R. Sinatra, C. Song, and D. Wang, created for "Quantifying the Evolution of Individual Scientific Impact," *Science* (November 4, 2016)

Pages 127–31
The Art Network, by A.-L. Barabási, S.P. Fraiberger, A. Grishchenko (pages 127, 128–129, 131), M. Nauro (page 130), M. Resch, C. Riedl, and R. Sinatra, created for "Quantifying Reputation and Success in Art," *Science* (November 16, 2018)

Pages 133–35
The Cosmic Web, by K. Albrecht, A.-L. Barabási, B. C. Coutinho, A. Dey, L. Hernquist, P. Torrey, and M. Vogelsberger, as published in "The Network Behind the Cosmic Web," arxiv.org (April 12, 2016)

Page 137–41
The Flavor Network (page 137) and *Gurgas* (pages 138–41), by A.-L. Barabási, N. Dehmami, A. Grishchenko, and S. Milanlouei, as published in "A Structural Transition in Physical Networks," *Nature* (November 28, 2018)
Photographs on pages 139 and 143 courtesy of Peter Puklus

Page 143
Data sculpture of a large Barabási-Albert network, by A.-L. Barabási, A. Grishchenko, and N. Dehlami, 2018
Photograph courtesy of Peter Puklus

Pages 144–49
Data sculptures of random and scale-free networks in plastic (pages 143–45) and bronze (pages 146, 147, 149), by A.-L. Barabási, N. Dehlami, A. Grishchenko, and M. Martino.
The image on pages 146–47 was published as the cover of *Nature* (November 29, 2018)
Photographs by Alice Grishchenko

Pages 153–57
The Mouse Connectome, by A.-L. Barabási, J. Brum, N. Dehmami, A. Grishchenko, and E. Towlson, created in 2019 to accompany a forthcoming paper

Pages 159–63
Fake News, by A.-L. Barabási, M. Martino, N. Dehmami, O. Varol. This work was part of the Wonder Net project and was shown in the IEEE Info Vis 2018 Art Exhibition, Berlin, October 23–26, 2018
Photograph on page 163 courtesy of Peter Puklus

Pages 165–71
150 *Years of Nature* cover art (page 165) and video stills, by A.-L. Barabási, A. J. Gates, A. Grishchenko, Q. Ke, M. Martino (pages 168–69), and O. Varol, as published in "*Nature*'s Reach: Narrow Work Has Broad Impact," *Nature* (November 6, 2019)

Pages 173–77
Heat, by A.-L. Barabási, N. Dehmami, and Y. Liu, for "Isotopy and Energy of Physical Networks," in *Nature Physics* (forthcoming in 2020)
Photograph on page 177 courtesy of Peter Puklus

Pages 179–81
The Art Board, by A.-L. Barabási, Cs. Both, A. Grischenko, A. Gates, and L. Shekhtman, 2019

Pages 182, 184
Courtesy of Peter Puklus

Inside back cover
The Art Board, Version I, by A.-L. Barabási, Cs. Both, A. Grishchenko, A. Gates, and L. Shekhtman, 2019
Photographs courtesy of Peter Puklus

ACKNOWLEDGMENTS

This book came together across continents and in the midst of a once-in-a-century pandemic. Its very existence is a testament to our engagement with and dependence on networks of all kinds—social, cultural, professional, electronic, not to mention viral.

We are especially indebted to Mónica Bello, Julia Fabényi, Kathleen Forde, József Készman, Isabel Meirelles, Carlo Ratti, Matthew Ritchie, and Peter Weibel for their revelatory essays, which locate the work of the BarabásiLab in historic, artistic, and personal context. And to Peter Puklus, whose illuminating photographs offer a unique perspective on the lab and its artifacts.

We are grateful, too, to András Szántó, a fellow eastern European emigré in the United States who has been a trusted friend and professional interlocutor, and something of a guide into the complicated networks and customs of the global art world.

For bringing together so much information and incorporating so many voices in a single volume, we thank Alanna Stang, cofounder of Well Said NYC. Her role extended well beyond that of an editor, helping put into words the historical evolution of the BarabásiLab and its breakthroughs, as well as capturing the meaning and relevance of the images in the plates section of this book.

Designer Ferenc Eln worked brilliantly, speedily, and calmly to give unifying form to the many disparate pieces of this complex project. His keen eye and smart solutions made this book sensible and beautiful. We are deeply appreciative that he brought his prodigious talents to this endeavor.

We also wish to thank Lena Kiessler and her team at Hatje Cantz for seeing the value in bringing the BarabásiLab's two and a half decades of data-and-network-visualization work to an international audience. Thomas Lemaître was especially helpful in making the book's production process smooth and the end result beautiful.

The works presented here are the results of a deeply collaborative and interactive process between scientists and designers. Special thanks to Kim Albrecht, Alice Grishchenko, Mauro Martino, and Gabriele Musella, the designers who have helped shape the visual journey of the BarabásiLab. Their creations have been fueled by the tireless work of many researchers, whose names appear in the credits section and who have, at times, moonlighted as artists and designers in the lab's collective effort to generate so many of the visuals presented in this book and the exhibition it accompanies.

Over the past decade, József Bartha, Részegh Botond, Péter Kullői, Viola Lukács, Rudolf Pacsika, Zsuzsanna Szegedi-Varga, Tijana van Roosmalen-Stepanovic, and many others have contributed to the work of the BarabásiLab in the form of ideas, discussions, and know-how. We are grateful to them all for helping shape the bridge between networks and art.

The Ludwig Museum wishes to thank Csilla Bogdán, Zsuzsanna Fehér, and Imola Részegh.

ZKM extends its gratitude to Anne Däuper, Anett Holzheid, Clara Runge, and Philipp Ziegler.

This book is published in conjunction with the exhibition *BarabásiLab: Hidden Patterns* at the Ludwig Museum in Budapest, Hungary, from October 10, 2020 to January 17, 2021, and then at ZKM | Center for Art and Media, in Karlsruhe, Germany, from February 27 to August 8, 2021.

Ludwig Museum, Budapest
https://www.ludwigmuseum.hu
10.10.2020–17.01.2021

ZKM | Center for Art and Media, Karlsruhe
https://zkm.de/de
27.02.2021–08.08.2021

Editor
Alanna Stang, Well Said NYC

Project management
Adam Jackman, Hatje Cantz

Authors
Albert-László Barabási, Mónica Bello, Julia Fabényi, Kathleen Forde, József Készman, Isabel Meirelles, Carlo Ratti, Matthew Ritchie, András Szantó, Peter Weibel

Copyediting
Myles McDonnell

Graphic design and typesetting
Ferenc Eln

Typeface
FF Infra by Gabriel Richter

Production
Thomas Lemaître, Hatje Cantz

Reproductions
DLG Graphic, Paris

Printing and binding
Livonia Print, Riga

Paper
Magno Matt, 150 g/m²

Published by
Hatje Cantz Verlag GmbH
Mommsenstraße 27
10629 Berlin
www.hatjecantz.de
A Ganske Publishing Group Company

ISBN 978-3-7757-4862-9

Printed in Latvia

Cover image:
Heat, 2020. Part of a series of visual studies the BarabásiLab created to illustrate the "network temperature" concept, the cover image is a rendering of how heat changes the physicality of a network. A zero-temperature network has only straight links. The links of a hot network, such as this lattice, by contrast, swerve and curve as they reach their destination. See pages 172–77 for more on the BarabásiLab's *Heat* project.

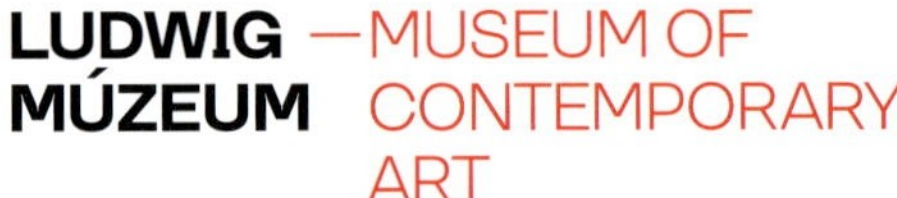

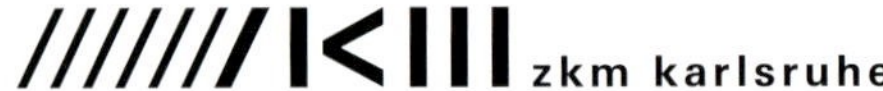

BarabásiLab

Center for Complex Research (CCNR)

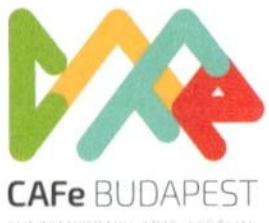

The exhibition is organised as part of the CAFe Budapest Contemporary Arts Festival.

Main sponsor: Magyar Telekom

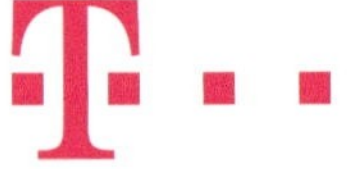

Sponsors:

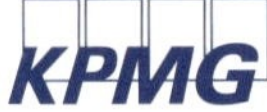

SAMSUNG

Partners:

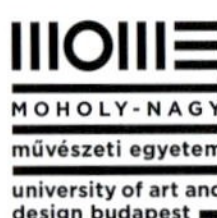

müpa
Budapest

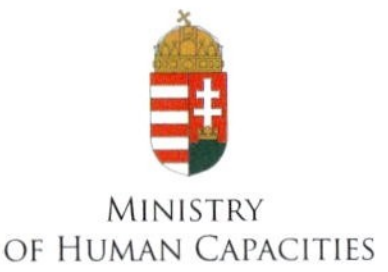

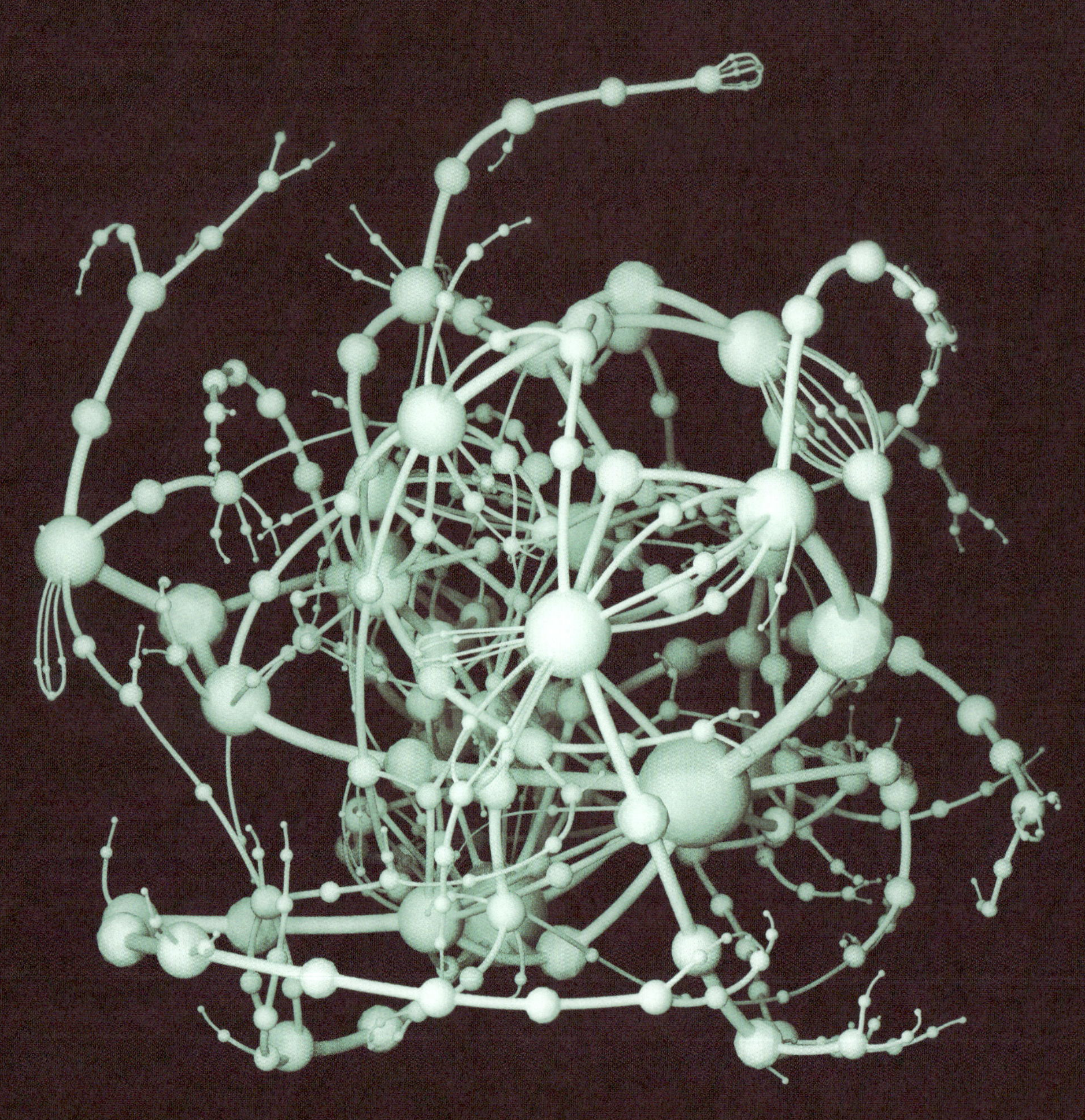